Communications in Computer and Information Science 1640

More information about this series at https://link.springer.com/bookseries/7899

Xiaofeng Meng · Qi Xuan · Yang Yang ·
Yang Yue · Zi-Ke Zhang (Eds.)

Big Data and Social Computing

7th China National Conference, BDSC 2022
Hangzhou, China, August 11–13, 2022
Revised Selected Papers

Editors
Xiaofeng Meng
Renmin University of China
Beijing, China

Qi Xuan
Zhejiang University of Technology
Hangzhou, China

Yang Yang
Zhejiang University
Hangzhou, China

Yang Yue
Shenzhen University
Shenzhen, China

Zi-Ke Zhang
Hangzhou Normal University
Hangzhou, China

ISSN 1865-0929   ISSN 1865-0937 (electronic)
Communications in Computer and Information Science
ISBN 978-981-19-7531-8   ISBN 978-981-19-7532-5 (eBook)
https://doi.org/10.1007/978-981-19-7532-5

This Springer imprint is published by the registered company Springer Nature Singapore Pte Ltd.
The registered company address is: 152 Beach Road, #21-01/04 Gateway East, Singapore 189721, Singapore

Preface

Since the development of mobile internet applications and big data, there has been explosive growth in the volume of data. Therefore, how to dig out insightful information from big data has become a crucial matter. In general, big data analysis includes data capturing, data storage, data analysis, search, sharing, transfer, visualization, querying, updating, and information privacy. Moreover, with the popularization of artificial intelligence algorithms and big data technology in the last decade, social computing has emerged, becoming a crossing field of computer science. For example, blogs, email, instant messaging, social network services, wikis, online gaming, and other instances of what is often called "social software" all evolve the idea of social computing. Nowadays, big data technology and the idea of social computing have been gradually applied to more industries, including internet searches, fintech, healthcare analytics, genomics, geographic information systems, urban informatics, and business informatics. We believe that in the near future, big data will become a part of everyday life.

This volume contains the papers presented at the China National Conference on Big Data & Social Computing (BDSC 2022), held in August, 2022, in Hangzhou, China. This was held as the seventh conference in its series with an emphasis on the state-of-the-art advances in big data and social computing. The main conference received 99 submissions, out of which 24 papers were accepted as regular papers and are presented here. All papers underwent a rigorous peer review process in which each paper was reviewed by 2 to 3 experts. The accepted papers, together with our invited speeches and flash mob videos, led to a vibrant technical program. The Program Committee shairs, Zi-Ke Zhang, Yang Yue and Yang Yang, supervised the review process of the technical papers and compiled a high-quality technical program. Meanwhile, we have also invited leading scholars in the field to deliver keynote speeches based on the theme of the conference, Digital Transformation and Common Prosperity. Besides, we organize a variety of academic events, including the Social Computing Innovation Competition, the Rising Stars Scholars Forum, and the Frontiers Workshop. These activities have played a positive role in promoting academic progress and dissemination. We are looking forward to future events in this conference series.

The conference would not have been successful without help from so many people. We would like to thank the Organizing Committee for their hard work in putting together the conference. First, we would like to express our sincere thanks to the guidance from the general assembly co-chairs: Jianxing Yu, Yi-Ke Guo and Yi-Cheng Zhang. We would like to express our deep gratitude to organizing chair Chao Wu for his support and promotion of this event. We greatly appreciate the excellent support and hard work of the chairs of Frontiers in the Social Computing workshop: Xiangjie Kong and Jianguo Liu; publicity chairs: Xiang Gao and Liming Suo; publication chair Qi Xuan; membership/committee development chair Yong Li; registration chair Hao Li and thematic chairs Jiayin Qi and Xiaolin Zhou. Most importantly, we would like to thank the authors for submitting their papers to BDSC 2022 conference.

We believe that the BDSC conference provides a good forum for both academic researchers and industrial practitioners to discuss advanced topics on big data and social computing. We also expect that the future BDSC conference will be as successful as indicated by the contributions presented in this volume.

August 2022

Xiaofeng Meng
Qi Xuan
Yang Yang
Yang Yue
Zi-Ke Zhang

Organization

General Co-chairs

Jianxing Yu   Zhejiang University, China
Zhejiang Gongshang University, China
Yike Guo   Hong Kong Baptist University, China and
Imperial College London, UK
Yicheng Zhang   University of Fribourg, Switzerland

Program Committee Chairs

Zike Zhang   Hangzhou Normal University, China
Yang Yue   Shenzhen University, China
Yang Yang   Zhejiang University, China

Organizing Committee Chair

Chao Wu   Zhejiang University, China

Frontiers in Social Computing Workshop Chairs

Xiangjie Kong   Zhejiang University of Technology, China
Jianguo Liu   Shanghai University of Finance and Economics,
China

Publicity Chairs

Xiang Gao   Zhejiang University, China
Liming Suo   Nankai University, China

Publication Chair

Qi Xuan   Zhejiang University of Technology, China

Member/Committee Development Chair

Yong Li   Northwest Normal University, China

Registration Chair

Hao Li   Zhejiang University, China

Thematic Chairs

Jiayin Qi   Shanghai University of International Business and
                                Economics, China
Xiaolin Zhou   Peking University, China

PC Members

Bin Zhou   Nanjing University of Information Science &
                                Technology, Nanjing, China
Changping Zhang   Guilin University of Technology, Guilin, China
Chenbo Fu   Zhejiang University of Technology, Hangzhou,
                                China
Chuang Liu   Hangzhou Normal University, Hangzhou, China
Dajun Zeng   Chinese Academy of Sciences, China
Dongwei Xu   Zhejiang University of Technology, Hangzhou,
                                China
Feng Xia   Federation University Australia, Ballarat,
                                Australia
Haibo Hu   Hong Kong Polytechnic University, Hong Kong,
                                China
Haimeng Liu   Institute of Geographic Sciences and Natural
                                Resources Research, Chinese Academy of
                                Sciences, Beijing, China
Hu Yang   Central University Of Finance And Economics,
                                China
Ji Liu   Xinjiang University Of Finance, China
Jiajun Zhou   Zhejiang University of Technology, Hangzhou,
                                China
Jiangao Deng   Hohai University, China
Jianguo Liu   Shanghai University of Finance and Economics,
                                Shanghai, China
Jianzhang Zhang   Hangzhou Normal University, Hangzhou, China
Jiayin Qi   Shanghai University of International Business and
                                Economics, Shanghai, China
Jinhuan Wang   Zhejiang University of Technology, Hangzhou,
                                China
Jinyin Chen   Zhejiang University of Technology, Hangzhou,
                                China
Junfeng Zhou   Donghua University, China

Kuangshi Huang	China population and Development Research Center, China
Lan You	Hubei University, China
Li He	Xi'an Jiaotong University, China
Peng Lu	Central South University, China
Quanhui Liu	Sichuan University, China
Ruiqi Li	Beijing University of Chemical Technology, China
Shanqing Yu	Zhejiang University of Technology, Hangzhou, China
Shuo Wang	Hebei University, China
Tao Jia	Southwest University, China
Tun Lu	Fudan University, China
Wei Xu	Renmin University of China
Weiwei Gu	Beijing University Of Chemical Technology, China
Wen Zhang	Beijing University Of Technology, China
Xiaoke Xu	Dalian Minzu University, Dalian, China
Xiaoxue Gao	East China Normal University, China
Xiu-Xiu Zhan	Hangzhou Normal University, Hangzhou, China
Yan Yu	Renmin University of China, China
Yang Chen	Fudan University, China
Ye Wu	Beijing Normal University, Zhuhai, China
Yijie Peng	Peking University, China
Ying Fan	Beijing Normal University, China
Yong Li	Northwest Normal University, Lanzhou, China
Youzhong Ma	Luoyang Normal University, China
Zeyu Wang	Zhejiang University of Technology, Hangzhou, China
Zhidong Cao	Chinese Academy of Sciences, China
Zhongyuan Ruan	Zhejiang University of Technology, Hangzhou, China

Contents

Social Network and Group Behavior

Digital Society and Public Security

Digital Government and Public Big Data

Urban Computing and Social Governance

Resilience-Based Epidemic Strategy Evaluation Method Under Post-Covid-19

Chenyang Wang, Rui Ba, and Hui Zhang[✉]

Institute of Public Safety Research, Tsinghua University, Beijing 100084, China
zhhui@mail.tsinghua.edu.cn

Abstract. COVID-19 has heavily attacked the urban system and has continued to cause economic losses and human fatalities worldwide. Methodologies to properly evaluate the advantages and disadvantages of epidemic prevention strategies are urged, and to develop mitigation and improvement are required post-COVID. The urban system includes many elements; existing epidemic prevention and control strategy evaluation only focus on the effectiveness of containing confirmed cases. Therefore, a new resilience concept by combing multifaceted effectiveness is proposed for evaluating how epidemic prevention strategy influences urban system. The approach reflects the short-term factual effectiveness for epidemic mitigation and long-term value, including urban social and institutional resilience improvement and PDCA-cycle-based dynamic adjustability. An integrated model is used to evaluate prevention and control strategies in Shenzhen and Shanghai, China. The scores obtained are consistent with the facts and indicate that Shenzhen has more reasonable strategies for urban system than Shanghai. The strategy evaluation framework based on resilience proposed in this paper presents an innovative approach for assessing public health emergencies more comprehensively.

Keywords: Strategy evaluation · Urban resilience · Epidemic · Integrated mode · Post-Covid-191

1 Introduction

City as a complex system is increasingly studied and simplified into several subsystems when assessed [1]. Transportation and mobility networks, Internet, mobile phone networks, power grids, social and contact networks, and neural networks were the forms that reflected that complex systems were organized under the form of networks where nodes and edges were embedded in space. Tyler, S. and M. Moench thought that the framework included the characteristics of urban systems, the agents that depend on and manage those systems, and institutions that link systems and agents [2]. Sharifi, A. and Y. Yamagata were categorized into five themes: infrastructure, resources, land use, urban geometry and morphology, governance, socio-demographic aspects, and human behavior [3]. A proposed framework of the urban FEW nexus was from resource interdependency, resource provision, and system integration [4].

Cities as a complex system face a wide variety of threats. Therefore, Resilience, as the ability to anticipate, absorb, accommodate, or recover from the effects of a hazardous event in a timely and efficient way for a system and its component, is increasingly valued [5]. Urban Resilience is proposed to resist climate change for the first time. Furthermore, Lovell, S. T. and J. R. Taylor [6] applied it to urban ecosystem services assessment and multifunctional green infrastructure resilience planning. Bene, C. et al. [7] thought that resilience had become popular in ecology. Rink, E. et al. [8] used it in climate change adaptation [9], urban planning, and governance [10]. Policymakers and international development agencies also increasingly referred to it. The core competencies of Resilience were resistance, recovery, and adaptation.

Moreover, there was a tendency to expand from a narrow definition to a system theory. Research on resilience has focused on urban ecosystems and green space planning for ages [11]. Then the theoretical studies have been refined from the initial definition to a massive system concept encompassing the complex network structure of urban systems [12] with 11 characteristics [13]. The complexity of resilience is recognized when it is studied as a scientific issue rather than theoretical studies [14]. Furthermore, the interests change from a city or even an entire complex ecosystem to the resilience of a community and individuals [15]. It is defined more broadly as the concentration of psychological resilience of a group [16]. There is consensus that resilience is essentially an improvement of capacity, policies must guide, and studies have begun to include policy assessment, decision support, and governance [17]. The short history of resilience development and the overly complex theoretical framework [18] have resulted in a lack of quantitative assessment methods.

Policy evaluation includes prior, concurrent, and ex-post evaluation and is narrowly defined as ex-post evaluation. Policy evaluation has evolved from objective evaluation to a combination of objective and value evaluation. Public health events such as pandemics cause a large number of casualties and greatly impact economies. The COVID-19 which emerged in 2019 attacks urban health system and harms public physical and psychological health. Because changes in confirmed cases are mainly determined by strategies which also influence the open market policy and economic growth in the post-COVID. Studies focus on available strategy evaluation methods to help evaluate and promote strategies for outbreak prevention and control.

Strategy evaluations are based on emergency control effectiveness previously. However, an epidemic impacts the total urban system [19], which requires consideration of more aspects, especially urban system resilience when evaluation [20]. Exploring the strategy impact on urban resilience for a major dynamic event in a city over a period of time taking strategy evaluation for the epidemic as a public health emergency as an example. Therefore, an integrated approach to evaluating strategy for public health emergencies the post-COVID is proposed. The new method evaluates epidemic prevention and control strategies in short-term effectiveness and long-term urban system resilience capacity recovery or improvement.

2 Theoretical Basis

2.1 Urban Subsystems Applied to Resilience

A city is a complex system that includes multiple forms of connections between people, information, and materials and is classified into economic, natural, physical, social, and institutional subsystems. The institutional and social subsystems are the focuses because they show the importance of strategy and adequate directions and are strongly correlated with each other when studying public health emergency, which has essentially no damage to urban infrastructure but the society. Moreover, the urban health system is significantly influenced by strategies under epidemic. The social subsystem consists of eight indicators: human capital, lifestyle and community competence, social and economy, community capital, social and cultural capital, population and demographics, environmental, and risk knowledge. The institutional subsystem consists of seven indicators: governance, mitigation policies, organized governmental services, management, warning and evacuation, emergency response, and disaster recovery. The description and division of the urban system are shown in Fig. 1 [21].

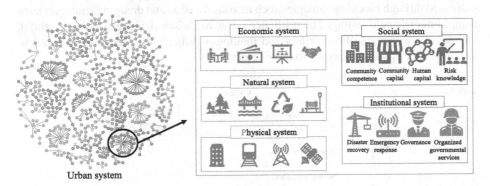

Fig. 1. Urban system and the division.

U = urban system;
μ_i = urban subsystem, including economic, natural, physical, social, and institutional subsystems.

$$\mu_4 = \{\mu_{41}, \mu_{42}, \mu_{43}, \mu_{44}, \mu_{45}, \mu_{46}, \mu_{47}, \mu_{48}\}$$

μ_{4i} = social subsystems, including human capital, life style and community competence, social and economy, community capital, social and cultural capital, population and demographics, environmental, and risk knowledge.

$$\mu_5 = \{\mu_{51}, \mu_{52}, \mu_{53}, \mu_{54}, \mu_{55}, \mu_{56}, \mu_{57}\}$$

μ_{5i} = institutional subsystem, including governance, mitigation policies, organized governmental services, management, warning and evacuation, emergency response, and disaster recovery.

2.2 Resilience Concept Applied to Urban System

Urban resilience refers to the ability of an urban system and all its constituent social networks across temporal and spatial scales to maintain a dynamic balance of desired functions. Characteristics of urban resilience include redundancy, diversity, efficiency, robustness, connectivity, adaptation, resources, independence, innovation, inclusion, and integration. The characteristics including efficiency, connectivity, adaptation, resources, independence, innovation, inclusion, and integration are most important when considering urban system resilience under epidemics.

Resilience curves are employed to express the resilience quantitatively. The qualitative resilience value is typically treated as a fixed one represented by the area S under the curve in each time range dt, as shown in Fig. 2(A). However, the resilience value is treated not as a fixed value S_2, but as an interval that contains top S_{21} and bottom S_{20} values, more like a strip in the paper, as shown in Fig. 2(B). The bottom value is determined by physical conditions such as infrastructure and economic prosperity. The urban social system consists of people, and personal decisions also affect the resilience value, which is an uncertainty value dS_2. When resilience is applied to the epidemic, the dredging and blocking strategy used to mitigate the flood is appreciated. Resilience is addressed through blocking strategies such as zone division and dredging strategies such as rapid nucleic acid testing. The resilience curve has a low strike resistance threshold, leading to a disaster spillover effect and making it difficult for dredging strategies to work once the epidemic spreads to more regions.

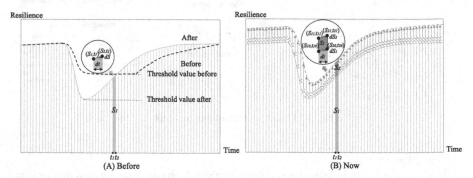

Fig. 2. The resilience curve diagram.

2.3 Strategy Evaluation Method Applied to Urban Resilience

The effectiveness of strategies includes short-term effectiveness in response to the emergency and long-term value in maintaining and improving urban resilience in the future for public health emergencies. Therefore, the epidemic response strategy evaluation is divided into factual assessment, which relies on infrastructural improvements and economic development already existing, and value evaluation which applies to improve the urban social subsystem and institutional subsystem for the epidemic in this paper. Moreover, the value evaluation includes the resilience indexes representing the static characteristics such as the reasonability and PDCA-cycle indexes representing dynamic characteristics such as timeliness and adjustability.

3 Strategy Evaluation Framework

The evaluability of epidemic prevention and control strategies is analyzed by 11 guidelines for investing in policy evaluation proposed by B.Bozeman and J.Massey, and the evaluability determination report should be passed. Ten inspection criteria for identifying whether the strategy is evaluable are developed based on the 11 guidelines, as shown in Table 1. Whether the strategy is evaluable is scored by the criteria, with yes being one point and no being zero. There is necessary to be evaluated when the scores are more remarkable than five points.

Table 1. Inspection criterions for evaluable strategies.

No	Inspection criterions	Yes	No
1	Direction of causality is apparent		
2	Direct effects are more significant than "spillover" effects		
3	Short-run benefits		
4	Have generalizability		
5	Evaluation in late stage		
6	The costs and stake of strategies are major		
7	Effectiveness can be manipulated or controlled		
8	Treatment can be clearly specified		
9	Parties are supportive		
10	Possible funding sources		

Then the strategy evaluation method of short-term factual assessment for the public health emergency is studied, and the index system of urban system resilience capacity assessment is proposed. The principal objective of strategies for public health emergencies is to prevent infections and deaths caused by the emergency and reduce economic losses and costs. Therefore, short-term factual assessment of strategies for public health emergencies is based on the typical critical indicators of the emergency, and different assessment methods are applied to different emergencies.

Principles for evaluation index selection concentrate on short-term and medium to long-term effects on improving the urban public health system resilience in response to similar emergencies. On one hand, we consider whether strategies consider various aspects of personnel, materials, and information influenced by the emergency, representing the degree of coverage and completeness of the strategies based on urban resilience. The evaluation reflects the strategy's resilience characteristics, including diversity, robustness, inclusion, redundancy, and integration. The elements included in the urban social and institutional subsystem selected above are employed to obtain the index system applied for epidemic prevention and control strategy evaluation, as shown in Table 2. The index system refers to China's GB/T 40947–2021.

Table 2. Urban public health system resilience of social subsystem index.

Subsystem	ID	Inspection criterions	Index
Social	μ_{41}	Human capital	Number of medical personnel
	μ_{42}	Life style and community competence	Diversity of residents
	μ_{43}	Social and economy	The per capita budget
	μ_{44}	Community capital	Self-organizing Capacity
	μ_{45}	Social and cultural capital	Group expectation
	μ_{46}	Population and demographics	The ratio of the elderly and children
	μ_{47}	Environmental	Green cover coverage
	μ_{48}	Risk knowledge	Successful experience
Institutional	μ_{51}	Governance	Government capacity
	μ_{52}	Mitigation policies	Reasonableness of strategies
	μ_{53}	Organized governmental services	Ability to secure the necessities
	μ_{54}	Management	Community and other lower management level
	μ_{55}	Warning and evacuation	Warning and placement
	μ_{56}	Emergency response	Timely response

On the other hand, the PDCA cycle is a dynamic process to assess the epidemic prevention and control strategy's efficiency, adaptation, innovation, and timeliness characteristics. PDCA-cycle contains seven essential elements, including the organization's environment, leadership and employee engagement, planning, support, operation, performance evaluation, and improvement, as shown in Fig. 3. The operation pattern follows the plan-do-check-action cycle and continuous improvement management model referred to as ISO4 45001 of China.

The development of public health emergencies relies heavily on the timeliness and effectiveness of strategies. Each stage of the PDCA cycle contains the elements that

Fig. 3. PDCA-cycle.

contribute to this closed-loop success, characterized by indexes to assess whether public health emergency strategies have been adjusted timely and are beneficial for urban resilience construction in the future, as shown in Table 3.

Table 3. Urban public health system resilience of PDCA-cycle assessment index.

First level index	Second level index	Third level index
Strategies efficiency, adaptation, innovation, and timeliness	Plan	Consideration of various sections of society
		Information completeness
		Risk assessment
		Multi-objective
	Do	Comprehensive budget
		Information platform and communication
		Human and material resource guarantee
		Cultural and psychological needs
		Development Strategy
	Check	Goal achievement
		Economic expenditure
		Sustainability
		New risks
	Action	Feedback on evaluation results
		Improvement measures
		Post-improvement evaluation

The scores obtained above are normalized and integrated reasonably for the corresponding emergency to obtain a comprehensive quantitative value of the strategy evaluation.

The key steps include a. determining whether epidemic prevention and control strategy is evaluable, b. strategies factual assessment by adapting appropriate assessment methods corresponding to various characteristics of different emergencies, c. constructing public health system resilience index through urban social subsystem and institutional subsystem, d. PDCA-cycle assessment for dynamic processes such as strategy adaptability and continuous improvement. The framework of epidemic prevention and control strategies evaluation is shown in Fig. 4.

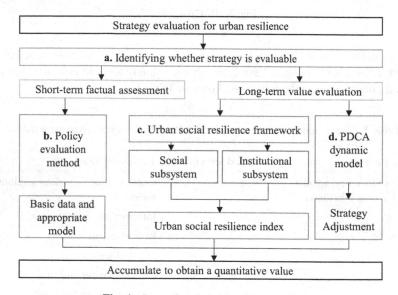

Fig. 4. Strategies evaluation framework.

4   Case Analysis and Discussion

In this paper, the strategies are chosen to be evaluated by the method proposed above, for which outbreaks in Shenzhen and Shanghai caused by the Omicron strain. The Shenzhen outbreak began in February 2022 and ended in April. Moreover, the Shanghai outbreak began in late March 2022 and lasted through June. The public in Shenzhen rapidly resumed everyday life. At the same time, Shanghai suffered a significant effect under different strategies taken by local governments, which make sense to evaluate their epidemic prevention and control strategies.

4.1   Identifying Evaluable Strategies

Whether the prevention and control strategies for outbreaks are evaluable is determined through the inspection criteria which are identified above. Results show they are evaluable because the score obtained is eight points out of five points, as shown in Table 4.

Table 4. Identify whether outbreak prevention strategies are evaluable.

No	Inspection criterions	Yes	No
1	Direction of causality is apparent	✓	
2	Direct effects are more significant than "spillover" effects	✓	
3	Short-run benefits	✓	
4	Have generalizability	✓	
5	Evaluation in late stage	✓	
6	The costs and stake of strategies are major		✓
7	Effectiveness can be manipulated or controlled	✓	
8	Treatment can be clearly specified	✓	
9	Parties are supportive	✓	
10	Possible funding sources		✓

4.2 Identifying Evaluable Strategies

The short-term factual assessment of outbreak prevention and control strategies indicates their effectiveness. Therefore, key parameters such as infection and fatality rates obtained from the coronavirus case trajectories fitting are essential to assess the strategies. The SEIR model is selected for curve fitting in this paper, proposed as Eq. (1).

$$\frac{dS(t)}{dt} = -\beta S(t)\frac{I(t)}{N}$$

$$\frac{dE(t)}{dt} = \beta S(t)\frac{I(t)}{N} - \gamma_1 E(t)$$

$$\frac{dI(t)}{dt} = \gamma_1 E(t) - \gamma_2 I(t)$$

$$\frac{dR(t)}{dt} = \gamma_2 I(t)$$

$$N = S(t) + I(t) + R(t) + E(t) \tag{1}$$

$S(t)$ is the number of susceptible cases;
$I(t)$ is the number of infected cases;
$R(t)$ is the number of recovered cases;
$E(t)$ is the number of exposed cases;

β is the infection rate;
$1/\gamma_1$ is incubation period;
$1/\gamma_2$ is infection period.

The β in SEIR model is improved to be a dynamic value which is correlated with the strategies and varies over time. It is imposed as Eq. (2).

$$\beta(t) = \begin{cases} \beta, t < \tau \\ \beta_0 + (\beta - \beta_0)e^{-k(t-\tau)}, t \geq \tau \end{cases} \tag{2}$$

β_0 is the initial value of infection rate;
k is the attenuation coefficient used to measure strategy intensity;
τ is the end time of free diffusion.

It is assumed that the first data collected corresponds to the time when the strategy is released. The preceding time is the epidemic's exponential transmission phase, and the following one is the strategy intervention phase. It is assumed to be a segmented function related to the strategy effectiveness for epidemic prevention. The image is shown in Fig. 5.

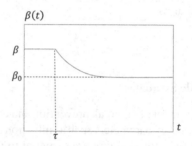

Fig. 5. Dynamic value of infection rate.

The time intervals used for fitting follow the periods of rapid growth and decline of the epidemic in Shanghai and Shenzhen, from March 31 to May 24 and February 20 to April 30, respectively. The $S(0)$ is the resident population in the two urbans. The $I(0)$ is the sum of exposed cases within seven days from the fitting day. The $1/\gamma_1$ and $1/\gamma_2$ are five days and 14 days, respectively. The coronavirus case trajectories fitting is fitted by the static value β_0 and improved $\beta(t)$, respectively, and the effectiveness of the strategy k is obtained, and results are shown in Fig. 6.

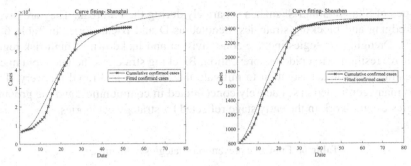

Fig. 6. Fitting results in Shanghai and Shenzhen.

The β_{01} is 0.018 when no strategy applied to the outbreak in Shanghai, while the β_1 is 0.18 and k_1 is 0.135 when strategies apply. The β_{02} is nearly zero when no strategy applied to the outbreak in Shenzhen, while the β_2 is 0.11 and k_2 is 0.085 when strategies apply (Table 5).

Table 5. Fitting results in Shanghai and Shenzhen.

City	Shanghai	Shenzhen
Time (Date)	31-Mar to 24-May	20-Feb to 30-Apr
$S(0)$ (Person)	25000000	17000000
$I(0)$ (Person)	2500	200
$R(0)$ (Person)	1677	162
$E(0)$ (Person)	5039	650
$1/\gamma_1$ (Day)	5	5
$1/\gamma_2$ (Day)	14	14
β_0	0.018	5.00E-05
k	0.135	0.085
τ	3	3
β	0.18	0.11

The strategy effectiveness in Shanghai $S_{f1} = \frac{\beta_1 - \beta_{01}}{\beta_1} = 0.9$. The strategy effectiveness in Shenzhen $S_{f1} = \frac{\beta_1 - \beta_{01}}{\beta_1} = 1$.

4.3 Resilience Capacity Index System of Urban Social System Under Epidemic

For the long-term value evaluation, it is essential to assess the comprehensiveness of the strategy, including the diversity, robustness, inclusion, redundancy, and integration of the urban resilience capacity index system constructed above. This paper collates the strategies of Shanghai and Shenzhen separately during the outbreak. They are divided into dredging and blocking strategies, denoted as D and B categories in Table 6 and Table 7. Dredging strategies include zone division and lockdown of high-risk regions to improve resilience to epidemic prevention. Blocking strategies include rapid nucleic acid testing and contact isolation to mitigate the outbreak and rapid recovery. There are too many confirmed cases densely concentrated in communities, and the grooming strategies cannot work in the early stage reflected by strategy categories.

Table 6. Epidemic prevention strategies in Shanghai.

Date	Strategies	Categories
1-Mar	Imported cases region as medium-risk region	D
11-Mar	Traceability results	B
12-Mar	Close primary and middle school	B
13-Mar	Universities closed-off management	B
16-Mar	Grading nucleic acid testing	B
26-Mar	COVID-19 antigen self-test citywide	B
28-Mar	Close-off management in Pudong	D
1-Apr	Close-off management in Puxi	D
4-Apr	Nucleic acid testing citywide	B
11-Apr	Lockdown, control and precaution Zone management	D
16-Apr	Strategy for work resumption	/
22-Apr	Zero community transmission policy	B
30-Apr	Strategy for work resumption	/
3-May	Regular nucleic acid detection point construction	B
6-May	Dynamic zero-COVID policy	B
7-May	NEMT postponement	B
9-May	Aid whole process management	B
11-May	Notarization service help	/
15-May	Crackdown on illegal group purchases	/
16-May	Optimize government processing	/
18-May	Traffic support	B
21-May	Resume public traffic	/
22-May	Restore catering trade/ Epidemic prevention in building industry	B
24-May	Help employment difficulty/ Restore farm fairs	/

Table 7. Epidemic prevention strategies in Shenzhen.

Date	Strategies	Categories
9-Feb	Frontline workers providing needed services	/
10-Feb	Guidelines for handling imported items	D
21-Feb	Online teaching for primary and middle school	B
24-Feb	Use of an integrated code citywide	B
28-Feb	Organizations are investigated for violating anti-epidemic rules/ Ensure consumers sufficient food supplies	B
1-Mar	More lockdown areas designated/ Consultations offered to pregnant women and offline medical care/ Doctor offers advice on lockdown anxiety	D
2-Mar	Multiple measures to ensure border security/ More lockdown areas/ Free nucleic acid tests offered to yellow health code holders	B
3-Mar	City ensures essential services for quarantined residents/ Rapid COVID test results for cross-border truckers	B
4-Mar	Tech innovations bolster city's against COVID	B
7-Mar	Entry requires 48th negative COVID test results	D
9-Mar	Criteria for lifting lockdown/ HK launches platform for submitting rapid test results	D
10-Mar	Guarantee salaries of quarantined employees	/
13-Mar	Suspend bus, metro services/ Contact three rounds of mass COVID tests	B
15-Mar	Medical services uninterrupted	B
17-Mar	Majority of government services accessible online/ Closed-loop management implemented for cross border trucks	D
18-Mar	Five district-level areas back to normal life/ Free cultural events offered to citizens	B
21-Mar	City reopens business, public transport/ Ensure business operations, aid companies	B
22-Mar	Back to normal pace in orderly manner	/
23-Mar	Measures to help COVID-affected business/ Metro service returns to normal capacity	D
28-Mar	Measures to help industry and services	/
29-Mar	Citizens returning to Shenzhen required to take COVID tests/ Relief measures help boost wholesale, retail enterprises/ Realign lockdown, control and prevention areas	D
31-Mar	Railway arrivals required to take on-site tests	D

(continued)

Table 7. (*continued*)

Date	Strategies	Categories
1-Apr	Inbound travelers required to declare travel records	D
6-Apr	Negative 72-h COVID test results required for access to public places/ Schools prepare for opening amid strict COVID-19 rules	B
7-Apr	72th COVID test result needed for leaving Shenzhen/ System in use to facilitate epidemiological investigation	B
11-Apr	Senior high school students return to campus	/
19-Apr	COVID hospital ensures zero medical staff infection	B
22-Apr	Lowers COVID-19 nucleic acid test cost	B
27-Apr	Against unnecessary holiday travel	B
29-Apr	Advise citizens to stay put during May Day holiday/ Park visits require negative 72th test results	B
6-May	Smart devices and techs help COVID fight	B

The strategies in Shanghai and Shenzhen are rated zero-one, and the aggregate point is 15, with yes being one point and no being zero. The strategy evaluation results of the Shenzhen and Shanghai epidemic obtained by the urban social resilience index are shown in Table 8. The total scores S_{v1} for Shanghai and Shenzhen are seven points and 15 points, respectively.

Table 8. Urban social resilience in Shanghai and Shenzhen.

ID	Index	Shanghai	Shenzhen
μ_{41}	Much number of medical personnel	1	1
μ_{42}	Diversity of residents	1	1
μ_{43}	High the per capita budget	1	1
μ_{44}	Strong self-organizing Capacity	0	1
μ_{45}	Group expectation congruency	0	1
μ_{46}	Low ratio of the elderly and children	1	1
μ_{47}	High green cover coverage	1	1
μ_{48}	Successful experience	1	1
μ_{51}	Government capacity	0	1
μ_{52}	Reasonableness of strategies	0	1
μ_{53}	Ability to secure the necessities	0	1
μ_{54}	Community and other lower management level	0	1

(*continued*)

Table 8. (*continued*)

ID	Index	Shanghai	Shenzhen
μ_{55}	Warning and placement	0	1
μ_{56}	Timely response	0	1
μ_{57}	Reasonable recovery	1	1
Total S_{v1}		7	15

It is also essential to assess the strategies' efficiency, adaptation, innovation, and timeliness characteristics. The PDCA-cycle process is selected to evaluate the strategies in Shanghai and Shenzhen.

The interim strategies of Shanghai and Shenzhen for outbreak prevention and control are shown in Figs. 7 and 8. Moreover, three days after a strategy release is treated as the time when it begins working. The figures reflect the strategy's effectiveness in controlling new confirmed cases and the timeliness of its adjustment.

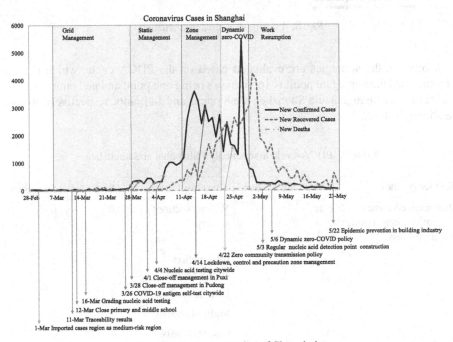

Fig. 7. Interim strategies of Shanghai.

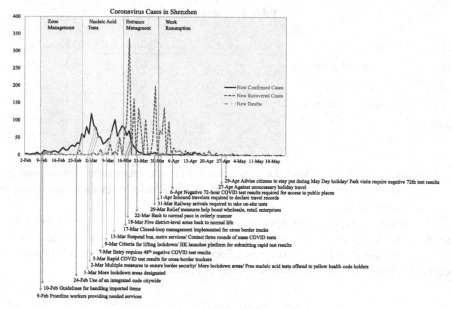

Fig. 8. Interim strategies of Shenzhen.

Moreover, the strategies are evaluated based on the PDCA cycle, which is rated zero-one, and the aggregate point is 16, with yes being one point and no being zero. The total scores for Shanghai and Shenzhen are 8 points and 14 points, respectively. Results are shown in Table 9.

Table 9. PDCA-cycle assessment of Shanghai and Shenzhen.

First level index	Second level index	Third level index	Shanghai	Shenzhen
Strategies efficiency, adaptation, innovation, and timeliness	Plan	Various sections of society	0	0
		Information completeness	0	1
		Risk assessment	1	1
		Multi-objective	1	1
	Do	Comprehensive budget	1	1
		Information platform and communication	1	1

(continued)

Table 9. (*continued*)

First level index	Second level index	Third level index	Shanghai	Shenzhen
		Human and material resource guarantee	0	1
		Cultural and psychological needs	1	1
		Development Strategy	1	1
	Check	Goal achievement	0	1
		Economic expenditure	1	1
		Sustainability	1	1
		New risks	0	1
	Action	Feedback on evaluation results	0	1
		Improvement measures	0	1
		Post-improvement evaluation	0	0
Total S_{v2}			8	14

4.4 Accumulation

Resilience value is treated as an interval that contains top and bottom values. Furthermore, the bottom value is determined by accurate assessment results, and the top value is associated with the results obtained by the value evaluation. The scores obtained are normalized and accumulated, and the formula is shown in Eq. (3). Short-term evaluation scores are weighted as one as well as long-term evaluation results, whose both sub-index results take a weight of 0.5, for a total score of 2 points.

$$S_f \leq T \leq S_f + \frac{\sum_{i=1}^{2} \omega_i S_{vi}}{\sum_{i=1}^{2} \omega_i} \tag{3}$$

Strategy assessment results show that Shanghai's internal is more significant than 0.90 points less than 1.38 points, and Shenzhen is more significant than 1.00 points less than 1.94 points. The results show that the strategies of Shenzhen scored higher in the three aspects, including short-term prevention and control effectiveness for the outbreak, designing urban social resilience, and adjustability in response to the active outbreak. In contrast, Shanghai scored lower in all of them. Shanghai will have a high score if assessed through the previous indicator system method, mainly based on the assessment of social resources, including public health infrastructure and economic development status. However, such a result is inconsistent with the practical outbreak prevention and control situation. Moreover, the confirmed cases in Shanghai decreased unreasonably, which requires more aspects of data to evaluate the strategies. Therefore, it is evident that the comprehensive evaluation method proposed in this paper is more reasonable than before. COVID-19 is extraordinarily contagious and has complex harm to urban society while strongly influencing urban governance strategies and mass decision-making. Furthermore, much case-based data is desired to reasonably grade the strategy assessment results.

4.5 Discussion

A promotion strategy is presented based on the evaluation results. Strategies should have short-term effectiveness for the emergency needed to respond at first, and further could be updated in time to adapt to the dynamic situation. The evaluation framework proposed in the paper differs from previous method to present a more refined way. It focuses not only on the short-term effects of the epidemic measures, but also consider the long-term effects on urban resilience. And the timeliness such as dynamic adjustment of the strategies is considered. It should also be improved in covering various sections of the society, such as disadvantaged groups in society, and targeted measures for teachers and students in higher education institutions. The strategies should not for coping with the current situation and cause a lot of economic waste, which does not promote the urban resilience improvement and undermine future urban advancement.

5 Conclusion

Urban public health system resilience is not a fixed value but is in a range of intervals. Therefore, epidemic prevention and control strategy evaluation should be based on the substantial effects and the value of promoting urban public health system resilience for future emergencies. A more likely result can be obtained by accumulating the results in the two aspects.

A new evaluation framework is proposed for epidemic prevention and control strategy evaluation. The framework includes an assessment for evaluability of strategy, a short-term factual assessment, a long-term value evaluation based on indicators of urban subsystem resilience, and the PDCA-cycle model index. The three aspects reflect the goal achievement, diversity, robustness, inclusion, redundancy, integration, efficiency, adaptation, innovation, and timeliness of strategies. Furthermore, it is accumulated into a quantitative result.

Strategy evaluation in the post-COVID is a priority issue. An integrated approach is applied to access the strategies for post-COVID prevention in Shanghai and Shenzhen, China. Results indicate that score of epidemic prevention strategies in Shenzhen is high, instead of the previous results of Shanghai scoring higher. It is more consistent with the facts and validates that the assessment method proposed in this paper is reasonable. The results suggest that the prevention and control strategy of public health emergencies such as COVID-19 should not just be a reactive response but should be an active strategic adjustment and consider the needs of all various sections of society to respond successfully and be beneficial for the future urban resilience.

The framework should be upgraded in the quantification approach to obtain more reasonable quantitative results in the future. Additional case studies are required to obtain grading criteria for strategy evaluation scores.

Acknowledgements. This work is supported by National Key R&D Program of China (No. 2021ZD0111200), National Science Foundation of China (Grant No. 72174099), High-tech Discipline Construction Fundings for Universities in Beijing (Safety Science and Engineering).

References

1. Barthelemy, M.: Spatial networks. Phys. Rep.-Rev. Section Phys. Lett. **499**(1–3), 1–101 (2011)
2. Tyler, S., Moench, M.: A framework for urban climate resilience. Clim. Dev. **4**(4), 311–326 (2012)
3. Sharifi, A.: Urban sustainability assessment: An overview and bibliometric analysis. Ecol. Ind. **121**, 107102 (2021)
4. Zhang, P., et al.: Food-energy-water (FEW) nexus for urban sustainability: a comprehensive review. Resour. Conserv. Recycl. **142**, 215–224 (2019)
5. Bene, C., et al.: Resilience as a policy narrative: potentials and limits in the context of urban planning. Clim. Dev. **10**(2), 116–133 (2018)
6. Lovell, S.T., Taylor, J.R.: Supplying urban ecosystem services through multifunctional green infrastructure in the United States. Landscape Ecol. **28**(8), 1447–1463 (2013)
7. Bene, C., et al.: Review article: resilience, poverty and development. J. Int. Dev. **26**(5), 598–623 (2014)
8. Brink, E., et al.: Cascades of green: a review of ecosystem-based adaptation in urban areas. Glob. Environ. Change-Human Policy Dimensions **36**, 111–123 (2016)
9. Sandifer, P.A., et al.: Exploring connections among nature, biodiversity, ecosystem services, and human health and well-being: opportunities to enhance health and biodiversity conservation. Ecosyst. Serv. **12**, 1–15 (2015)
10. Broto, V.C.: Urban governance and the politics of climate change. World Dev. **93**, 1–15 (2017)
11. Calkin, D.E., et al.: Negative consequences of positive feedbacks in US wildfire management. For. Ecosyst. **2**(1), 1–10 (2015)
12. Meerow, S., et al.: Defining urban resilience: a review. Landsc. Urban Plan. **147**, 38–49 (2016)
13. Ribeiro, P.J.G., Gonçalves, L.A.P.J.: Urban resilience: a conceptual framework. Sustain. Cities Soc. **50**, 101625 (2019)
14. Elmqvist, T., et al.: Sustainability and resilience for transformation in the urban century. Nat. Sustain. **2**(4), 267–273 (2019)
15. De Kock, J.H., et al.: A rapid review of the impact of COVID-19 on the mental health of healthcare workers: implications for supporting psychological well-being. BMC Pub. Health **21**(1), 1–18 (2021)
16. Hudelson, C., Cluver, L.: Factors associated with adherence to antiretroviral therapy among adolescents living with HIV/AIDS in low- and middle-income countries: a systematic review. Aids Care-Psychol. Socio-Med. Aspects AIDS/HIV **27**(7), 805–816 (2015)
17. Aldridge, J.M., McChesney, K.: The relationships between school climate and adolescent mental health and wellbeing: a systematic literature review. Int. J. Educ. Res. **88**, 121–145 (2018)
18. Sharifi, A., Yamagata, Y.: Principles and criteria for assessing urban energy resilience: a literature review. Renew. Sustain. Energy Rev. **60**, 1654–1677 (2016)

19. Liu, H., et al.: Evaluating the real-time impact of COVID-19 on cities: China as a Case Study. Complexity **2020** (2020)
20. McClelland, A G., Jordan, R., Parzniewski, S., et al.: Post-COVID recovery and renewal through whole-of-society resilience in cities. J. Saf. Sci. Resilience (2022)
21. Min, G.C., Frank, K.A., Pokhrel, Y., et al.: Natural infrastructure in sustaining global urban freshwater ecosystem services. Nat. Sustain. **4**, 1068–1075 (2021)

The Effects of Intervention Strategies for COVID-19 Transmission Control on Campus Activity

Yina Yao[1](✉), Hui Zhang[1], Rui Yang[1], Lida Huang[1], and Qing Deng[2]

[1] Department of Engineering Physics, Tsinghua University, Beijing 100084, China
yaoyina123@163.com
[2] School of Civil and Resource Engineering, University of Science and Technology, Beijing, Beijing 100083, China

Abstract. University is one of the most likely environments for the cluster infection due to the long-time close contact in house and frequent communication. It is critical to understand the transmission risk of COVID-19 under various scenario, especially during public health emergency. Taking the Tsinghua university's anniversary as a representative case, a set of prevention and control strategies are established and investigated. In the case study, an alumni group coming from out of campus is investigated whose activities and routes are designed based on the previous anniversary schedule. The social closeness indicator is introduced into the Wells-Riley model to consider the factor of contact frequency. Based on the anniversary scenario, this study predicts the number of the infected people in each exposure indoor location (including classroom, dining hall, meeting room and so on) and evaluates the effects of different intervention measures on reducing infection risk using the modified Wells-Riley model, such as ventilation, social distancing and wearing mask. The results demonstrate that when applying the intervention measure individually, increasing ventilation rate is found to be the most effective, whereas the efficiency of increased ventilation on reducing infection cases decreases with the increase of the ventilation rate. To better prevent COVID-19 transmission, the combined intervention measures are necessary to be taken, which show the similar effectiveness on the reduction of infected cases under different initial infector proportion. The results provide the insights into the infection risk on university campus when dealing with public health emergency and can guide university to formulate effective operational strategies to control the spread of COVID-19.

Keywords: COVID-19 · Infection risk · Intervention strategies · Wells-Riley model · Campus

1 Introduction

The coronavirus disease 2019 (COVID-19) spreads throughout the world, which has become a public health emergency of global concern [1, 2]. Indoor environment is critical for the occupants' safety in epidemic [3], especially when crowd conditions occur [4]. Due to the close contact and long-time presence of the same people in closed indoor environment, university campus is considered as a high-risk environment for the spread of infectious disease [5–8]. A university campus includes different functional indoor environments, where occupant density, ventilation rate and activity level are inconsistent, resulting in difference in virus transmission [9, 10]. Thus, the infection risk at various confined spaces on university campus should be evaluated separately.

Three transmission routes of COVID-19 are primarily discovered: contact, droplet, and airborne transmission. The droplet transmission and contact transmission have been identified as the major transmission routes [11]. Virus-containing droplets are released when an infector breaths, talks, sneezes, or coughs [12]. Some studies believed that the large respiratory droplets are deposited on the floor within 2m [13]. Whereas small infectious droplets/particles in the form of nucleus are dispensed and suspended over a long distance [14, 15]. Contact transmission is resulted from contacting a surface contaminated by the virus; droplet transmission is due to the inhalation of the respiratory droplets generated by infected person; airborne transmission is accomplished though inhaling the droplet nuclei [16, 17].

The Wells-Riley model and dose-response model are two kinds of models for quantitative evaluation of the infection risk. The dose-response model is related to the exposure amount to the virus [18], which is costly to obtain through experimental measurements or simulation results. The Wells–Riley model has been extensively used to perform risk assessment even when the infectious dose data of the pathogen are unavailable [19–21]. Since the infection dose cannot be obtained accurately, the Wells-Riley model is used in our study for quick risk evaluation. In the Wells-Riley model, the quantum is used as the minimum dose of airborne virus to cause the infection [22, 23]. According to the previous studies, the infection risk in various confined spaces has been investigated using the Wells-Riley model, such as buses, hospitals, schools, and aircraft cabins [24–26]. Dai et al. [27] estimated the infection risks for different closed spaces with various ventilation rates and evaluated the ventilation rate required to achieve a low infection risk of 1%. To further study the effect of social distancing, Sun et al. [28] introduced the social distance probability into the WR model and assessed the infection risk in confined indoor environment with various occupancy densities.

Some studies have been carried out on the evaluation of the infection risk on campus [10, 29, 30]. Xu et al. [29] estimated the infection risk of COVID-19 in U.S. schools and evaluated the effect of intervention measures on reducing the infection risk, including enhanced ventilation, air filtration, and hybrid learning. Shen et al. [30] proposed a approach to evaluate the effectiveness of indoor air quality measures for reducing the infection risk in various spaces. Various studies investigated the impacts of the intervention measures, which suggested that improved ventilation, air filtration and social distancing played essential roles in the reduction of infection risk [27, 31, 32]. Although some researchers have studied the infection risk of COVID-19 on campus, they focused mainly on the infection risk of individuals in different confined indoor environments base on daily activities. The spread of COVID-19 on campus during the large event with a large number of people coming from outside such as school anniversary remains elusive, when overcrowding and poorly-ventilation are more likely to occur.

In this study, different prevention and control measures are formulated to deal with public health emergency during a large event. Specially, the spread of COVID-19 during the university's anniversary is studied, taking Tsinghua University as an example. The activities and routes for an alumni group of 50 people coming from outside are designed. Based on the schedule of the alumni group, the number of infected people generated in different exposure locations is calculated utilizing the modified Wells-Riley model. The efficacy of different intervention measures on reducing the infected people number is investigated, including ventilation, social distancing and masks wearing. The results provide the insights for formulating effective intervention measures and individuals' self-protection.

2 Methodology

2.1 Model of Infection Risk

In this section, the Wells-Riley model is used to evaluate the infection risk of COVID-19. The WR model is shown as below:

$$P = 1 - \exp\left(-\frac{Iqpt}{Q}\right) = 1 - \exp\left(\frac{qptB}{Q/N}\right) \tag{1}$$

where P is the infection probability; I is the number of infectors; p is the pulmonary ventilation rate of susceptible individuals; q is the quanta generation rate (h^{-1}), which is estimated to be ranged from 14 to 48 h^{-1} by Dai [27] using a back-calculation form. Therefore, q is defined as the average value of 31 h^{-1} in this study [33], meaning a medium likelihood of being infected; t is the exposure time (h); Q is the ventilation rate (m^3/h); B is the proportion of infectors in the crowd, $B=I/N$ where N is the total number of occupants. Q/N is the fresh air volume per person ($m^3/h \cdot per$).

To investigate the impact of social distance on airborne disease infection risk, Sun et al. [28] developed a critical index-social distance probability into the WR model and has been widely used. The social distance index P_d represents the relationship between the statistical probability of virus-containing droplets and their transmission distances.

$$P_d = (-18.19\ln(d) + 43.276)/100 \tag{2}$$

where d is the social distance (m). Considering the filtration effect of the mask, mask index E_M is developed, which represents the mask effects on reducing the infection risk of susceptible individuals. Wearing a mask can not only reduce the amount of virus generated by infectors but also diminish the amount of virus inhaled by susceptible person. The E_M can be represented as:

$$E_M = (1 - f_I\eta_I)(1 - f_S\eta_S) \tag{3}$$

where η_I is the filtration efficiency for exhalation; η_S is the filtration efficiency for respiration. f_I and f_S are the proportion of infectors and susceptible individuals wearing masks, whose values are assumed to be same in this study. According to previous studies, the filtration efficiency of masks is proposed to be 50% [34], both filtration efficiencies of the masks are assumed to be 50% in this study.

Previous studies have proposed that simple epidemic-like models cannot generate the structure of real-world diffusion trees. Zhou et al. suggested that the real-world social networks lead to the discrepancy in the real spread and model spread [33]. The real-world social network has effect on the transmission of COVID-19. In our study, the studied alumni group has the same schedule during the simulation, who contact with each other for a long time and the infection risk among them is high. Thus, the effect of social contact closeness is also considered by the indicator ψ. If the susceptible individual is one in the alumni group, the value of ψ is assumed to be 2, otherwise $\psi = 1$. Integrating the social distance index P_d, mask index E_M and social closeness indicator ψ into Eq. (1), the modified WR model is derived as:

$$P_m = 1 - \exp\left(-P_d E_M \psi \frac{qpt\phi}{Q/N}\right) \tag{4}$$

2.2   Case Design

When facing public health crisis, it is a significant challenge for universities to carry out systematic prevention and control strategies to ensure the safety of people on campus. This study establishes a set of prevention and control strategies to deal with public health emergency during a large event under the influence of epidemic. First, the campus is divided into several areas generally, including teaching area, office area, dormitory area, and sports area. Second, according to the characteristics of various people on campus, people on campus are classified into several roles. Then the region-specific and role-specific management can be carried out to inhibit the cross-infection.

Taking the event of celebrating university's anniversary (Tsinghua university is chosen) as a representative case, the detailed prevention and control measures are demonstrated and investigated. During the anniversary, the crowd can be classified to several roles, including students, teachers, staff, and alumni. Since alumni is the most representative group in the anniversary, an alumni group with 50 people is selected as a key research object, who plays as a team. According to the anniversary schedule lasting three days on the last weekend of April (4/22–4/24, 2022), the routes and activities for the alumni group is designed, as shown in Fig. 1. The alumni group will visit several typical locations, including dining hall, classroom, museum, auditorium and so on. This study aims at evaluating the risk of epidemic brought by the alumni group during the anniversary by assessing the infection risk of each location where alumni have gone to. To achieve this target, the scene at each location should be specified, which includes the information on the exposure time, human behavior, total number of occupants and the number of people with different roles. The scenes for the alumni group are presented in Table 1. It should be noted that the infection risk in the hotel is neglected in this study.

The input parameters used in the baseline case are listed in Table 2. Since the pulmonary ventilation rate is closely related to human behavior, we consider the occupants' actives in the scene are sitting, whispering, eating, respectively. Duan [33] reported that $p = 0.3m^3/h$ when people are sitting, whispering, or participating in light activities. The value of pulmonary ventilation rate is then assigned as 0.3 or 0.78 based on the preset activity type [36]. The fresh air volume per person is determined according to the JGJ/1

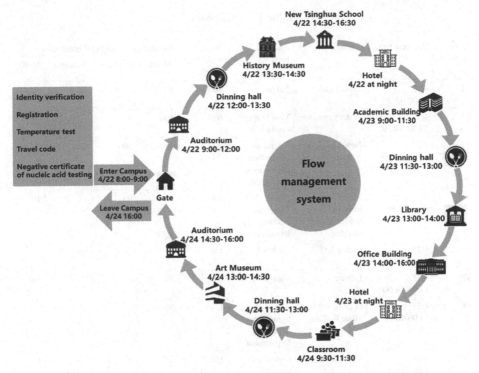

Fig. 1. Illustration of the route for the alumni group during the anniversary

309–2013 [37] standard, which provides the designed guideline of ventilation rates for different types of buildings. It should be noted that the fresh air volume per person presented in Table 2 is obtained according to the required minimum ventilation rate for each functional type of rooms. The actual ventilation rate (including natural ventilation and mechanical ventilation) may be much larger, which reduces the infection risk. For example, Park suggested that the ventilation rates were measured at 22.43 ACH [37] (equivalent to about 107–155 m^3/h·per) with the window opening ratio of 100% for the summer season. Moreover, the social distance is estimated according to the designed regulation (GB 9673–1996 1996) assuming that the seats are 100% occupied.

Table 1. The scenes for the alumni group at each location during anniversary

Scene number	Exposure time	Locations	Alumni behavior	Total number of people	Number of people in different roles			
					Alumni	Students	Teachers	Staff
S1	4/22 9:00–12:00	Auditorium	Watch the special performance for graduation anniversary	800	700	-	-	100

(continued)

Table 1. (*continued*)

Scene number	Exposure time	Locations	Alumni behavior	Total number of people	Number of people in different roles			
					Alumni	Students	Teachers	Staff
S2	4/22 12:00–13:30	Dining hall	Eat lunch	200	50	-	50	50
S3	4/22 13:30–14:30	History museum	Visit history exhibition	60	50	-	-	10
S4	4/22 14:30–16:30	New Tsinghua School	Attend the celebration for university's anniversary	2000	600	600	600	200
S5	4/23 9:00–11:30	Multifunctional room in academic Building	Attend Tsinghua information frontier Forum	150	50	90	-	10
S6	4/23 11:30–13:00	Dining hall	Eat lunch	150	50	-	50	50
S7	4/23 13:00–14:00	Library	Visit	60	50	-	-	10
S8	4/23 14:00–16:00	Lecture hall in office Building	Attend alumni Symposium held by Department	100	50	-	40	10
S9	4/24 9:30–11:30	West Classroom	Listen to the speech	150	50	60	30	10
S10	4/24 11:30–13:00	Dining hall	Eat lunch	200	50	-	100	50
S11	4/24 13:00–14:30	Art Museum	Visit Art Exhibition	60	50	-	-	10
S12	4/24 14:30–16:00	Auditorium	"Humanities Tsinghua" special lecture	800	200	300	200	100

The impacts of different intervention measures are investigated through modifying the input parameters. The intervention measures include increasing the ventilation rate (measure A1–A4), increasing social distance (measure B1–B4), wearing mask (measure C1–C4) and the combination of these three measures. The input parameters are as presented in Table 2, where the symbol '-' represents that the parameter values of the case are the same as those of the baseline case. Since it is impossible for individuals to wear masks during eating at the dining hall, the assumption that people are not wearing masks at the dining hall is made. Thus, when applying measure of wearing masks, the locations are divided into the dining hall and other locations, as shown in Table 2.

Table 2. Input parameters for baseline case and other cases which apply different intervention measures

Cases	Locations	fresh air volume per person, Q/N(m³/h·per)	Social distance, d(m)	Proportion of masks wearing
Baseline Case	Auditorium	12	0.78	0%
	Dining hall	25	0.9	0%
	History museum	16	0.76	0%
	New Tsinghua School	12	0.78	0%
	Multifunctional room in academic building	12	1	0%
	Library	17	0.76	0%
	Meeting room in office Building	12	1	0%
	West Classroom	24	1	0%
	Art Museum	16	0.76	0%
Measure A1	All locations	25	-	-
Measure A2	All locations	35	-	-
Measure A3	All locations	45	-	-
Measure A4	All locations	55	-	-
Measure B1	All locations	-	1	-
Measure B2	All locations	-	1.5	-
Measure B3	All locations	-	2	-
Measure B4	All locations	-	2.5	-
Measure C1	Dining hall	-	-	0%
	Other locations	-	-	40%
Measure C2	Dining hall	-	-	0%
	Other locations	-	-	60%
Measure C3	Dining hall	-	-	0%
	Other locations	-	-	80%
Measure C4	Dining hall	-	-	0%
	Other locations	-	-	100%
Measure A1 + B1 + C1	Dining hall	25	1	0%

(continued)

Table 2. (*continued*)

Cases	Locations	fresh air volume per person, $Q/N(m^3/h\cdot per)$	Social distance, $d(m)$	Proportion of masks wearing
	Other locations	25	1	40%
Measure A2 + B1 + C1	Dining hall	35	1	0%
	Other locations	35	1	40%
Measure A1 + B3 + C1	Dining hall	25	2	0%
	Other locations	25	2	40%
Measure A1 + B1 + C4	Dining hall	25	1	0%
	Other locations	25	1	100%

3   Results

3.1   The Transmission of COVID-19 Caused by the Alumni Group for the Baseline Case

For the baseline case, two initial infectors in alumni are assumed. As the number of the alumni group studied in this paper is 50, the initial infection portion is obtained as 4%. The modified WR model in Sect. 2.1 is applied to predict the transmission of COVID-19 for the baseline case. Figure 2 shows the total number of infected people generated in each scene and the number of infected students, teachers, staff, other alumni, respectively. As the alumni group of 50 people (research object in this study) act together, the number of infected people included in the alumni group at previous scene is treated as the number of initial infectors for the next scene, whereas the actions of other people are random whose route is not tracked. The type of infected people is determined according to the proportion of different roles included in each scene. In Fig. 2, it indicates that the infected people generated on April 22–24 are 8, 18 and 41, respectively. There is a rapid spread of virus on April 24 due to more initial infected alumni. The total number of infected people after three-day's activities is 68, including 27 people in the alumni group, 10 students, 15 teachers, 9 staff and 6 other alumni. Except the alumni group, the role with the largest number of infectors is teacher. This is because alumni are only allowed to eat in the teachers' dining hall according to the role-specific management. Besides, since the results are obtained based on the required minimum ventilation rate, the total number of infected people may be bigger than that for the actual situation. To further investigate the effect of ventilation, social distancing and wearing mask on reducing the infection risk, this case is regarded as the baseline case.

3.2   The Effect of Ventilation, Social Distancing and Wearing Mask on COVID-19 Transmission

As anticipated, the ventilation, social distancing and wearing mask are important measures in controlling the transmission of COVID-19. In this study, the effects of different

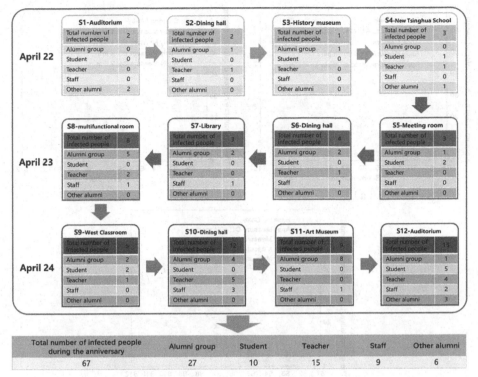

Fig. 2. The predicted results of baseline case: the number and type of infected people generated in each scene during the anniversary

intervention measures are investigated. The considered measures are summarized in Table 2.

Figure 3(a) shows that accumulative number of the infected people after increasing the ventilation rates in all scenes to 25 m³/h·per, 35 m³/h·per, 45 m³/h·per and 55 m³/h·per. As shown in Fig. 3(a), the number of infected people present an exponential increase in different scenes approximately. After the increase at ventilation rate, the number of infected people varies linearly, which results in a rapid decrease in the total number of infected people. When increasing ventilation rate to 35 m³/h·per, the total number of infected people is reduced to 16, representing a reduction of 76%. Increasing ventilation rate further to 45m³/h·per and 55 m³/h·per, the total number of infected people reduces to less than 10, indicating that enhanced ventilation is the effective measure to retard the spread of COVID-19. Moreover, with the increase of the ventilation rate, the efficiency of enhancing ventilation decreases: the total number of infected people is reduced by 38% when increasing the ventilation rate from 25 to 35 m³/h·per, which only be reduced by 1.5% when increasing the ventilation rate from 45 to 55 m³/h·per. Therefore, to further reduce the total number of infected people, only increasing the ventilation rate is not the most efficient measure when energy consumption is considered.

Social distancing can effectively reduce the infection risk of susceptible individuals. Figure 3(b) shows the variation in the accumulative number of infected people under

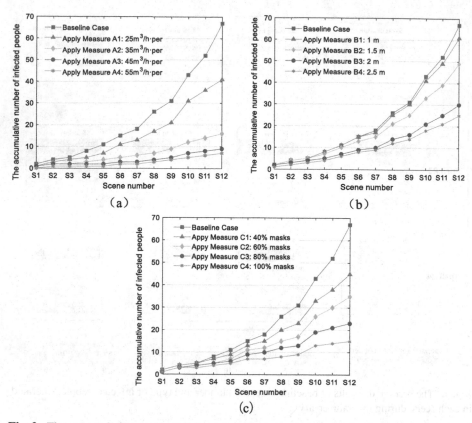

Fig. 3. The accumulative number of the infected people undern the implementation of three intervention measures: (a) increasing ventilation rate; (b) social distancing; (c) wearing mask

different conditions of increasing social distance to 1 m, 1.5 m, 2 m, and 2.5 m, respectively. It should be noted that although increasing social distance to 2 m or 2.5 m is not practical for the most cases, their effects on reducing the number of infected people are also studied. When increasing social distance to 1 m, the variation of infected people shows the similar trend with the baseline case, in which the number of the infected people only reduced by 7.5% compared with that for the baseline case. While when the distance is increased to more than 1.5 m, there is a significant reduction in the number of infectors. The number of infectors reduces to 46, 30 and 25 under social distances of 1.5 m, 2 m, and 2.5 m, respectively, representing a reduction of 32%, 55%, 63%. Since the social distance is restricted by the size of confined space, the decrease of infection risk is limited. Thus, only increasing social distance is not enough to achieve low infection risk (infected people less than 10).

The effect of wearing mask to control infection during the anniversary is investigated and the results are presented in Fig. 3(c). It can be observed that when 40%, 60%, 80% and 100% of individuals wear masks, the total number of infected people is reduced to 45, 35, 23 and 15, representing a reduction of 33%, 48% and 65% and 78% respectively. With the increase in the proportion of people wearing masks, the total number of infected people decreases proportionally approximately. Even when all people (100%) wear masks, the total number of infected people could not be reduced to the small, targeted number of 10. It is attributed to the assumption that no people wear masks at the dining hall (as mentioned above in Sect. 2.2), resulting in the failure to inhibit the transmission of virus. Thus, wearing mask measure should be combined with other measures to minimize the infection risk for all indoor spaces.

3.3 The Impact of Combined Intervention Measures on the COVID-19 Transmission

Figure 4 illustrates the variation in the accumulative number of infected people under combined intervention strategies. The results show that the combination of the strategies has a good performance on the control of transmission of COVID-19. Firstly, the measure A1 + B1 + C1 is applied, and the total number of infected people decreases to 24. Then we strengthen one kind of measures and keep other two kinds of measures unchanged to achieve the small, targeted number of infected people. After prediction by the modified WR model, it is found that implementing the combined measures of A2 + B1 + C1, A1 + B3 + C1 and A1 + B1 + C4 can reduce the total number of infected people to less than 10. The effects of these three combined measures reducing the infected cases are the same. It can be observed that when apply the measure A1 + B1 + C4, the majority infections happen at the dining hall (the scene of S5 and S9), suggesting that wearing mask can substantially diminish the infection at most locations except the dining hall. Compared with Fig. 3, it can be proposed that combined measures can lead to the adoption of lighter intervention measures, consequently improving the feasibility and people's comfort. The results are obtained by assuming that there are two initial infectors in alumni group. If more initial infectors exist in the alumni group, more restrictive strategies should be carried out to maintain the infection risk at a low level. According to the analysis, the university may select different strategies to control the spread of COVID-19 while considering other factors at the same time, such as manpower, energy efficiency, the difficulty of the implementation.

To achieve a targeted small number of infected people (lower than 10 in this study), the combined relationship of ventilation, social distancing and wearing mask is further clarified. The required minimum ventilation rate is estimated by different social distances (varying from 0.5 m to 3 m) and different proportions of individuals wearing masks (varying from 0% to 100%), as shown in Fig. 5. Under different measures of wearing masks, the required minimum ventilation rate shows similar trends with the increasing social distance. With the increase of the social distance, the efficiency of social distancing on reducing the required minimum ventilation rate decreases. For instance, among all the cases, the total number of infected people decreases by 12.9%–13.2% with the social distance increasing from 0.5 m to 0.75 m, which only decreases 5.4%–6.4% when the distance increases from 2.75 m to 3 m. Thus, adequate social distance should be kept based on the actual ventilation situation of confined space. Figure 5 shows that with the increase in the proportion (from 0% to 100%) of masks wearing, the required minimum ventilation decreases. When more than 40% of people wear masks, a rapid decrease in the total number of infected people occurs, indicating the necessity to ensure at least

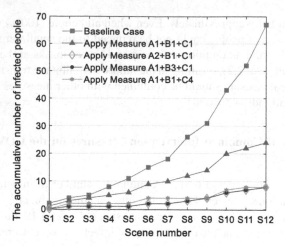

Fig. 4. The accumulative number of infected people under combined intervention measures

40% of people wear masks. The results can provide guideline for policymakers to select appropriate combination of these intervention measures according to actual situation.

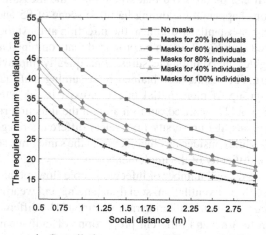

Fig. 5. The minimum required ventilation rate under different social distances and different proportions of people wearing masks to achieve the targeted small number of infected people (less than 10)

4 Discussion

4.1 The Transmission Risk Brought by Staff During the Anniversary

Different from other roles, staff always work at a fixed place and contact with many people, who may bring high infection risk once they are infected. Thus, the transmission of COVID-19 caused by infected staff is further investigated in this part. As dining hall is the location where the virus is most likely to spread, the infection caused by staffs of dining hall is selected and discussed as an example. Based on the results of baseline case in 3.1, there are 3 staffs are infected among 50 staffs in the dining hall. The number of people eating breakfast, lunch and dinner in the dining hall is supposed to be 200, respectively. The exposure time is set as 2.5 h. The modified WR model is used to predict the infection risk and the indicator of social contact closeness among staff is set as 2 similarly. Since people are unable to wear masks at the dining hall, only the measures of ventilation and social distancing can be taken. After applying the measure A2–A4 (increase ventilation rate from 35 to 55 m^3/h·per), the total number of infected people decreases to 11, 8,7. And applying the measure B2–B4 (increase social distance from 1.5 to 2.5m), the total number of infected people also decreases to 13, 11, 9, indicating that both measures are essential in reducing the infection risk in the dining hall. Meanwhile, since no people wear masks, more strict intervention measures should be carried out to ensure low infection risk, including but not limited to enhancing ventilation, social distancing, disinfection and staggering the dining hour.

4.2 The Comparison of Cases with Different Initial Infector Proportions

For the baseline case, the initial infector proportion is assumed to be 4%. To investigate the effect of initial infector proportion, three other initial infector proportions are designed. Figure 6 shows the accumulative number of infected people in each scene with different initial infector proportions. The total number of infected people under initial infector proportion of 2%, 4%, 6% and 8% is 47, 67, 94 and 125. It can be indicated that the total number of infected people increases linearly approximately with the increasing initial infector proportion. According to previous studies, when the dose of virus inhaled by susceptible individuals is small, the infection risk calculated by the WR model (Eq. (4)) is approximate to the linear form. Thus, the infection risk is proportional to the infector proportion in this study due to the small dose of inhaled virus, which can explain the trend shown in Fig. 6. The dotted line in the figure represents the number of infected people after applying intervention measure A1 + B1 + C1. The number has been reduced to 10, 23, 29 and 38 after applying the measure, representing a reduction of 78%, 66%, 69% and 70%, which suggests that the combined intervention measures show similar effectiveness on the reduction for infected cases under different initial infector proportions. Based on analysis, it can be indicated that conclusions obtained from the baseline case (4% initial infection proportion) are also applicable for the cases with different initial infection proportions.

4.3 The Limitations of This Study

Some limitations are remained in this paper. First, taking the anniversary scenario as a presentative case, the results in this study are obtained based on a fixed designed schedule for alumni, which might be different from actual situation. The probability of continuous contact between alumni and other people in different scenes is ignored, which may result in the underestimation of the results. Second, although the indicator representing the social closeness among individuals is introduced in the Wells-Riley model, an

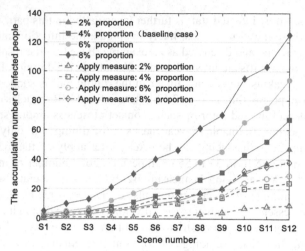

Fig. 6. The accumulative number of infected people under different initial infector proportion

empirical value is assigned for simplification due to the lack of actual data. The effect of social closeness will be investigated further in the future. Third, only the transmission of COVID-19 caused by the alumni group is tracked continuously, the possible transmission results from other infected people are not further predicted and discussed. Last but not the least, SARS-CoV-2 is known to transmit through contact, droplets, and aerosols. The droplet and aerosol transmission are considered in our modified Wells-Riley model, whereas the contact transmission is not involved in this study.

5 Conclusions

The spread of COVID-19 has been estimated under the anniversary scenario of Tsinghua University. Based on the designed alumni activities lasting for three days, the number of infected people generated in each scene during the anniversary is calculated. Multiple intervention strategies are modeled to assess their effectiveness in reducing the infection risk, including ventilation, social distancing, and wearing mask. Different initial infection proportions are also considered. The results are obtained as follows, which could provide the guideline for university to adopt appropriate intervention strategies to mitigate the spread of COVID-19 during a large event.

1. A social closeness indicator is introduced into the Wells-Riley model to evaluate the infection risk among alumni and other people. The number of infected people generated for different scenes are predicted based on the initial infector proportion of 4% in the alumni group using the modified WR model.

2. The respective effects of ventilation, social distancing and wearing mask on diminishing the spread of COVID-19 are evaluated. The results show that the efficiency of enhanced ventilation decreases with the increasing ventilation rate. When implementing the intervention measure individually, the required ventilation rate should reach more than 45 m^3/h to achieve the targeted small number of infected people (less than 10),

which is hard and costly to achieve by most current ventilation system. Nevertheless, the measures of only increasing social distance or wearing masks are not sufficiency to achieve the targeted small number of infected people.

3. The results show that the combination of the intervention measures has a good performance on the transmission of COVID-19. Meanwhile, the required minimum ventilation rate is estimated to achieve the small infection number (less than 10). The results propose that with the increase in social distance, its effect on the required minimum ventilation rate reduces. Besides, the required minimum ventilation rate decreases proportionally with increasing proportions of individuals wearing masks (20%–80%).

4. Since the conclusions obtained are based on the initial infector proportion of 4%, more cases with different initial proportions (i.e., 2%, 6%, 8%) are discussed. The results suggests that the total number of infected people increases linearly approximately with the increasing initial infector proportion. Moreover, the combined strategies show similar effectiveness on the reduction of infected cases under different initial infector proportions.

Acknowledgments. This work is supported by National Key R&D Program of China (No. 2021ZD0111200), National Natural Science Foundation of China (Grant No. 72174099, 72004113, 72104123), High-tech Discipline Construction Fundings for Universities in Beijing (Safety Science and Engineering).

References

1. Jahan, Y., Rahman, A.: COVID-19: Challenges and viewpoints from low-and-middle- income asian countries perspectives. J. Saf. Sci. Resil. 1 (2), 70–72 (2020)
2. Cucinotta, D., Vanelli, M.: WHO declares COVID-19 a pandemic. Acta bio-medica: Atenei Parmensis **91**(1), 157–160 (2020)
3. Ronchi, E., Lovreglio, R.: EXPOSED: An occupant exposure model for confined spaces to retrofit crowd models during a pandemic. Safety Sci. **130**, 104834 (2020)
4. Dong, B., Yan, D., Li, Z., et al.: Modeling occupancy and behavior for better building design and operation-A critical review. Build. Simul. **11**, 899–921 (2018)
5. D'Orazio, M., Bernardini, G., Quagliarini, E.: A probabilistic model to evaluate the effectiveness of main solutions to COVID-19 spreading in university buildings according to proximity and time-based consolidated criteria. Build. Simul. **14**(6), 1795–1809 (2021). https://doi.org/10.1007/s12273-021-0770-2
6. Anderson, R.M., Heesterbeek, H., Klinkenberg, D., et al.: How will country-based mitigation measures influence the course of the COVID-19 epidemic? Lancet **395**(10228), 931–934 (2020)
7. Bruinen de Bruin Y, Lequarre A-S, McCourt J, et al.: Initial impacts of global risk mitigation measures taken during the combatting of the COVID-19 pandemic. Safety Sci. 128, 104773 (2020)
8. Yang, Y., Peng, F., Wang, R., et al.: The deadly coronaviruses: The 2003 SARS pandemic and the 2020 novel coronavirus epidemic in China. J. Autoimmun. **109**, 102434 (2020)
9. Huan, X., Gang, Z., Peng, Z.: HVAC design for campus buildings. Heating Ventilating & Air Conditioning **36**(1), 8 (2006)
10. Li, J., Cheng, Z., Zhang, Y., et al.: Evaluation of infection risk for SARS-CoV-2 transmission on university campuses. Sci. Technol. Built. En. **27**, 1165–1180 (2021)

11. NHC. 2020. COVID-19 Diagnosis and Treatment Plan (Trial Eighth Edition), http://www.nhc.gov.cn/yzygj/s7653p/202008/0a7bdf12bd4b46e5bd28ca7f9a7f5e5a.shtml
12. CDC (2020a). Centers for disease control - "How COVD-19 spreads, https://www.cdc.gov/oronavirus/209-110ncov/prevent-getting-sick/how-covid-spreads
13. Shinohara, N., Sakaguchi, J., Kim, H., et al.: Survey of air exchange rates and evaluation of airborne infection risk of COVID-19 on commuter trains. Environ. Int. **157**, 106774 (2021)
14. Wells, W.: On air-borne infection: study II droplets and droplet nuclei. Am. J. Epidemiol. **20**(3), 611–618 (1934)
15. Xie, X., Li, Y., Chwang, A., Ho, P., et al.: How far droplets can move in indoor environments – revisiting the Wells evaporation–falling curve. Indoor Air **17**, 211–225 (2007)
16. WHO. Director-General's opening remarks at the media briefing on COVID-19 - March 11, 2020. World Health Organization, Geneva
17. WHO, 2021. Coronavirus Disease (COVID-19) Dashboard; World Health Organization, Geneva. https://covid19.who.int/ (accessed 28 March 2022)
18. To, G., Chao, C.: Review and comparison between the Wells-Riley and dose-response approaches to risk assessment of infectious respiratory diseases. Indoor Air **10**, 2–16 (2020)
19. Qian H, Zheng X.: Ventilation control for airborne transmission of human exhaled bio-aerosols in buildings. J. Thorac Dis. 10 (2018)
20. Ai, Z., Melikov, A.: Airborne spread of expiratory droplet nuclei between the occupants of indoor environments: a review. Indoor Air **28**(4), 500–524 (2018)
21. Zhang, S., Lin, Z.: Dilution-based evaluation of airborne infection risk - Thorough expansion of Wells-Riley model. Build. Environ. **194**, 107674 (2021)
22. W.F. Wells.: Airborne Contagion and Air Hygiene: an Ecological Study of Droplet Infection.Harvard University Press, Cambridge, MA, 1955
23. Li, C., Tang, H.: Study on ventilation rates and assessment of infection risks of COVID-19 in an outpatient building. J. Build. Eng. **42**, 103090 (2021)
24. Yan, Y., Li, C., Shang, Y., et al.: Evaluation of airborne disease infection risks in an airliner cabin using the Lagrangian-based Wells-Riley approach. Build. Environ. **121**, 79–92 (2017)
25. You, R., Lin, C., Wei, D., et al.: Evaluating the commercial airliner cabin environment with different air distribution systems. Indoor Air **29**, 840–853 (2019)
26. Qian, H., Li, Y., Nielsen, P., et al.: Spatial distribution of infection risk of SARS transmission in a hospital ward. Build. Environ. **44**, 1651–1658 (2009)
27. Dai, H., Zhao, B.: Association of the infection probability of COVID-19 with ventilation rates in confined spaces. Build. Simul. **13**(6), 1321–1327 (2020). https://doi.org/10.1007/s12273-020-0703-5
28. Sun, C., Zhai, Z.: The efficacy of social distance and ventilation effectiveness in preventing COVID-19 transmission. Sustain. Cities Soc. **62**, 102390 (2020)
29. Xu Y, CAI J, Li S, et al.: Airborne infection risks of SARS-CoV-2 in U.S. schools and impacts of different intervention strategies. Sustain. Cities Soc. 74, 103188 (2021)
30. Shen, J., Kong, M., Dong, B., et al.: A systematic approach to estimating the effectiveness of multi-scale IAQ strategies for reducing the risk of airborne infection of SARS-CoV-2. Build. Environ. **200**, 107926 (2021)
31. Kou, L., Wang, X., Li, Y., et al.: A multi-scale agent-based model of infectious disease transmission to assess the impact of vaccination and non-pharmaceutical interventions: The COVID-19 case. J. Saf. Sci. Resil. **2**, 199–207 (2021)
32. Niu, Y., Li, Z., Meng, L., et al.: The collaboration between infectious disease modeling and public health decision-making based on the COVID-19. J. Saf. Sci. Resil. **2**, 69–76 (2021)
33. Srivastavaa, S., Zhao, X., Manay, A., Chen, Q.: Effective ventilation and air disinfection system for reducing coronavirus disease 2019 (COVID-19) infection risk in office buildings. Sustain. Cities Soc. **75**, 103408 (2021)

34. Davies, A., Thompson, K.A., Giri, K., Kafatos, G., Walker, J., Bennett, A.: Testing the efficacy of homemade masks: would they protect in an influenza pandemic? Disaster Med. Public. **7**, 413–418 (2013)

35. Zhou, B., Pei, S., Muchnik, L., et al.: Realistic modelling of information spread using peer-to-peer diffusion patterns. Nat. Hum. Behav. **4**, 1198–1207 (2020)

36. EPA. (2011). Exposure factors handbook 2011 (Edition). Final Report

37. Park, S., Choi, Y., Song, D., Kim, E.: Natural ventilation Measure and related issues to prevent coronavirus disease 2019 (COVID-19) airborne transmission in a school building. Sci. Total Environ. **789**, 147764 (2021)

Social Resilience Assessment for Urban System: A Case Study of COVID-19 Epidemic

Rui Ba[1], Chenyang Wang[2], Luyao Kou[2], Xiaojing Guo[2], and Hui Zhang[2(✉)]

[1] School of National Security, People's Public Security University of China, Beijing 100038, China

[2] Institute of Public Safety Research, Tsinghua University, Beijing 100084, China
zhhui@mail.tsinghua.edu.cn

Abstract. With the surge of deep uncertainties and multi-dimensional impacts of crisis events, social resilience assessment needs to advance the analysis of dynamic influencing process for urban system. To this end, this paper investigates the resilience assessment method of social resilience by using the differences analysis between capacities and demands. A gap analysis-based assessment method for social resilience is developed to quantify the resilience gap and levels, and a systemic resilience analysis framework is proposed to support overall analysis of urban systems. To verify the proposed method, we apply it to the novel coronavirus 2019 (COVID-19) epidemic in Shanghai during the period of February to May, 2022. Based on the data analysis of COVID-19-related cases, we compared the capacities and demands in urban medical system of patients transferring, admission and healing procedure. The fluctuations of resilience levels are examined and discussed. In addition, the resilience analysis of social systems and governance capacity in COVID-19 crisis are further carried out, and three-layer measures and procedure optimizations are introduced to build social resilience. The proposed resilience assessment method and systemic resilience management measures have potential implications and applications in the practical epidemic prevention and control.

Keywords: Resilience · Capacities and demands · Social governance · Data analysis · COVID-19 epidemic

1 Introduction

Resilience receives extensive attentions in recent years, which is applied in urban planning, social governance, economic development and anthropic status. According to risks at different levels [1], the connotations of resilience range from national, urban, social, community, infrastructure, organizational, psychological scales [2–5]. Among them, social resilience is more concentrated with the resistance and recovery of human society from crisis events to guarantee social security and stable development [6]. Especially, under the continuous and repetitive disruptions, social resilience becomes particularly important.

Social resilience reflects the ability of urban system to adapt, response and recover from disruptions with combined effects of social, economic, political, integrated, valued and other urban elements [7]. The disturbances of disasters to social resilience have been widely investigated in respects to threat type and system type, such as seismic resilience [8], flood resilience [9], multi-hazards [10], or supply system [11], transportation system [12], power system [13, 14] and economic system [15]. Among them, the social actions and impacts are increasingly emphasized to advance social resilience. For example, to enhance social-ecological resilience exposed to abrupt coastal disasters, Adger et al. [16] summarized local- and regional-scale actions to mitigate risks of hazard, maintain system functionality, and improve adaptive capacity, including measures of sustainable use, diverse mechanisms, governance organizations and social capital. In addition, Imperiale et al. [17] analyzed multi-dimensional social impacts affected by disasters and categorized them into eight aspects (health, community, culture, livelihoods, infrastructure, housing, environment and land). A paradigm of resilience building and disaster risk reduction (DRR) was also proposed to overcome cultural and political barriers in social-ecological governance. With the deepening and enrichment of research, social resilience further incorporated the roles of power, politics and participation in the context of threats and uncertainties [18]. Moreover, city's values (like diversity and sustainability) are also emphasized in the British standard [19] to guide resilience assessment and prioritization process.

Social resilience may suffer multiple, continuous and cascading impacts provoked by shocks, stress and resilience. The stakeholders comprise people, groups and organizations, while a variety of operating systems can affect resilience or be affected by the disruptions. For example, in the context of epidemic, health and medical system is the first and foremost disturbed in social system to cope with significantly increasing patients. Haldane et al. [20] used a health systems resilience framework to analyze domains of governance and financing, health workforce, community engagement and other efforts to contain and mitigate epidemic spread. Four elements of comprehensive responses, adaptation capacity, functions and resources preservation, and vulnerability reduction were further proposed to enhance system resilience. Besides, the supply chain [11, 21] and logistics [22] system in various scales of provincial, regional and international chain has gained prominent attentions. The resilience strategies, such as prepositioning extra-inventory and a backup supplier, were simulated and compared the abilities to meet demands [23]. To explain the factors fostering social resilience, Juan Sebastián et al. [24] conducted a survey in Spain, and the findings highlighted the importance of political communication, that is the governance system. Moreover, Ba and Zhang et al. [3, 10] integrated the cognitive domain (e.g., spirit and culture) which is a vital part in disaster response and resilience building beyond the physical system aspects of cities. In the face of diverse demands of social communities, McClelland et al. [25] emphasized the top-down and bottom-up collaboration of stakeholders across informal and formal approaches to promote whole-of-society resilience.

To quantitatively assess and describe social resilience, several kinds of assessment methods were developed, mainly consisting of scorecard [26], models [4], indicator system [7, 27] and procedure analysis [25]. The United Nations International Strategy for Disaster Reduction (UNISDR) proposed a disaster resilience scorecard, which is comprised of ten essentials and 117 indicator criteria [26]. The calculation of resilience triangle area [8, 28] was commonly used to measure both of functionality changes and recovery rapidity. In addition, Kameshwar et al. [4] developed a probabilistic resilience assessment model by incorporating decision-support framework and Bayesian networks to quantify the joint probability of achieving robustness and rapidity. Meanwhile, a set of indicators were also introduced to quantify the resilience of criminogenic ecosystems [27], and the community resilience to multi-hazards [7], such as FEMA's population- and community-focused measures [29]. Furthermore, the International Standard Organization (ISO) conducted practice-based initiatives to construct technical specification of "ISO/TS 22393 - Guidelines for planning Recovery and Renewal" [25]. It provides a framework to assess the COVID-19 impacts on communities, and guide the development of recovery plans and renewal strategies to build resilience. These resilience assessment methods significantly promoted effective analysis of social resilience, whereas the impacts of disruption on dynamic system process still lacks resilience analysis and quantitative characterization.

In view of the deficiency of dynamic process resilience assessment for urban system, this paper aims to propose a fast, quantitative and applicable method to analyze social resilience gap and fluctuations of resilience levels. We propose a gap analysis-based assessment method by incorporating the comparisons of capacities and demands, and a systemic resilience analysis framework. The method is applied to the case study of COVID-19 epidemic in Shanghai. The procedure of medical system and the systemic resilience analysis is carried out to develop resilience management measures.

2   Gap Analysis-Based Assessment Method

In contrast to the performance-based resilience assessment methods like resilience triangle [8], the gap between demands and capacities is analyzed and used to assess social resilience. Figure 1 shows the conceptual model for resilience assessment. Inspired by the British standard of city resilience guide [19], we revised the resilience assessment method based on resilience gap analysis between system capacity and demands, as illustrated in Fig. 1(a). The social resilience stakeholder groups in urban system consist of the sectors, agencies, organizations, systems and citizens. System capacities represent that the current system already has measures in place to mitigate, adapt and response to the effects of shocks and stresses. It mainly comprises the adaptive, integrated, valued and durable measures, where partial sub-categories of each capacity are listed in Fig. 1(a). System demands refer to the overall risk with dynamic changes of probability and impact to the system provoked by shocks, stresses and challenges, including multiple effects of external and internal, conflicts, emergencies, ongoing disturbances and etc. Based on the comparison analysis of system capacities and demands, the resilience gap can be used as an indicator to evaluate social resilience levels, so as to determine major strategies, prioritized actions and implemented measures for resilience management and improvement. Following the shocks, stresses or challenges, typical changing trends over time in system capacities (green curve), system demands (blue curve) and their differences to represent resilience gap (gray curve) are shown in Fig. 1(b). The vertical axis in the figure represents the changes of monitoring values of social systems (like the number of supplies of medical system, the number of vehicles of public services) from the start time (n_i) to recovery time (n_j) under disruptions. According to gap analysis between capacities and demands, the resilience levels can be identified, such as three kinds of high, middle and low resilience.

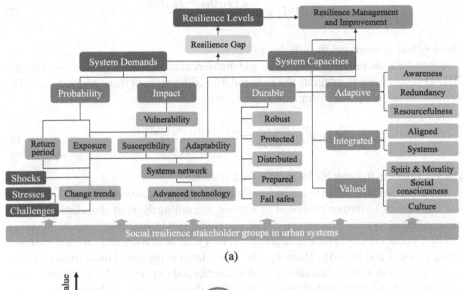

(a)

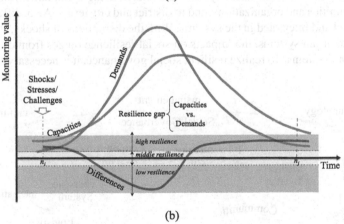

(b)

Fig. 1. Conceptual model of resilience assessment method. (a) Resilience assessment and prioritization process (revised from the BSI standard [19]); (b) Resilience gap over time by comparing demands and capacities following shocks or stresses.

In order to quantificationally represent the resilience gap, the Relative Difference in resilience levels (RD) [27] is used to calculate the amount of demands relative to the actual capacities of social system in the n-th day (Eq. 1). It can be used to measure the fluctuations of relative difference level.

$$RD = \frac{Y_C(n) - Y_D(n)}{Y_{C(n)}} \qquad (1)$$

where Y_C and Y_D refer to actual capacities and demands in n-th day.

To realize resilience assessment in a period of time, an indicator namely Capacities-Demands Difference Resilience Indicator (CDDRI) is further developed to calculate the cumulative differences as the Eq. 2 shown.

$$CDDRI = \frac{\sum_{n_i}^{n_j}(Y_C(n) - Y_D(n))}{\sum_{n_i}^{n_j} Y_C(n)} \tag{2}$$

where n_i and n_j represent the i-th day to j-th day.

Since there are multiple subsystems and measurements in social system, the indicator CDDRI is necessary to integrate the accumulative differences of these comparisons. The corresponding function is formulated as follows:

$$CDDRI = \sum_1^r \frac{\sum_{n_i}^{n_j}(Y_{Cr}(n) - Y_{Dr}(n))}{\sum_{n_i}^{n_j} Y_{Cr}(n)} \tag{3}$$

where r refers to the specific items in social system.

Based on social resilience assessment for urban systems, a systemic resilience analysis framework is further proposed to support overall analysis of interdependent and interconnected systems. As shown in Fig. 2, typical systems consist of medical, infrastructure, economic, cyberspace, logistics, ecological, education and cultural systems, public services and so forth. These systems are related to the social units from individuals to communities and organizations, and to district and city levels. Also, different cities are connected and integrated in the systems. With the disruptions of shocks, stresses and challenges to urban systems, the impacts on social resilience ranges from different levels, scales and systems. To realize resilient social governance, it is necessary to combine

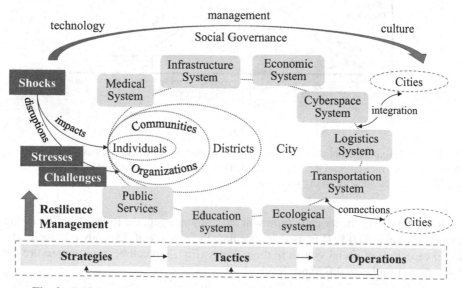

Fig. 2. Social resilience assessment for urban system: subsystems and governance.

three dimensions of technology, management and culture, while three-layer measures of strategies-tactics-operations are developed to carry out resilience management for urban system.

3   Case Analysis of COVID-19 Epidemic

3.1   Materials and Methods

Study Area and Data. Since the outbreak of COVID-19 epidemic in Shanghai, China in early March 2022, daily new COVID-19 cases rise from a few to thousands. In order to assess social resilience from the point of capacities and demands comparison, the data of COVID-19-related cases are used to derive actual demands, which is acquired from official statistics of the Shanghai Municipal Health Commission (https://wsjkw. sh.gov.cn/). It is worth noting that some realistic data in reference to the capacities of medical system has not yet been publicly available or detailed statistics at this stage. Despite this, we collect the data reported in official statistics and news report, and some hypothetical data is also used to characterize system capacities to further validate our method in resilience analysis. A few statistics data related to the original condition of medical system are accessed from the Shanghai Municipal Bureau of Statistics (http:// tjj.sh.gov.cn/).

Resilience Assessment Method. The proposed resilience assessment method described in Sect. 2 is adopted to the resilience gap analysis for medical system. As shown in Fig. 3, main procedure of patients transferring, admission and healing in medical system is illustrated to support systemic analysis and resilience assessment. According to the COVID-19 diagnosis and treatment plan (ninth trial version) [30], Fig. 3(a) presents four kinds of COVID-19-related patients (*a* to *d*) in the ideal procedure of system network scenario. These kinds of patients are transferred, admitted and healed among urban communities, centralized isolation sites, Fangcang shelter hospitals and designated hospitals. In addition, Fig. 3(b) demonstrates the topological structure of medical system network and necessary demands in critical nodes. In order to realize resilience assessment, the number of vehicles and drivers are used for representing the capacity of patients transferring, the amount of treatment beds and nutrient of energy measures patients admission capacity, while the staffs, equipment and drugs are responsible for the assessment of patients healing capacity. The evaluation indicators for resilience assessment of medical system are listed in Table 1.

3.2   Data Analysis Results

According to the daily official statistics of local COVID-19-related cases, Fig. 4(a) shows the number of daily new confirmed patients (red color), asymptomatic infections (navy color) and recovery cases (green color) in Shanghai since February 26 to May 30, 2022. As interpreted in Table 1, the recovery cases include the cured and discharged cases as well as asymptomatic infections released from medical observation. The existing cumulative cases are a comprehensive representation of the sum of confirmed, asymptomatic

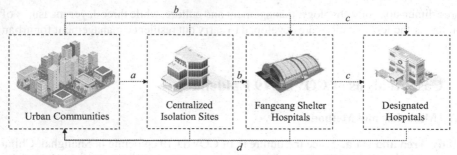

Legends: *a* - suspected patients or close contacts; *b* - patients with mild to moderate symptoms or asymptomatic infection; *c* - patients with moderate to severe symptoms; *d* - recovered COVID-19 patients.

(a) ideal procedure of patients in medical system network scenario

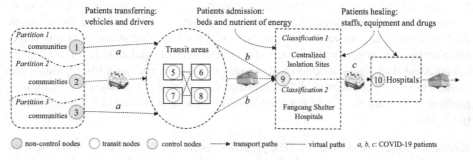

(b) topological structure and necessary demands in critical nodes

Fig. 3. Main procedure of patients transferring, admission and healing in medical system.

Table 1. Evaluation indicators for resilience assessment of medical system.

Indicator	Subcategory	Interpretation	Calculation
Existing COVID-19-related cases (P)	confirmed cases (P_c)	Confirmed COVID-19 cases, it also includes the cases turned from asymptomatic infections (P_{ac})	$P(n) = P_c(n) + P_a(n) + P_s(n)\text{-}P_{ac}(n)\text{-}P_r(n)\text{-}P_d(n)$
	asymptomatic infections (P_a)	COVID-19 asymptomatic infections are with the positive nucleic acid test, but no clinical symptoms	

(continued)

Table 1. (*continued*)

Indicator	Subcategory	Interpretation	Calculation
	suspected cases (P_s)	Suspected cases are people with any one of epidemiological history, and any two of clinical symptoms in [30]	
	recovery cases (P_r)	Recovery cases also include the cured patients (P_{rc}) and asymptomatic infections released from medical observation (P_{ra})	
	hospitalized cases (P_h)	Hospitalized cases are people who are still being treated in hospital	
	deaths (P_d)	Deaths due to COVID-19	
	cases at social community (P_{sc})	COVID-19 cases detected at the social community level, i.e., the cases outside of isolation and control	
Patient transferring capacity (*PT*)	vehicles (PT_v)	Negative pressure ambulances and buses used to transfer patients, in principle an ambulance only transfer one confirmed case, except for those infected with same COVID-19 strain. Assuming a maximum of 40 patients in a bus and 5 patients in an ambulance	$PT_v(n) =$ $(P_c(n)\text{-}P_{ac}(n)\text{-}P_d(n)\text{-}P_{rc}(n)\text{-}P_h(n))/5 +$ $(P_a(n) + P_s(n) + P_{rc}(n))/40$

(*continued*)

Table 1. (*continued*)

Indicator	Subcategory	Interpretation	Calculation
	drivers (PT_d)	Suppose a car is staffed with three drivers and three workers, one driver and one worker each time for 8 h, working three shifts a day	$PT_d(n) = PT_v(n) \times 6$
Patient admission capacity (*PA*)	beds (PA_b)	Treatment beds in the designated hospitals, Fangcang shelter hospitals and centralized isolation sites, herein one patient with one bed	$PA_b(n) = P(n)$
	nutrient of energy (PA_e)	Nutrient of energy refers to the minimum daily food requirements per person, which is 2100 kcals according to the UNHCR emergency food assistance standard [31]	$PA_e(n) = P(n) \times 2100$
Patient healing capacity (*PH*)	staff (PH_s)	Doctors and nurses are served for patients according to the principle of minimum requirements: 10 patients with 1 doctor and 1 nurse on average [32]	$PH_s(n) = P(n)/10 \times 2$
	equipment (PH_e)	Equipment is used for patient treatment, suppose the requirement per person is M_e, and 5% of patients requires the equipment like ventilator	$PH_e(n) = P_c(n) \times 0.05 \times M_e$
	drugs (PH_d)	Drugs for medical treatment, suppose the amount of fundamental medicine required per person is M_d	$PH_d(n) = P(n) \times M_d$

Note: UNHCR is the United Nations High Commissioner for Refugees; the number of COVID-19-related cases are reported by the Shanghai Municipal Health Commission infected and suspected cases minus the sum of confirmed cases turned from asymptomatic infections, recovery cases and deaths. Figure 4(b) presents the development trend of existing cumulative cases. It can be seen that the number of existing cumulative cases peaked on April 17 with a number of 293,290 and then declined gradually, as the fluctuation of recovery cases increased and that of confirmed cases and asymptomatic infections decreased. Compared to the statistics data in Fig. 4(a) and (b), new social community cases detected outside isolation and control (Fig. 4(c)) is more practical for the analysis and judgment of epidemic development trend, management and control, and resilience recovery. The data shows that the cases at social community level experienced a rapid development phase since March 9, and remained at a high level from late March to late April. From the May 14, the social community cases tend to zero transmission with occasional daily single-digit cases. This indicates that the spread risk of the epidemic in social community level is controllable, so that the orderly recovery of production and life can be gradually promoted.

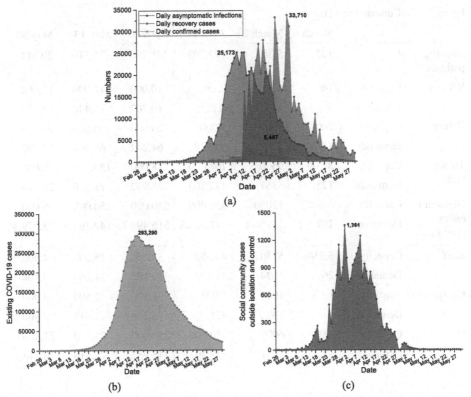

Fig. 4. Daily number of new confirmed, asymptomatic infected and recovered COVID-19 cases (a), the existing cumulative cases (b) and new social community cases detected outside isolation and control (c) in Shanghai since February 26 to May 30, 2022.

Based on the initial data of social and medical system reported in the news reports and official statistics, the hypothetical data in several time points is used to validate the proposed resilience assessment model for the analysis of main changes in COVID-19 patient transferring, admission and healing procedure (Table 2). The values of resilience indicator CDDRI at several time points and the analysis of resilience level are presented in Fig. 5. The CDDRI values (red line with red dot symbol) have a sharp decrease since the outbreak of epidemic due to insufficient capacity to meet rapidly growing demands. Then, it gradually increases as capacities improve and demands decrease. Accordingly, the resilience level changes from high resilience to middle and low level, then recovers to middle resilience. It is worth noting that social resilience in the context of an epidemic is not only related to medical system, but also to multiple other urban systems including logistics, infrastructure, public services and so forth. The capacities for transferring, admission and healing of patients comprehensively affect the building of social resilience.

Table 2. Main changes in patient transferring, admission and healing procedure.

Items	Comparison	Date					
		March 6	March 23	April 9	April 26	May 13	May 30
Existing patients	/	125	5,361	177,203	245,952	71,316	20,514
Vehicles	Capacity	140	160	2,180	10,000	11,000	12,000
	Demands	3	143	4,123	10,707	11,444	11,632
Drivers	Capacity	200	300	5,000	20,000	60,000	70,000
	Demands	18	858	24,738	64,242	68,664	69,792
Treatment beds	Capacity	8,000	9500	168,000	218,000	150,000	50,000
	Demands	125	5361	177,203	245,952	71,316	20,514
Nutrient of energy (10^3 kcal)	Capacity	3,000	12000	350,000	550,000	150,000	50,000
	Demands	262.5	11258.1	372,126.3	516,499.2	149,763.6	43,079.4
Staff	Capacity	5,350	5350	43,350	53,000	15,000	4,500
	Demands	26	1074	35,442	49,192	14,264	4,104
Equipment (M_e)	Capacity	1,000	1000	1,000	1,800	2,500	3,000
	Demands	1	13	321	2,228	2,848	2,900
Drugs (M_d)	Capacity	3,000	6000	150,000	250,000	75,000	21,000
	Demands	125	5361	177,203	245,952	71,316	20,514

3.3 Resilience Analysis

To explore the impacts of COVID-19 epidemic on social resilience and urban systems, based on the proposed systemic resilience analysis framework, Fig. 6 systematizes and reveals the interrelationships, relevance risks, coupling effects and response measures for medical system and other related urban systems. The ability to contain the epidemic actually reflects capacity of social governance including dimensions of technology, management and culture. When an epidemic occurs, the medical system bears the brunt and is closely interrelated to other systems. For example, infrastructure system provides water, electricity, gas security and the construction of temporary hospitals; logistics system and public services carry the functions of patients transfer and material logistics for human society; cyberspace covers the dissemination of information about epidemic, social public opinion and its guidance and governance; cultural system refers to people's awareness of self-protection, social safety culture and degree of policy cooperation. In

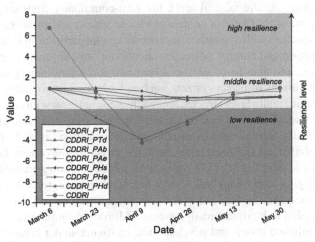

Fig. 5. CDDRI results and resilience assessment for medical system under COVID-19 epidemic.

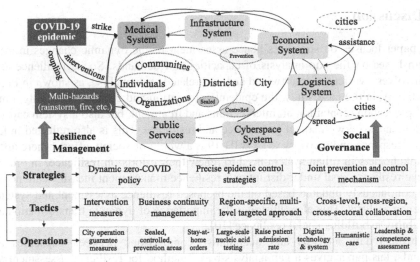

Fig. 6. Social resilience assessment for urban system: three-layer measures of strategies-tactics-operations.

addition, the multi-hazard risks superimposed by epidemic and disasters (e.g., rainstorm, fire) exacerbate the complexity and instability of social system. The internal cascading effects and interactions from medical system to other social systems, as well as external connections with other cities need to be considered and managed at a global level to enhance social resilience.

Three-layer measures of strategies-tactics-operations are developed to carry out resilience management. For the overall strategies, dynamic zero-COVID policy is a resilient epidemic prevention policy that should be followed at current stage of China due to the insufficient medical resources and masses of elderly people. It is necessary to combine and apply the precise epidemic control strategies and joint prevention and control mechanism. At the tactical level, the zero-community transmission policy is an operational, available tactic to contain epidemic spread and promote recovery and renewal, in conjunction with dynamic adjustment of spatial partition and classification for epidemic prevention and control. Managers should not only implement epidemic intervention measures, but also focus on social business continuity management to ensure fundamental operations of urban systems, such as logistics system and public services. The region-specific, multi-level targeted approach in conjunction with cross-level, cross-region and cross-sectoral collaboration are also vital tactics to epidemic prevention and control. Specifically, the operations of epidemic interventions include the classification of sealed, controlled and prevention areas, the stay-at-home orders, large-scale and normalized nucleic acid testing [33], along with social operating guarantee measures. Among them, digital technology and system is crucial to trace, record and identify the COVID-19 contacts, but the leadership and competence with or without these technologies are also needed to be dynamically assessed. Moreover, humanistic care is of great importance to enhance moral and psychological resilience under community or urban lockdown.

4 Discussion

This paper focuses on social resilience assessment of the dynamic changes in urban system based on the gap analysis of capacities and demands. Social resilience actually involves a variety of intertwined and interrelated systems [34], as shown in Fig. 2. Specifically, in the case study, the epidemic prevention and control is not only a matter of prevention, containment, interventions and treatment, but also a system capacity and demand issue with social governance and resilience. This is also reflected in [25] that the response and recovery to COVID-19 is a whole-of-society effort, where different stakeholders in urban system need to renew their efforts on resilience. In order to achieve resilience goal under disruptions, resilience management measures are needed to be continuously updated based on the proposed resilience assessment and systemic resilience analysis. This also illustrates the importance of dynamic transformation and learnability in building social resilience [10].

Through data analysis and quantitative comparisons between capacities and demands, this paper gives a gap analysis-based method for resilience assessment and systemic resilience analysis framework (Figs. 1 and 2). Based on the resilience analysis for medical system procedure with the proposed assessment method (Table 1 and Fig. 5), it is reasonable to believe that redundancy or excess capacity is significant for building social resilience, which is also emphasized in [4, 12]. Meanwhile, business continuity planning or management is proved to be critical in the process of epidemic prevention and control [26], because of the close interrelationships among urban systems. To enhance the restorative rapidity of social resilience, it is crucial to make efforts to realize zero-community transmission as soon as possible (Fig. 4). In practical, it also served as an indicator for the resumption of work and production. Besides, it is thus demanding to sort out and guarantee urban critical businesses during the period of epidemic prevention and control. Simultaneously, it is necessary to ensure that all these businesses are operated in a separate system, like closed-loop management, to coordinate citizens' lives, economic development, and epidemic prevention and control. We believe that the proposed multilayered measures of strategies-tactics-operations are helpful to resilience management so as to improve social resilience.

Towards the procedure scenario of patient transferring, admission and healing of urban medical system illustrated in Fig. 3, several kinds of procedure optimizations are introduced to promptly balance system capacities to increasing system demands. The first is to reduce the number of people entering node 9. In view of the significantly increased demands of transferring vehicles, drivers, admission beds and medical staffs, the stay-at-home isolations for the close and secondary contacts are worth trying and applying, even for asymptomatic infections in case of run out of medical resources. Definitely, it is necessary to guarantee the isolation hardware facilities and support conditions in advance, and ensure the living materials and medicines for the people in home isolation (nodes 1, 2 and 3). Secondly, it is possible to increase the number of people out of the hospitals (nodes 9 and 10) by shortening the length of hospital stay, thereby accelerating the turnover of admission beds and increasing the admission rate of patients. As the new regulations stated [35], the principles of isolation time and discharge criteria has been optimized and standardized. In addition, it is important to enhance the construction capacity of temporary hospitals, the number of medical staff and the supply of materials through the support of other cities and the central government, so as to improve resourcefulness and recovery rapidity. Moreover, in the nodes 4 to 8 of patient transfer process, it is crucial for rational planning and unified transfer of COVID-19-related cases by geographic region, floors and units, and by patient type and severity. This kinds of classification, partition and stratification of patients help to effectively advance capacity of patient transferring.

In addition to the impacts of epidemic on medical system and physical domain, the mental blow of individuals and effects on social consciousness is also of importance to social resilience. According to the five-stage process of denial, anger, bargaining, depression and acceptance of Kubler-Ross theory [36], the personal spiritual and social consciousness status in the context of the Shanghai epidemic is also divided into five stages. At the first stage, there was denial and panic emotions mixed with curious attitude during the initial city lockdown. With the increase of lockdown time and the consumption of household supplies, extreme angry spread and dominated. Supplies shortage of logistics system induced the changes of social mood. Afterwards, the irritability state develops and depression emotion increases, while people's focuses range from epidemic to work. At the fifth stage, acceptance to the life may be a kind of popular condition, with fewer concerns about unlock or not. The recovery of cultural system may take a long time in view of the complexity of emotional changes. More attention should be paid to people's well-being, psychological care and stimulus actions to create a culture of moral resilience [37].

Limitations: The resilience assessment mainly focused on the macroscale analysis of capacities and demands based on the limited and hypothetical data of COVID-19 local cases in Shanghai. It should be stated that cases imported to Shanghai from abroad are not considered because they are under closed-loop management after entering the city. Besides, more detailed and realistic data is actually needed to validate and improve the proposed resilience assessment method. For example, once the true number of transferred patients among nodes 1–3, 9 and 10 is obtained, the actual demands can be determined for comparison with real capacities. Also, the relationship of causality, influence and interaction among the indicators of medical systems are necessary to be further explored. By integrating fine-grained data of system capacities and detailed procedure network data related to epidemic, future investigations will be devoted to refined modeling and analysis of social resilience.

5 Conclusion

To solve the deficiency of resilience assessment for dynamic system process, we propose a gap analysis-based assessment method to analyze resilience gap and level with the comparisons between capacities and demands. The advantages of the proposed model come from quantitative comparison assessment and applicable resilience analysis for various aspects of dynamic system process. A systemic resilience analysis framework is also developed to carry out social resilience analysis of urban system, which contributes to improve the resilience management and social governance.

The method is then applied to the case of COVID-19 epidemic in Shanghai, and investigated the procedure of patients transferring, admission and healing in medical system. Results show that with the development of the epidemic, the resilience levels experienced fluctuations from high to low level, and then recovering to middle resilience. Meanwhile, through the resilience analysis of social system and governance capacity, the interrelationships, relevance risks and coupling effects of medical system and related urban systems are systematically revealed. We emphasize on the resilience-building efforts during the epidemic, including the improvement of capacities to meet demands, and overall resilience management of interrelated systems, cities and transboundary risks. Furthermore, three-layer measures of strategies-tactics-operations and several kinds of procedure optimization plans are introduced to promote resilience management. Future research will be devoted to microscale resilience analysis by using network partitions, agent-based modeling and fine-grained multi-dimensional data.

Acknowledgments. This work is supported by National Key R&D Program of China (No. 2021ZD0111200), National Science Foundation of China (Grant No. 72204134, 72174099) and High-tech Discipline Construction Fundings for Universities in Beijing (Safety Science and Engineering).

References

1. Anna, K., McLeod Logan, T.: Resilience: lessons to be learned from safety and acceptable risk. J. Saf. Sci. Resilience **2**, 253–257 (2021)
2. Kimhi, S., Eshel, Y., Marciano, H., Adini, B.: Fluctuations in national resilience during the COVID-19 pandemic. Int. J. Environ. Res. Public Health **18**, 3876 (2021)
3. Ba, R., Zhang, Y., Liu, Y., Zhang, H.: Three-layer and four-domain scenario analysis method and its application to urban complex disasters. Qinghua Daxue Xuebao/J. Tsinghua Univ. 1–12 (2022). https://doi.org/10.16511/j.cnki.qhdxxb.2022.22.029
4. Kameshwar, S., et al.: Probabilistic decision-support framework for community resilience: incorporating multi-hazards, infrastructure interdependencies, and resilience goals in a Bayesian network. Reliab. Eng. Syst. Saf. **191**, 106568 (2019)
5. Denckla, C.A., et al.: Psychological resilience: an update on definitions, a critical appraisal, and research recommendations. Eur. J. Psychotraumatol. **11**, 1822064 (2020)
6. Ghesquiere, F.D., Simpson, A.L., Phillips Solomon, E., Toro, J., Balog-Way, S.A.B., Aaserud, J.L.: Understanding risk-Building evidence for action: proceedings from the 2016 UR forum. The World Bank (2016)
7. Tian, C.S., Fang, Y.P., Yang, L.E., Zhang, C.J.: Spatial-temporal analysis of community resilience to multi-hazards in the Anning River basin, Southwest China. Int. J. Disaster Risk Reduction **39**, 101144 (2019)
8. Bruneau, M., et al.: A framework to quantitatively assess and enhance the seismic resilience of communities. Earthq. Spectra **19**, 733–752 (2003)
9. Matczak, P., Hegger, D.: Improving flood resilience through governance strategies: gauging the state of the art. WIREs Water **8**, e1532 (2021)
10. Ba, R., Deng, Q., Liu, Y., Yang, R., Zhang, H.: Multi-hazard disaster scenario method and emergency management for urban resilience by integrating experiment–simulation–field data. J. Saf. Sci. Resilience **2**, 77–89 (2021)
11. Ossevorth, F., et al.: Resilience in supply systems – What the food industry can learn from energy sector. J. Saf. Sci. Resilience **3**, 39–47 (2022)
12. Tonn, G., Reilly, A., Czajkowski, J., Ghaedi, H., Kunreuther, H.U.S.: transportation infrastructure resilience: influences of insurance, incentives, and public assistance. Transp. Policy **100**, 108–119 (2021)
13. Umunnakwe, A., Huang, H., Oikonomou, K., Davis, K.R.: Quantitative analysis of power systems resilience: standardization, categorizations, and challenges. Renew. Sustain. Energy Rev. **149**, 111252 (2021)
14. Ankit, A., Liu, Z., Miles, S.B., Choe, Y.U.S.: Resilience to large-scale power outages in 2002–2019. J. Saf. Sci. Resilience **3**, 128–135 (2022)
15. Xie, W., Rose, A., Li, S., He, J., Li, N., Ali, T.: Dynamic economic resilience and economic recovery from disasters: a quantitative assessment. Risk Anal. **38**, 1306–1318 (2018)
16. Adger, W.N., Hughes Terry, P., Folke, C., Carpenter Stephen, R., Rockström, J.: Social-ecological resilience to coastal disasters. Science **309**, 1036–1039 (2005)
17. Imperiale, A.J., Vanclay, F.: Conceptualizing community resilience and the social dimensions of risk to overcome barriers to disaster risk reduction and sustainable development. Sustain. Dev. **29**, 891–905 (2021)
18. Keck, M., Sakdapolrak, P.: What is social resilience? Lessons learned and ways forward. Erdkunde **67**, 5–19 (2013)
19. British Standards Institution. BS 67000:2019 City resilience. Guide. BSI: BSI Standards Limited (2019)
20. Haldane, V., et al.: Health systems resilience in managing the COVID-19 pandemic: lessons from 28 countries. Nat. Med. **27**, 964–980 (2021)

21. Ivanov, D.: Viable supply chain model: integrating agility, resilience and sustainability perspectives—lessons from and thinking beyond the COVID-19 pandemic. Ann. Oper. Res. (2020)https://doi.org/10.1007/s10479-020-03640-6

22. Yang, S., Ning, L., Jiang, T., He, Y.: Dynamic impacts of COVID-19 pandemic on the regional express logistics: evidence from China. Transp. Policy **111**, 111–124 (2021)

23. Moosavi, J., Hosseini, S.: Simulation-based assessment of supply chain resilience with consideration of recovery strategies in the COVID-19 pandemic context. Comput. Ind. Eng. **160**, 107593 (2021)

24. Fernández-Prados, J.S., Lozano-Díaz, A., Muyor-Rodríguez, J.: Factors explaining social resilience against COVID-19: the case of Spain. Eur. Soc. **23**, S111–S121 (2021)

25. McClelland, A.G., Jordan, R., Parzniewski, S., Shaw, D., O'Grady, N., Powell, D.: Post-COVID recovery and renewal through whole-of-society resilience in cities. J. Saf. Sci. Resiliencehttps://doi.org/10.1016/j.jnlssr.2022.03.003

26. United Nations International Strategy for Disaster Reduction. Disaster Scorecard Resilience for Cities (2017)

27. Borrion, H., Kurland, J., Tilley, N., Chen, P.: Measuring the resilience of criminogenic ecosystems to global disruption: a case-study of COVID-19 in China. PLOS One **15**, e0240077 (2020)

28. Chang, S.E., McDaniels, T., Fox, J., Dhariwal, R., Longstaff, H.: Toward disaster-resilient cities: characterizing resilience of infrastructure systems with expert judgments. Risk Anal. **34**, 416–434 (2014)

29. Tan, S.B.: Measuring community resilience: a critical analysis of a policy-oriented indicator tool. Environ. Sustain. Indic. **12**, 100142 (2021)

30. National Health Commission of the People's Republic of China. COVID-19 diagnosis and treatment plan (ninth trial version). http://www.gov.cn/zhengce/zhengceku/2022-03/15/content_5679257.htm. Accessed on 10 Apr 2022

31. Sphere Association. The Sphere Handbook: Humanitarian Charter and Minimum Standards in Humanitarian Response, fourth edition, Geneva, Switzerland (2018)

32. Yanling, Z., Delu, Y., Hejun, Z., Tianmu, C.: Construction and operation of COVID-19 lsolation sites in primary healthcare institutions: a case study of Wuhan. Chin. Gen. Pract. **24**, 1179–1182+1197 (2021)

33. Li, Z., et al.: Comprehensive large-scale nucleic acid–testing strategies support China's sustained containment of COVID-19. Nat. Med. **27**, 740–742 (2021)

34. Hagenlocher, M., Banerjee, S., Bermudez-Zambrano, D.A., et al.: Understanding and managing cascading and systemic risks: lessons from COVID-19. United Nations Office for Disaster Risk Reduction (2022)

35. Shanghai Municipal Health Commission. Press Conference on Epidemic Prevention and Control in Shanghai (2022). https://wsjkw.sh.gov.cn/xwfb/20220413/daf72a696f0541e5817ef6fd79dcdf17.html. Accessed on 15 Apr 2022

36. Cholbi, M.: Regret, resilience, and the nature of grief. J. Moral Philos. **16**, 486–508 (2019)

37. Gujral, H., Rushton, C.H., Rosa, W.E.: Action steps toward a culture of moral resilience in the face of COVID-19. J. Psychosoc. Nurs. Ment. Health Serv. **58**, 2–4 (2020)

Prediction of Female Fertility Structure and Population Change in China by Modified SIR Model

Qi Zhang[1,2], Difeng Zhu[3], Hui Zhang[1], Jianguo Chen[1(✉)], and Heng Zhang[1]

[1] Department of Engineering Physics, Tsinghua University, Beijing 100084, China
chenjianguo@tsinghua.edu.cn
[2] Tsinghua Shenzhen International Graduate School, Tsinghua University, Shenzhen 518055, China
[3] Beijing Institute of Technology, Beijing 100081, China

Abstract. With the development of the economy, the global fertility rate has generally decreased, and even led to negative population growth in some developed countries. In recent years, China, where family planning is implemented, has also gradually shown such a trend. The decline of fertility rate limits the further development of the society. In this paper, based on the SIR infectious disease model, we improve the SIR fertility structure model applicable to the prediction of female fertility structure based on the state transformation process existing in the female fertility stage, and forecast the female fertility structure, female population, and total population of China from 2018–2027 with the data related to the female population in 2017. Compared with the prediction results of the three classical models of Grey model (1, 1), BP Neural Network model and Logistic model, the SIR fertility structure and population prediction model in this paper can predict the female fertility structure in the short term in the future and deduce the population size accordingly, which has better prediction accuracy and the total population accuracy rate can reach 99.945%. The model can provide reference and basis for population prediction under the condition of low fertility level.

Keywords: Population prediction · Fertility structure · Population model · SIR model · Chinese population

1 Introduction

The growth rate of Chinese population has been declining since family planning policy, and the Seventh National Population Census in 2020 also indicates that China has entered the ranks of ultra-low fertility rate [1, 2]. The low fertility rate has led to a reduction in the labor force and an aging population, which has made China's economic development seriously limited for a long time, and how to improve the fertility willingness of women and increase fertility rate has become the focus of social attention [3, 4]. The "comprehensive two-child" policy, which allows one couple to have two children, was proposed by China to address these issues and has had a good impact in the early stage since its

X. Meng et al. (Eds.): BDSC 2022, CCIS 1640, pp. 57–79, 2022.
https://doi.org/10.1007/978-981-19-7532-5_4

implementation on January 1st, 2016. Wang et al. analyzed the effectiveness of the comprehensive two-child policy in slowing down the total population decline by exploring the changes in the age structure of the population under different fertility patterns [5]. However, with the decline of the "two-child effect", the fertility rate is still declining rapidly, and in 2017, Wang et al. simulated the trend of labor population change under the "two-child" policy, and the results showed that the impact of the fertility policy on the working population was not significant in the long run [6]. Based on these assessments and facts, China implemented the "three-child" policy on August 20th, 2021. In 2021, Chen analyzed the trends in China's fertility levels under the Seventh National Population Census of China and found through demographic decomposition that the delayed marriage of young women was an important cause of fertility decline and that the implementation of the "three-child" policy could limit its impact [7]. In addition, scholars have analyzed and summarized the causes of low fertility rates in China and worldwide [8–14].

Current research on population issues focuses on the prediction of population structure and population size. Commonly used population forecasting models include Logistic model, Grey model (1, 1), BP Neural Network model, Leslie model, etc. Logistic functions are suitable for variables that satisfy exponential growth with increasing hysteresis, and the resulting population models use the total population as an indicator for forecasting, which is not sufficiently detailed to consider a single factor [15–17]. The Grey model (1, 1) speculates on future numerical changes by studying the patterns of variable observations, and are well adapted to the lack of information [18]. The BP Neural Network model is trained to obtain the desired output value by learning the rules for a given input value through the gradient descent method. The Leslie model improves the Keyfitz matrix to achieve dynamic prediction of population age composition and quantity based on the age composition structure and migration of the population [19]. In addition, Bayesian, double exponential smoothing (DES), autoregressive integrated moving average (ARIMA) models, and cohort factors and other methods have also been extensively studied in the prediction of population structure and quantity in recent years, and relatively good results have been obtained [20–27]. Classical population prediction models focus on predicting changes in total population data through simple mathematical models, while Bayesian, DES and other methods have higher requirements for data sets, so the prediction accuracy is limited when the statistics are incomplete. At present, scholars' research is less concerned with the effect of female fertility structure, which is one of the main reasons for the current general decline in fertility, and the relevant demographic structure and prediction models need to be studied urgently.

The infectious disease model represented by SIR was proposed by Kermack and McKendrick in 1927, which illustrates the dynamics of infectious disease epidemics through the language of mathematical models and was widely used in the field of epidemiology [28–30]. Krylova described the transmission of childhood diseases and vaccination process through the SIR model [31]. Han used the SIR model to better explain the spread of SARS in Beijing and Hong Kong [32]. Cooper demonstrated that the SIR model is goodly interpretive of the COVID-19 propagation process [33]. In other fields, the improved SIR model has also been well applied: Francis used the nature of SIR model to tax the effect of vaccination [34]; Rosati used the SIR model to fit the download time series of popular songs and found that the popular process of songs is more similar to the mechanism of infectious disease transmission [35]; Feng et al. proposed an improved SIR model in combination with the infectious disease model computer virus model to better simulate the virus transmission and immunization process in computer networks [36]. It can be seen that the infectious disease model can reflect the transmission law of specific problems from the perspective of dynamics, and can well reflect the process of transmission and state change.

This paper adopts the method of SIR infectious disease model to simulate the state transition of female fertility process, and improves a SIR fertility structure and population prediction model for the study of population problems, focusing on the influence of female fertility structure on population birth rate, improving the accuracy for population prediction, and putting forward a new idea for the improvement of population prediction model.

As following Fig. 1 shows that the first section of this paper introduces the current status of China's population development and investigates the currently used population prediction models and the application of infectious disease models. The second section of this paper improves and constructs a new SIR fertility structure and population prediction model based on the state transition process existing in the female fertility stage, starting from the similarity between the SI model and the Logistic model. Section 3 describes and sets the initial values and parameters of the model based on data from the National Bureau of Statistics of China and the United Nations Population Division. Section 4 uses this paper's improved SIR population model to forecast the female fertility structure and population situation in China from 2018–2021, and verifies the validity of this paper's SIR model from an error perspective by comparing it with three classical population forecasting models, and then forecasts and analyses the female fertility structure as well as the population situation in China in the next five years, analyzing the Chinese population situation from 2018–2027. Section 5 summarizes the work done in this paper and makes suggestions for further population prediction.

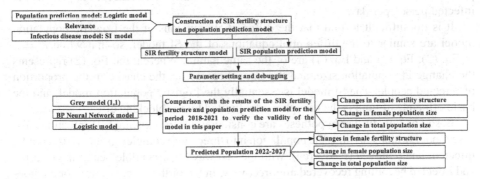

Fig. 1. Flow chart of this paper.

2 SIR Fertility Structure and Population Prediction Model

2.1 Model Front

In demography, the Logistic population model, as a classical population prediction model, considers the hysteresis effect of objective conditions such as resources and environmental factors on the natural population growth rate, and its differential equation is:

$$\frac{dN_t}{dt} = rN_t\left(1 - \frac{N_t}{K}\right) \tag{1}$$

$$N_t = \frac{KN_0}{N_0 + (K - N_0)e^{-rt}} \tag{2}$$

where N_t is the total population size, N_0 is the initial population size, K is the stable population size allowed by environmental resources, and r is the natural population growth rate.

In infectious diseases, for the basic transmission process of infectious diseases, the SI infectious disease model divides the population into susceptible and infected people (only the susceptible people are infected). The differential equations for the law of evolution between the two groups are:

$$\frac{di}{dt} = \lambda i(1 - i) \tag{3}$$

$$i = \frac{1}{1 + \left(\frac{1}{i_0} - 1\right)e^{-\lambda t}} \tag{4}$$

where $i(t)$ is the proportion of infected persons, $s(t)$ is the proportion of susceptible persons, and λ is the average number of effective contacts with susceptible persons per infected person per day.

It is not difficult to find that the differential equations of the Logistic population model are similar to the differential equations of the SI model, so that while $K = 1$ in Eq. (2), Eq. (2) and Eq. (4) are of the same nature. Wherein the Eq. (2) represents the change in population size, and the Eq. (4) represents the change in the proportion of infected people. The SI model is essentially the Logistic population model, and the basic principle of both is the growth model limited by the blocking effect.

Based on this, further hypotheses are considered for the existing SIR infectious disease model, which classifies the population into three more complex groups, susceptible, infected, and removed (recovered), with the pathway of susceptible becoming infected and infected becoming recovered after recovery. In the birth rate prediction for the population, the three groups are women of childbearing age, gravidas, and removers. The SIR fertility structure model is constructed by taking the entire process of a woman of childbearing age becoming pregnant and giving birth to a child, with a time step of one day, and the mth day of the n year is denoted as t_m^n.

Female States and State Transitions in the Model

At some point in time t_m^n, existing women in China may be in one of the following three states:

1. S (Susceptible): refers to women aged 15–49 years who are of childbearing age (fertile) at the time t_m^n and who are not yet pregnant but may become pregnant, called Women of Childbearing Age. The number of women of childbearing age at the time of t_m^n is recorded as $S(t_m^n)$, the $S(t_m^n)$ to the total female population at this moment in time is recorded as $s(t_m^n)$, $(s(t_m^n) \geq 0)$.
2. I (Infected): refers to women who is pregnant at the time t_m^n, called Gravidas. The number of gravidas at the moment of time t_m^n is recorded as $I(t_m^n)$, the $I(t_m^n)$ to the total female population at this moment in time is recorded as $i(t_m^n)$, $(i(t_m^n) \geq 0)$.
3. R (Removed): refers to the group of women other than the first two at the time t_m^n, called Removers. This includes (i) women who are under childbearing age (<15 years old), (ii) women who have completed childbirth, and (iii) women who are over childbearing age (>49 years old), and the number of removers at the time t_m^n is recorded as $R(t_m^n)$, the $R(t_m^n)$ to the total female population at that time is recorded as $r(t_m^n)$, $(r(t_m^n) \geq 0)$.

Over the years, the status of women transitions according to the following rules:

1. For a woman in state S, once she becomes pregnant the woman is transformed from state S to state I.
2. If a woman in state S is over 49 years old but still not pregnant, she will be converted directly from state S to state R.
3. For women in state I, they can enter state R through childbirth.

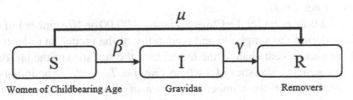

Fig. 2. SIR fertility structure model.

Each square bracket in Fig. 2 indicates the state in which women are in, the line with an arrow indicates the transition path from one state to another for women, and the mathematical symbols above the line with an arrow indicate the state transition parameters, where:

β indicates the pregnancy rate for the group of women of childbearing age.

γ indicates the rate of delivery in the group of gravidas.

μ indicates the probability that the group of women of childbearing age will lose their fertility to the group of removers because they are over childbearing age and have not given birth.

Model Assumptions

1. Assume that $s(t_m^n) + i(t_m^n) + r(t_m^n) = 1$, the overall female population at each moment is recorded as 1. In the model, the overall female population is remained unchanged and the proportions of the three groups are increased or decreased according to the model dynamics mechanism to reflect female state changes.
2. In the short term (10 years), pre-existing females aged 0–14 years among newborn females and removers(R) will be converted to females aged 10–24 years. The peak age of female pregnancy is concentrated at 25–34 years due to Chinese national considerations. And the age of pregnancy has been delayed in recent years due to the increase in work pressure and cost of living, so women aged 10–24 have a lower chance of pregnancy and are neglected in this model. Therefore, the group of women who may become pregnant in the short term is all concentrated among women of childbearing age S.
3. Since the number of gravidas per year is not published in China, it is assumed that an average of 99 women in China will have one twin: the pregnant woman population of the current year equals to the population of newborns in the following year/k_1, (k_1 is the ratio of births to the corresponding gravidas, $k_1 = 100/99$):

$$I(T_n) = B(T_{n+1})/k_1 \tag{5}$$

4. The number of females who died is not part of the overall female population and therefore excluded from the model. In later prediction of the total female population, the female mortality rate is referenced to the average of the last five years of mortality, which is 7.1 per 1,000.
5. The standard time point for the Chinese census is 00:00 on November 1 of the census year. Considering the simplicity and readability of the model, in order to avoid the possible impact of year change, the model uses the statistics of the last day of each year to represent the statistics of a whole year, i.e. $T_n = t_{365}^n$. The initial parameter settings are based on the number of women of childbearing age, the number of gravidas, and the total female population in the previous year.

2.2 Basic Prediction Model

The SIR fertility structure and population prediction model in this paper is built according to the mathematical model in this section and implemented through python 3.8 platform.

SIR Fertility Structure Model

Based on the transition of women's status in Fig. 2, a SIR fertility structure model is established:

$$\begin{cases} \dfrac{dS}{dt} = -\beta * s * i - k * s \\[2mm] \dfrac{dI}{dt} = \beta * s * i - \gamma * i \\[2mm] \dfrac{dR}{dt} = \gamma * i + \mu * s \end{cases} \tag{6}$$

where S, R, and I satisfy:

$$s(t_m^n) + i(t_m^n) + r(t_m^n) = 1 \tag{7}$$

By substituting the female fertility structure data $s(t_m^n)$, $i(t_m^n)$, $r(t_m^n)$ on day m of year n into Eqs. (6) and (7), we can obtain the female fertility structure data $s(t_{m+1}^n)$, $i(t_{m+1}^n)$, $r(t_{m+1}^n)$ on the latter day (day m + 1 of year n).

SIR Population Prediction Model

The population prediction model in this paper focuses on predicting the future annual births, female population and total population in China based on the proportion of gravidas population obtained from the above SIR fertility structure model. T_n is the current year and T_{n+1} is the subsequent year.

Knowing the female population P_f (T_n), the male population P_m (T_n), the total population P (T_n) and the corresponding fertility structure s (T_n), i (T_n), r (T_n) in the year T_n, the number of gravidas in the year T_n can be obtained as:

$$I(T_n) = P_f(T_n) * i(T_n) \tag{8}$$

According to Eq. (8), the newborn population B (T_{n+1}) in the year T_{n+1} is:

$$B(T_{n+1}) = I(T_n) * k_1 \tag{9}$$

According to the sex ratio k_2 (male/female) of China's birth population in recent years, the female birth population B_f (T_{n+1}) in the year T_{n+1} is:

$$B_f(T_{n+1}) = B(T_{n+1}) * \frac{1}{k_2 + 1} \tag{10}$$

According to the mortality rate d (T_n) and the sex ratio k_3 (male/female) of the death population in China in recent years, the female death population D_f (T_{n+1}) in T_{n+1} is:

$$D_f(T_{n+1}) = P(T_n) * d(T_{n+1}) * \frac{1}{k_3 + 1} \tag{11}$$

So the female population P_f (T_{n+1}) in the year T_{n+1} is:

$$P_f(T_{n+1}) = P_f(T_n) + B_f(T_{n+1}) - D_f(T_{n+1}) \tag{12}$$

Recursively, the female population can be predicted for a certain time. The male population is predicted similarly, where: the male birth population $B_m(T_{n+1})$ in year T_{n+1} is:

$$B_m(T_{n+1}) = B(T_{n+1}) * \frac{k_2}{k_2 + 1} \tag{13}$$

The male mortality population $D_m(T_{n+1})$ in the year T_{n+1} is:

$$D_m(T_{n+1}) = P(T_n) * d(T_{n+1}) * \frac{k_3}{k_3 + 1} \tag{14}$$

The male population $P_m(T_{n+1})$ in the year T_{n+1} is:

$$P_m(T_{n+1}) = P_m(T_n) + B_m(T_{n+1}) - D_m(T_{n+1}) \tag{15}$$

Thus, the total population $P(T_{n+1})$ of China in the year T_{n+1} is:

$$P(T_{n+1}) = P_f(T_{n+1}) + P_m(T_{n+1}) \tag{16}$$

2.3 Parameters of the Model

The parameters of the SIR fertility structure and population prediction model (The following is called the SIR population model and will not be explained) in this paper are shown in Table 1.

3 Data Source and Parameter Setting

3.1 Data Sources

The comprehensive two-child policy has been into effect since January 1st, 2016, and based on the population growth curve, the two-child policy has had some impact on the demographic issue. Due to the consideration of the time it takes for people to decide on the length of the fertility period and the length of the pregnancy period, this paper will predict the number of pregnancies from 2017, through substituting the 2017 Chinese female population, the number of women of childbearing age and the 2017 gravidas data derived from the newborn population in 2018 into the SIR population model by adjusting the parameters for optimization to obtain the fertility structure of Chinese women in the next 10 years, including the proportion of women of childbearing age, the proportion of gravidas and the proportion of removers. Then, the calculation methods introduced in the previous section are used to obtain the birth population, female population and total population of China in 2018–2021 to compare the differences between the predicted calculation results and the actual population data in 2018–2021, and finally predict the birth population, female population, and total population of China in 2022–2027.

The data on Chinese females, males, births and deaths from 1949–2021 are from the National Bureau of Statistics of China for mainland China (excluding Hong Kong, China, Macau, China, and Taiwan, Province of China) [37].

Table 1. Parameter settings in the model of this paper.

Parameter	Meaning
t_m^n	The mth day of the nth year is denoted as t_m^n
T_n	$T_n = t_{365}^n$
$S(t_m^n)$	The number of women of childbearing age at the moment of t_m^n
$s(t_m^n)$	The ratio of the number of women of childbearing age at t_m^n to the total female population at that time
$I(t_m^n)$	The number of pregnant women at t_m^n
$i(t_m^n)$	The ratio of the number of pregnant women at t_m^n to the total female population at that time
$R(t_m^n)$	The number of removers at t_m^n
$r(t_m^n)$	The ratio of the number of removers at t_m^n to the total female population at that time
β	Pregnancy rate for the group of women of childbearing age
γ	Birth rate for the group of pregnant women
μ	Probability that a group of women of childbearing age is incapacitated to become a group of removers because they are over childbearing age and have not given birth
k_1	Ratio of births to corresponding pregnant women
k_2	Sex ratio of the birth population in China in recent years (male: female)
k_3	Sex ratio of the death population in China in recent years (male: female)
$P_f(T_n)$	Female population in the T_n year
$P_m(T_n)$	Male population in the T_n year
$P(T_n)$	Total population in the T_n year
$B_f(T_{n+1})$	Female birth population in the T_{n+1} year
$B_m(T_{n+1})$	Male birth population in the T_{n+1} year
$B(T_{n+1})$	Total birth population in the T_{n+1} year
$D_f(T_{n+1})$	Female mortality in the T_{n+1} year
$D_m(T_{n+1})$	Male mortality in the T_{n+1} year
$d(T_n)$	Mortality rate of China's population in recent years

Since the National Bureau of Statistics of China has less data on China's population by age group, the data on the female fertility structure of China in 2017–2018 were obtained from the United Nations Population Division, The 2019 Revision of World Population Prospects, for mainland China (excluding Hong Kong, China, Macao, China, and Taiwan, Province of China) female age group headcount statistics [38], and scaled according to the female population data from the Bureau of Statistics, making the age-specific percentages of the female population consistent with the UN data.

3.2 Parameter Setting

Pregnancy to Population Ratio
According to statistical data, on average one out of 99 women in China will give birth to one twin. Considering the special situation, the ratio of births to the corresponding gravidas k_1 needs to be set. The ratio of the pregnant population k_1 is:

$$k_1 = 100/99 = 1.010101 \tag{17}$$

Population Sex Ratio
In recent years, the sex ratio at birth in China k_2 (male/female) and sex ratio at death in China k_3 (male/female) from UN statistics on sex ratio at birth and number of male and female deaths in mainland China (excluding Hong Kong, Macau and Taiwan Province of China) for 2015–2020, where:

$$k_2 = 1.13 \tag{18}$$

$$k_3 = 28423/22249 = 1.277514 \tag{19}$$

Model Initial Values
The SIR population model needs to set the initial value, that is, to consider the proportion of each group in the female fertility structure in 2017, and the female population in 2017 in the National Bureau of Statistics is 683.61 million. And the female population in 2017 in the United Nations data is 691.559 million, of which 333.134 million (48.17%) is the female population from 0 to 14 and over 50 years old, and 358.424 million (51.83%) is the female population of childbearing age from 15 to 49 years old. Therefore, after processing, we can get that the actual female population of 0–14 as well as 50 years old and above in China in 2017 is 329.306 million, accounting for 48.17%, which is the initial value of R (Removed).The female population of reproductive age is 354.304 million (51.83%), of which the population of gravidas in 2017 can be obtained from the national newborn population of 15.205 million in 2018: 15.205 / k_1 = 15.053 million (2.20%), which is the initial value of I(Infected).

So the population of non-pregnant women of childbearing age in 2017 was 339,251,000(49.63%), which is the initial value of S (Susceptible).

4 Analysis of Empirical Results

This chapter is divided into three parts: firstly, the prediction of female fertility structure and population situation in China for 2018–2021 based on the SIR population model in this paper; secondly, the validity and superiority of the SIR population model is tested by comparing this paper's model with three classical population prediction models from the perspective of prediction error using the population situation for 2018–2021 as the validation set; thirdly, the prediction and comparison of China's future population situation using the above four models using 2022–2027 as the test set; the results of female fertility structure and population prediction obtained from the SIR population model are analyzed.

4.1 SIR Population Model Prediction Analysis

Changing Trends in Female Fertility Structure

Using 2017 as the initial year to set parameters, the SIR population model was used to predict the female fertility structure from 2018–2021, and the results are shown in Table 2. It shows that the proportion of females of childbearing age decreases from 49.63% to 46.56% and the proportion of removers increases from 48.17% (2017) to 52.09% (2021) from 2017 to 2021. It indicates that the number of gravidas as a proportion of the female population of childbearing age decreases gradually, developing from 1/22 in 2017 to about 1/40 in 2021, which shows that the proportion of women of childbearing age converting to gravidas has lower conversion rate, making the fertility rate in China show a decreasing trend.

Table 2. Predicted female fertility structure, 2018–2021.

Year	Female fertility structure ratio (%)		
	S: Women of childbearing age	R: Removers	I: Gravidas
2017	49.626	48.172	2.202
2018	48.835	49.216	1.949
2019	48.061	50.215	1.724
2020	47.303	51.172	1.525
2021	46.561	52.09	1.348

Based on the proportion of female fertility structure obtained from the SIR population model, the female population for 2018–2021 can be predicted according to the population prediction model in Sect. 2.2.2, followed by the number of female groups with different fertility structures for each year. As shown in Table 3 below, for women with different fertility structures, the error between the predicted and actual values from 2018 to 2021 is relatively small, with a maximum error rate of 7.6% (the predicted number of gravidas in 2018 is considered an outlier because the error rate is too different from the other averages). Among them, the prediction error rate for women of childbearing age (S) is stable at 0.2%; the prediction error of gravidas (I) varies greatly in different years, but excluding the outlier point in 2018, the prediction errors of 2019 and 2020 are only 0.2% and 0.04%, and the prediction error of removers (R) is maintained near 0.15%, which shows that the prediction of the SIR population model established in this paper are in good agreement with the actual female fertility structure and the population of each group as a whole, which reflects the validity of the model.

It is worth noting that the large prediction error of the number of pregnant women in 2018 may be due to the effect of the two-child policy adopted by China in 2016, which led to a sudden increase in the number of pregnant women in 2018, but this effect gradually stabilizes after 2019. The SIR population model in this paper is consistent with the prediction results of female fertility structure after 2019, so that future female population prediction can be made.

Table 3. Predicted effects of female fertility structure, 2018–2021.

Year		2018	2019	2020	2021
Predicted number of people (10,000 people)	S: Women of childbearing age	33520.01939	33083.28185	32621.14073	–
	I: Gravidas	1337.68720	1186.90159	1051.67383	930.58880
	R: Removers	33781.83531	34566.15353	35288.95216	35950.45450
Actual number of people (10,000 people)	S: Women of childbearing age	33444.50116	33152.50882	32565.13301	–
	I: Gravidas	1448.40149	1189.37428	1051.29510	–
	R: Removers	33784.09735	34627.11691	35238.57189	35893.61116
Prediction error rate (%)	S: Women of childbearing age	0.22580	0.20881	0.17199	–
	I: Gravidas	7.64389	0.20790	0.03603	–
	R: Removers	0.00670	0.17606	0.14297	0.15837

In Fig. 3, the number of women of childbearing age decreases by a total of more than 10 million, the number of gravidas decreases by more than 6 million, and the number of removers increases by 20 million over the five-year period from 2017 to 2021. Both the predicted and actual values are more consistent and can reflect the changing trend.

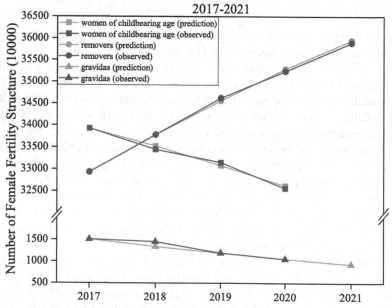

Fig. 3. Actual versus predicted female fertility structure, 2017–2021.

Trends in Female Population and Total Population

Based on the female fertility structure ratio obtained from the SIR population model, the female population as well as the total population change from 2018 to 2027 can be deduced, as shown in Table 4 and Table 5.

Table 4 shows the error between the predicted and actual female population of this model between 2018 and 2021, and the prediction error for all four years did not exceed 0.2%. Among them, the error between the predicted and observed female population in 2018 is 374,581,000, with a prediction error rate of 0.0545%, which is a relatively accurate prediction; the error between the predicted and observed female population in 2019 is 1,326,630,000, with a prediction error rate of 0.1924%, which is a relatively slightly worse prediction.

Table 5 shows the errors between the total population predicted by this model and the observed during 2018–2021, in which the prediction error for 2018 is 9107 people, with a prediction error rate of 0.0006%, which is basically consistent with the observed value. The prediction errors for 2019, 2020 and 2021 are relatively larger, with an error rate of about 0.08%. The overall forecast between 2018 and 2021 is very consistent with the actual situation, therefore, the future population prediction made it more effective and had certain reference value.

Table 4. Female population error, 2018–2021.

Year	Predicted number of women (10,000 people)	Actual number of women (10,000 people)	Forecast error (10,000 people)	Prediction error rate (%)
2018	68639.5419	68677.0000	37.4581	0.0545
2019	68836.3370	68969.0000	132.6630	0.1924
2020	68961.7660	68855.0000	− 106.7660	0.1551
2021	69015.6292	68949.0000	− 66.6292	0.0966

Table 5. Total population error, 2018–2021.

Year	Predicted total population (10,000 people)	Actual total population (10,000 people)	Forecast error (10,000 people)	Prediction error rate (%)
2018	140540.0893	140541.0000	0.9107	0.0006
2019	140894.7241	141008.0000	113.2759	0.0803
2020	141097.3690	141212.0000	114.6310	0.0812
2021	141146.4805	141260.0000	113.5195	0.0804

4.2 Model Prediction Error Validation Analysis

To verify and reflect the effectiveness and superiority of the SIR population model in this paper, three classical population models, namely, Grey model (1, 1), BP Neural Network model, and Logistic model, are selected and compared to forecast Chinese females and total population to analysis the forecasting errors and patterns of different models in this section.

Female and Total Population Prediction Results for the Classical Models
For the three classical models, seven sets of population data from 1949–2017, 1960–2017, etc. were trained as training sets, and then the prediction were made for the female as well as total population from 2018–2021.Table 6 and Table 7 show the prediction and errors for female as well as total population under the three classical models for the period 2018–2021. For the seven data sets of different lengths, there are significant differences in the effects of female as well as total population prediction. Overall, the smaller the length of the data (e.g., the known years are 2012–2017) and the closer the data are to the prediction year (2018), the smaller the error rate of the prediction results and the more accurate the prediction. For the different three classical models, BP Neural Network model has the relatively best prediction results: the overall prediction error rate for the female population is basically no more than 2%, and the overall prediction error rate for the total population is basically no more than 1%.

Table 6. Female population predicted by three classical models vs. actual, 2018–2021.

Grey model (1, 1)	Known year						
	Forecast year	1949–2017	1960–2017	1970–2017	1980–2017	1990–2017	2000–2017	2012–2017
Predicted number of people (10,000 people)	2018	75230.8	73624.0	71740.0	70502.2	69006.0	68726.8	68776.5
	2019	76218.7	74502.0	72471.0	71124.0	69469.0	69155.3	69205.5
	2020	77219.6	75390.0	73210.0	71751.4	69935.0	69586.5	69637.1
	2021	78233.6	76288.0	73957.0	72384.2	70404.0	70020.3	70071.4
Prediction error rate (%)	2018	9.5429	7.2033	4.4600	2.6576	0.4791	0.0725	0.1449
	2019	10.5115	8.0224	5.0776	3.1246	0.7250	0.2701	0.3429
	2020	12.1481	9.4910	6.3249	4.2065	1.5685	1.0624	1.1359
	2021	13.5564	10.7156	7.3121	5.0158	2.1244	1.5642	1.6388
BP Neural Network model	Known year						
	Forecast year	1949–2017	1960–2017	1970–2017	1980–2017	1990–2017	2000–2017	2012–2017
Predicted number of people (10,000 people)	2018	68721.3	68635.5	68784.5	68596.0	68335.2	68866.5	68617.0
	2019	69040.5	68882.5	69198.5	69019.1	68422.8	69419.1	68639.5

(*continued*)

Table 6. (*continued*)

Grey model (1, 1)	Known year						
	Forecast year	1949–2017	1960–2017	1970–2017	1980–2017	1990–2017	2000–2017	2012–2017
	2020	69333.6	69140.4	69596.0	69129.6	68674.5	70005.9	68640.2
	2021	69605.3	69359.2	69971.9	69656.0	68746.9	70505.2	68640.2
Prediction error rate (%)	2018	0.0645	0.0604	0.1565	0.1179	0.4977	0.2759	0.0874
	2019	0.1037	0.1254	0.3328	0.0726	0.7920	0.6526	0.4778
	2020	0.6951	0.4145	1.0762	0.3988	0.2621	1.6715	0.3120
	2021	0.9583	0.5989	1.4935	1.0323	0.2951	2.2722	0.4509

Logistic model	Known year						
	Forecast year	1949–2017	1960–2017	1970–2017	1980–2017	1990–2017	2000–2017	2012–2017
Predicted number of people (10,000 people)	2018	69014.5	68525.2	68407.6	68450.4	71503.5	68783.3	68815.3
	2019	69397.7	68824.7	68696.4	68737.3	71596.9	69202.0	69261.1
	2020	69771.7	69113.9	68975.2	69013.8	71685.7	69620.9	69713.0
	2021	70136.6	69393.3	69244.2	69280.4	71770.2	70039.9	70171.2
Prediction error rate (%)	2018	0.4914	0.2210	0.3923	0.3300	4.1156	0.1548	0.2014
	2019	0.6216	0.2092	0.3953	0.3359	3.8103	0.3378	0.4235
	2020	1.3313	0.3760	0.1746	0.2306	4.1111	1.1123	1.2461
	2021	1.7340	0.6487	0.4310	0.4839	4.1192	1.5928	1.7845

Table 7. Total population predicted by three classical models vs. actual, 2018–2021.

Grey model (1, 1)	Known year						
	Forecast year	1949–2017	1960–2017	1970–2017	1980–2017	1990–2017	2000–2017	2012–2017
Predicted number of people (10,000 people)	2018	154377.2	151223.6	147239.0	144658.5	141874.6	140692.9	140851.3
	2019	156389.6	153019.4	148726.5	145917.8	142839.8	141499.4	141683.8
	2020	158428.1	154836.4	150229.0	147188.1	143811.6	142310.5	142521.3
	2021	160493.3	156675.1	151746.7	148469.5	144789.9	143126.2	143363.7
Prediction error rate (%)	2018	9.8450	7.6011	4.7659	2.9297	0.9489	0.1081	0.2208
	2019	10.9083	8.5182	5.4738	3.4819	1.2991	0.3485	0.4793
	2020	12.1917	9.6482	6.3854	4.2320	1.8409	0.7779	0.9272
	2021	13.6155	10.9126	7.4237	5.1037	2.4989	1.3211	1.4892

BP Neural Network model	Known year						
	Forecast year	1949–2017	1949–2017	1960–2017	1970–2017	1980–2017	1990–2017	2000–2017

(*continued*)

Table 7. (*continued*)

Grey model (1, 1)		Known year						
	Forecast year	1949–2017	1960–2017	1970–2017	1980–2017	1990–2017	2000–2017	2012–2017
Predicted number of people (10,000 people)	2018	140657.8	140577.3	140712.9	140743.2	140667.8	140358.8	140195.8
	2019	141178.0	140916.7	141328.0	141377.8	141225.5	140736.4	140251.3
	2020	141581.3	141028.9	141860.1	141911.9	141686.5	140990.6	140184.2
	2021	141879.6	140921.4	142311.0	142330.0	142055.8	141118.2	140186.6
Prediction error rate (%)	2018	0.0831	0.0258	0.1223	0.1439	0.0902	0.1297	0.2456
	2019	0.1206	0.0648	0.2270	0.2623	0.1543	0.1926	0.5367
	2020	0.2616	0.1297	0.4590	0.4956	0.3360	0.1568	0.7279
	2021	0.4387	0.2397	0.7440	0.7574	0.5633	0.1004	0.7599
Logistic model		Known year						
	Forecast year	1949–2017	1949–2017	1960–2017	1970–2017	1980–2017	1990–2017	2000–2017
Predicted number of people (10,000 people)	2018	141499.8	140620.1	140129.1	140209.7	140147.1	149059.6	155814.5
	2019	142287.5	141245.4	140695.8	140770.0	140686.5	149895.6	156394.9
	2020	143056.7	141850.3	141242.2	141309.2	141205.3	150734.2	156966.7
	2021	143807.8	142435.1	141768.9	141828.1	141704.0	151575.3	157529.8
Prediction error rate (%)	2018	0.6822	0.0563	0.2931	0.2357	0.2803	6.0613	10.8676
	2019	0.9074	0.1684	0.2214	0.1688	0.2280	6.3029	10.9121
	2020	1.3064	0.4520	0.0214	0.0689	0.0048	6.7432	11.1568
	2021	1.8036	0.8319	0.3603	0.4021	0.3143	7.3023	11.5176

Table 6 and Table 7 above show that the four-year female population prediction error rates for the best performing traditional BP network model are 0.0604%, 0.1254%, 0.4145%, and 0.5989% (data set is 1960–2017), and the four-year total population prediction error rates are 0.1297%, 0.1926%, 0.1568%, and 0.1004% (data set is 2000–2017); while comparing Table 4 and Table 5 show the SIR fertility structure of this paper and the four-year female population prediction error rates of 0.0545%, 0.1924%, 0.1551%, and 0.0966% for the population prediction model, and the four-year total population prediction errors are 0.0006%, 0.0803%, 0.0812%, and 0.0804%, which shows that Both in terms of overall prediction stability and prediction accuracy by year, the SIR population model in this paper outperformed the three traditional population prediction models.

Error Comparison Between SIR and Classical Models

In order to more intuitively compare the overall errors of the population prediction of each model, this paper uses three error values of RMSE, MAE, and MAPE to characterize the overall error of the SIR population model and the three classical models in predicting the female and total population for 2018–2021, as shown in Table 8 below.

From the error comparison of the results of the above four population models, it can be seen that the SIR population model in this paper outperform the three classical models in each error index of RMSE, MAE, and MAPE, with lower error rate levels, regardless of the female population or total population. Table 9 below shows the optimal

Table 8. Comparison of classical model and SIR population model errors.

Classic model	Known year	Female			Total population		
		RMSE	MAE	MAPE (%)	RMSE	MAE	MAPE (%)
Grey model (1, 1)	1949–2017	7932.20839	7863.15610	11.41710	16540.46500	16416.80093	11.64012
	1960–2017	6157.39482	6088.50000	7.91973	13054.11771	12933.36314	8.20119
	1970–2017	4052.53199	3982.00000	5.30052	8598.16978	8480.03003	5.49753
	1980–2017	2653.53977	2577.94413	3.52973	5673.42587	5553.23375	3.70668
	1990–2017	954.15748	841.00000	1.17124	2467.38908	2323.71246	1.58023
	2000–2017	655.73693	509.72500	0.72699	1112.85932	901.97576	0.62594
	2012–2017	695.93367	560.12500	0.80341	1293.52305	1099.78680	0.77201
BP Neural Network model	1949–2017	408.30821	312.67500	0.44791	375.14014	318.95316	0.22357
	1960–2017	254.42175	205.90000	0.29666	198.63875	162.33879	0.11462
	1970–2017	644.13351	525.22500	0.75908	643.53819	547.74593	0.38868
	1980–2017	382.20582	278.17500	0.39878	673.11255	585.46464	0.41264
	1990–2017	349.49476	317.65000	0.46022	480.03393	403.63726	0.28435
	2000–2017	998.10189	836.67500	1.21867	209.79801	204.23799	0.14447
	2012–2017	251.82669	228.27500	0.32665	851.55272	800.81056	0.56833
Logistic model	1949–2017	798.18898	717.62500	1.04553	1764.25527	1657.68028	1.18237
	1960–2017	277.62269	249.82500	0.35811	680.22288	532.47573	0.37152
	1970–2017	249.23794	239.35000	0.34713	362.98805	315.81340	0.22314
	1980–2017	244.98768	237.12500	0.34434	353.05238	308.65866	0.21879
	1990–2017	2777.90355	2776.57500	4.03154	337.53884	291.54593	0.20679
	2000–2017	678.64835	549.02500	0.76563	9335.85018	9310.90898	6.60464
	2012–2017	763.93490	627.65000	0.90014	15676.05391	15671.23421	10.42437
SIR population model	2017	93.32875	85.87908	0.12352	98.56369	85.58428	0.05453

error results of each classical population prediction model selected for comparison and validation with the prediction results of the SIR population model.

Table 9. Comparison of errors of the optimal classical models and the SIR population model.

Types of models	Female population prediction			Total population prediction		
	RMSE	MAE	MAPE (%)	RMSE	MAE	MAPE (%)
Grey model (1, 1)	655.73693	509.72500	0.72699	1112.85932	901.97576	0.62594
BP Neural Network model	254.42175	205.90000	0.29666	198.63875	162.33879	0.11462
Logistic model	244.98768	237.12500	0.34434	337.53884	291.54593	0.20679
SIR population model	93.32875	85.87908	0.12352	98.56369	85.58428	0.05453

Table 9 shows that the SIR population model in this paper has only 36.68% of the RMSE value of the best-performing BP neural network for female population prediction for 2018–2021; and 49.62% of the best-performing BP neural network model for total population prediction.

It can be seen that the SIR population model in this paper significantly outperforms the classical Grey model (1, 1), BP Neural Network model, and Logistic model in predicting the female population and total population size in China, with lower levels of RMSE, MAE, MAPE. Thus the SIR population model in this paper has higher accuracy and requires less data set than the three classical models in predicting female population structure and population size, and has better performance and potential in the population prediction problem.

4.3   Model Prediction of Future Population Scenarios

As described in the previous section, the SIR population model in this paper has a much better prediction accuracy for the female fertility structure as well as the population for 2018–2021. Therefore, further prediction of the future (2022–2027) population can be carried out.

Each Model Analysis of Prediction Results
In this section, according to the female population and the total population in 2018–2027, the set of prediction with better performance of RMSE and MAPE are selected from the prediction results of the three classical models to compare with the prediction results of the SIR population model, as shown in Fig. 4(a) (b), where the black line represents the actual total population size.

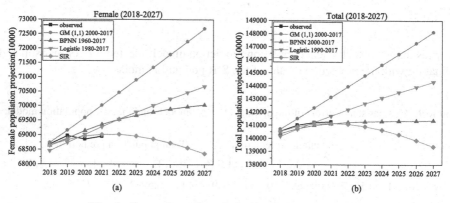

Fig. 4. Comparison of prediction results of four models.

Figure 4(a) shows the prediction of the four models for the female population. Compared with the actual female population, the Grey model (1, 1) represented by the red line is overly optimistic, with a linear upward trend and a large deviation from the actual one, with a MAPE of 0.727%; the Logistic model represented by the green line and the

BP Neural Network model represented by the blue line also have a linear upward trend and a large deviation from the actual one, with MAPEs of 0.344% and 0.297%. The SIR population model represented by the purple line and the prediction results are more consistent with the actual female population change, with a minimum MAPE of only 0.124% and a four-year prediction accuracy of 99.876%, and well reflect the fluctuating decrease trend of the female population in recent years.

Figure 4(b) shows the prediction of the four models for the total population. Compared with the actual total population, the prediction results of Grey model (1, 1) and Logistic model are still more linear in growth, which are not consistent with the reality and have a larger error rate, with MAPE of 0.626% and 0.207%, respectively; the results of BP Neural Network model have a fast and then slow growth trend, which is consistent with the reality, but the overall deviation rate is relatively too large, with MAPE of 0.145%; and the SIR population model prediction results in this paper are most consistent with the actual trend and error, with a MAPE of only 0.055% and a four-year prediction accuracy rate of 99.945%, which is relatively the best prediction result.

Analysis of SIR Population Model Prediction Results
Using the SIR population model in this paper to forecast the female fertility structure in 2022–2027, and combining its results with the data from 2017–2021, which are shown in Fig. 5.

Since 2017, the proportion of women of childbearing age in China has become a continuous downward trend. It is foreseeable that without favorable changes in population policies, the proportion of females of childbearing age will continue to decline after 2022, possibly from 45.83% (2022) to 42.40% (2027). This change could lead to a decrease in the population of pregnant women, which, according to the model results, could decrease from 1.192% (2022) to 0.640% (2027) of the female population in China when β (the pregnancy rate in the reproductive age group) is constant. This figure is alarming and suggests that the pregnant population in 2027 could be half of what it is at this stage. Further, this will directly lead to a decline in the number of births, and thus a decline in the total population, bringing about various problems such as population aging.

Figure 6 shows the changes in the female population and the total population predicted by the model during 2018–2027, with an increasing trend in the number of females from 2018 to 2022 and a gradual decrease in the female population from 2023 onwards. It can be found that the decline in the total population and the change in the number of females follows the same trend, peaking in 2021–2022 and then gradually decreasing.

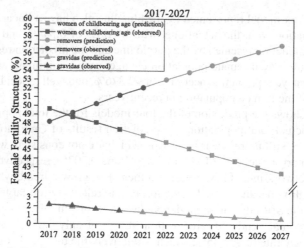

Fig. 5. Predicted of female fertility structure vs. observed, 2017–2027.

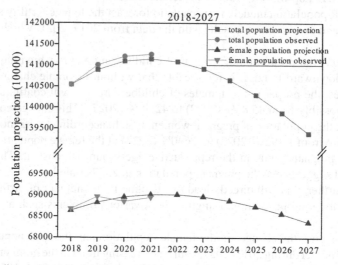

Fig. 6. Predicted change in female population and total population vs. observed, 2018–2027.

5   Conclusion

This study explores the application of SIR infectious disease model in population prediction analysis, introduces the SIR infectious disease model into the field of prediction
of population structure and population size, and improves the new SIR fertility structure
and population prediction model based on the state transition of female fertility process,
and predicts the female fertility structure, birth population, female population and total
population in China during 2018–2027. The results are compared with three classical
population forecasting models, and we find that the SIR population model in this paper
has better population forecasting ability:

1. The prediction accuracy is more accurate compared with other classical models: the prediction results of the SIR fertility structure and population prediction model are very consistent with the changes in the actual female population and the actual total population, and the four-year prediction accuracy rate reaches 99.876% and 99.945% respectively, which well reflects the decline in fluctuations in the female population in recent years and the trend of the gradual increase in the total population.
2. Good prediction of the change of female fertility structure: The classical model for population prediction shows the prediction of population size, but lacks consideration of the change of fertility structure due to the influence of female fertility factors. While SIR fertility structure and population prediction model can better solve this problem.

The improved SIR fertility structure and population prediction model in this paper focuses on the current female fertility downturn in China, however, the decrease in female fertility is only one of the causes of population aging and negative growth. Therefore, further research can look at factors such as the increasing age of individuals in order to explore more accurate and applicable population prediction models. This study provides an example of the application of the SIR infectious disease model in birth population prediction studies, and it is hoped that this model will be better developed in this field.

References

1. Shu, W., Yuzhu, M., Qing, Z.: Low fertility rate, cohort gender structure and children's education level. Financ. Econ. Ser. 1–13 (2022). https://doi.org/10.13762/j.cnki.cjlc.2022030 3.001
2. Jiaju, C., Yongai, J.: The history of changes in world fertility levels and future prospects: comparison of trends and summary of patterns. J. Popul. **43**(06), 41–53 (2021). https://doi.org/10.16405/j.cnki.1004-129X.2021.06.004
3. Zhigang, G., Siyu, T.: The impact of contemporary young women's late marriage on low fertility levels. Youth Res. (06), 16–25+91 (2017)
4. Xiang, L.: Analysis of the impact of low fertility on China's economic growth. Huaqiao University (2020). https://doi.org/10.27155/d.cnki.ghqiu.2020.000639
5. Jinying, W., Yanxia, G.: Population development trends in China under the implementation of comprehensive two-child policy. Popul. Res. **40**(06), 3–21 (2016)
6. Fei, W.: China's family planning policies and their labor market consequences. J. Popul. Econ. **30**(1), 31–68 (2016)
7. Wei, C.: Low fertility rate and three-child policy in China–an analysis based on the data of the seventh national census. Popul. Econ. (05), 25–35 (2016)
8. Xin, Y., Sjian, Z.: The impact of catastrophic events on fertility: historical experience and practical considerations. Popul. Stud. **46**(01), 70–81 (2022)
9. Xiaodong, Z., Yalu, Z., Guoping, J., Mengjun, T., Gong, C., Lei, Z.: Progress of low fertility research in China: a literature review. Popul. Dev. **27**(06), 9–21 (2021)
10. Jun, W., Guangzhou, W.: A study on the differences in fertility intention and fertility behavior under low fertility level in China. J. Popul. **38**(02), 5–17 (2016). https://doi.org/10.16405/j.cnki.1004-129X.2016.02.001
11. Manxiao, O., Heyun, L., Yang, Y.: Fertility intention and influencing factors of urban residents in Liaoning Province under the "two-child policy". China Public Health **38**(02), 224–227 (2022)

12. Zhilei, S., Yunyan, Y.: Fertility intentions and fertility behaviors of families eligible for the "separate two-child" policy. Popul. Res. **38**(05), 27–40 (2014)
13. Baochang, G.: Fertility intention, fertility behavior and fertility level. Popul. Res. **35**(02), 43–59 (2011)
14. Lee, R.: The outlook for population growth. Sci. (Am. Assoc. Adv. Sci.) **333**(6042), 569–573 (2011)
15. Marchetti, C., Meyer, P.S., Ausubel, J.H.: Human population dynamics revisited with the logistic model: how much can be modeled and predicted? Technol. Forecast. Soc. Change **52**(1), 1 (1996)
16. Miranda, L.C.M., Lima, C.A.S.: On the logistic modeling and forecasting of evolutionary processes: application to human population dynamics. Technol. Forecast. Soc. Change **77**(5), 699–711 (2010)
17. Xuan, H.Y., Zhang, A.Q., Yang, N.N.: A model in Chinese population growth prediction. Appl. Mech. Mater. **556–562**, 6811–6814 (2014)
18. Gao, H., Yao, T., Kang, X.: Population forecast of Anhui province based on the GM(1, 1) model. Grey Syst. **7**(1), 19–30 (2017)
19. Qiang, R., Dadao, H.: Stochastic methods for population forecasting: based on Leslie matrix and ARMA model. Popul. Res. **35**(02), 28–42 (2011)
20. Bryant, J.R., Graham, P.J.: Bayesian demographic accounts: subnational population estimation using multiple data sources. Bayesian Anal. **8**(3), 591–622 (2013)
21. Wheldon, M.C., Raftery, A.E., Clark, S.J., Gerland, P.: Reconstructing past populations with uncertainty from fragmentary data. J. Am. Stat. Assoc. **108**(501), 96–110 (2013)
22. Wiśniowski, A., Smith, P.W., Bijak, J., Raymer, J., Forster, J.J.: Bayesian population forecasting: extending the Lee-Carter method. Demography **52**(3), 1035–59 (2015)
23. Alias, A.R., Zainun, N.Y., Rahman, I.A.: comparison between ARIMA and DES methods of forecasting population for housing demand in Johor. In: MATEC Web of Conferences 2016. EDP Sciences (2016)
24. Peng, D., Long, L.: Long-term trend forecast of population aging in China in the new era. J. Renmin Univ. China **35**(01), 96–109 (2021)
25. Raftery, A.E., et al.: Bayesian probabilistic population projections for all countries. Proc. Natl. Acad. Sci. **109**(35), 13915–13921 (2012)
26. Hyndman, R.J., Booth, H.: Stochastic population forecasts using functional data models for mortality fertility and migration. Int. J. Forecast. **24**(3), 323–342 (2008)
27. Wiśniowski, A., et al.: Bayesian population forecasting: extending the Lee-Carter method. Demography **52**(3), 1035–1059 (2005)
28. Kermack, W.O., McKendrick, A.G.: A contribution to the mathematical theory of epidemics. Proc. R. Soc. London A: Math. Phys. Eng. Sci. **115**(772), 700–721 (1932)
29. Kermack, W.O., McKendrick, A.G.: Contributions to the mathematical theory of epidemics. II. The problem of endemicity. Proc. R. Ser. A Math. Phys. Eng. Sci. **138**(834), 55–83 (1932)
30. Kermack, W.O., McKendrick, A.G.: Contributions to the mathematical theory of epidemics. III. Further studies of the problem of endemicity. Proc. R. Soc. London. Ser. A Containing Pap. Math. Phys. Character **141**(843), 94–122 (1933)
31. Krylova, O., Earn, D.J.D.: Effects of the infectious period distribution on predicted transitions in childhood disease dynamics. J. R. Soc. Interface **10**(84), 20130098 (2013)
32. Han, W., Wabg, J., Liu, X.: Back analyzing parameters and predicting trend of SARS transmission. Adv. Earth Sci. **19**(6), 925–930 (2004)
33. Cooper, I., Mondal, A., Antonopoulos, C.G.: A SIR model assumption for the spread of COVID-19 in different communities. Chaos Solitons Fractals **139**, 110057 (2020)
34. Francis, P.J.: Optimal tax/subsidy combinations for the flu season. J. Econ. Dyn. Control **28**(10), 2037–2054 (2004)

35. Rosati, D.P., Woolhouse, M.H., Bolker, B.M.: Modelling song popularity as a contagious process. Proc. R. Soc. Math. Phys. Eng. Sci. **477**(2253), 20210457 (2021)
36. LiPing, F., Hongbin, W., Suqin, F.: An improved SIR computer virus propagation model. Comput. Appl. **31**(7), 1891–1893 (2011). https://doi.org/10.3724/sp.j.1087.2011.01891
37. National Bureau of Statistics Homepage. https://data.stats.gov.cn/easyquery.htm?cn=C01. Accessed 30 Dec 2021
38. UN Population Division Homepage. https://population.un.org/wpp/Download/. Accessed 2019

Generative Adversarial Network for Imputation of Road Network Traffic State Data

Dongwei Xu[1,2], Zefeng Yu[1,2], Tian Tian[3], and Yanfang Yang[4(✉)]

[1] Institute of Cyberspace Security, Zhejiang University of Technology,
Hangzhou 310023, China
[2] College of Information Engineering, Zhejiang University of Technology,
Hangzhou 310023, China
[3] Hangzhou Zhongao Technology Company Limited, Hangzhou 310000, China
[4] China Academy of Transportation Sciences, Beijing 100029, China
yangyf@motcats.ac.cn

Abstract. The loss of traffic state data is a common problem in intelligent transportation system. To improve the imputation accuracy and robustness of road traffic data, a novel generative adversarial network for the imputation of road network traffic data is proposed in this paper, i.e., GAE-GAN-LSTM. The spatiotemporal characteristics were extracted using a improved graph auto-encoder (GAE), followed by a generative adversarial network (GAN) to generate the complete spatiotemporal characteristics on the basis of the missing features. The internal structure of the generator was a long short-term memory network (LSTM), and the internal structure of the discriminator was a fully connected neural network (FCN). Finally, the traffic state data could be recovered by the decoder of GAE. The experimental results revealed that the performance of the proposed method was better than that of the other methods at any data loss ratio considered. The main innovations of the proposed method include two aspects. One, an improved GAE for the imputation of road network data was presented by redefining the loss function of GAE, which could effectively extract the potential spatiotemporal features of a road network. Two, the GAN was used to generate the spatiotemporal characteristics of the traffic state data by using the strong data generation ability of GAN.

Keywords: Data imputation · Graph auto-encoder · Generative adversarial network · Road traffic state data

1 Introduction

With the increase in urbanization, urban road traffic problems are becoming worse. Traffic management and control engineering need complete and precise road traffic state data, which mainly includes vehicle speed and traffic flow.

These traffic state data are not only temporally correlated, but also spatially correlated on adjacent lanes; therefore, road traffic state data are critical for intelligent transport systems [1]. Because of a road detector or transmission failure and other reasons [2], the road traffic state data may be missing, which may have an adverse effect on an intelligent transportation system. Therefore, data imputation has become a research hotspot of transportation [3].

Over the years, there have been many methods of traffic state data imputation, which contains three types of methods, that is, prediction-based data imputation method, interpolation-based data imputation method, and statistical-based data imputation method [4].

The prediction-based data imputation method predicts the missing data from the relationship among the historical data to realize the imputation of traffic state data, such as the autoregressive integrated moving average (ARIMA) model [5], the feed-forward neural network method [6,7], and support vector regression (SVR) [8], as well as some of their variants [9]. Although some improved methods can also improve the precision of imputation of traffic state data, the precision of data imputation decreases when there is continuous missing data or a large proportion of missing data.

The interpolation-based data imputation method filling the loss data depends on the historical data, such as, moving average method, exponential smoothing method, historical average method, local least squares (LLS) [10], and k-nearest neighbor method (KNN) [11,12] and its variant [13]. The interpolation-based data imputation can provide better imputation results by relying on the assumption that the adjacent traffic state data are similar. However, the adjacent traffic state data do not always meet this assumption, as the traffic state data change in the time series. Therefore, there are some shortcomings of this method, which result in unsatisfactory data imputation results.

The statistical-based data imputation method presets the probability distribution model according to the data and then fills in the loss data according to the distribution of the maximum probability of the model, such as Markov chain Monte Carlo (MCMC)-based interpolation method [14,15], probabilistic principal component analysis-based interpolation method (PPCA) [16], functional principal component analysis-based interpolation method(FPCA) [17], and kernel probabilistic principal component analysis (KPPCA) [18]. The statistics-based data imputation method needs the data to satisfy the probabilistic distribution; therefore, the method has a shortcoming that the data do not always meet the probability distribution model.

In addition, deep learning has also been used in intelligent transport system and data imputation, which has a stronger ability of data extraction and data generation. The deep learning methods are also gradually applied to imputation of traffic state data, such as denoising stacked autoencoder method (DSAE) [19] and importance-weighted autoencoder (MIWAE) [20]. GAN [21], proposed in 2014, is a framework of deep learning. GAN consists of two parts: one is generator and the other is discriminator. The generator can generate data, and the discriminator can judge the authenticity of the generated data. GAN is widely used in image super-resolution [22], image dataset synthesis [23] and text generation. Recently, GAN gradually applied to data imputation [24,25]. GAN has the problems of unstable training and mode collapse, but the above methods can not solve these problems. Thus, in this paper, we use Wasserstein-GAN (WGAN) to address this challenge. In the field of Intelligent Transport Systems, GAN has made a considerable contribution to traffic state data imputation [25] and traffic flow prediction [26,27]. Moreover, LSTM has extensive applications in traffic speed prediction [28]. However, these methods in processing of traffic state data can not accurately extract the graph structure of traffic state data and spatiotemporal characteristics. Graph auto-encoder (GAE), serving as a variant of Graph convolution Network (GCN), takes GCN as the encoder, and thus, the graph structure of traffic state data can be extracted effectively.

For these problems and challenges, to improve the precision and the robustness of traffic state data imputation, a novel generative adversarial network for the imputation of road network traffic state data has been proposed, i.e., GAE-GAN-LSTM. Firstly, GAE has been used to extract the spatiotemporal characteristics of the missing dataset, followed by GAN to generate the spatiotemporal characteristics of the complete dataset according to the characteristics of the missing dataset. In particular, the internal structure of the generator is LSTM, and the internal structure of the discriminator is a fully connected neural network. Finally, the traffic state data imputation can be realized by the decoder of GAE.

Our innovations are as follows:

(1) By redefining the loss function of graph autoencoder, we developed an improved graph autoencoder suitable for road network data repair, which can effectively extract the potential spatiotemporal characteristics of the road network.
(2) Because of the strong data generation ability of the generated adversarial network, we used this network to generate the spatiotemporal characteristics of the traffic state data.
(3) Compared with other models, the proposed model can enhance the precision of data repair, and maintain good performance and strong robustness in a high loss ratio.

2   Methodology

Figure 1 shows the framework of our method. First, a GAE model was applied to extract the spatiotemporal characteristics of the incomplete traffic state data. Second, the complete traffic spatiotemporal characteristics were generated according to the spatiotemporal characteristics of the incomplete data by GAN. The generator and the discriminator were the LSTM and the fully connected neural network, respectively. The generator is to generate the Spatiotemporal characteristics of the complete data according to the spatiotemporal characteristics of the incomplete data. The function of the discriminator is to judge the authenticity of the Spatiotemporal characteristics generated by generator, so as to ensure that the spatiotemporal features generated are similar to the spatiotemporal features of the complete data. Finally, the complete data were generated using the decoder of GAE, and the imputation of the traffic state data was realized.

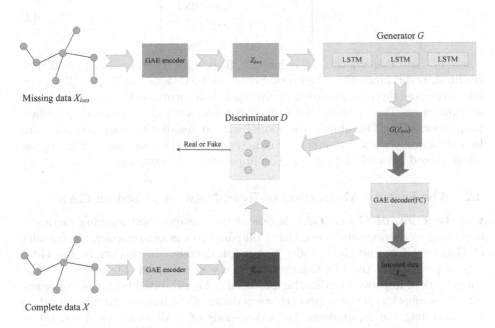

Fig. 1. Proposed generative adversarial network for imputation of road network traffic state data

2.1   Data Preprocessing

Observing that the spatial relationship of different detectors and the temporal relationship between the data of each detector, we modeled the road network as $\mathcal{G} = (\mathcal{V}, \mathcal{E})$. $\mathcal{V} = \{v_i\}_{i=1}^N$ denotes N detectors and $\mathcal{E} = \{e_{ij}\}_{i,j=1}^n$ denotes connection relationship between two corresponding links. $|\mathcal{V}| = N$ denotes the number of nodes. If v_i and v_j are spatially adjacent, $e_{ij} = 1$; else, $e_{ij} = 0$. The traffic state data can be described as follows:

$$X = \begin{bmatrix} x_{11} & x_{21} & \dots & x_{N1} \\ x_{12} & x_{22} & \dots & x_{N2} \\ \vdots & \vdots & \dots & \vdots \\ x_{1M} & x_{2M} & \dots & x_{NM} \end{bmatrix} \tag{1}$$

where N denotes the number of traffic detectors and M represents the number of traffic state data items when the time interval of sampling is t. x_{ij} represents the j-th traffic state data of the detector i. By normalization processing, we translated the elements of X between 0 and 1. In addition, the missing mask matrix Q of the traffic state data with a certain loss ratio could be described as follows:

$$Q = \begin{bmatrix} q_{11} & q_{21} & \cdots & q_{N1} \\ q_{12} & q_{22} & \cdots & q_{N2} \\ \vdots & \vdots & \cdots & \vdots \\ q_{1M} & q_{2M} & \cdots & q_{NM} \end{bmatrix} \tag{2}$$

where q_{it} indicates whether x_{it} is missing. If so, $q_{ij} = 1$; otherwise, $q_{ij} = 0$. The traffic state data including the missing data can be denoted as $X_{loss} = X_{true} * Q$, and $*$ denotes the multiplication operation of the corresponding elements of the two matrices. The training and testing datasets were divided under a certain proportion of p. The aim of the model was to repair the road network data by extracting the spatiotemporal characteristics of the road network using the missing road network data X_{loss}. The imputation data was denoted as X_{rec}.

2.2   The Feature Abstraction of Road Network Based on GAE

Construction of GAE. GAE is one of the unsupervised learning methods, including an encoder and a decoder. Compared to the autoencoder, the encoder of GAE is GCN and the decoder is a graph decoder. In this study, the GAE was improved and the loss function of GAE was redefined. Figure 2 shows the framework of improved GAE. The improved GAE exhibited better performance for extracting the spatiotemporal characteristics of the road network by encoding and decoding the input data. The expressions of GAE could be described as follows:

$$Z = GCN(X, A) \tag{3}$$

$$\hat{X} = \sigma_2(W_{D1}(\sigma_1(W_{D0}Z + B_{D0})) + B_{D1}) \tag{4}$$

$$\hat{A} = \sigma_3(ZZ^T) \tag{5}$$

where traffic state data X represents the input matrix of the encoder; A is the adjacent matrix, which is equivalent to $\mathcal{E}$. Z represents the spatiotemporal characteristics extracted after encoding. $\hat{X}$ represents the new traffic state output data matrix of the decoder. σ_1, σ_2, σ_3 represent the activation function. W_{D0} and W_{D1} are the weighted matrices of the decoder. B_{D0} and B_{D1} represent the bias matrix. $\hat{A}$ is the new adjacent matrix of the decoder's output. Z^T is the transposed matrix of Z. By minimizing the difference between $\hat{A}$ and the real adjacency matrix A, the potential spatiotemporal characteristics Z in the traffic state data is extracted. The extracted spatiotemporal characteristics Z can be decoded by a fully connected neural network and the new traffic state data $\hat{X}$ is obtained. The encoder can also be described as follows:

$$\tilde{A} = D^{-\frac{1}{2}} A D^{-\frac{1}{2}} \tag{6}$$

$$GCN(A, X) = \tilde{A}\sigma_4(\tilde{A}XW_{G0})W_{G1} \tag{7}$$

where W_{G0} and W_{G1} represent the weighted matrix of the encoder and σ_4 represents the activation function. D is the degree matrix.

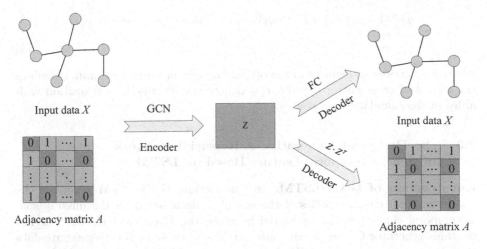

Fig. 2. The framework of the improved GAE

Loss Function of GAE. In this paper, we reconstruct the decoder of GAE to meet our work, which not only retains the decoding of adjacency matrix, but also adds the decoding of traffic state data, so that GAE can not only give play to the advantages of extracting graph features, but also be used to decode traffic state data. Therefore, the loss function of GAE should be composed of two parts, one is the loss function suitable for traffic state data decoding, L_D, and the other is the loss function suitable for adjacency matrix decoding, L_A. They are connected by a super parameter α to obtain the final loss function of gae, L_G:

$$L_G = L_D + \alpha L_A \tag{8}$$

where L_D was constructed by mean square error:

$$L_D = \frac{1}{p} \sum_{i=0}^{p} (\hat{X} - X)^2 \tag{9}$$

where p denotes the number of data items. In this paper, the loss function of weighted cross entropy with logits was used to construct L_A:

$$q = \frac{N^2 - \sum_{i=1}^{N} \sum_{j=1}^{N} a_{ij}}{\sum_{i=1}^{N} \sum_{j=1}^{N} a_{ij}} \tag{10}$$

$$l = (1 + (q - 1) * \hat{A}) \tag{11}$$

$$r = \frac{N^2}{N^2 - 2 \sum_{i=1}^{N} \sum_{j=1}^{N} a_{ij}} \tag{12}$$

$$g = (1 - A) * \hat{A} + l * (log(1 + exp(-abs(\hat{A}))) + max(\hat{A}, 0)) \tag{13}$$

$$L_A = r \frac{g}{N^2} \tag{14}$$

where a_{ij} denotes an element of the original matrix in x row j column, q denotes the weight of cross entropy, and l, r, g denote the intermediate transition variables in the calculation process.

2.3   The Design of Generative Adversarial Network for Spatio-Temporal Feature Based on LSTM

Construction of GAN-LSTM. In this section, GAN-LSTM generates the spatiotemporal characteristics of the complete data based on the missing spatiotemporal characteristics extracted by using the GAE method. GAN-LSTM contains generator G and discriminator D. The purpose of G is to generate data that D supposes to be true. While the purpose of D is to distinguish the real data as true and the data generated by the generator as false. Through constant adversarial training, G can generate data that are more similar to the real data.

The internal structure of generator G is LSTM, followed by a fully connected network to obtain the output. The expression of LSTM can be described as follows:

$$f_t = \sigma(W_f[h_{t-1}, x_t] + b_f) \tag{15}$$

$$i_t = \sigma(W_i[h_{t-1}, x_t] + b_i) \tag{16}$$

$$\tilde{C}_t = tanh(W_c[h_{t-1}, x_t] + b_C) \tag{17}$$

$$C_t = f_t * C_{t-1} + i_t * \tilde{C}_t \tag{18}$$

$$o_t = \sigma(W_o[h_{t-1}, x_t] + b_o) \tag{19}$$

$$h_t = o_t * tanh(C_t) \tag{20}$$

where W_f, W_i, W_c, W_o and b_f, b_i, b_C, b_o represent the weight matrix and bias matrix, respectively. f_t, i_t and o_t represent the output of the forget gate, input gate, and the output gate, respectively. $\tilde{C}_t$ and C_t represent the temporary and the new states of the memory cell, respectively. σ represent the Sigmoid function. $tanh(\cdot)$ can be described as follows:

$$tanh(\varepsilon) = \frac{e^\varepsilon - e^{-\varepsilon}}{e^\varepsilon + e^{-\varepsilon}} \tag{21}$$

The generator G is implemented using LSTM, followed by a fully connected network to obtain G_Z:

$$G_Z = \sigma(W_G h_t + b_G) \tag{22}$$

where W_G and b_G denote the weighted and bias matrix, respectively. The internal structure of discriminator D is an n-layer fully connected network whose first layer is as follows:

$$Y_R^{(1)} = W_d^{(1)} Z + B_1 \tag{23}$$

$$Y_F^{(1)} = W_d^{(1)}G_Z + B_1 \tag{24}$$

The expressions of the i-layer fully connected network are as follows:

$$Y_R^{(i)} = W_d^{(i)}Y_R^{(i-1)} + B_i \tag{25}$$

$$Y_F^{(i)} = W_d^{(i)}Y_F^{(i-1)} + B_i \tag{26}$$

Finally, $Y_F^{(i)}$ and $Y_R^{(i)}$ represent the results of the i-layer fully connected network of generator G_Z and the hidden layer feature matrix of GAE, respectively.

Loss Function of Generative Adversarial Network. In this section, Wasserstein-GAN is used to replace GAN. Different from the traditional GAN, WGAN uses the Wasserstein distance rather than the JS divergence to estimate the similarity of the data distribution, because WGAN can deal with the vanishing gradient problem in the training process and ensure the diversity of the generated samples. The loss functions of G and D can be listed as follows:

$$D_L = \frac{1}{k}\sum_{i=1}^{k} y_F^{(n)(i)} - \frac{1}{k}\sum_{i=1}^{k} y_R^{(n)(i)} \tag{27}$$

$$G_L = \frac{1}{k}\sum_{i=1}^{k} y_F^{(n)(i)} - \frac{1}{p}\sum_{i=1}^{p} (G_i - Z_i) \tag{28}$$

where k and p denote the output number of discriminator D and generator G, respectively. $y_F^{(n)(i)}$, $y_R^{(n)(i)}$, G_i and Z_i represent the i-th element of $Y_F^{(n)}$, $Y_R^{(n)}$, G_Z and Z respectively. D_L and G_L represent the loss function of discriminator D and generator G, respectively.

2.4 The Imputation of Road Network Data Based on GAE-GAN

To better apply GAE to road network data imputation, data decoding was added to the decoder of GAE. Fully connected layers were used for the data decoding. and the traffic state data imputation was realized through GAE decoding based on G_Z. The decoding process can be described as follows:

$$X_{rec} = \sigma(W_{D1}(ReLU(W_{D0}G_Z + B_{D0})) + B_{D1}) \tag{29}$$

Finally, X_{rec} was de-normalized to obtain the traffic states data imputation.

3 Experiment

3.1 Experimental Design

The dataset of the Seattle expressway network, which include traffic speed, was used for our experiment. The traffic state data of 23 road detectors were selected from January 1, 2017 to March 1, 2017, and the data sampling interval was 5 min.

In the experiment, the data missing patterns were categorized as missing completely at random (MCAR) or MCAR in space (MCARS). In addition, the missing ratio ranged from 10% to 90%. Figure 3 shows the complete dataset and the data heat map under the MCAR and MCARS data missing modes with different data missing ratios. The X-axis denotes the time on January 1 and the Y-axis denotes the detectors. The left and right subfigures of Figs. 3(b and c) denote the missing patterns of MCAR and MCARS, respectively. Finally, the proposed model was compared with the other baselines under the two data missing patterns.

3.2   Parameter Setting and Model Index

To test the precision of the proposed model, some baselines were compared with the proposed model. First, to prove the effectiveness of GAE's extraction features, the proposed model was compared with GAN-LSTM. In the GAN-LSTM model, the hidden layer of LSTM in generator was 1, and its units was 64. The hidden layer of FCN of discriminator was 3, and its units was [32, 64, 128]. Second, to verify the effectiveness of the generator LSTM, the structure of the generator was revised to FCN, i.e., GAE-GAN-BP. In the GAE-GAN-BP model, D and G each had 3 hidden layers, and their units were [32, 64, 128]. Finally, some typical baselines were compared with the proposed method, such as KNN, DSAE, and LSTM. Both BP and DSAE had 3 hidden layers, and their units were [32, 64, 128]. The value of k in KNN was 5. The LSTM had one hidden layer, and the number of hidden layer units was 64. In the structure of GAE-GAN-LSTM, the units of encoder was [32, 16] and the units of decoder was 32. Other parameters are the same as GAN-LSTM. The α value was 0.0001. σ_1 and σ_4 were the ReLU functions. σ_2 and σ_3 were the Sigmoid functions.

To compare models, three typical evaluation indices, namely root mean square error (RMSE), mean absolute error (MAE), and mean absolute percentage error (MAPE), were adopted in this paper, which are shown as follows:

$$\text{RMSE} = [\frac{1}{n} \sum_{i=1}^{n} (y_i - \tilde{y}_i)^2]^{\frac{1}{2}} \tag{30}$$

$$\text{MAE} = \frac{1}{n} \sum_{i=1}^{n} |y_i - \tilde{y}_i| \tag{31}$$

$$\text{MAPE} = \frac{1}{n} \sum_{n=1}^{n} |\frac{y_i - \tilde{y}_i}{y_i}| \tag{32}$$

where y_i and $\tilde{y}_i$ denote the true and the imputed values in the missing locations, respectively.

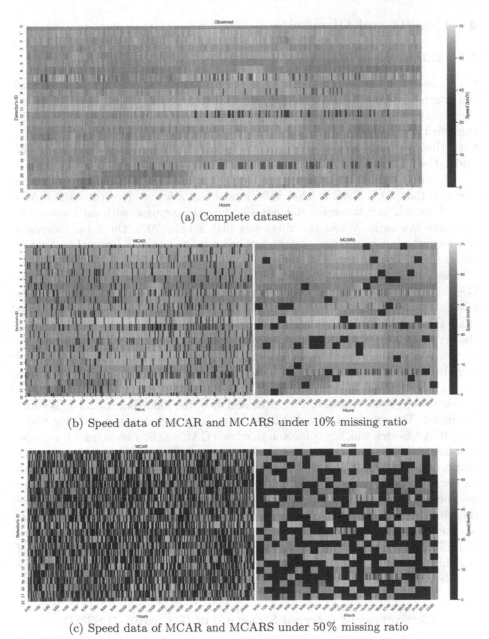

(a) Complete dataset

(b) Speed data of MCAR and MCARS under 10% missing ratio

(c) Speed data of MCAR and MCARS under 50% missing ratio

Fig. 3. Speed data heat map of Seattle expressway network dataset on January 1, 2015

4   Results and Discussion

4.1   Effectiveness of GAE

Compared with the traditional GAE model, the data decoder was merged into the graph decoder of GAE to reconstruct the loss function, which made GAE further extract the spatiotemporal characteristics of the traffic state data. To verify the effectiveness of GAE, the index results of GAE-GAN-LSTM were compared with those of GAN-LSTM. The results of GAE-GAN-LSTM and GAN-LSTM under the MCAR and MCARS modes are shown in Fig. 4.

Figure 4(a) shows that under the MCAR mode, when the data loss ratio was less than 70%, GAE-GAN-LSTM model had a lower error than the GAN-LSTM model, and the error did not significantly increase with an increase in the data loss ratio. When the ratio was higher than 70%, the error increased significantly, but it remained in the low error range and was lower than that of the GAN-LSTM model.

Figure 4(b) shows that under the MCARS mode, the index results of GAE-GAN-LSTM model were similar to those of the MCAR mode. When the data loss ratio was less than 70%, the errors of GAE-GAN-LSTM model were lower than those of GAN-LSTM model. When the data loss was greater than 70%, the errors of GAE-GAN-LSTM were close to those of the GAN-LSTM model. In particular, when the data loss ratio was 90%, the errors of the proposed model were higher than those of GAN-LSTM, but most of the data loss ratio conditions were still satisfied.

From the results shown in Figs. 4(a) and 4(b), the following conclusions could be drawn. The proposed model showed lower error and stronger stability under the MCAR model, which was inseparable from GAE's ability to extract the graph features and the spatiotemporal characteristics of the data. Under the MCARS mode, when the data loss ratio was less than 70%, the model accuracy was higher. When the data loss was higher than 70%, the model precision began to decline, which might be associated with the internal generator of LSTM. Under the MCARS mode, the higher data loss ratio would lead to a continuous data loss phenomenon in the time dimension, which reduced the feature extraction ability of LSTM. Note that the proposed model showed strong stability irrespective of whether the data loss ratio was high or low, which showed the effectiveness of the GAE to extract the spatiotemporal characteristics of the road network data.

4.2   Effectiveness of Internal Structure of Generator (LSTM)

The internal structure of the generator in the proposed model was LSTM. In this paragraph, the internal structure of the generator was revised to a fully connected neural network for comparison, that is, GAE-GAN-BP. The index results of GAE-GAN-LSTM and GAE-GAN-BP under the MCAR and MCARS modes are shown in Fig. 5.

Figures 5(a) and 4(b) show that the accuracy of the GAE-GAN-LSTM was considerably higher than that of GAE-GAN-BP under the two data loss modes

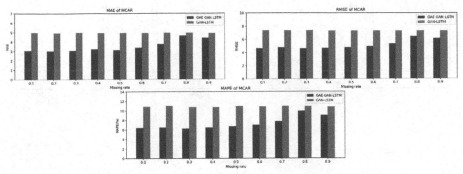

(a) Histogram results of GAE-GAN-LSTM and GAN-LSTM under the MCAR mode

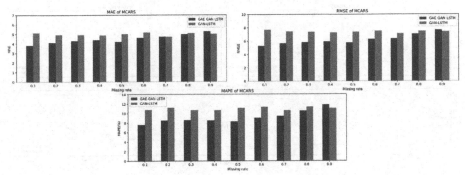

(b) Histogram results of GAE-GAN-LSTM and GAN-LSTM under the MCARS mode

Fig. 4. Histogram results of GAE-GAN-LSTM and GAN-LSTM under different data loss mode

and all the data loss ratios, which was related to the characteristics of the LSTM and BP models. LSTM inherited most of the characteristics of the RNN model and was very suitable for feature extraction in the time series. Therefore, LSTM was suitable as the generator to generate the characteristics. Compared with LSTM, BP was not very sensitive to the characteristics in the time series. Moreover, BP exhibited good performance in the training process but poor performance in the testing process, which was related to the weak ability of generalization. Based on the above analysis, as the internal structure of the generator, LSTM could effectively enhance the precision of the imputation.

4.3 Comparison with Other Models

Some baselines were compared with the proposed methods under the MCAR and MCARS modes. The loss ratio of the baselines was 10%, 50%, and 90%; Tables 1 and 2 show the corresponding index.

In Table 1, the errors increased with the loss ratio increased. At the low loss ratio of 10%, the proposed models, both BP and LSTM, had a high accuracy.

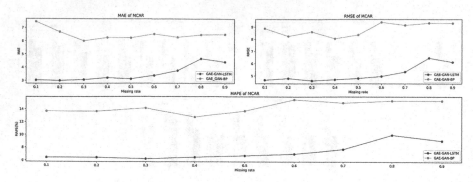

(a) Results of GAE-GAN-LSTM and GAE-GAN-BP under the MCAR mode

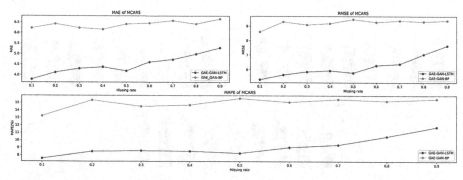

(b) Results of GAE-GAN-LSTM and GAE-GAN-BP under the MCARS mode

Fig. 5. Results of GAE-GAN-LSTM and GAE-GAN-BP under different data loss modes

However, when the loss ratio was increased to 90%, the accuracy of BP declined rapidly. However, the accuracy of the proposed model and LSTM did not decline very quickly and maintained a certain stability, which demonstrated that LSTM had an advantage in the feature extraction in the time-series data. Moreover, as GAE could extract the graph characteristics, the proposed model had better stability than LSTM. However, both the KNN and the DSAE models demonstrated poor accuracy and stability, which might be attributed to the fact that the KNN model required the daily data to have a relative similarity. Moreover, DSAE's generalization ability was not strong.

In Table 2, under the MCARS mode, the errors of most of the models increased, which could be attributed to the characteristics of the MCARS and MCAR modes. Figure 3(b) and 3(c) show that compared with the MCAR mode, under the MCARS mode, the large-area continuous data loss phenomenon was more likely to occur. However, the missing data under the MCAR mode were relatively discrete, which increased the difficulty of feature extraction for the models listed in Table 2, reducing the precision of the models. As for stability, with the loss ratio increased, the error trend under the MCARS mode was similar to the error trend under the MCAR mode, and the proposed model still had the best effect among the baselines.

Table 1. Index results under MCAR mode

Model	Loss rate								
	10%			50%			90%		
	MAE	RMSE	MAPE (%)	MAE	RMSE	MAPE (%)	MAE	RMSE	MAPE (%)
GAE-GAN-LSTM	**3.04**	**4.66**	**6.44**	**3.11**	**4.8**	**6.72**	**4.39**	**6.12**	**9.05**
BP	3.43	4.96	6.9	4.78	7.03	10.03	5.79	8.84	12.42
KNN	5.6	7.95	11.38	6.22	9.13	12.77	6.32	9.49	13.7
DSAE	5.95	7.22	10.61	6.16	8.23	13.27	6.52	9.16	15.08
LSTM	3.47	5.11	7.45	3.92	5.86	8.68	4.9	7.28	10.71

Table 2. Index results under MCARS mode

Model	Loss rate								
	10%			50%			90%		
	MAE	RMSE	MAPE (%)	MAE	RMSE	MAPE (%)	MAE	RMSE	MAPE (%)
GAE-GAN-LSTM	**3.79**	**5.3**	**7.58**	**4.18**	**5.77**	**8.26**	**5.28**	**7.64**	**11.78**
BP	5.12	7.1	9.71	5.7	8.34	13.04	5.72	8.27	12.83
KNN	7.39	10.46	14.87	6.48	9.86	13.83	6.57	9.86	14.01
DSAE	6.92	9.60	16.44	6.70	9.49	15.81	6.58	9.31	15.27
LSTM	4.71	7.10	10.9	4.88	7.16	10.63	5.96	8.39	12.01

5 Conclusions

Aiming to improve the low precision of road traffic state data imputation, a novel generative adversarial network for the imputation of road network traffic state data was proposed. First, considering that the traffic state data had certain graph structure characteristics, we extracted the spatiotemporal characteristics of the incomplete traffic state data by GAE. Second, owing to the powerful data generation ability of GAN, GAN was applied to generate the features characteristics of the complete data. The internal structure of the generator adopted LSTM, which improved the ability of generating spatiotemporal characteristics. Finally, the data decoding was completed based on the spatiotemporal characteristics generated by the improved decoder of GAE, and the road network traffic state data were repaired. From the analysis, we drew the following conclusions:

1) The decoder of GAE was improved to make GAE suitable for the decoding of road network data. Moreover, the GAE could enhance the performance of the model.

2) LSTM was used in the generator part of GAN. Compared with the internal structure of the fully connected neural network, LSTM had a better effect on the data imputation and improved the imputation accuracy of the model.
3) Compared with the traditional data imputation method, GAE-GAN-LSTM had a higher imputation accuracy. Moreover, the model maintained high imputation precision with high loss ratios. The stability of the proposed model was incomparable to that of the traditional models.
4) Because of the strong stability, the proposed model could better satisfy the requirements of a road traffic network with large-scale data missing, which makes a considerable contribution to road traffic state data imputation.

In the future, other datasets will be considered for verification, and the parameters will be modified to improve the repair accuracy. Meanwhile, some parameters will be simplified to make the model more concise and further improve the practicability of the model.

Acknowledgment. This work was supported in part by the National Natural Science Foundation of China under Grant (61903334), in part by the Zhejiang Provincial Natural Science Foundation under Grant (LY21F030016, LQ16E080011), in part by the China Postdoctoral Science Foundation under Grant 2018M632501, and in part by Open Foundation of Key Laboratory of Transport Industry of Big Data Application Technologies for Comprehensive Transport (2020B1205).

References

1. Wang, F.Y.: Parallel control and management for intelligent transportation systems: concepts, architectures, and applications. IEEE Trans. Intell. Transp. Syst. **11**(3), 630–638 (2010)
2. Ni, D., Leonard, J.D., Guin, A., Feng, C.: Multiple imputation scheme for overcoming the missing values and variability issues in ITS data. J. Transp. Eng. **131**(12), 931–938 (2005)
3. Xie, K., et al.: Accurate recovery of internet traffic data: a sequential tensor completion approach. IEEE/ACM Trans. Netw. **26**(2), 793–806 (2018)
4. Li, H., Li, M., Lin, X., He, F., Wang, Y.: A spatiotemporal approach for traffic data imputation with complicated missing patterns. Transp. Res. Part C: Emerg. Technol. **119**, 102730 (2020)
5. Zhong, M., Sharma, S., Lingras, P.: Genetically designed models for accurate imputation of missing traffic counts. Transp. Res. Rec. **1879**(1), 71–79 (2004)
6. Dia, H.: An object-oriented neural network approach to short-term traffic forecasting. Eur. J. Oper. Res. **131**(2), 253–261 (2001)
7. Karlaftis, M.G., Vlahogianni, E.I.: Statistical methods versus neural networks in transportation research: differences, similarities and some insights. Transp. Res. Part C: Emerg. Technol. **19**(3), 387–399 (2011)
8. Zhang, Y., Liu, Y.: Data imputation using least squares support vector machines in urban arterial streets. IEEE Signal Process. Lett. **16**(5), 414–417 (2009)
9. Elshenawy, M., El-Darieby, M., Abdulhai, B.: Automatic imputation of missing highway traffic volume data. In: 2018 IEEE International Conference on Pervasive Computing and Communications Workshops (PerCom Workshops), pp. 373–378. IEEE (2018)

10. Gang, C., Qiaoyun, W., Lei, L.: Missing data imputataion for traffic flow based on weighted local least squares (2012)
11. Xu, D.W., Wang, Y.D., Jia, L.M., Li, H.J., Zhang, G.J.: Real-time road traffic states measurement based on kernel-KNN matching of regional traffic attractors. Measurement **94**, 862–872 (2016)
12. Xu, D.W., Wang, Y.D., Jia, L.M., Zhang, G.J., Guo, H.F.: Real-time road traffic states estimation based on kernel-KNN matching of road traffic spatial characteristics. J. Central S. Univ. **23**(9), 2453–2464 (2016)
13. Zhang, S., Li, X., Zong, M., Zhu, X., Cheng, D.: Learning K for KNN classification. ACM Trans. Intel. Syst. Technol. (TIST) **8**(3), 1–19 (2017)
14. Ni, D., Leonard, J.D.: Markov chain monte Carlo multiple imputation using Bayesian networks for incomplete intelligent transportation systems data. Transp. Res. Rec. **1935**(1), 57–67 (2005)
15. Farhan, J., Fwa, T.: Airport pavement missing data management and imputation with stochastic multiple imputation model. Transp. Res. Rec. **2336**(1), 43–54 (2013)
16. Qu, L., Li, L., Zhang, Y., Hu, J.: PPCA-based missing data imputation for traffic flow volume: a systematical approach. IEEE Trans. Intell. Transp. Syst. **10**(3), 512–522 (2009)
17. Chiou, J.M., Zhang, Y.C., Chen, W.H., Chang, C.W.: A functional data approach to missing value imputation and outlier detection for traffic flow data. Transportmetrica B: Transp. Dyn. **2**(2), 106–129 (2014)
18. Li, L., Li, Y., Li, Z.: Efficient missing data imputing for traffic flow by considering temporal and spatial dependence. Transp. Res. Part C: Emerg. Technol. **34**, 108–120 (2013)
19. Duan, Y., Lv, Y., Kang, W., Zhao, Y.: A deep learning based approach for traffic data imputation. In: 17th International IEEE Conference on Intelligent Transportation Systems (ITSC), pp. 912–917. IEEE (2014)
20. Mattei, P.A., Frellsen, J.: MIWAE: deep generative modelling and imputation of incomplete data sets. In: International Conference on Machine Learning, pp. 4413–4423. PMLR (2019)
21. Goodfellow, I., et al.: Generative adversarial nets. Adv. Neural Inf. Process. Syst. **27** (2014)
22. Ledig, C., et al.: Photo-realistic single image super-resolution using a generative adversarial network. In: Proceedings of the IEEE Conference on Computer Vision and Pattern Recognition, pp. 4681–4690 (2017)
23. Shrivastava, A., Pfister, T., Tuzel, O., Susskind, J., Wang, W., Webb, R.: Learning from simulated and unsupervised images through adversarial training. In: Proceedings of the IEEE Conference on Computer Vision and Pattern Recognition, pp. 2107–2116 (2017)
24. Yoon, J., Jordon, J., Schaar, M.: GAIN: missing data imputation using generative adversarial nets. In: International Conference on Machine Learning, pp. 5689–5698. PMLR (2018)
25. Chen, Y., Lv, Y., Wang, F.Y.: Traffic flow imputation using parallel data and generative adversarial networks. IEEE Trans. Intell. Transp. Syst. **21**(4), 1624–1630 (2019)
26. Xu, D., Peng, P., Wei, C., He, D., Xuan, Q.: Road traffic network state prediction based on a generative adversarial network. IET Intel. Transport Syst. **14**(10), 1286–1294 (2020)

27. Xu, D., Wei, C., Peng, P., Xuan, Q., Guo, H.: GE-GAN: a novel deep learning framework for road traffic state estimation. Transp. Res. Part C: Emerg. Technol. **117**, 102635 (2020)
28. Ma, X., Tao, Z., Wang, Y., Yu, H., Wang, Y.: Long short-term memory neural network for traffic speed prediction using remote microwave sensor data. Transp. Res. Part C: Emerg. Technol. **54**, 187–197 (2015)

Artificial Intelligence and Cognitive Science

Improving Events Classification with Latent Space Clustering-Based Similarities

Jiaxuan Wu[1,2], Jianghao Gao[3(✉)], Yongdan Fan[3], Yuanjie Cheng[3], Peng Zhu[1], and Dawei Cheng[1,2]

[1] Collaborative Innovation Center of Internet Finance Safety, Tongji University, Shanghai 201804, China
{1853924,dcheng}@tongji.edu.cn
[2] Department of Computer Science and Technology, Tongji University, Shanghai 201804, China
[3] System Security Department, Shanghai Financial Futures Information Technology Co., Ltd., Shanghai 200122, China
{gaojh,fanyd,chengyj}@cffex.com.cn

Abstract. The research on event intelligent analysis based on big data refers to the intelligent classification of monitoring events through the analysis of monitoring event alarm information in the operation and maintenance platform, to automatically recommend monitoring event processing solutions according to the event knowledge base. However, there are currently few methods to classify monitoring events. To solve this problem, our method relies on the BERT model and the Jieba word segmentation tool to perform keyword extraction, keyword word vector transformation and event representation vector generation for event information in training data. We then pre-classify the training data using the clustering algorithm and similarity to obtain information about each cluster. We establish the relationship between clusters and event classifications based on the pre-classification results and the classification labels of the training data. Finally, we process and analyze the new monitoring events that appear in the operation and maintenance platform, and effectively classify the new events according to the model training results. In addition, our method can periodically train the model to optimize the classification performance based on dynamically added data from the monitoring event database. We perform experiments on the real-life datasets and the results validate the effectiveness of our proposed method.

Keywords: Event keywords · Bert · Clustering algorithm · Similarity measurement · Event classification

1 Introduction

Automated operation and maintenance (O&M) [15] is the current mainstream O&M technology. It refers to the use of tools to replace the operations of some

X. Meng et al. (Eds.): BDSC 2022, CCIS 1640, pp. 99–113, 2022.
https://doi.org/10.1007/978-981-19-7532-5_6

people to realize large-scale and batch operations. In the automatic O&M mode, the decision-making and processing of professionals is the key part of the O&M. But only relying on manual processing will limit the stability, accuracy and efficiency of the operation and maintenance system. So the traditional O&M method is difficult to provide more complex systems with high-quality O&M services. Intelligent O&M method [22], on the other hand, uses artificial intelligence algorithms such as machine learning to simulate the operations of professionals for analyzing emergency, and then help professionals make operation and maintenance decisions. At the same time, intelligent O&M method can, like professionals, continuously learn the rules and improve the efficiency of exception handling through the accumulated analysis experience in the past.

The traditional machine learning classification method [12] is to split the intelligent analysis process of events into two parts: feature engineering [25] and classification. Feature engineering obtains the key text data of events and converts them into vector data through three parts: data preprocessing, feature extraction and text representation. And according to the classification requirements, the appropriate feature weight calculation method is used for the key text, so as to obtain its weight features. Use the training data set after feature engineering to train traditional machine learning models, such as KNN methods [5], decision trees [17], etc., to obtain event classification models. The most important thing for deep learning [14] to solve large-scale text classification problems is the vector representation of event text data, and its features are automatically obtained by using network structures such as CNN [19]. The Huffman tree [10] is established according to the frequency of the category label. When predicting the event category, the output of the hidden layer is calculated with each Huffman tree node vector.

For the specific situation of this project, due to the lack of training data, the model cannot obtain good training results whether using traditional machine learning classification methods or deep learning classification methods [24], which result in poor classification accuracy of the model in predicting emergency monitoring events. At the same time, before accumulating a large amount of training data with classification labels, the classification model trained by traditional methods cannot dynamically optimize the classification effect. Repeated prediction [2] and classification errors will often occur, which will have a certain impact on the efficiency of professionals in dealing with emergencies. Therefore, according to the existing situation, this paper proposes a monitoring event classification algorithm that can meet the two requirements of optimizing the monitoring event classification effect, dynamically adjusting the classification model through the text clustering algorithm and the similarity measurement method.

The main methods of this paper are as follows: 1) We use the TF-IDF algorithm and the Bert pre-training model to establish a keyword dictionary with word weights and word vector representations, and a word vector matrix of event categories. 2) Based on the DBSCAN clustering algorithm, we use the optimized parameters to cluster the training data. 3) According to the clustering results or noise data and its corresponding event category, we use the Attention mechanism and similarity measurement method to update the classification parameters of each event category. 4) Based on the new contents accumulated in the monitoring event database and event knowledge base, we periodically train to update the key parameters of the model and optimize the classification effect. Overall, when events with similar key information are aggregated together by clustering and labeled with event categories. Our approach hopes to achieve the effect that unclassified surveillance events can be successfully classified by finding similar clusters of surveillance events. In calculating word weights, we use IDFs that emphasize the distinguishing ability of word weights to participate in generating a more effective vector of keyword representatives. Our method can quickly form the correspondence between new clusters and event categories by means of clustering and similarity measures after adding a small amount of similar noise data, thus flexibly and dynamically adjusting the model classification effect. We perform extensive experiments on the real-life dataset, and the experimental results verify the effectiveness of the method.

2 Related Work

For the text classification task, we mainly study the work in the two fields of keyword extraction and text clustering.

2.1 Keyword Extraction

TF-IDF [16] is commonly used in the keyword extraction part of the participating text classification tasks. For classification tasks in different situations, the TF-IDF method is improved to obtain more effective keywords and their weights. For example, studies have shown that the introduction of information entropy and word length information to improve the TF-IDF algorithm can effectively improve classification accuracy [8]. At the same time, the TF-IDF method has been improved for different fields [13], and its keyword extraction ability for short texts have been greatly improved. Therefore, it can be competent for keyword extraction tasks in text classification. BERT [3] is an important tool for word vector transformation in text classification tasks. Studies have shown that when BERT is used as the input of the embedding layer for text classification through deep learning, word vectors are effectively optimized [18]. Moreover, through the research on the principle of the BERT model and its main improved models [20], we believe that the dynamic word embedding pre-training model, that is, the BERT pre-training model, is more suitable for word vector transformation tasks.

2.2 Text Clustering

For text clustering [1], the more commonly used algorithms are K-Means [7], DBSCAN [6] and BIRCH [23] clustering algorithms. Through the study of text clustering tasks, the difficulty of text clustering tasks is often the determination of clustering parameters. The advantage of the K-Means clustering algorithm is that it is fast and simple, and has high efficiency for large data sets, but its disadvantage is that it is easily affected by the K value, the selection of initial class centroid samples or the initial class division. The optimal K value often takes a lot of time resources [11]. A reasonable range of clustering parameters can be obtained by using the adaptive DBSCAN clustering algorithm, which can effectively improve the clustering accuracy [21]. At the same time, since the DBSCAN clustering algorithm can eliminate the noise data of the training samples and reduce the format of the training samples, it can reduce the calculation amount of the text classification to a certain extent [9]. The BIRCH clustering algorithm is more suitable for analyzing a wide variety of text clustering scenarios. However, the high-dimensional features of text data will greatly reduce the clustering effect of the BIRCH algorithm. Additionally, the limit on the number of clustering features per node may cause the clustering results to be different from the real category distribution [4].

3   Method

According to the corresponding relationship between clusters and event categories as well as the classification similarity threshold of event categories, the algorithm realizes the classification of monitoring events through the similarity measurement method. At the same time, the algorithm can optimize the model effect according to the accumulated data in the event knowledge base and monitoring event base. The general framework diagram of the method is shown in Fig. 1.

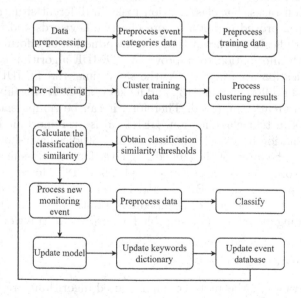

Fig. 1. The general framework diagram of the method.

3.1 Data Preprocessing

Preprocess Textual Descriptions of Event Categories. 1) Event category text description data segmentation Build a custom dictionary, adding certain fixed phrases to it in advance. At the same time, use regular expressions to dynamically identify phrases connected by underscores or hyphens contained in the text numbers, and add them to the custom dictionary. By loading the custom dictionary and stop word list, use the jieba word segmentation tool to obtain word segmentation results. 2) The purpose of establishing the keyword dictionary is to accurately extract the keywords of unclassified monitoring events. The text description of each event category is set as a document, and the TF-IDF method is used to calculate the IDF value of each word in the word segmentation result. The IDF value of each word in the word segmentation is calculated as follows:

$$weight_i = \lg \frac{|D|}{|j : t_i \in d_j|} \tag{1}$$

In Eq. (1), $|D|$ is the total number of text descriptions of all event categories, and $|j : t_i \in d_j|$ represents the number of text descriptions of event categories containing the word t_i. The IDF value of each word is used as the weight feature of the word segmentation and is stored in the keyword dictionary together with the word segmentation. Use the Bert pre-training model to calculate the word vectors of all the segmented words in the keyword dictionary in advance, and store them in the keyword dictionary. Through Fig. 2, we can see the basic structure of Bert and the process of generating the semantically enhanced word vectors. Bert is formed by stacking Transformer Encoder modules layer by layer. There are several important part in Transformer Encoder: (1) The Multi-head Self-Attention part in the Transformer Encoder module uses different Self-Attention modules to obtain the enhancement of each word in the text in different semantic spaces semantic vector, and linearly combine multiple enhanced semantic vectors of each word to obtain a final enhanced semantic vector with the same length as the original word vector. (2) Through the residual connection, the input and output of the Multi-head Self-Attention module are directly added and used as the input of the Layer Normalization module. (3) The Layer Normalization module completes the standardization of 0 mean and 1 variance for a certain layer of neural network nodes. (4) Two linear transformations are performed on the enhanced semantic vector of each word to enhance the expressive ability of the entire model. The semantically enhanced word vector generation process is shown in the right figure in Fig. 2. The yellow circle represents each word segment, represented by a vector, as the input text. Each word segment generates a multi-dimensional vector consisting of multiple purple circles, and then passes through multiple Encoder modules in the Transformer. Finally, each semantically enhanced word vector is generated. The semantically enhanced word vector of the participle t_i, which we define as $v_i = v_{(i,1)}, \ldots, v_{(i,768)}$. Since the keywords extracted from the monitoring event are all word segmented in the keyword dictionary, the word vector conversion of the monitoring event keywords can be achieved by querying the keyword dictionary, which shortens the word vector conversion time of the monitoring event keywords. 3) According to the word segmentation results and word vectors of the text description of each event category, a three-dimensional word vector matrix E is established to measure the similarity between monitoring events and different event category.

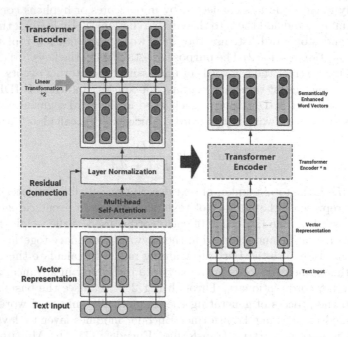

Fig. 2. The structure of the Bert model.

Preprocess Training Data. The training data used for model learning is a small amount of data with classification labels from the monitoring event database. Before extracting the keywords of the training data, it is first necessary to use regular expressions to identify and delete redundant information (such as time, date, etc.) according to the fixed format, so as to improve the efficiency of word segmentation and keyword extraction. By dynamically updating and loading custom dictionaries and stop word lists, use the jieba word segmentation tool to obtain the segmentation results of the training data. According to the keyword dictionary, the word segmentation with the top ten weights in the word segmentation result is found as the keyword of the alarm information of the monitoring event. Find word vectors and word weights corresponding to all keywords in the training data in the keyword dictionary, and use the weighted average method to generate a representative vector of the training data. The formula to generate the representative vector is as follows:

$$v = \frac{\sum_{i=1}^{n}(v_i * weight_i)}{n} \qquad (2)$$

The representative vectors of training and testing data are generated using Eq. (2) in order to participate in clustering and similarity measurement tasks.

3.2   Initialize Clustering of the Training Data

Obtain Training Data Clustering Results. 1) Using the T-SNE method to visualize the training data, it can be observed that the training data set is an irregular dense data set, and there is no specific fixed number of clusters, so the DBSCAN clustering algorithm is suitable for the situation for clustering. 2) The clustering effect is evaluated by using the silhouette coefficient S and the noise rate R. The silhouette coefficient is one of the indicators used to evaluate the clustering effect, and it can be considered as an indicator used to describe the clarity of the outline of each cluster, including two concepts of cohesion and separation. Cohesion can reflect the degree of closeness between a sample point and other elements in the same cluster; while separation degree can reflect the degree of closeness between a sample point and other elements outside the cluster. For the sample point i, $a(i)$ is the average value of the distance from the sample point i to all the sample points in the same cluster, $b(i)$ and is the average value of the distance from the sample point i to all the sample points outside the cluster, then the silhouette coefficient corresponding to the sample point i is:

$$S(i) = \frac{b(i) - a(i)}{\max(a(i), b(i))} \tag{3}$$

It can be seen from formula (1) that when the silhouette coefficient is close to 1, the degree of separation and cohesion are relatively good, that is, the clustering contour is more clear; the average of the silhouette coefficients of all sample points is obtained. The overall silhouette coefficient of the overall clustering results. The noise rate represents the proportion of sample points that are not clustered successfully (noise points) after using the DBSCAN algorithm. The calculation equation of the evaluation result is as follows:

$$Score = S - R \tag{4}$$

The meaning of $Score$ in Eq. (3) is that while the silhouette coefficient is expected to be close to 1, the data noise rate is expected to be lower. In the algorithm, the difference between the two is used to evaluate the clustering results, and the larger the value is, the better the clustering effect is. 3) There are two ways to optimize the parameters of the clustering algorithm: By setting a reasonable range of eps and min_samples, the best combination of two different combinations is found by using the $Score$ obtained by the method of clustering result evaluation. Using the KANN-DBSCAN adaptive algorithm, we use T-SNE to reduce the dimension of the training data representative vector. With the change of the parameter K, if the number of clusters does not change three consecutive times in a row, the eps and min_samples corresponding to the largest K are considered to be the best clustering parameters.

Process Clustering Results. 1) According to the category label group of monitoring events in the training data set, all clusters are divided into a new clustering result. At this time, all monitoring events in each cluster only correspond to the same group, that is, the cluster number and group label should have a one-to-one or many-to-one relationship, and a cluster group is generated according to the cluster number and group label. Chart. After the secondary division, the cluster number to which the training data belongs is updated, and the cluster number of −1 is the noise data that has not been successfully clustered. 2) According to the new clustering results, the K-means algorithm is used for each cluster to obtain the cluster center's vector to represent the cluster. And calculate the minimum value of cosine similarity from all points in each cluster to their cluster center vector, set it as the similarity threshold of each cluster, and generate the cluster center vector table and cluster similarity threshold table. The equation for calculating the similarity threshold of each cluster is as follows:

$$cluster\_threshold_i = \min\{\frac{(x_{i,j} * Center_i)}{\sqrt{(x_{i,j})^2} * \sqrt{(Center_i)^2}} | j = 1, \ldots n\} \qquad (5)$$

In Eq. (4), $cluster\_threshold_i$ is the minimum value of the cosine similarity from all points $X_i = x_{i,1}, \ldots, x_{i,n}$ in the cluster to the cluster center $Center_i$ which is the similarity threshold of clusters. 3) The cluster center vector table and the cluster similarity threshold table are connected through the cluster number and the cluster-group comparison table to form a cluster information table in the database, which is convenient for querying when classifying monitoring events.

3.3   Calculate the Classification Similarities of Event Categories

Generate Representative Vectors of Event Categories. In this step, by using the Attention mechanism and the word vector matrix of the event category, a representative vector P of the corresponding event category is generated according to each cluster center or noise data. The Attention mechanism structure is shown in Fig. 3.

$$P = Attention(Q, K, V) = softmax(QK^T)V \qquad (6)$$

In Eq. (5), Q is the cluster center vector or the noise data vector. K is the keyword word vector list of a certain event category in the word vector matrix E. And V is the same as K. The representative vector P of a certain event category can be calculated by the cluster center vector or the noise data vector Q. According to Fig. 3 and the Eq. (5), it can be analyzed that, the Attention mechanism can use the weighted average to generate the representative vector of each event category, so that in all the word segmentation described by the event category text, the weight of the word segmentation related to the corresponding cluster center or noise data is higher, thereby reducing those related to clustering. The influence of class-center-independent word segmentation in forming representative vectors.

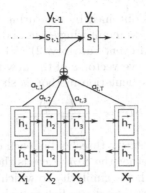

Fig. 3. The structure of the Attention mechanism.

Calculate Classification Similarity Thresholds for Event Categories.
Calculate the cosine similarity between each cluster center vector or noise data
vector and its corresponding event category representative vector. The equation
is as follows:

$$Sim_{x_i,y_i} = \frac{(x_i * y_i)}{\sqrt{(x_i)^2} * \sqrt{(y_i)^2}} \tag{7}$$

Sim_{x_i,y_i} in formula (6) is the cosine similarity between the cluster center vector
or noise data vector x_i and the representative vector y_i of the corresponding
event category. Then, using the minimum similarity value corresponding to each
event category as a threshold, a classification similarity threshold table of event
categories is generated. The equation is as follows:

$$group\_threshold_i = \min\{Sim_{j,i} | j \in i\} \tag{8}$$

In Eq. (7), $Sim_{j,i}$ is the cosine similarity between the representative vector v_i
of the event category i and the vector v_j of the cluster center j it contains.
$group\_threshold_i$ represents the classification similarity threshold of event category i. The $group\_threshold_i$ can ensure that the cluster center or noise data
belonging to the category i can be correctly classified into the category i.

3.4   Process New Monitoring Event

Preprocess New Monitoring Event. According to the method of preprocessing training data, the alarm information of unclassified new monitoring events
is segmented, keywords are extracted, and representative vectors are generated.

Classify New Monitoring Event. In this step, the classification result of
the new monitoring event is obtained by measuring the similarity between the
representative vector of the new monitoring event and each cluster center and
the representative vector of each event category. 1) The classification result of

the new monitoring event is obtained by measuring the similarity between the representative vector of the new monitoring event and each cluster center and the representative vector of each event category. 2) Calculate the cosine similarity Sim between the representative vector v of the new monitoring event and each cluster center vector c. The calculation method is shown in Eq. (8):

$$Sim = \frac{(v * c)}{\sqrt{(v)^2} * \sqrt{(c)^2}} \tag{9}$$

According to the cluster similarity threshold of each cluster in the cluster information table, determine whether the Sim exceeds the similarity threshold, and find the top five clusters with the similarity to which the new monitoring event belongs. Referring to the correspondence between clusters and event categories in the clustering information table, the classification results of the new monitoring events are given. If it fails to be divided into any cluster, it will be marked as noise data ($noise_label = True$). 3) Calculate the cosine similarity between the representative vector of the noise data and each event category. Using the Attention mechanism, the cosine similarity between the representative vector of each event category generated by the noise data and the noise data is calculated. Compare the result with the classification similarity threshold of each event category in the event knowledge base, and recommend event categories that meet the classification similarity threshold and have the top five similarities as the classification result. 4) Combined with expert experience, after the classification result of the new monitoring event is revised, it and its category label are automatically added to the monitoring event database as training data for subsequent model updates.

3.5　Update Event Knowledge Database

Update Event Category. If there is no event category that matches the new monitoring event in the event knowledge base, a professional is required to add an event category, describe it in text and describe its processing plan, and automatically add it to the event knowledge base. Besides, for the new word segmentation in the keyword dictionary, use the Bert pre-training model to obtain its word vector and add it to the word vector table.

Update Keyword Dictionary. After adding an event category, the content in the keyword dictionary will change. It is necessary to update the content in the keyword dictionary by building a keyword dictionary according to the text descriptions of all event categories in the event knowledge base.

Update Monitoring Event Database. As the keyword dictionary is updated, the representative vectors of all events in the monitoring event database may change. In order to obtain correct training data, it is necessary to re-extract the keywords of all events in the monitoring event database, generate a new representative vector according to the new weight, and then update the content in the monitoring event database.

Update the Word Vector Matrix. According to the new keyword dictionary and the word segmentation result of the text description of each event category, according to the method in the step of generating the word vector matrix, the word vector matrix is regenerated and completed.

Overall Mode Update. At the same time, the clustering information table learned by the model during the learning process and the classification similarity table of all event categories in the event knowledge base also need to be updated. Using the data in the monitoring event database as training data, re-run the steps in the algorithm implementation Sect. 3.3 to 3.4 to retrain the model. Once the update is complete, the task of classifying new monitoring events can be processed.

3.6 Process Accumulated Noise Data

When the marked noise data rate in the monitoring event database reaches or is higher than the artificially set threshold, some noise data may already meet the conditions for forming new clusters, then all existing noise data need to be clustered. form a new cluster. According to the newly formed clusters and their corresponding category labels, the cluster information table and the event category classification similarity threshold table are updated according to the above method.

3.7 Optimal Learning of the Model

When more data is accumulated in the monitoring event database, the data in the monitoring event database is used as training data, and the model can be retrained by re-running the steps in the algorithm implementation Sect. 3.3 to 3.4. This step can optimize the classification effect of the model with richer training data.

4 Experimental Results and Discussion

4.1 Experimental Datasets

A small amount of emergency monitoring event alarm information data with category labels in the monitoring event database provided by the CFFEX operation and maintenance platform is used as the dataset. The training and testing datasets are obtained by dividing the dataset by a ratio of 4:1. There are 2752 monitoring event data in the training dataset, and 689 monitoring event data in the test data. The meta-information in the table structure of the experimental data set after data preprocessing is shown in the Fig. 4.

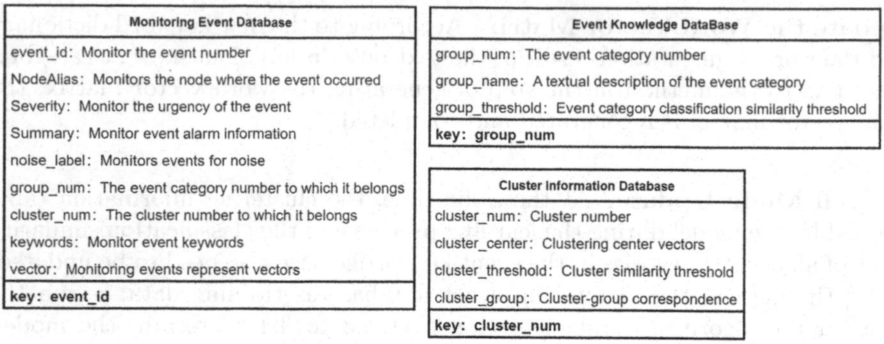

Monitoring Event Database
event_id: Monitor the event number
NodeAlias: Monitors the node where the event occurred
Severity: Monitor the urgency of the event
Summary: Monitor event alarm information
noise_label: Monitors events for noise
group_num: The event category number to which it belongs
cluster_num: The cluster number to which it belongs
keywords: Monitor event keywords
vector: Monitoring events represent vectors
key: event_id

Event Knowledge DataBase
group_num: The event category number
group_name: A textual description of the event category
group_threshold: Event category classification similarity threshold
key: group_num

Cluster Information Database
cluster_num: Cluster number
cluster_center: Clustering center vectors
cluster_threshold: Cluster similarity threshold
cluster_group: Cluster-group correspondence
key: cluster_num

Fig. 4. The meta-information in the table structure of the experimental dataset.

4.2   Baseline Models and Parameter Settings

Baseline Models. We compare our model with the two models on the valuation datasets. K-Means [7]: which is a clustering algorithm based on Euclidean distance, which considers that the closer the distance between two targets, the greater the similarity. BIRCH [23]: which is a comprehensive hierarchical clustering algorithm.

Parameter Settings. When clustering the training data, the parameter of the DBSCAN clustering algorithm used in this paper are set as follows: the "eps" is set to 0.01 and the "min_samples" is set to 2. When calculating the cluster center of the clustering result, the parameter of the K-Means clustering algorithm used in this paper are set as follows: the "n_clusters" is set to 1, the "init" is set to "k-means++", and the "precompute_distances" is set to "auto". When using T-SNE to reduce the dimension of word vectors, the parameters are set as follows: the "n_components" is set to 2, the "init" is set to "pca", and the "random_state" is set to 0. When using the attention mechanism, the parameters are set as follows: the "use_scale" is set to "False", the "causal" is set to "False".

4.3   Overall Performance

We used the three most commonly used algorithms for text clustering on the training data set for clustering, and judged the most suitable clustering algorithm according to the clustering effect. By using the silhouette coefficient for evaluation, the clustering parameters with the best clustering effect of each of the three clustering algorithms are found. Comparing the three clustering algorithms, it can be seen from Table 1 that the contour coefficients of the three do not differ significantly. However, the number of clusters generated by DBSCAN is significantly less, which can effectively reduce the amount of calculation when classifying new data. Therefore, we believe that the DBSCAN algorithm should be selected as the clustering algorithm for monitoring events.

Table 1. Comparison of the effects of three clustering algorithms.

Clustering algorithm	The number of clusters	Silhouette coefficient
K-Means	243	0.98582
BIRCH	229	0.98605
DBSCAN	191	0.97624

Table 2. Display of partially correctly classified test data.

Summary	Group_name	Group_num	Group
Process keepalived instance number is abnormal	The number of process instances is abnormal	10	[10]
The number of ports is abnormal, it should be equal to 1	The number of listen ports is abnormal	9	[9]
Tradefrt3 system CPU usage is abnormal	Abnormal system CPU usage	8	[8]
WARNING pub_session ::on_peer_close	Pub_session on_peer_close are reported	29	[29]

Then we use the DBSCAN algorithms to obtain the clustering results of the training data and construct the classification model according to the methods mentioned above. Use the model to classify the test data. The "group" field in Table 2 is the classification result given by the model. Meanwhile, in order to compare the impact of different clustering algorithms on the classification effect, We use K-Means, BIRCH and DBSCAN clustering algorithms to cluster the representative vectors of the training data, respectively, to compare the impact of different clustering methods on the event classification effect. The key parameters of the K-Means and BIRCH clustering algorithms are determined according to the elbow method and the silhouette coefficient. The parameter K of K-Means is 243, and the parameter branching_factor of BIRCH is 40. The DBSCAN clustering algorithm uses the parameter tuning method mentioned above to get the optimal eps and min_samples values. After using the above three clustering algorithms to obtain the clustering results of the training data, continue to construct three classification models according to the methods mentioned above. Use them to classify the test data and get the classification accuracy of each model. According to Table 2 and Table 3, it can be seen that the model trained by DBSCAN algorithm can classify most of the test data with the same classification result as its original event category label.

According to the tables, This paper believes that the classification accuracy of this model is good. For the case that more than one classification result occurs during classification, the order is arranged in descending order of matching similarity. As can be seen from Table 3, although the original event category labels of monitoring events are included in the classification results, the classification results of the maximum matching degree of some data are different from the

Table 3. Test data classification accuracy display.

Method	Number of correctly classified data	Number of incorrectly classified data	Accuracy
K-Means	667	22	0.96806
BIRCH	669	20	0.97097
DBSCAN	687	2	0.99709

original event category labels. There are two reasons for the inaccurate classification of data: 1) The same data does not appear in the monitoring event database. 2) Inaccurate keyword extraction leads to the inability to find similar clusters of monitored events, and thus to their correct classification.

5   Conclusion

In this paper, we propose the use of IDF as word weights to address the validity of representative vectors for monitoring events. At the same time, we propose a method to establish the correspondence between monitoring event clusters and event categories, which solves the problems of classification accuracy and stability. Finally, we propose a method for clustering noisy data, which solves the problem of flexibility in model optimization. We conduct extensive experiments on real-life datasets to validate the effectiveness of the proposed method. The result demonstrates that our method significantly outperforms existing approaches in the application of real scenarios.

References

1. Aggarwal, C.C., Zhai, C.: A survey of text clustering algorithms. In: Aggarwal, C., Zhai, C. (eds.) Mining Text Data, pp. 77–128. Springer, Boston, MA (2012). https://doi.org/10.1007/978-1-4614-3223-4_4
2. Cheng, D., Niu, Z., Tu, Y., Zhang, L.: Prediction defaults for networked-guarantee loans. In: 2018 24th International Conference on Pattern Recognition (ICPR), pp. 361–366. IEEE (2018)
3. Devlin, J., Chang, M.W., Lee, K., Toutanova, K.: BERT: pre-training of deep bidirectional transformers for language understanding. arXiv preprint arXiv:1810.04805 (2018)
4. Fahad, A., et al.: A survey of clustering algorithms for big data: taxonomy and empirical analysis. IEEE Trans. Emerg. Top. Comput. **2**(3), 267–279 (2014)
5. Guo, G., Wang, H., Bell, D., Bi, Y., Greer, K.: Using KNN model for automatic text categorization. Soft. Comput. **10**(5), 423–430 (2006). https://doi.org/10.1007/s00500-005-0503-y
6. Hahsler, M., Piekenbrock, M., Doran, D.: DBSCAN: fast density-based clustering with R. J. Stat. Softw. **91**, 1–30 (2019)
7. Hartigan, J.A., Wong, M.A.: Algorithm AS 136: a k-means clustering algorithm. J. Roy Stat. Soc. Ser. C (Appl. Stat.) **28**(1), 100–108 (1979)

8. Jin, Y., Huang, J.: Improved TFIDF algorithm based on information entropy and word length information. J. Zhejiang Univ. Tech. **49**(2), 203–209 (2021)

9. Jing, Y., Gou, H., Zhu, Y.: An improved density-based method for reducing training data in KNN. In: 2013 International Conference on Computational and Information Sciences, pp. 972–975. IEEE (2013)

10. Knuth, D.E.: Dynamic Huffman coding. J. algorithms **6**(2), 163–180 (1985)

11. Kwale, F.M.: A critical review of K means text clustering algorithms. Int. J. Adv. Res. Comput. Sci. **4**(9), 27–34 (2013)

12. Liang, X., Cheng, D., Yang, F., Luo, Y., Qian, W., Zhou, A.: F-HMTC: detecting financial events for investment decisions based on neural hierarchical multi-label text classification. In: IJCAI, pp. 4490–4496 (2020)

13. Liu, C.Z., Sheng, Y.X., Wei, Z.Q., Yang, Y.Q.: Research of text classification based on improved TF-IDF algorithm. In: 2018 IEEE International Conference of Intelligent Robotic and Control Engineering (IRCE), pp. 218–222. IEEE (2018)

14. Minaee, S., Kalchbrenner, N., Cambria, E., Nikzad, N., Chenaghlu, M., Gao, J.: Deep learning-based text classification: a comprehensive review. ACM Comput. Surv. (CSUR) **54**(3), 1–40 (2021)

15. Okogbaa, G., Huang, J., Shell, R.L.: Database design for predictive preventive maintenance system of automated manufacturing system. Comput. Indust. Eng. **23**(1–4), 7–10 (1992)

16. Qaiser, S., Ali, R.: Text mining: use of TF-IDF to examine the relevance of words to documents. Int. J. Comput. Appl. **181**(1), 25–29 (2018)

17. Sakakibara, Y., Misue, K., Koshiba, T.: Text classification and keyword extraction by learning decision trees. In: Proceedings of 9th IEEE Conference on Artificial Intelligence for Applications, p. 466. IEEE (1993)

18. Sun, H., Chen, Q.Y.: Chinese text classification based on BERT and attention. J. Chin. Comput. Syst. **43**(1), 22–26 (2022)

19. Tu, Y., Niu, L., Chen, J., Cheng, D., Zhang, L.: Learning from web data with self-organizing memory module. In: Proceedings of the IEEE/CVF Conference on Computer Vision and Pattern Recognition, pp. 12846–12855 (2020)

20. Wang, C., Nulty, P., Lillis, D.: A comparative study on word embeddings in deep learning for text classification. In: Proceedings of the 4th International Conference on Natural Language Processing and Information Retrieval, pp. 37–46 (2020)

21. Wang, G., Lin, G.: Improved adaptive parameter DBSCAN clustering algorithm. Comput. Eng. Appl. **56**(14), 45–51 (2020)

22. Yang, H., Zhan, K., Yao, Q., Zhao, X., Zhang, J., Lee, Y.: Intent defined optical network with artificial intelligence-based automated operation and maintenance. Sci. China Inf. Sci. **63**(6), 1–12 (2020). https://doi.org/10.1007/s11432-020-2838-6

23. Zhang, T., Ramakrishnan, R., Livny, M.: BIRCH: an efficient data clustering method for very large databases. ACM Sigmod Rec. **25**(2), 103–114 (1996)

24. Zhu, P., Cheng, D., Luo, S., Xu, R., Liang, Y., Luo, Y.: Leveraging enterprise knowledge graph to infer web events' influences via self-supervised learning. J. Web Semant. **74**, 100722 (2022)

25. Zhu, P., et al.: Improving Chinese named entity recognition by large-scale syntactic dependency graph. IEEE/ACM Trans. Audio Speech Lang. Process. **30**, 979–991 (2022)

SubGraph Networks Based Entity Alignment for Cross-Lingual Knowledge Graph

Shanqing Yu[1,2]([✉]), Shihan Zhang[1,2], Jianlin Zhang[1,2], Jiajun Zhou[1,2],
Yun Sun[3], Bing Li[3], and Qi Xuan[1,2]

[1] Institute of Cyberspace Security, Zhejiang University of Technology,
Hangzhou 310023, China
yushanqing@zjut.edu.cn
[2] College of Information Engineering, Zhejiang University of Technology,
Hangzhou 310023, China
[3] Hangzhou Zhongao Technology Company Limited, Hangzhou 310000, China

Abstract. Entity alignment is the task of discovering entities representing the equal real-world object in two knowledge graphs (KGs). Cross-lingual knowledge graph entity alignment aims to discover the cross-lingual links in the multi-language KGs, which is of wonderful value to solve the NLP problems and integrate multi-language KGs. In the task of aligning cross-language knowledge graphs, the structures of the two graphs are very similar, and the equivalent entities often have the same subgraph structure characteristics. The traditional GCN method neglects to obtain structural features through representative parts of the original graph and the use of adjacency matrix is not enough to effectively represent the structural features of the graph. In this paper, we introduce the subgraph network (SGN) method into the GCN-based cross-lingual KG entity alignment method. In the method, we extracted the first-order subgraphs of the KGs to expand the structural features of the original graph to enhance the representation ability of the entity embedding and improve the alignment accuracy. Experiments show that the proposed method is advanced in the task of entity alignment.

Keywords: Knowledge graph · Entity alignment · Cross-language · Graph neural network · Subgraph network

1 Introduction

The knowledge graph, which aims to organize human knowledge in a structured form, is playing an increasingly important role as an infrastructure in the field of artificial intelligence and natural language processing [1]. A knowledge graph is a collection of a series of knowledge facts, usually represented by a triple. With the vigorous development of multilingual knowledge graphs such as YAGO [18,19], DBpedia [12] and BabelNet [15], the structured knowledge provided by these KGs is widely used as a priori for applications such as language modeling [2].

© The Author(s), under exclusive license to Springer Nature Singapore Pte Ltd. 2022
X. Meng et al. (Eds.): BDSC 2022, CCIS 1640, pp. 114–128, 2022.
https://doi.org/10.1007/978-981-19-7532-5_7

However, these multilingual knowledge graphs are difficult to integrate effectively due to different language codes. In order to effectively utilize the knowledge contained in KGs from different languages, more and more researches are focused on the alignment of cross-language knowledge graphs which aim to automatically discover and match the equivalent entities in multilingual knowledge graphs.

The multilingual knowledge graphs contains rich cross-language links. These links match the equivalent entities in different languages KG, and play an important role in completing the multilingual graph. Traditional cross-language graph alignment methods usually use machine translation or define independent features of various languages to discover cross-language links. Such methods are challenging to practice on a massive scale. With the popularity of knowledge graph embedding methods, many alignment methods primarily based on embedding have been proposed.

The knowledge graph embedding can map the entities and relationships in the graph to a continuous low-dimensional vector space, and retain some semantic information. Recently, many representative works have appeared in the field of knowledge graph embedding. Among them, TransE [3] is one of the most classic knowledge graph embedding methods. It regards the relationship in the triple (h, r, t) as the translation from the head entity vector to the tail entity vector, and makes each triple must satisfy $h + r \approx t$. The model learns embedding by minimizing the Euclidean distance between the vectors $h + r$ and t. The TransE model is simple and powerful, and excels in the tasks of link prediction and triple classification. However, due to the problem of insufficient expression ability of the model, it cannot handle the one-to-one, one-to-many, and many-to-many relationships well. Researchers have proposed some improved models based on TransE. For example, TransH [22] solves the problem that the TransE model cannot handle one-to-many and many-to-one issues by projecting the vector representations of h and t corresponding to each relationship onto different hyperplanes. TransR [13] adds entity attribute information during the embedding process. TransD [9] solves the vector representation problem of multiple semantic relations after embedding through dynamic matrix. TransA [24] changes the distance metric in the loss function to Mahalanobis distance, and sets different weights for each dimension of learning. HyTE [5] considers the time validity of the establishment of triples. The above models have improved the expressive ability of TransE to a certain extent.

JE [8] uses an embedding-based method to map the entities into a low-dimensional space by given two knowledge graphs and a set of pre-aligned entities, and then matches the equivalent entities according to their embedding vectors. MTransE [4] increases the embedding of relations, so training the model needs to provide pre-aligned triples in two knowledge graphs. JAPE [20] adds entity attribute embedding on the basis of MTransE to enhance the alignment effect. Wang [23] and others first transferred the method of graph convolutional neural network to knowledge graph for entity alignment. However, none of the existing models take full advantage of the subgraph network [25] information of the knowledge graph. Since the network structure of cross-linguistic knowledge graphs is very similar, the use of adjacency matrix is not enough to effectively represent the structural features of the graph. By extracting its subgraph features, it can effectively make up for its lack of features.

In view of the above situation, this paper proposes a cross-language knowledge graph alignment model combining subgraph features. This method combines the knowledge model and the alignment model to learn the representation of the multilingual knowledge graph. Among them, the knowledge model uses the graph convolutional neural network to encode the feature information of the entity to obtain the node-level embedding vector. The alignment model comprehensively considers the structural embedding, the subgraph structural embedding and attribute embedding of the KG to find the equivalent entity. The main contributions of this paper are as follows:

- A method is proposed to expand the structural features of the original KG by using the sub-graph features, and make the structural embedding vector more suitable for the discovery of equivalent entities.
- Combining the SGN and the GCN method proves the effectiveness of the subgraph feature embedding in the task of aligning entities of the structurally similar knowledge graph.

The rest of this paper is arranged as follows. In Sect. 2, we present some basic methods for GCN, SGN and knowledge graph alignment based on embedding. In Sect. 3, we introduce a method of entity alignment in cross-language knowledge graph based on subgraph network. In Sect. 4, we introduce the dataset and experiment extensively. In Sect. 5, we conclude the paper.

2   Related Work

2.1   GCN

The convolutional neural network (GCN) [6,11] is a neural network that can run directly on the graph data. In the method of this article, input the adjacency matrix of the graph and the feature vector of the entity to the GCN, and then the domain information of the entity can be encoded as a real-valued vector. In the task of aligning entities of the cross-language knowledge graph, equivalent entities generally have similar structural features. Therefore, GCN model can effectively aggregate these two types of information and map entities to a low-dimensional vector space. And make the equivalent entities have similar vector representations. The GCN model consists of several fixed GCN layers, and its $l+1$ layer depends on the output of the previous layer, with the specific convolution calculated as follows:

$$H^{(l+1)} = \sigma(\widehat{Q}^{-\frac{1}{2}} \widehat{P} \widehat{Q}^{-\frac{1}{2}} H(l) W(l)), \tag{1}$$

where P is the adjacency matrix and n is the number of nodes. $\widehat{P} = P + I$, I is the identity matrix, $\widehat{Q}$ is $\widehat{P}$ diagonal nodal matrix, $H(l)$ is the vertex feature matrix input to the first layer of the GCN model, $W(l)$ is the weight matrices of the neural network of the first layer of various features, and σ is similar to RELU's nonlinear activation function.

2.2   SGN

Many real-world structures can be naturally represented by networks, such as collaborative networks [16,26] and social networks [7,10]. Knowledge graph also contains rich network structure. The entities in KG can be regarded as nodes in the network, relationships can be regarded as edges in the network. Therefore, the knowledge graph can be regarded as a heterogeneous network in essence.

Subgraphs are the basic components of a network, so studying the substructur of a network is an effective way to analyze a network [21]. Recently, Word2vec [14], DeepWalk [17] and other graph embedding algorithms have been widely used in node classification and other tasks. However, the embedded vector obtained by such models contains only local structure information around nodes, while ignoring the global structure information of the entire network. The SGN proposal effectively solves this problem, Xuan et al. [25] designed the algorithm used to build first-order and second-order SGN, and can be easily extended to build high-order subgraph network. Experiments show that the structural characteristics of SGN can complement the structural characteristics of the original network, so as to higher elevate out downstream tasks such as node classification and network classification.

2.3   Knowledge Graph Alignment Based on Embedding

Currently, the alignment of knowledge graph based on embedding can be divided into two categories: alignment based on the TransE model and alignment based on the GCN [11] model. This section will briefly introduce some of the most representative models and discuss the differences between them.

The JE [8] model merges the pre-aligned entities into the same KG, and jointly learns the representation of multiple KGs in a unified vector space, and then aligns the entities in the knowledge map according to the embedded vector.

MTransE [4] combines the knowledge model and the alignment model to align the knowledge graph. This method uses TransE to train two knowledge graphs separately, and encodes entities and relationships in independent spaces. Then use some pre-aligned triples for training, and the alignment model considers three cross-language alignment representations based on distance-based axis calibration, translation vector and linear transformation.

Sometimes, the structural information of the KG cannot be used to obtain a good alignment effect, so some scholars have proposed an alignment method combining attribute information. The JAPE [20] model combines structure embedding and attribute embedding to match entities in different KGs. The model uses TransE to learn the structural features of the two KGs, and the Skip-gram model to capture attribute features, which improves the performance of MTransE to a certain extent.

The above methods all rely on the TransE model to learn entity embedding. Such methods are often limited by the expressive ability of the TransE model. Therefore, Wang [23] and others proposed a method of graph convolutional neural network. This method uses the GCN model to embed the entities in different

KGs into a unified vector space, so that the aligned entities are as close as possible. Unlike TransE-based models such as MTransE and JAPE, this method does not require pre-aligned triples, but only needs to focus on pre-aligned entities.

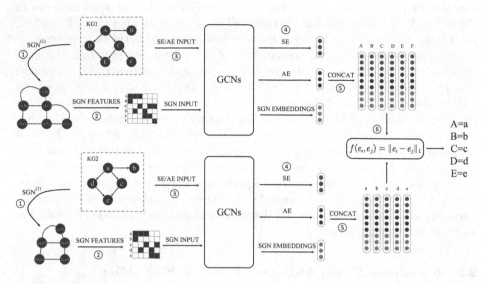

Fig. 1. The framework of sub-GCN, which consists of six steps. First, convert the original KG into a first-order SGN; secondly, extract first-order subgraph features for entities of the original network; third, obtain the structure and attribute features of the original knowledge graph as input; fourth, obtain the structure, attributes and SGN embedding vectors by training GCN models; fifth, concatenate the three embedding vectors according to different weights; sixth, align the entities in the two knowledge graphs according to the scoring function.

3   Methodology

The graph alignment framework proposed in this paper is shown in Fig. 1, which can be summed up in three parts: subgraph feature extraction, entity embedding model and entity alignment model. For a given KG_1 and KG_2 knowledge graph in two different languages and a set of known alignment entity pairs $S = \{(e_{i1}, e_{i2})\}_{i=1}^{m}$. The subgraph feature extraction part uses the first-order SGN algorithm to extract the subgraph network from the original KG, and then performs the subgraph feature encoding for each entity. Entity embedding uses the GCN model to encode the entities in the KG, and embeds entities from different languages into a unified vector space. After training, the distance between equivalent entities will be as close as possible. Finally, the candidate entities are ranked by a predefined distance function to find the corresponding equivalent entity of each entity.

3.1 Problem Definition

The knowledge graph stores knowledge in the real world in the form of triples. In this article, we divide the graph into two types: relation triples and attribute triples. For example, in the DBP15K data set, $(Ren'Py, operatingSystem, Linux)$ is a relational triplet, and its format is $(entity_1, relation, entity_2)$. $(GaryLocke, dateOfBirth, 1950)$ is an attribute triplet, The format is $(entity, attribute, value)$. Formally, we express the knowledge graph as $KG = E, R, A, T_R, T_A$, where E, R, A represent the set of entities, relations and attributes, and $T_R \subseteq (E \times R \times E)$ represents the relationship triplet set, $T_A \subseteq (E \times A \times V)$ represents the relationship triplet set, and V represents the set of attribute values.

For $KG_1 = \{E_1, R_1, A_1, T_1^R, T_1^A\}$ and $KG_2 = \{E_2, R_2, A_2, T_2^R, T_2^A\}$ two knowledge graphs in different languages, we define the task of cross-language knowledge graph alignment as finding new alignment entity pairs in KG through existing known entities. This experiment uses a set of pre-aligned entity pairs $S = \{(e_{i1}, e_{i2}) | e_{i1} \in E_1, e_{i2} \in E_2\}_{(i=1)}^m$ to train the GCN model, and then discover new aligned entity pairs based on the distance function, where the pre-aligned entity pairs are constructed by cross-language links in DBpedia.

3.2 Enhanced Structure Embedding Based on Subgraph Feature

Subgraph Networks [25] can effectively expand the structural feature space of the original network, and integrating this structural information can improve the performance of subsequent algorithms based on network structure. In the task of aligning cross-language knowledge graphs, the structures of the two graphs are very similar, and the equivalent entities often have the same subgraph structure characteristics.Therefore, extracting subgraph features to supplement the structural information of the original KG can effectively improve the accuracy of the entity alignment task. This paper extracts the first-order subgraph network of the original KG, and encodes the first-order subgraph feature for each entity. Specific steps are as follows:

- Detect subgraphs from the original network. In the method, the most basic sub-graphs (i.e. lines) are selected as sub-graphs due to the fact they are simple and relatively frequent in most networks.
- Use subgraphs to construct SGN. After extracting adequate subgraphs from the original network, a connection is established between them according to certain rules to construct SGN. Here, for simplicity, as long as two subgraphs share the same node or link in the original network, connect them.
- Use SGN to construct the subgraph features of the original network. The new node in SGN is regarded as the encoding object of ont-hot encoding. If the entity in the original knowledge graph belongs to one of the subgraphs, it is marked as 1 at the corresponding position.

Algorithm 1: Constructing Subgraph Feature.

Input: A Knowledge Graph $KG(E, R, T_R)$ with entity set E, relation set R and relation triples $T_R \subseteq (E \times R \times E)$.

Output: Subgraph Feature Matrix h_{sgn}.

1 Initialize a network $G(V', E')$ with node set $V' \subseteq E$ and link set $E' \subseteq (V' \times V')$ by $KG(E, R, T_R)$;

2 $L = \{l_1, l_2, ..., l_3\} \leftarrow$ extracting lines as subgraphs;

3 **for** $i, j \in L$ **do**

4 $\quad$ **if** i, j *share a common node* $\in V'$ **then**

5 $\quad\quad$ | $\quad$ add the link(i, j) into $\widetilde{E}$

6 $\quad$ **end**

7 **end**

8 get the $SGN^{(1)}$ denoted by $G(L, \widetilde{E})$;

9 **for** *each* $e \in E$ **do**

10 $\quad$ **if** *if any subgraph* $\in L$ *contains* e **then**

11 $\quad\quad$ | $\quad$ marked subgraph feature vector as 1 at the corresponding position

12 $\quad$ **end**

13 **end**

14 **return** Subgraph Feature Matrix h_{sgn};

3.3 GCN-Based Entity Embedding

In this paper, three GCN models was trained by the structural features, attribute features and subgraph features of the knowledge graph. The parameters of the three GCN models are shown in Table 1. Each GCN model consists of multiple fixed GCN layers, and the $l + 1$ layer depends on the output of the previous layer, with the specific convolution calculated as follows:

$$[H_s^{(l+1)}; H_a^{(l+1)}; H_{sgn}^{(l+1)}] = \sigma(\hat{Q}^{-\frac{1}{2}} \hat{P} \hat{Q}^{-\frac{1}{2}} [H_s(l) W_s(l); H_a(l) \ W_a(l); H_{sgn}(l) W_{sgn}(l)]), \qquad (2)$$

where P in this paper adopts the adjacency matrix calculation method for knowledge graph proposed by Wang. $H_s(l)$, $H_a(l)$ and $H_{sgn}(l)$ are the vertex feature matrix, attribute feature matrix and subgraph feature matrix input To the first layer of the GCN model, $W_s(l)$, $W_a(l)$ and $W_{sgn}(l)$ are the weight matrices of the neural network of the first layer of various features. The GCN model embeds the structural features and attribute features of different language entities into a unified vector space. This paper designs the following embedding method to enhance structural features to improve accuracy, which reduces the difference between equivalent entities.

3.4 Model Training

In order to make the embedding vectors of equivalent entities as close as possible in the vector space, this paper uses a set of pre-aligned entity pairs S as the training set of the GCN model, and trains model by minimizing the following loss function based on marginal ranking:

$$L_s = \sum_{(e,v) \in S} \sum_{(e',v') \in S} [f(h_s(e), h_s(v)) + \gamma_s - f(h_s(e'), h_s(v'))]_+, \qquad (3)$$

$$L_a = \sum_{(e,v) \in S} \sum_{(e',v') \in S} [f(h_a(e), h_a(v)) + \gamma_a - f(h_a(e'), h_a(v'))]_+, \qquad (4)$$

$$L_{sgn} = \sum_{(e,v) \in S} \sum_{(e',v') \in S} [f(h_{sgn}(e), h_{sgn}(v)) + \gamma_{sgn} - f(h_{sgn}(e'), h_{sgn}(v'))]_+, \qquad (5)$$

where $[x]_+ = max\{0, x\}$, $f(x, y) = \|x - y\|_1$, $S'_{(e,v)}$ is to randomly replace the aligned entity pairs. The negative sample set constructed by an entity in (e, v). The replaced entity is randomly selected from KG_1 and KG_2. γ_s, γ_a, $\gamma_{sgn} > 0$ is a hyperparameter used to control the degree of positive and negative alignment entities. L_s, L_a, and L_{sgn} are the loss functions of structural embedding, attribute embedding, and subgraph embedding, respectively. They are independent of each other, so they will be optimized using stochastic gradient descent respectively.

3.5   Knowledge Graph Entity Alignment Prediction

Knowledge Graph entity alignment is predicted based on the distance between two entities in vector space. For the entity e_i in KG_1 and the entity e_j in KG_2, the distance between them is calculated by the following formula:

$$D(e_i, e_j) = \alpha \frac{f(h_s(e_i), h_s(e_j))}{d_s} + \beta \frac{f(h_a(e_i), h_a(e_j))}{d_a} + \gamma \frac{f(h_{sgn}(e_i), h_{sgn}(e_j))}{d_{sgn}}, \qquad (6)$$

where $h_s(e)$, $h_a(e)$, $h_{sgn}(e)$ represent vectors after structural embedding, attribute embedding, and first-order subgraph embedding, d represents their dimensions. α, β, γ are the parameter to balance the three embedding vectors and need to satisfy $\alpha + \beta + \gamma = 1$. For entity e_i in KG_1, this method calculates the distance from all entities in KG_2 to e_i and ranks them as candidate equivalent entities. In addition, the alignment from KG_2 to KG_1 can also be performed. The results of the alignment in both directions are given in the next section.

Table 1. Parameters of Three GCNs

	Parameter	KG_1	KG_2
	Initial Structure Feature Matrices	$H_{s1}^{(0)} \in \mathbb{R}^{|E_1| \times d_s}$	$H_{s2}^{(0)} \in \mathbb{R}^{|E_2| \times d_s}$
	Weight Matrix for Structure Features in Layer 1	$W_s^{(1)} \in \mathbb{R}^{d_s \times d_s}$	
GCN_{SE}	Weight Matrix for Structure Features in Layer 2	$W_s^{(2)} \in \mathbb{R}^{d_s \times d_s}$	
	Output Structure Embeddings	$H_{s1}^{(2)} \in \mathbb{R}^{|E_1| \times d_s}$	$H_{s2}^{(2)} \in \mathbb{R}^{|E_2| \times d_s}$
	Initial Attribute Feature Matrices	$H_{a1}^{(0)} \in \mathbb{R}^{|E_1| \times |A_1|}$	$H_{a2}^{(0)} \in \mathbb{R}^{|E_2| \times |A_2|}$
GCN_{AE}	Weight Matrix for Attribute Features in Layer 1	$W_a^{(1)} \in \mathbb{R}^{|A_1| \times d_a}$	
	Weight Matrix for Attribute Features in Layer 2	$W_a^{(2)} \in \mathbb{R}^{d_a \times d_a}$	
	Output Attribute Embeddings	$H_{a1}^{(2)} \in \mathbb{R}^{|E_1| \times d_a}$	$H_{a1}^{(2)} \in \mathbb{R}^{|E_2| \times d_a}$
	Initial Subgraph Feature Matrices	$H_{sgn1}^{(0)} \in \mathbb{R}^{|E_1| \times |SGN|}$	$H_{sgn2}^{(0)} \in \mathbb{R}^{|E_2| \times |SGN|}$
GCN_{SGN}	Weight Matrix for Subgraph Features in Layer 1	$W_{sgn}^{(1)} \in \mathbb{R}^{|SGN| \times d_{sgn}}$	
	Weight Matrix for Subgraph Features in Layer 2	$W_{sgn}^{(2)} \in \mathbb{R}^{d_{sgn} \times d_{sgn}}$	
	Output Subgraph Embeddings	$H_{sgn1}^{(2)} \in \mathbb{R}^{|E_1| \times d_{sgn}}$	$H_{sgn2}^{(2)} \in \mathbb{R}^{|E_2| \times d_{sgn}}$

4   Experiments

4.1   Experimental Setting

Here, we will explain the experimental setting. To prove the effectiveness of Sub-GCN, we performed an entity alignment task in the DBP15K dataset and compared it with some of the latest baseline methods. For all alignment models, we use 30% of the pre-aligned entity links as the training set, and the remaining 70% for testing. The parameters in the sub-GCN are set to $d_s = 200$, $d_{sgn} = d_a = 100$; $\gamma_s = \gamma_{sgn} = \gamma_a = 3$; $epochs = 5000$; $\alpha = 0.72$; $\beta = 0.2$; $\gamma = 0.08$; the number of negative samples for each positive seed parameter $k = 20$. The results GCN[Wang] obtained from Wang et al. [23], and * marked result parameter settings are as follows: $d_s=200$, $d_a=100$; $\gamma_s = \gamma_a = 3$; $epochs = 5000$; $\alpha = 0.8$; $\beta = 0.2$; $k = 20$.

4.2   DataSet

The data set in the experiment is DBP15K, which was constructed by Sun [20] and others. The DBP15K data set comes from DBpedia, which is a large-scale multilingual knowledge map from which DBP15K extracts a subset of the KG in Chinese, English, Japanese, and French. The description of the data set is shown in Table 2. Each data set consists of two knowledge graphs in specific languages and 15,000 equivalent entity links.

Table 2. Details of the datasets

Datasets		Entities	Relations	Attributes	Rel.triples	Attr.triples
DBP15K_ZH-EN	Chinese	66,469	2,830	8,113	153,929	379,684
	English	98,125	2,317	7,173	237,674	567,755
DBP15K_JA-EN	Japanese	65,744	2,043	5,882	164,373	354,619
	English	95,680	2,096	6,066	233,319	497,230
DBP15K_FR-EN	French	66,858	1,379	4,547	192,191	528,665
	English	105,889	2,209	6,422	278,590	576,543

4.3   Result

In the experiment, we mainly compared our method with the recent work based on GCN [23], and also compared some methods based on TransE embedding, such as JE, MTransE and JAPE models. The experimental results are shown in Tables 3,4,5, where SE means that only structural information is used for embedding, SE+AE means that both structure and attribute information are used for embedding. The sub-GCN is the model proposed in this paper which uses three types of information: structure, attributes and subgraph features. We use Hits@k as an evaluation indicator to evaluate the performance of all methods. Hits@k represents the hit rate of the correct entity among the top k candidate entities.

Table 3. Results comparison of cross-lingual KG alignment (ZH-EN)

DBP15K_ZH-EN		ZH-EN			EN-ZH		
		Hits@1	Hits@10	Hits@50	Hits@1	Hits@10	Hits@50
JE		21.27	42.77	56.74	19.52	39.36	53.25
MTransE		30.83	61.41	79.12	24.78	52.42	70.45
JAPE	SE w/o neg	38.34	68.86	84.07	31.66	59.37	76.33
	SE	39.78	72.35	87.12	32.29	62.79	80.55
	SE+AE	41.18	74.46	**88.90**	40.15	71.05	**86.18**
GCN[Wang]	SE	38.42	70.34	81.24	34.43	65.68	77.03
	SE+AE	41.25	74.38	86.23	36.49	69.94	82.45
*GCN[Wang]	*SE	40.22	69.53	78.76	37.81	67.30	76.95
	*SE+AE	44.71	75.89	86.51	42.14	73.92	84.78
sub-GCN		**45.01**	**76.48**	87.02	**42.97**	**75.30**	85.72

Table 4. Results comparison of cross-lingual KG alignment (JA-EN)

DBP15K_JA-EN		JA-EN			EN-JA		
		Hits@1	Hits@10	Hits@50	Hits@1	Hits@10	Hits@50
JE		18.92	39.97	54.24	17.80	38.44	52.48
MTransE		27.86	57.45	75.94	23.72	49.92	67.93
JAPE	SE w/o neg	33.10	63.90	80.80	29.71	56.28	73.84
	SE	34.27	66.39	83.61	31.40	60.80	78.51
	SE+AE	36.25	68.50	85.35	38.37	67.27	82.65
GCN[Wang]	SE	38.21	72.49	82.69	36.90	68.50	79.51
	SE+AE	39.91	74.46	86.10	38.42	71.81	83.72
*GCN[Wang]	*SE	41.90	72.73	81.43	39.72	69.06	77.82
	*SE+AE	45.19	77.10	87.63	42.83	74.02	85.96
sub-GCN		**45.46**	**78.15**	**88.98**	**43.50**	**75.46**	**87.18**

Table 5. Results comparison of cross-lingual KG alignment (FR-EN)

DBP15K_FR-EN		FR-EN			EN-FR		
		Hits@1	Hits@10	Hits@50	Hits@1	Hits@10	Hits@50
JE		15.38	38.84	56.50	14.61	47.25	54.01
MTransE		24.41	55.55	74.41	21.26	50.60	69.93
JAPE	SE w/o neg	29.55	62.18	79.36	25.40	56.55	74.96
	SE	29.63	64.55	81.90	26.55	69.39	78.71
	SE+AE	32.39	66.68	83.19	32.97	65.91	82.38
GCN[Wang]	SE	36.51	73.42	85.93	36.08	72.37	85.44
	SE+AE	37.29	74.49	86.73	42.50	76.78	87.92
*GCN[Wang]	*SE	42.07	76.34	85.66	40.33	73.71	83.90
	*SE+AE	43.44	79.21	88.93	42.44	76.85	87.88
sub-GCN		**43.67**	**79.65**	**89.68**	**42.93**	**77.38**	**88.93**

Sub-GCN vs. JAPE. According to the data in the table, the sub-GCN alignment model is superior to JAPE in the alignment of the $DBP15K_{JA-EN}$ and $DBP15K_{FR-EN}$. This shows that in the cross-language knowledge graph, the GCN model based on the graph structure is easier to capture the characteristics of the entity than the model using TransE embedding. The effect of the sub-GCN alignment model on the alignment of $DBP15K_{ZH-EN}$ is not better than that of JAPE on the hits@50 index. This may be because the embedding of the JAPE model can use the triples of relations and attributes at the same time, so higher consequences can be received on data sets with multiple relations and attributes. But this also increases the cost of pre-labeling, and the training of the model requires pre-aligning the entire triplet. In this regard, GCN-based embedding only needs to label aligned entities, which is appropriate for the alignment of massive knowledge graphs.

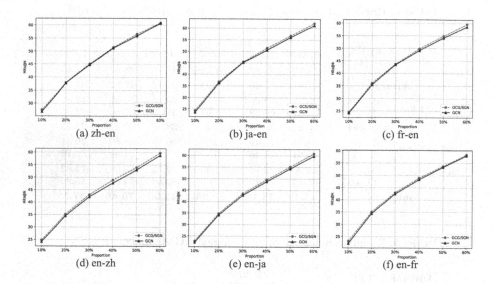

Fig. 2. GCN(AE+SE) and sub-GCN using different sizes of training data; vertical coordinates: Hits@1

Sub-GCN vs. GCN(SE+AE). Compared with GCN (SE+AE), sub-GCN outperforms GCN (SE+AE) on the three datasets. After extracting the first-order subgraph of the knowledge graph to enhance the structural information, the alignment ability of the GCN model has been improved. Experiments show that in the task of aligning cross-language knowledge graphs, the subgraph feature can effectively expand and expand the structural information of the original graph to obtain a better alignment effect.

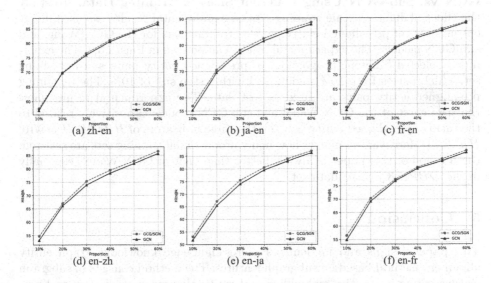

Fig. 3. GCN(AE+SE) and sub-GCN using different sizes of training data; vertical coordinates: Hits@10

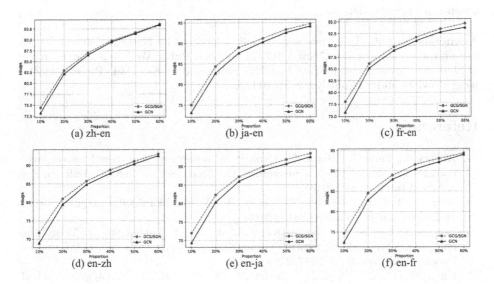

Fig. 4. GCN(AE+SE) and sub-GCN using different sizes of training data; vertical coordinates: Hits@50

GCN vs. Sub-GCN Using Different Sizes of Training Data. To study the effect of different scale training sets on experimental results, we used different numbers of pre-aligned entity pairs as training sets for the GCN[Wang] and sub-GCN models. The experimental results can be seen in Figs. 2,3,4. The experiment selected different proportions of pre-aligned entity pairs as the training set, which ranges from 10% to 60% and with a step size of 10%. The remaining pre-aligned entity pairs are used as test data. The experimental results show that the effect of the GCN[Wang] and sub-GCN models is positively related to the ratio of pre-aligned entity pairs on the three indicators of $Hits@1$, $Hits@10$, $Hits@50$. Moreover, no matter how many proportional training sets are selected, the method of this paper is always better than that of GCN[Wang], especially in the $DBP15K_{JA-EN}$ data set.

5   Conclusion

This paper designs and implements a cross-language knowledge graph entity alignment method based on subgraph features. The method consists of subgraph feature extraction, entity embedding and entity alignment prediction, and performed entity alignment tasks on multiple real multilingual knowledge graphs. The experimental results show that the method can enhance the structural information of the original KG and obtain a higher hit rate, which provides a new approach for the alignment of the cross-language knowledge graph. In our future work, we will explore effective and fast subgraph feature extraction methods for second or higher order.

Acknowledgment. This work was partially supported by National Natural Science Foundation of China under Grant 62103374, by Basic Public Welfare Research Project of Zhejiang Province under Grant LGF20F020016, and by Key R&D Projects in Zhejiang Province under Grant No. 2021C01117.

References

1. Aditya, S., Yang, Y., Baral, C.: Explicit reasoning over end-to-end neural architectures for visual question answering. In: Thirty-Second AAAI Conference on Artificial Intelligence (2018)
2. Ahn, S., Choi, H., Pärnamaa, T., Bengio, Y.: A neural knowledge language model. arXiv preprint arXiv:1608.00318 (2016)
3. Bordes, A., Usunier, N., Garcia-Duran, A., Weston, J., Yakhnenko, O.: Translating embeddings for modeling multi-relational data. In: Advances in Neural Information Processing Systems, pp. 2787–2795 (2013)
4. Chen, M., Tian, Y., Yang, M., Zaniolo, C.: Multilingual knowledge graph embeddings for cross-lingual knowledge alignment. arXiv preprint arXiv:1611.03954 (2016)
5. Dasgupta, S.S., Ray, S.N., Talukdar, P.: Hyte: hyperplane-based temporally aware knowledge graph embedding. In: Proceedings of the 2018 Conference on Empirical Methods in Natural Language Processing, pp. 2001–2011 (2018)

6. Defferrard, M., Bresson, X., Vandergheynst, P.: Convolutional neural networks on graphs with fast localized spectral filtering. In: Advances in Neural Information Processing Systems, pp. 3844–3852 (2016)

7. Fu, C., et al.: Link weight prediction using supervised learning methods and its application to yelp layered network. IEEE Trans. Knowl. Data Eng. **30**(8), 1507–1518 (2018)

8. Hao, Y., Zhang, Y., He, S., Liu, K., Zhao, J.: A joint embedding method for entity alignment of knowledge bases. In: Chen, H., Ji, H., Sun, L., Wang, H., Qian, T., Ruan, T. (eds.) CCKS 2016. CCIS, vol. 650, pp. 3–14. Springer, Singapore (2016). https://doi.org/10.1007/978-981-10-3168-7_1

9. Ji, G., He, S., Xu, L., Liu, K., Zhao, J.: Knowledge graph embedding via dynamic mapping matrix. In: Proceedings of the 53rd Annual Meeting of the Association for Computational Linguistics and the 7th International Joint Conference on Natural Language Processing (Volume 1: Long Papers), pp. 687–696 (2015)

10. Kim, J., Hastak, M.: Social network analysis: characteristics of online social networks after a disaster. Int. J. Inf. Manag. **38**(1), 86–96 (2018)

11. Kipf, T.N., Welling, M.: Semi-supervised classification with graph convolutional networks. arXiv preprint arXiv:1609.02907 (2016)

12. Lehmann, J., et al.: Dbpedia-a large-scale, multilingual knowledge base extracted from Wikipedia. Semantic Web **6**(2), 167–195 (2015)

13. Lin, Y., Liu, Z., Sun, M., Liu, Y., Zhu, X.: Learning entity and relation embeddings for knowledge graph completion. In: Twenty-Ninth AAAI Conference on Artificial Intelligence (2015)

14. Mikolov, T., Chen, K., Corrado, G., Dean, J.: Efficient estimation of word representations in vector space. arXiv preprint arXiv:1301.3781 (2013)

15. Navigli, R., Ponzetto, S.P.: Babelnet: the automatic construction, evaluation and application of a wide-coverage multilingual semantic network. Artif. Intell. **193**, 217–250 (2012)

16. Nguyen, D., Luo, W., Nguyen, T.D., Venkatesh, S., Phung, D.: Learning graph representation via frequent subgraphs. In: Proceedings of the 2018 SIAM International Conference on Data Mining, pp. 306–314. SIAM (2018)

17. Perozzi, B., Al-Rfou, R., Skiena, S.: Deepwalk: online learning of social representations. In: Proceedings of the 20th ACM SIGKDD International Conference on Knowledge Discovery and Data Mining, pp. 701–710 (2014)

18. Rebele, T., Suchanek, F., Hoffart, J., Biega, J., Kuzey, E., Weikum, G.: YAGO: a multilingual knowledge base from Wikipedia, wordnet, and geonames. In: Groth, P., et al. (eds.) ISWC 2016. LNCS, vol. 9982, pp. 177–185. Springer, Cham (2016). https://doi.org/10.1007/978-3-319-46547-0_19

19. Suchanek, F.M., Kasneci, G., Weikum, G.: YAGO: a large ontology from Wikipedia and wordnet. J. Web Semantics **6**(3), 203–217 (2008)

20. Sun, Z., Hu, W., Li, C.: Cross-lingual entity alignment via joint attribute-preserving embedding. In: d'Amato, C., et al. (eds.) ISWC 2017. LNCS, vol. 10587, pp. 628–644. Springer, Cham (2017). https://doi.org/10.1007/978-3-319-68288-4_37

21. Ullmann, J.R.: An algorithm for subgraph isomorphism. J. ACM (JACM) **23**(1), 31–42 (1976)

22. Wang, Z., Zhang, J., Feng, J., Chen, Z.: Knowledge graph embedding by translating on hyperplanes. In: Twenty-Eighth AAAI Conference on Artificial Intelligence (2014)

23. Wang, Z., Lv, Q., Lan, X., Zhang, Y.: Cross-lingual knowledge graph alignment via graph convolutional networks. In: Proceedings of the 2018 Conference on Empirical Methods in Natural Language Processing, pp. 349–357 (2018)

24. Xiao, H., Huang, M., Hao, Y., Zhu, X.: Transa: an adaptive approach for knowledge graph embedding. arXiv preprint arXiv:1509.05490 (2015)
25. Xuan, Q., et al.: Subgraph networks with application to structural feature space expansion. IEEE Trans. Knowl. Data Eng. 33(6), 2776–2789 (2019)
26. Xuan, Q., Zhang, Z.Y., Fu, C., Hu, H.X., Filkov, V.: Social synchrony on complex networks. IEEE Trans. Cybern. 48(5), 1420–1431 (2017)

A Secured Deep Reinforcement Learning Model Based on Vertical Federated Learning

Jie Ge[1], Xinyi Xie[1], Haibin Zheng[2(✉)], Jinyin Chen[1,2], Hu Li[3], Ling Pang[3], and Wenhong Zhao[4]

[1] College of Information Engineering, Zhejiang University of Technology, Hangzhou 310023, China
[2] Institute of Cyberspace Security, Zhejiang University of Technology, Hangzhou 310023, China
haibinzheng320@gmail.com
[3] Key Laboratory of Information System Security Technology, Beijing 100101, China
[4] College of Information Engineering, Jiaxing Nanhu University, Jiaxing 314001, China

Abstract. Deep reinforcement learning (DRL) has been widely used in diverse applications, which combines the key technologies of reinforcement learning and deep learning. In this work, a secured DRL based on vertical federated learning (VFL), named VF-DRL, is proposed to protect the model's information. Specifically, in the proposed VF-DRL, each client trains a partial local model, and uploads the feature embedding cooperatively to a server for global model aggregation. In this way, if one of the client attempts to construct an adversarial attack on the VF-DRL, it cannot be easily succeeded with only its own features of data and local model alone. Meanwhile, the server aggregates the output embedding of each client to accomplish the global model training in a distributed fashion. Extensive experiments are carried out to testify the robustness of VF-DRL. The results show that the VF-DRL achieves the state-of-the-art defensibility compared with base-lines.

Keywords: Deep reinforcement learning · Vertical federated learning · Defense · Adversarial attack · Robustness

Supported by organization the National Natural Science Foundation of China (No. 62072406), the National Key Laboratory of Science and Technology on Information System Security (No. 61421110502), the Key R&D Projects in Zhejiang Province (No. 2021C01117), the 2020 Industrial Internet Innovation Development Project (No.TC200H01V), "Ten Thousand Talents Program" in Zhejiang Province (No. 2020R52011).

X. Meng et al. (Eds.): BDSC 2022, CCIS 1640, pp. 129–142, 2022.
https://doi.org/10.1007/978-981-19-7532-5_8

1   Introduction

Deep reinforcement learning (DRL) [23] was first proposed by DeepMind in 2013 for the Atari [2] game scenario. Combining deep learning (DL) and reinforcement learning (RL), it was the first DRL framework so that machines can explore and learn automatically as humans do.

Benefiting from the satisfying performance that DRL brings, the security critical applications are also suffered from the malicious attack conducted on DRL. In early works [3,8,14,16,27], DL has been proved vulnerable towards adversarial attacks, i.e., by carefully crafting malicious samples with imperceptible perturbation added on the clean environmental state to fool the DL model to make totally wrong decision. Specifically, DRL is mainly designed to address the issue of decision-making and control. The agent uses the well-trained policy to select the optimal action according to the state of the environment. Then the environment feeds back the corresponding rewards to the action to evaluate the agent's behavior. During the reasoning phase of DRL, if the input state, policy or environment is maliciously interfered [29], it will lead to the decision-making failure. In actual scenarios, such as autonomous driving scenarios [20], if the environmental road conditions are maliciously disturbed (e.g., patched road signs), the victim vehicle may perform abnormal actions, such as crossing the line or even crashing into other vehicles.

To address the problem, numerous defense approaches have been proposed. For example, Gu et al. [9] proposed a learning framework against Actor-Critic (A3C). Through the game training with the hostile agent, the target agent finally reaches the Nash equilibrium, which makes the A3C model more robust and more adaptive to the environment. Lin et al. [19] proposed an action conditional frame prediction model. However, these methods assume the possible presence of the attacker in the environment, which leads to increased training costs and decreased agent accuracy. Consequently, the main challenge is to accomplish the DRL training in a distributed way, i.e., keeping partial data and model locally, and maintain policy well-training. Motivated by it, we propose a secured vertical federated deep reinforcement learning, referring to VF-DRL. We explore the application of vertical federated learning (VFL) in DRL scenarios by dividing the local model into multiple clients, and ensuring that the input data features of each agent shares minimal or no overlap. Then, when one of the agents is a malicious party (i.e., an attacker), but only can access to the data and model of its own part, its attack ability towards the whole DRL model will be degraded. Moreover, the input for the global model will be the implicit features up-loaded by each client, to provide protection for both the data and the model.

This paper makes the following research contributions.

- We propose a DRL model based on VFL, denoted as VF-DRL, and explore the learning performance of VF-DRL.
- We evaluate the overall performance of the VF-DRL model and verify the robustness of the VF-DRL model against four attack methods by making comparison of three DRL models.

2   Related Works

This section briefly introduces the existing DRL models, attacks and defenses on DRL.

2.1   Deep Reinforcement Learning

Since the first DRL framework proposed by Mnih [23], various modified versions for RL have been increasingly proposed, including double deep Q-network (DDQN) [11], prioritized DQN [24], dueling DQN [28], etc. The policy-based RL algorithms have asynchronous or synchronous advantages Actor-Critic (A3C or A2C) [22], trust region policy optimization (TRPO) [25], and proximal policy optimization (PPO) algorithms [26].

Specifically, the DDQN [11] uses a DQN to alleviate the problem of DQN's overestimation of Q value. The prioritized DQN [24] prioritizes the training samples in the experience pool for sampling, increasing the use of rare samples, but the training process is unstable. The dueling DQN [28] solves the problem of an unstable training process, but cannot handle continuous actions. The policy-based A3C/A2C [22] can handle continuous actions, but the memory consumption is large and the variance in updating the policy is unstable. The TRPO [25] uses the Kullback & Leible (KL) divergence to limit the policy update to ensure that the policy is updated in the direction of optimization, and its computational cost is large. The PPO [26] is easier to implement than TRPO, and also requires fewer mediation parameters. In all, most of the existing research on DRL methods focuses on the policy rather than its robustness improvement and risk evaluation.

2.2   Defense for Deep Reinforcement Learning

Several defense methods have been proposed for DRL's security improvement. Gu et al. [9] proposed a learning framework for A3C. This adversarial learning framework introduces a hostile agent in the learning process to simulate possible unstable factors in the environment. Lin et al. [19] proposed an action conditional frame prediction model. By comparing the difference between the action distribution of the target policy on the prediction frame and the current frame, it determines whether the current frame is an adversarial sample. If the current frame is judged to be an adversarial sample, the agent uses the prediction frame as input and performs the action. In addition, Marc Fischer et al. [6] proposed a network architecture called Robust Student-DQN (RS-DQN), which allows online robustness training to be parallel to the Q-network while maintaining competitive performance. Combining RS-DQN with adversarial training and robust training, it can resist attacks during training and testing.

At the model structure level. Behanzadan et al. [1] proved that adding noise to the DQN model parameters and retraining the original model can resist attacks. In addition, Havens et al. [12] proposed a meta-learning advantage hierarchy framework, which determines whether to continue to execute the current sub-policy by measuring the return of the sub-policy within a certain period. Based on this framework, Lee et al. [17] further explored the feasibility of using it as a defense framework and realized the defense against DRL.

At present, some RL models combine federated learning [30] to achieve data privacy protection. Zhuo et al. [31] proposed a RL method that considers privacy, which uses federated learning and differential privacy to achieve the model in multi-agent route planning scenarios and data protection. Hu et al. [13] proposed a reward shaping based on federated reinforcement learning (FRS) based on reward shaping for grid world scenarios. Since only high-level information is shared between the client and the server, and no communication occurs between the clients, FRS can protect privacy from client to server and client to client. Researchers have also done related work in the edge computing of network communication. Lim et al. [18] proposed a new FRL architecture for edge computing environments and proposed an effective gradient sharing and model transfer program. They also use edge computing to solve network problems that occur when training multiple real devices.

3   VF-DRL

3.1   Overview

For VF-DRL, data samples are divided in multiple clients for training, each client inputs different feature data and outputs hidden layer features. This prevents the attacker from observing the complete model and data, thus reducing the possibility of being attacked by one agent.

The system of VF-DRL is shown in Fig. 1. The red solid line represents forward propagation, and the red dashed line is back-propagation. The simulation environment can be various RL scenarios. The environment in this paper uses a consecutive action game scenarios shown in Fig. 1.

In the model training phase, the state is sampled first and then the state is split and distributed to each client. Each client owns data with different features to establish a cooperatively training framework. After each client gets the data, it will train each one's local model. And then each client uploads the hidden layer features output by the local model to the server. The server first uses an aggregator to aggregate the hid-den layer features, and then inputs it to the global model for training.

In the model testing phase, when the adversarial attack takes place, the trained models are distributed on each client, so they are difficult to be manipulated at the same time. If the attacker can access to the model and data from one of the clients, and add noise to the input through various attack strategies, this operation is more difficult to conduct, which has an obvious effect on the overall task.

3.2   Global Model

In the server, the global model is constructed based on the PPO [26] algorithm. The overall block diagram of the global model is shown in Fig. 2, and the attack

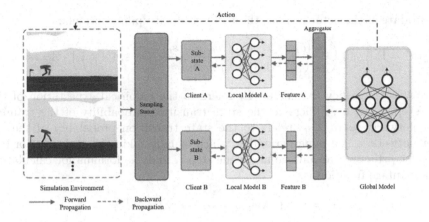

Fig. 1. The main framework of the secured VF-DRL model.

and defense are based on this model. The Markov decision process of the model is described by a tuple (S, A, P, R, γ), where $S = \{s_1, s_2, s_3, \ldots, s_t\}$ is the finite state set and $A = \{a_1, a_2, a_3, \ldots, a_t\}$ is the finite action set, P is the state transition probability, R is the reward function, and γ is the discount rate, which is used to calculate the long-term cumulative reward.

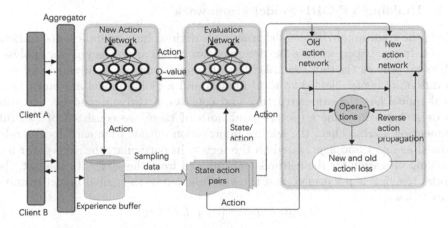

Fig. 2. The framework of global model aggregation on the server.

The global model based on the PPO algorithm uses importance based sampling to solve the difficult problem of sampling, so it is proposed to sample from another distribution that is easy to sample. When PPO combines importance sampling with the actor-critic framework, the agent is composed of two parts. One is an actor, which is responsible for interacting with the environment to collect samples. The other is a critic, which is responsible for judging the actor.

The update of the actor can use the PPO gradient update formula:

$$J_{ppo}^{\theta'}(\theta) = \hat{E}_t \left[\min \left(\frac{p_\theta\left(a_t \mid s_t\right)}{p_{\theta'}\left(a_t \mid s_t\right)}, \text{clip}\left(\frac{p_\theta\left(a_t \mid s_t\right)}{p_{\theta'}\left(a_t \mid s_t\right)}, 1 - \varepsilon, 1 + \varepsilon \right) \right) \cdot A_{\theta'}\left(s_t, a_t\right) \right]$$

$$(1)$$

where θ is the policy parameter, $\hat{E}_t$ refers to the empirical expectation of the time step, $p_\theta\left(a_t \mid s_t\right)$ refers to the state transition probability of the training actor-network, $p_{\theta'}\left(a_t \mid s_t\right)$ refers to the state transition probability of the old actor-network, ε is a hyperparameter which usually taking the value 0.1 or 0.2, A_t is the estimated advantage at a time step t, and the formula for calculating the advantage function is:

$$A_t = \delta_t + (\gamma\lambda)\delta_{t+1} + \cdots + (\gamma\lambda)^{T-t+1}\delta_{T-1} \qquad (2)$$

where $\delta_t = r_t + \gamma V\left(s_{t+1}\right) - V\left(s_t\right)$, $V\left(s_{t+1}\right)$ is the state value function calculated by the critic network at t, and r_t is the reward value at t. The loss of critic is calculated as follows:

$$L_c = \left(r + \gamma\left(\max\left(Q\left(s', a'\right)\right)\right) - Q(s, a)\right) \qquad (3)$$

where $\gamma\left(\max\left(Q\left(s', a'\right)\right)\right)$ is the objective value function, $Q(s, a)$ is the prediction value, s is the state and a is the action.

3.3   Building VF-DRL Model Framework

First, the traditional DRL model training is divided into several clients and one server. In this paper, we take the design of two clients as an example for analysis. Then we process the data, sampled from the environment, are divided and sent to different clients. Next, two local models and a global model are built. Each local model has the same structure and consists of two sub-models. The sub-models share the same structure, and both of them are consisted of two full connection layers. Then, the feature information output from each local model is used as input and aggregated on the server. In particular, the aggregator is a stacking operation for the features transmit-ted from the server. In the last, the model training is performed, and the loss function of the global model training is as follows:

$$L_{\theta'}(\theta) = L_{\theta'}^{\text{actor}}(\theta) + L_{\theta'}^{\text{critic}}(\theta) \qquad (4)$$

where $L_{\theta'}^{\text{actor}}(\theta)$ is the loss function of the action network, $L_{\theta'}^{\text{critic}}(\theta)$ is the loss function of the discriminator network, θ is the global model parameter, and the loss function of the action network is as follows:

$$L_{\theta'}^{actor}(\theta) = -A_t^{\theta'} \min \left(\frac{p_\theta\left(a_t \mid s_t\right)}{p_{\theta'}\left(a_t \mid s_t\right)}, \text{clip}\left(\frac{p_\theta\left(a_t \mid s_t\right)}{p_{\theta'}\left(a_t \mid s_t\right)}, 1 - \varepsilon, 1 + \varepsilon \right) \right) \qquad (5)$$

where $p_\theta\left(a_t \mid s_t\right)$ is the state transition probability of the action network, $p_{\theta'}\left(a_t \mid s_t\right)$ is the state transition probability of the old action network, ε is a hyperparameter, and A_t is the estimated advantage at t step. The loss function of the discriminator network is as follows:

$$L_{\theta'}^{\text{critic}}(\theta) = \lambda_1 \left(r + \gamma \left(\max \left(Q\left(s', a'\right)\right)\right)\right) - \lambda_2 Q(s, a) \qquad (6)$$

where $r + \gamma \left(\max \left(Q\left(s', a'\right)\right)\right)$ is the objective value function, $Q\left(s, a\right)$ is the prediction value, s is the state and is the action, λ_1 and λ_2 are hyperparameters. Each local model also uses the loss feedback of the global model to update the local model parameters. Although the global model training loss function is similar to the PPO model, the network model is different. The server's action network and evaluation network are both constructed with a layer of full connection and Tanh activation function.

3.4 Model Training and Implementation

First, build a VF-DRL model. And then, in the model training phase, sample the state from the environment, divide the sampled state into two parts evenly, and distribute them to different clients. The two clients build local models respectively. Each local model outputs the hidden layer features and uploads them to the server. The server aggregates the acquired features and uses them as the input of the global model. The server mapping function is:

$$a = f(\text{cat}(embedding_A, embedding_B)) \qquad (7)$$

where cat $(\cdot)$ is the aggregation function in order to splices the hidden layer features uploaded by the server, a is the execution action, $embedding_A$ and $embedding_B$ is the hidden layer features output by client A and client B. Then the global model parameters are updated according to Eq. 4.

4 Experiment and Analysis

In this section, three DRL baselines are compared with VF-DRL. At the same time, four attack methods are adopted to verify the robustness of VF-DRL model.

4.1 Experiment Setup

Experiment Scene. BipedalWalkerHardcore-v2 (the continuous action biped robot in the box2d scene in Gym [2]).

DRL Baselines. Three contrast DRL baselines are used in VF-DRL, including TD3 [7], SAC [10] and PPO [26].

Attack Methods. In the testing phase, the robustness of the model is verified against the attack, including RandomNoise [5], the fast gradient sign method (FGSM) [15], the momentum iterative fast gradient sign method (MI-FGSM) [4] and the project gradient descent (PGD) [21].

Disturbance Metrics. Classic disturbance calculation methods are adopted, including L0-norm, L2-norm and L∞-norm. We use the L2-norm to measure the size of the disturbance, and the calculation for-mula is $\|X\|_2 = \sqrt{\sum_{i=1}^{N} x_i^2}$.

Experimental Platform. i7-7700K 4.20GHzx8 (CPU), TITAN 12GiBx2 (GPU), 16GBx4 RAM (DDR4), Ubuntu 16.04 (Operating System), Python 3.6, Pytorch-1.4.0 (DL Framework), gym-0.10.8, Box2D-2.3.10.

4.2   Environment of Experiment

The experimental scene is built on the gym platform developed by OpenAI [2]. It provides some built-in environments. This paper chooses a continuous action game scene on this platform, namely BipedalWalkerHardcorev2 biped robot walking.

The experimental scenes are shown in Fig. 3, which is a game scene of a biped robot walking. This environment requires the training robot to move forward, and a total of 300 points reward for walking to the farthest position. If the game player fall, the reward is -100. The state of the environment includes the hull angular velocity, angular velocity, horizontal velocity, vertical velocity, joint position and joint angular velocity, whether the legs are in contact with the ground and 10 lidar rangefinders. In Fig. 3(a), the robot walks normally. When the robot is attacked, the robot will not be able to walk normally. From Fig. 3(b), it can be seen that the robot will fall and can-not walk normally after being attacked.

(a)   (b)

Fig. 3. The game scenario of a biped robot. (a) The robot walks normally when not attacked. (b) The robot walks abnormally when attacked.

4.3   Training Model

Considering the overall performance of the VF-DRL model, firstly, the model is built and the hyperparameters are adjusted. The empirical buffer capacity is set to 3000 and the maximum time step of each round is set to 1500. The model training results are shown in Fig. 4. Three DRL baselines are compared in the figure. The VF-DRL model is built based on PPO. It can be seen from the results that it can achieve the same effect as PPO. And the training effect of the other two baselines is better than PPO, but their own defense ability still needs to be verified.

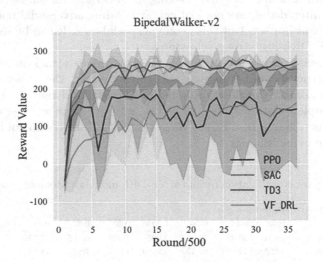

Fig. 4. Model training results in the biped robot scenario.

The model training results are shown in Fig. 4. Firstly, PPO and VF-DRL are com-pared. They can achieve equivalent results. The reward value of PPO and VF-DRL after training is lower than that of TD3 and SAC. But compared with VF-DRL and PPO, VF-DRL can achieve the same effect as PPO. TD3 and SAC are improved versions of DRL model, and their performance is better than PPO. But their robustness needs to be verified compared with VF-DRL.

4.4   Robustness Verification of VF-DRL Models

In order to verify the robustness of the model, we use four attack methods to verify in the testing phase, and compares three baselines. The experimental results are shown in Table 1. The first column in the table is four attack methods, and the second column is the model, the remaining columns correspond to the reward values of different disturbance sizes.

Firstly, by comparing PPO and VF-DRL models in Table 1, under all attack methods in the table, the reward value of VF-DRL model is the highest after being attacked, and there is almost no large fluctuation. Therefore, the roadside robustness of the VF-DRL model is greatly improved compared with PPO, and the defense ability of the improved model is strong. Secondly, compared with SAC and TD3, both of these baselines are improved versions of AC and are more stable in their own training. It can be seen from the table that the reward value of VF-DRL is the highest under four attack methods. Except that the corresponding reward value of the TD3 model after the FGSM attack is higher under the disturbance size of 0.18. But the reward value is 17.08 compared with the VF-DRL model, which is not very different. This large value fluctuation is inseparable from the exploration and learning of the agent itself, the trained model itself will fluctuate slightly. During the TD3 testing phrase, some states may be encountered that are not critical, and adding adversarial noise does not have a significant impact. But this is only a special case. It can be seen from the table that VF-DRL has strong robustness.

And the reason why VF-DRL is more resistant to attack is related to its own model structure and training data. In this paper, the attacker only gets one client, i.e., one of the clients is a malicious party, and the attacker does not know the complete data features, so he can only get some features of the same state. The experimental results also verify that these features do not have a great impact on the overall model.

Table 1. Robustness verification results of VF-DRL models under four attack methods.

Method	Model	Disturbance Size								
		0.12	0.14	0.16	0.18	0.20	0.22	0.24	0.26	0.28
FGSM	PPO	58.51	55.45	73.66	73.96	78.43	68.73	77.72	70.61	69.53
	SAC	161.58	123.19	98.27	136.69	142.75	70.31	78.15	−20.82	−35.65
	TD3	−53.48	−50.40	135.84	**254.86**	−51.41	−40.53	−67.13	−41.08	−70.74
	VF-DRL	**240.28**	**233.73**	**237.77**	237.98	**234.15**	**235.52**	**242.45**	**238.00**	**240.79**
PGD	PPO	84.51	93.02	84.80	85.91	89.07	85.63	91.15	80.12	80.88
	SAC	−89.85	−100.35	−99.66	−101.70	−100.21	−100.07	−104.02	−103.02	−105.63
	TD3	−42.67	−63.56	−30.98	23.62	−38.89	107.25	−99.91	−80.81	−38.81
	VF-DRL	**209.14**	**205.18**	**175.87**	**197.47**	**170.08**	**173.02**	**164.46**	**180.96**	**148.76**
MI-FGSM	PPO	73.16	65.73	56.80	74.82	82.98	73.40	51.21	74.60	53.34
	SAC	−92.22	−65.03	−58.64	−61.02	−61.90	−68.01	−69.15	−73.57	−77.79
	TD3	59.14	195.64	47.98	194.03	−71.64	−77.72	21.26	−101.57	−98.96
	VF-DRL	**234.99**	**240.50**	**247.20**	**243.18**	**236.35**	**243.86**	**232.49**	**239.88**	**247.31**
Random Noise	PPO	72.05	84.90	82.88	87.31	90.44	84.29	85.83	86.07	84.01
	SAC	−91.61	−96.17	−101.19	−102.22	−103.11	−103.90	−104.66	−104.76	−104.51
	TD3	5.94	−16.13	−40.79	−58.63	−74.20	−87.99	−94.57	−96.59	−99.94
	VF-DRL	**197.21**	**211.56**	**211.93**	**183.67**	**205.57**	**214.05**	**203.32**	**202.63**	**208.32**

Table 1 compares the reward values of different models for four attack methods. The disturbance size is in the range of 0.12 to 0.28. Whether adding a larger disturbance will produce different conclusions remains to be verified. In order to increase the credibility of the conclusion, we further increase the disturbance to prove the robustness of the VF-DRL model. The experimental results are shown in Fig. 5. The abscissa is the number of test rounds, and the ordinate is the corresponding reward value. As can be seen from the figure, the reward value of VF-DRL model is also decreasing with the increase of disturbance size. When the disturbance size of PGD attack is 0.82, the corresponding reward of VF-DRL and PPO model is almost equal. When the disturbance size of MI-FGSM attack is 1.02, the corresponding reward of VF-DRL and PPO model is also less different. In other cases, the VF-DRL model corresponds to a larger reward value, and the model is more robust.

Moreover, the PPO has a high reward value for individual fluctuation points, while VF-DRL is more stable and the overall reward is larger. It is speculated that individual clients of VF-DRL model are disturbed, and the overall performance will not fluctuate greatly. However, when the interference is too large, e.g., when the disturbance is 1.02, there will be significant performance degradation, but the overall performance is better than other models.

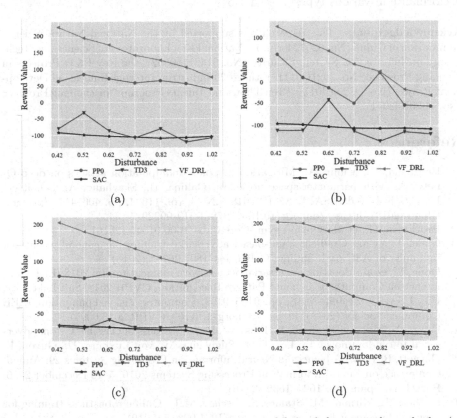

Fig. 5. Reward values corresponding to four models and four attack methods. (a) Reward curves of four DRL models under FGSM attack. (b) Reward curves of four DRL models under PGD attack. (c) Reward curves of four DRL models under MI-FGSM attack. (d) Reward curves of four DRL models under RandomNoise attack.

5   Conclusion

In this work, we research on the data protection policy of DRL, this paper uses the data protection function of VFL, explores the application feasibility of VFL in the RL, and proposes a VF-DRL model. The robustness of VF-DRL model is verified under four attack methods. At the same time, the structure of the VF-DRL model is analyzed, and the possible reasons why the model can realize DRL data protection are explained.

Although extensive experiments have testified the effectiveness of the proposed VF-DRL and the feasibility of the application of VFL in RL scenarios, there are still areas to be improved. This experiment compares three baselines and has not been verified in discrete action scenarios. Future work will further study the security of DRL and further improve the VF-DRL model, and improve performance in various types of scenarios.

Acknowledgements. This research was supported by the National Natural Science Foundation of China (No. 62072406), the National Key Laboratory of Science and Technology on Information System Security (No. 61421110502), the Key R&D Projects in Zhejiang Province (No. 2021C01117), the 2020 Industrial Internet Innovation Development Project (No.TC200H01V), "Ten Thousand Talents Program" in Zhejiang Province (No. 2020R52011).

References

1. Behzadan, V., Munir, A.: Mitigation of policy manipulation attacks on deep Q-networks with parameter-space noise. In: Gallina, B., Skavhaug, A., Schoitsch, E., Bitsch, F. (eds.) SAFECOMP 2018. LNCS, vol. 11094, pp. 406–417. Springer, Cham (2018). https://doi.org/10.1007/978-3-319-99229-7_34
2. Brockman, G., et al.: Openai gym. CoRR abs/1606.01540 (2016)
3. Chen, T., et al.: Gradient band-based adversarial training for generalized attack immunity of A3C path finding. CoRR abs/1807.06752 (2018)
4. Dong, Y., et al.: Boosting adversarial attacks with momentum. In: 2018 IEEE Conference on Computer Vision and Pattern Recognition, CVPR 2018, Salt Lake City, UT, USA, 18–22 June 2018, pp. 9185–9193. Computer Vision Foundation/IEEE Computer Society (2018). https://doi.org/10.1109/CVPR.2018.00957
5. Fawzi, A., Moosavi-Dezfooli, S., Frossard, P.: Robustness of classifiers: from adversarial to random noise. In: Lee, D.D., Sugiyama, M., von Luxburg, U., Guyon, I., Garnett, R. (eds.) Advances in Neural Information Processing Systems 29: Annual Conference on Neural Information Processing Systems 2016, 5–10 December 2016, Barcelona, Spain, pp. 1624–1632 (2016)
6. Fischer, M., Mirman, M., Stalder, S., Vechev, M.T.: Online robustness training for deep reinforcement learning. CoRR abs/1911.00887 (2019)
7. Fujimoto, S., van Hoof, H., Meger, D.: Addressing function approximation error in actor-critic methods. In: Dy, J.G., Krause, A. (eds.) Proceedings of the 35th International Conference on Machine Learning, ICML 2018, Stockholmsmässan, Stockholm, Sweden, 10–15 July 2018. Proceedings of Machine Learning Research, vol. 80, pp. 1582–1591. PMLR (2018)
8. Gleave, A., Dennis, M., Wild, C., Kant, N., Levine, S., Russell, S.: Adversarial policies: attacking deep reinforcement learning. In: 8th International Conference on Learning Representations, ICLR 2020, Addis Ababa, Ethiopia, 26–30 April 2020. OpenReview.net (2020)
9. Gu, Z., Jia, Z., Choset, H.: Adversary A3C for robust reinforcement learning. CoRR abs/1912.00330 (2019)

10. Haarnoja, T., Zhou, A., Abbeel, P., Levine, S.: Soft actor-critic: off-policy maximum entropy deep reinforcement learning with a stochastic actor. In: Dy, J.G., Krause, A. (eds.) Proceedings of the 35th International Conference on Machine Learning, ICML 2018, Stockholmsmässan, Stockholm, Sweden, 10–15 July 2018. Proceedings of Machine Learning Research, vol. 80, pp. 1856–1865. PMLR (2018)

11. van Hasselt, H., Guez, A., Silver, D.: Deep reinforcement learning with double Q-learning. In: Schuurmans, D., Wellman, M.P. (eds.) Proceedings of the Thirtieth AAAI Conference on Artificial Intelligence, 12–17 February 2016, Phoenix, Arizona, USA, pp. 2094–2100. AAAI Press (2016)

12. Havens, A.J., Jiang, Z., Sarkar, S.: Online robust policy learning in the presence of unknown adversaries. In: Bengio, S., Wallach, H.M., Larochelle, H., Grauman, K., Cesa-Bianchi, N., Garnett, R. (eds.) Advances in Neural Information Processing Systems 31: Annual Conference on Neural Information Processing Systems 2018, NeurIPS 2018, 3–8 December 2018, Montréal, Canada, pp. 9938–9948 (2018)

13. Hu, Y., Hua, Y., Liu, W., Zhu, J.: Reward shaping based federated reinforcement learning. IEEE Access 9, 67259–67267 (2021). https://doi.org/10.1109/ACCESS.2021.3074221

14. Huang, S.H., Papernot, N., Goodfellow, I.J., Duan, Y., Abbeel, P.: Adversarial attacks on neural network policies. In: 5th International Conference on Learning Representations, ICLR 2017, Toulon, France, 24–26 April 2017, Workshop Track Proceedings. OpenReview.net (2017)

15. Ilahi, I., et al.: Challenges and countermeasures for adversarial attacks on deep reinforcement learning. IEEE Trans. Artif. Intell. 3(2), 90–109 (2022). https://doi.org/10.1109/TAI.2021.3111139

16. Lee, X.Y., Ghadai, S., Tan, K.L., Hegde, C., Sarkar, S.: Spatiotemporally constrained action space attacks on deep reinforcement learning agents. In: The Thirty-Fourth AAAI Conference on Artificial Intelligence, AAAI 2020, The Thirty-Second Innovative Applications of Artificial Intelligence Conference, IAAI 2020, The Tenth AAAI Symposium on Educational Advances in Artificial Intelligence, EAAI 2020, New York, NY, USA, 7–12 February 2020, pp. 4577–4584. AAAI Press (2020)

17. Lee, X.Y., Havens, A.J., Chowdhary, G., Sarkar, S.: Learning to cope with adversarial attacks. CoRR abs/1906.12061 (2019)

18. Lim, H., Kim, J., Kim, C., Hwang, G., Choi, H., Han, Y.: Federated reinforcement learning for controlling multiple rotary inverted pendulums in edge computing environments. In: 2020 International Conference on Artificial Intelligence in Information and Communication, ICAIIC 2020, Fukuoka, Japan, 19–21 February 2020, pp. 463–464. IEEE (2020). https://doi.org/10.1109/ICAIIC48513.2020.9065233

19. Lin, Y., Liu, M., Sun, M., Huang, J.: Detecting adversarial attacks on neural network policies with visual foresight. CoRR abs/1710.00814 (2017)

20. Liu, F., Dai, S., Zhao, Y.: Learning to have a civil aircraft take off under crosswind conditions by reinforcement learning with multimodal data and preprocessing data. Sensors 21(4), 1386 (2021). https://doi.org/10.3390/s21041386

21. Madry, A., Makelov, A., Schmidt, L., Tsipras, D., Vladu, A.: Towards deep learning models resistant to adversarial attacks. In: 6th International Conference on Learning Representations, ICLR 2018, Vancouver, BC, Canada, 30 April - 3 May 2018, Conference Track Proceedings. OpenReview.net (2018)

22. Mnih, V., et al.: Asynchronous methods for deep reinforcement learning. In: Balcan, M., Weinberger, K.Q. (eds.) Proceedings of the 33nd International Conference on Machine Learning, ICML 2016, New York City, NY, USA, 19–24 June 2016. JMLR Workshop and Conference Proceedings, vol. 48, pp. 1928–1937. JMLR.org (2016)

23. Mnih, V., et al.: Playing atari with deep reinforcement learning. CoRR abs/1312.5602 (2013)
24. Schaul, T., Quan, J., Antonoglou, I., Silver, D.: Prioritized experience replay. In: Bengio, Y., LeCun, Y. (eds.) 4th International Conference on Learning Representations, ICLR 2016, San Juan, Puerto Rico, 2–4 May 2016, Conference Track Proceedings (2016)
25. Schulman, J., Levine, S., Abbeel, P., Jordan, M.I., Moritz, P.: Trust region policy optimization. In: Bach, F.R., Blei, D.M. (eds.) Proceedings of the 32nd International Conference on Machine Learning, ICML 2015, Lille, France, 6–11 July 2015. JMLR Workshop and Conference Proceedings, vol. 37, pp. 1889–1897. JMLR.org (2015)
26. Schulman, J., Wolski, F., Dhariwal, P., Radford, A., Klimov, O.: Proximal policy optimization algorithms. CoRR abs/1707.06347 (2017)
27. Tretschk, E., Oh, S.J., Fritz, M.: Sequential attacks on agents for long-term adversarial goals. CoRR abs/1805.12487 (2018)
28. Wang, Z., Schaul, T., Hessel, M., van Hasselt, H., Lanctot, M., de Freitas, N.: Dueling network architectures for deep reinforcement learning. In: Balcan, M., Weinberger, K.Q. (eds.) Proceedings of the 33nd International Conference on Machine Learning, ICML 2016, New York City, NY, USA, 19–24 June 2016. JMLR Workshop and Conference Proceedings, vol. 48, pp. 1995–2003. JMLR.org (2016)
29. Yan, X., Cui, B., Li, J.: Malicious domain name recognition based on deep neural networks. In: Wang, G., Chen, J., Yang, L.T. (eds.) SpaCCS 2018. LNCS, vol. 11342, pp. 497–505. Springer, Cham (2018). https://doi.org/10.1007/978-3-030-05345-1_43
30. Yang, Q., Liu, Y., Cheng, Y., Kang, Y., Chen, T., Yu, H.: Federated learning. Synthesis Lectures Artif. Intell. Mach. Learn. 13(3), 1–207 (2019). https://doi.org/10.2200/S00960ED2V01Y201910AIM043
31. Zhuo, H.H., Feng, W., Xu, Q., Yang, Q., Lin, Y.: Federated reinforcement learning. CoRR abs/1901.08277 (2019)

An Improved K-means Algorithm Based on the Bayesian Inference

Rumeng Chen[1,2,3], Feng Wang[1,2,3], and Feng Hu[1,2,3](✉)

[1] Computer College of Qinghai Normal University, Xining 810008, Qinghai, China
qhhuf@163.com
[2] The State Key Laboratory of Tibetan Intelligent Information Processing and Application,
Xining 810008, Qinghai, China
[3] Academy of Plateau Science and Sustainability, Xining 810016,
Qinghai, People's Republic of China

Abstract. As one of the most widely used algorithms in machine learning, the fs algorithm is known for its simplicity and efficiency. However, it also has certain limitations, including pre-selecting the K value, which leads to issues such as different cluster shapes and outlier effects. In addition, this clustering algorithm needs to select the initial cluster centers, which produces the phenomenon of local optimum. To alleviate these two types of problems, this paper propose a K-means variant combined with Bayesian inference, dubbed the Bayes-K-means. Firstly, use Bayesian parameter inference to identify parameters for initial cluster centers. According to the probability function of the prior distribution, recalculate the distance from the sample points to the cluster centers. Therefore, the algorithm realizes the global search in the iterative process, which helps to improve the global optimum ability of the algorithm and avoids the phenomenon of local search caused by the K-means algorithm. We verify the Bayes-K-means and theoretically analyze its convergence from the aspect of the posterior distribution and the expression of the clustering center, respectively. Finally, applying the collected and processed real datasets, experimental tests based on artificial datasets and UCI datasets, then comparing Bayes-K-means with K-means, K-means++ and Bisecting K-means experiments, aggregated the class results are consistent with the actual situation. The results show that the proposed algorithm can effectively improve the clustering accuracy, efficiency and generalization performance.

Keywords: Clustering · Bayesian parameter inference · K-means · Global optimum

1 Introduction

In contemporary society, with the continuous development of computing technology, it has become popular to obtain data and find its flaws in it. Machine learning, which becomes an important tool in these studies, is often classified into supervised learning and unsupervised learning [1]. Since the K-means clustering method is commonly used in unsupervised learning algorithms, it is often combined with deep learning, and a large

© The Author(s), under exclusive license to Springer Nature Singapore Pte Ltd. 2022
X. Meng et al. (Eds.): BDSC 2022, CCIS 1640, pp. 143–156, 2022.
https://doi.org/10.1007/978-981-19-7532-5_9

number of K-means variants have emerged [2–4]. The traditional K-means algorithm performs well in compact and spherical clustering. We focus on and expect to improve two main problems in the K-means algorithm: (1) cluster center sensitivity and K value, (2) more difficulties to handle other types of data. Therefore, this paper proposes a Bayes-K-means clustering algorithm for these two problems to improve the clustering efficiency and accuracy of the algorithm.

Bayes' theorem, which originated in 1763, is a classic theorem in probability and statistics. It is currently commonly used in machine learning. Among them, Bayesian inference [5] is the application of Bayes' theorem, which enables us to incorporate prior beliefs and use probability distributions to describe the uncertainties of many parametric variables, making them deterministic. After that, we revise the guess by making more observations and finally get the posterior distribution. Therefore, we usually use this method to scan the parameters of the data information. The main idea is optimizing and updating the posterior distribution of the objective function by continuously adding sample points for a given objective function, to better adjust the current parameters [6].

Due to the continuous increase of data and the continuous improvement and optimization of models, more and more people have begun to do parallel research on classification and clustering algorithms, and the progress has been rapid. For example, Olivier et al. [7] proposed an improved K-means++ algorithm, adding prior distribution information, and the algorithm has better robustness; Farivar et al. [8] introduced GPU on the basis of traditional K-means to realize parallel clustering operations; Mao et al. [9] introduced the Canopy algorithm, using the maximum and minimum principle to improve the center point selection, which improved the convergence speed; Chowdhury et al. [10] proposed an adaptive K-means algorithm based on MapReduce. Guo et al. [11] introduced the idea of high density, which improved the clustering effect of datasets with large differences, and also enhanced the stability of the K-means clustering algorithm. However, this method does not consider the problem of outliers. Huang et al. [12] used the method of distance and SSE to select reasonable initial cluster centers, and optimized K-means clustering to a certain extent, but the number of clusters K was uncertain. Wang et al. [13] used dimension-weighted Euclidean distance to measure the distance between sample points, which significantly reduced the number of iterations in the clustering process. However, there is a higher order time complexity due to finding the initial cluster centers.

Combined with the inspiration from the work of the above related scholars, we derived the Bayesian parameter inference model and combined it with the K-means algorithm, so that the Bayes-K-means algorithm has both the robustness of Bayesian inference and the efficiency of the K-means algorithm. Then, the conjecture is corrected through more observation, and finally, the posterior distribution is obtained.

This paper collects and processes data sets of graduates majoring in information and computing science, and uses the Bayes-K-means algorithm to analyze the training quality and career development of graduates in this major. Then compared with the traditional K-means algorithm, the results show that the clustering effect of the algorithm is better, more robust, and has a certain practical value. The key devotions of this paper are listed below.

- We propose an improved clustering method, which is a generalization of the traditional K-means algorithm in calculating distance and selecting initial cluster centers.
- We combine the Bayesian parameters to infer the relevant expressions and theoretically discuss the rationality and convergence of the method.
- Process the collected real data and apply the data to the improved method.
- Compared with the traditional K-means, K-means++ and Bisecting K-means algorithms, the feasibility and accuracy of the improved algorithm are demonstrated.

2 Bayes-K-means Clustering Algorithm

2.1 Improvement of K-means Algorithm

K-means algorithm is the most classic clustering algorithm in data mining, and it is a common unsupervised machine learning algorithm [14]. The basic idea of the algorithm is: select the initial cluster center, classify data points based on how far each data point is from the center of the cluster. After completing one iteration, update the center point of each category according to the clustering result, and then repeat the previous operation and iterate again until there is no difference between the two classification results before and after.

In this paper, the traditional K-means algorithm is improved through the following process:

Cluster-Based Bayesian Parameter Inference
Given a training sample set of data $Z = \{x_1, x_2, x_3, \ldots, x_n\}$ described by n attributes, calculate on all sample data in the dataset, The condition for assigning the sample Z of the unknown class to the class C_k is $p(C_k|Z) > p(C_j|Z), 1 \leq k \leq n, 1 \leq j \leq n, j \neq k$, which can be obtained by Bayesian inference:

$$p(C_k|Z) = \frac{p(C_k)p(Z|C_k)}{p(Z)} = \frac{p(C_k)}{p(Z)} \prod_{i=1}^{d} p(x_i|C_k) \qquad (1)$$

From this, using Bayesian parameter inference to estimate the prior probability $p(C_k)$ of the class based on the sample data set Z, and estimate the conditional probability $p(x_i|C_k)$ for each cluster, let A represent the C_k-th class sample set in the training data set Z, then:

$$p(C_k) = \frac{|Z_{C_k}|}{Z} \qquad (2)$$

For discrete attributes, let Z_{C_k, x_i} denote the set of samples whose value is x_i on the i-th attribute in Z_{C_k}, there are:

$$p(x_i|C_k) = \frac{|Z_{C_k}, x_i|}{Z_{C_k}} \qquad (3)$$

For continuous attributes, suppose $p(x_i|C_k) \sim N(\mu C_{k,i}, \delta^2 C_{k,i})$, where $\mu C_{k,i}$ and $\delta^2 C_{k,i}$ are the mean and variance of the value of the i-th attribute of the C_k-th sample, respectively, there are:

$$p(x_i|C_k) = \frac{1}{\sqrt{2\pi}\delta C_{k,i}} \exp(-\frac{(x_i - \mu C_{k,i})^2}{2\delta^2 C_{k,i}}) \tag{4}$$

It should be noted here that, in the above model [15], if a certain attribute value does not appear at the same time in the data, the probability value is zero, resulting in an error. The Laplace correction algorithm is used to solve this problem:

$$p(C_k) = \frac{|Z_{C_k}| + 1}{|Z| + N}, p(x_i|C_k) = \frac{|Z_{C_k, x_i}| + 1}{|Z_{C_k}| + N_i} \tag{5}$$

Among them, N represents the number of all possible categories in the data set, and N_i represents the number of possible values of the i-th attribute.

Calculate the Average Distance of All Sample Elements
Let d_{ij} denote the Euclidean distance between data objects x_i and x_j, and the prior distribution is uniform, then we have:

$$d_p = \frac{2}{n(n-1)} \sum_{i=1}^{n} \sum_{j=i+1}^{n} d_{ij} \tag{6}$$

Let d_{i1} and d_{i2} be the Euclidean distances from sample i to v_1 and v_2, respectively, and median takes the median. Therefore, the average distance can be expressed as:

$$dist_i = median(\{min(d_{i1}, d_{i2}, ..., d_{in})\})(i = 1, 2, ..., n) \tag{7}$$

Silhouette Coefficient
Silhouette coefficient is an index used to evaluate the degree of class density and dispersion [16]:

$$S(i) = \frac{b(i) - a(i)}{max\{a(i), b(i)\}} \tag{8}$$

In Eq. 8, $a(i)$ represents the internal aggregation degree of the sample, $b(i)$ represents the external aggregation degree of the sample, and the value of $S(i)$ is between $[-1, 1]$. If $S(i)$ is close to 1, it means that the cluster of the sample is reasonable. Otherwise, the sample should be divided into other clusters [17].

Improve Similarity Measurement

1. Constructing Bayesian parameters to infer the distribution of sample information.

$$p_j^{(i)} = 1 - (1 - \frac{x_j^{(i)}}{\sum_{j=1}^{n} x_j^{(i)}}) \approx \frac{x_j^{(i)}}{\sum_{j=1}^{n} x_j^{(i)}} \tag{9}$$

In the formula, n is the number of samples.

2. Next, calculate the posterior probability of the attribute:

$$q_i = 1 + \sum_{i=1}^{n} p_j^{(i)} \log p_j^{(i)} \tag{10}$$

3. Calculate the inferred probability value over the eigenvalues of the Bayesian parameter:

$$\chi_i = \frac{q_i}{\sum_{i=1}^{m} q_i} \tag{11}$$

In it, m is the sample attribute.

4. Definition of Cluster Probability Distance:

$$L_2(x_i, x_j) = \sqrt[2]{\sum_{l=1}^{m} \chi_i (x_i^{(l)} - x_j^{(l)})^2} \tag{12}$$

Based on the above model, this paper optimizes Eqs. 1, 2, 3, 4 to find the point where the prior probability value $p(C_k)$ and the position of the corresponding point in the sample, and selects the first initial cluster C_1 based on this. Then according to the Bayesian parameter inference and combined with the maximum and minimum distance criteria, select the remaining initial cluster centers. Pick out all the median of probability among them. Then taking this object as the second initial cluster center, the process is repeated until found all K initial cluster centers c_k.

The first is to use the Bayesian parameter in the sample data points as the similarity measurement between samples; that is, if the posterior probability q_i value of a certain feature value is larger, it means that the degree of discrimination is low, and the probability value will be assigned to the value with a smaller value. On the contrary, if the posterior probability is larger, a larger probability value is assigned to the value to improve the clustering effect [18].

2.2 Algorithm Steps

In summary, the specific calculation steps of the Bayes-K-means algorithm are as follows:

Algorithm Input: Data set Z;

Algorithm output: each cluster after clustering C_i, $i = 1,2,3,...,$K;

Step1: Select the best value of K according to the silhouette coefficient method;

Step2: Use the posterior probability distribution formula to calculate the distance from each sample point x_i in the data set to the cluster center c_i;

Step3: Calculate the probability $p(C_k)$ that each sample is selected as the next cluster center, and classify the sample data into clusters of each cluster according to the probability distance, so as to select k cluster centers;

Step4: Repeat steps Step2–3 until the updated cluster centers no longer change or reach the threshold of the number of runs, and use the similarity measurement to improve the clustering effect.

2.3 Algorithm Convergence

Similar to other improved algorithms based on the traditional K-means algorithm [19]. Under the premise of reasonable parameter settings, the Bayes-K-means algorithm converges (after a finite number of iterations). Since the method of dividing data sample points into K clusters is bound to be limited, that is, the distribution of attribute posterior probability values is limited [20]; Therefore, the posterior probability q_i ($i = 1,2,3,...,K$) that each attribute may be divided into may only appear once in the entire iterative process, and it will eventually converge.

Assuming $q^{t1} = q^{t2}(t_1 \neq t_2)$, where t_i represents the i time iteration, for a given q^{ti}, the calculation Eq. 9 can obtain p^{ti}; Therefore, for q^{t1} and q^{t2}, p^{t1} and p^{t2} can be obtained respectively (and both are equal because $q^{t1} = q^{t2}$). Further, χ^{t1} and χ^{t2} can be obtained by Eq. 10, (because of $q^{t1} = q^{t2}$ and $p^{t1} = p^{t2}$, the two are also equal), from this we get $L_2^{t_1} = L_2^{t_2}$. Since the clustering probability distance $L_2(\cdot, \cdot)$ is strictly monotonically decreasing [21], the Bayes-K-means algorithm will converge after a finite number of iterations.

3 Experimental Results and Analysis

In order to more objectively evaluate the improvement effect of the Bayes-K-means algorithm, this section conducts experimental analysis on the artificial self-made data set (see Sect. 3.1) and four UCI data sets (as shown in the Table 3), which are different from the traditional K-means, K-means++, Bisecting K-means algorithm for experimental comparison [22]. It is evaluated by three evaluation indicators [23]: Time, Acc, and NMI. Among them, Time measures the average length of time for the algorithm to run, and the smaller the value, the shorter the time required to run. Acc represents the accuracy of clustering, that is, whether the clustering results are consistent with the real results; NMI is the normalized mutual information, which is used to represent the degree of association between the two groups of data.

In order to exclude the influence of chance and random factors, 80 experiments were carried out, and the average value of the experimental results was obtained. The artificially self-made dataset comes from a questionnaire for graduates majoring in information and computing in a Chinese university from 2008 to 2020. Experimental environment: Python, Windows 11 64bit, CPU 3.40 GHz.

3.1 Data Acquisition and Processing

The data used in this paper comes from the real questionnaires filled out by the graduates of a university majoring in information and computing science from 2008 to 2020.

From March to May 2021, the author distributed a total of 217 questionnaires, all of which were successfully recovered, of which 209 were valid and valuable, with an effective rate of 96%. The specific questions of the questionnaire focus on 34 categories such as career choice, work direction, skill development, and future planning. In addition, the author also conducted interviews with students who are already on the job or continuing their studies. At the same time, the salary situation, school employment guidance A survey was conducted on job satisfaction and so on.

Then, perform data preprocessing, filter out useful data information [24], and perform word segmentation, text cleaning, standardization, etc.

After integrating and processing these data, more than 40,000 pieces of valid information are obtained a large visual screen was created using Python, and some data information was displayed as shown in Fig. 1.

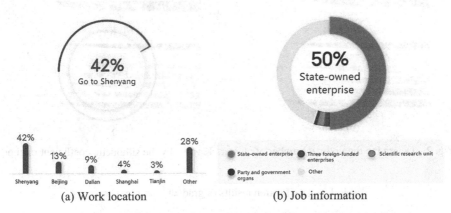

(a) Work location   (b) Job information

Fig. 1. Data graph display of graduate information part

3.2 Apply Bayes-K-means Algorithm to Cluster Dataset

In this paper, the data vectors in the required format are obtained from the original dataset through data preprocessing, and the improved K-means clustering module is used to build a clustering model in Python. First, after running the processed data, determine the K value using the silhouette coefficient method [25].

As shown in Fig. 2(a–f), from the silhouette diagram, when the K value is 4, all the silhouettes in the picture are more or less of similar thickness, so the sizes are similar, and it can be seen from the calculation that the $S(i)$ at this time is the largest locally, which can divide the graduate group in detail, so it is most reasonable to select K = 4.

The attributes of the sample data [26] can be specifically classified as skills (average/unit), graduation time (average/year), salary (average/yuan), work location (0 for foreign and domestic major cities, 1 for Other cities in China), position information (0–2 indicates the level of the position, 0 is the supervisor and above), current education (0–2, respectively indicates the undergraduate, master, doctoral and above), work direction (0 is related to the major, 1 other), postgraduate entrance examination status (0 means yes, 1 means no).

Using the Bayes-K-means algorithm to perform cluster analysis on the processed dataset, the samples are divided into the following 4 categories, as shown in Table 1 below:

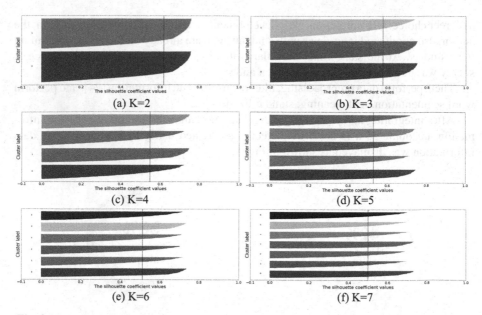

Fig. 2. Determine the optimal number of clusters K value by the silhouette coefficient method

Table 1. Classification results of graduate sample dataset

Cluster center	1	2	3	4
The proportion of graduates	19.32%	22.71%	40.59%	17.38%
Possess skill(s)	7	5	3	2
Graduation time (year)	8	6	4	3
Salary (yuan)	21143.46	9865.28	7653.70	5499.13
Work location	0	0	1	1
Job information	0	1	2	2
Current education	2	1	0	0
Work direction	0	1	0	1
Whether to the postgraduate entrance examination	0	0	1	1

According to the classification results obtained in Table 1, it is better to divide into four types of graduate groups [27]. Among them, the first type of graduate accounts for 19.32%, which is the longest among all graduates. The salary is also the highest, and most of them are concentrated in major developing cities abroad and China.

The second category of graduates accounted for 22.71%. Such graduates have graduated for a long time, have higher education and work experience. However, most of the jobs have nothing to do with their majors and have relatively large. The third type of graduates has the largest proportion among the four types of graduates, reaching

40.59%. It can be seen that the graduation time is not long and the position is generally low, resulting in a low average salary, and most of them are engaged in related majors. The fourth category of graduates accounted for 17.38%, which is the smallest among the four categories of graduates, with the lowest education, the least skills, and the work direction has nothing to do with the major, resulting in the lowest salary. Such graduates are the groups that the government and universities need to pay the most attention to and have the greatest benefit in improving the overall level of the major.

Based on the above, after analyzing the career development status of the graduate group, it is found that there is not much difference in the career development of the graduate group, which also shows that the graduates majoring in information and computing science are mainly engaged in industries related to their major after graduation [28]. It is beneficial to the development of graduates to improve their educational level as much as possible.

3.3 Experimental Results and Analysis on the Self-made Dataset

In this section, on the self-made dataset shown in Fig. 1 and Table 1, by comparing the Bayes-K-means algorithm with K-means algorithm, K-means++ algorithm and Bisecting K-means algorithm data simulation experiment, the results verify the effectiveness and accuracy of the new algorithm. The experimental evaluation indicators mainly include the number of iterations, the average running time (Time), the clustering accuracy (Acc) and the normalized mutual information (NMI).

From the comparison of clustering effects in Fig. 3, it can be seen that the traditional K-means algorithm has certain limitations in selecting the initial cluster center and calculating the distance [29], which easily leads to the problem of local optimization. The K-means++ algorithm [30] only improves the initial value, and the early calculation is more complicated; The Bisecting K-means algorithm [31] cannot guarantee convergence to the global optimal value; therefore, the above three algorithms are prone to problems such as local optimality, and Bayes-K-means algorithm can better avoid such problems.

Table 2 show the number of iterations, average running time (Time), clustering accuracy (Acc), and the normalized mutual information (NMI) of the proposed algorithm and the other three algorithms on the graduate dataset. It can be seen from the results that the experimental evaluation indicators of the Bayes-K-means algorithm are better than the other three algorithms.

3.4 Experimental Results and Analysis on the UCI Datasets

Compared with general artificial datasets, UCI datasets have more attributes, higher dimensions, and higher clustering difficulty. The advantage of choosing UCI datasets for testing is that, given their actual partitions, the algorithm performance can be evaluated by comparing the results obtained by the clustering algorithm with the known real partitions.

The UCI datasets used in the experiment is shown in Table 3. The experimental results on the average running time (Time) of the four algorithms on the four UCI datasets are shown in Table 4.

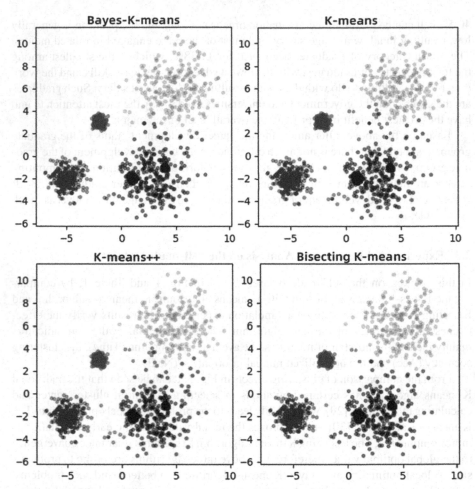

Fig. 3. Comparison of Bayes-K-means with K-means, K-means++ and Bisecting K-means clustering effects

Table 2. Comparison of clustering experiment results

Dataset	Graduate dataset			
Comparison indicators	Number of iterations	Time/s	Acc/%	NMI
K-means	11	3.574	81.5%	0.327
K-means++	11	3.218	88.2%	0.356
Bisecting K-means	10	2.663	90.3%	0.488
Bayes-K-means	**9**	**2.091**	**93.8%**	**0.781**

Table 3. Information on the 4 UCI datasets

Number	Dataset	Dataset size	Number of attributes	Number of clusters
1	Iris	150	4	3
2	Wine	178	13	3
3	Seeds	210	7	3
4	Glass	214	10	6

Table 4. Experimental results of the four algorithms on the average running time (Time) of the four UCI datasets (s)

Dataset	K-means	K-means++	Bisecting K-means	Bayes-K-means
Iris	0.53	0.33	0.39	**0.31**
Wine	2.79	2.41	2.29	**1.53**
Seeds	3.91	3.38	3.51	**2.45**
Glass	5.26	4.21	4.47	**3.09**

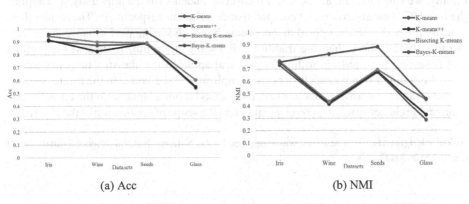

(a) Acc   (b) NMI

Fig. 4. Comparison of UCI datasets cluster evaluation indicators (Acc and NMI)

As can be seen from Table 4 and Fig. 4, in the small-scale datasets, the evaluation index values of all algorithms are not much different, but the Bayes-K-means algorithm has greater advantages; in larger-scale datasets, the K-means algorithm takes a long time, because when the algorithm is layered, the dimension of the dataset is higher, resulting in longer algorithm iteration time and thus lower Acc and NMI values. The K-means++ algorithm and the Bisecting K-means algorithm have similar clustering index values, but both are slightly lower than the Bayes-K-means algorithm because both algorithms only optimize the selection of the initial centroids [32]. Therefore, the indicators of the new algorithm proposed in this paper are better than the other three algorithms.

To sum up, the results show that the Bayes-K-means algorithm retains the advantages of the traditional K-means algorithm, at the same time, it eliminates the influence of bias when selecting the initial cluster center through Bayesian parameter inference, increases the stability of the clustering results and generalization performance, this is reflected in self-made dataset as well as UCI datasets. In addition, compared with the other three algorithms, the Bayes-K-means algorithm requires additional calculation of relevant probability values. Although this will increase a little computational cost, the amount of calculation is less than the K-means++ algorithm, and the subsequent clustering will converge faster. Therefore, Bayes-K-means algorithm can reduce the error generated by the classification results, and at the same time, the accuracy rate has also improved accordingly.

4 Conclusion

To overcome the shortcomings of the traditional K-means algorithm and adapt to the data sets with new characteristics, this paper proposes a new Bayes-K-means clustering algorithm based on Bayesian parameter inference. Firstly, the average distance calculation method is improved through the probability function of the prior distribution, and its eigenvalues are optimized, and then the similarity measure of the algorithm is improved. Finally, we collected and adopted real dataset of students from a university, and applied the four UCI datasets to conduct comparative experiments respectively. The results show that the Bayes-K-means algorithm can obtain better clustering performance and generalization performance than the traditional K-means algorithm, K-means++ algorithm and Bisecting K-means algorithm. In practical applications, the structural features of many high-dimensional data clusters are complicated and diverse. In the future, we plan to make further improvements to make the method more adaptable to the complex and changeable cluster structure, thereby expanding the scope of application of the algorithm.

Acknowledgments. This research was supported by the National Natural Science Foundation of China (61663041).

References

1. Breiman, L.: Stacked regressions. Mach. Learn. **24**, 49–64 (1996). https://doi.org/10.1023/A:1018046112532
2. Wang, H.B.: Research on clustering algorithm of multidimensional data deduplication in big data environment. In: Network Security Technology and Application, pp. 37–38 (2021)
3. Zhou, Z.H.: Machine Learning. Tsinghua University Press, Beijing (2017)
4. Zeng, J.: Analysis of data mining K-means clustering algorithm based on partitioning. Mod. Electron. Technol. **43**(03), 14–17 (2020)
5. Wang, F., Cai, J., Liu, J., Su, J.: A novel measurement-based method enabling rapid extraction of Bayesian inference-based behavioral model. In: IEEE MTT-S International Conference on Numerical Electromagnetic and Multiphysics Modeling and Optimization (NEMO), pp. 1–4 (2020). https://doi.org/10.1109/NEMO49486.2020.9343584

6. Gao, X.: An improved K-means clustering algorithm and a new clustering effective-ness index research. Anhui University, Hefei (2020)
7. Olivier, B., Mario, L.S., Hamed, H., Andreas, K.: Fast and provably good seedings for k-means. In: Proceedings of the 30th International Conference on Neural Information Processing Systems (NIPS 2016). Curran Associates Inc., Red Hook, NY, pp. 55–63 (2016)
8. Farivar, R., Rebolledo, D., Chan, E., et al.: A parallel implementation of K-means clustering on GPUs. In: Proceedings of the 2008 International Conference on Parallel and Distributed Processing Techniques and Applications, pp. 340–345. Springer-Verlag (2008)
9. Mao, D.H.: Improved canopy-kmeans algorithm based on MapReduce. Comput. Eng. Appl. **48**(27), 22–26 (2012)
10. Chowdhury, T., Mukherjee, A., Chakraborty, S.: An efficient MapReduce-based adaptive K-means clustering for large dataset. In: 2017 IEEE International Symposium on Nanoelectronic and Information Systems (iNIS), pp. 157–162. IEEE (2017)
11. Guo, Y.Y., et al.: K-means clustering algorithm for optimizing initial cluster centers. Comput. Eng. Appl. **56**(15), 172–178 (2020)
12. Huang, B.H., et al.: Differential privacy K-means clustering algorithm based on distance and error sum of squares. Inf. Netw. Secur. **20**(10), 34–40 (2020)
13. Wang, Z.L., Li, J., Song, Y.F.: Improved K-means algorithm based on distance and weight. Comput. Eng. Appl. **56**(23), 87–94 (2020)
14. Adnan, R.M., Khosravinia, P., Karimi, B., Kisi, O.: Prediction of hydraulics performance in drain envelopes using Kmeans based multivariate adaptive regression spline. Appl. Soft Comput. J. **100**, 107008 (2021)
15. Wang, G.Y.: A preliminary study on uncertainty-oriented data clustering. Jilin University, Changchun (2020)
16. Mehmood, R., El-Ashram, S., Bie, R., et al.: Clustering by fast search and merge of local density peaks for gene expression microarray data. Sci. Rep. **7**, 45602 (2017). https://doi.org/10.1038/srep45602
17. Jin, H.T., Ju, X.Z., Jian, H.G.: Recommendation algorithm for minority cultural resources based on MapReduce. In: Abstracts of 2019 IEEE International Conference on Computer Science and Educational Informatization (IEEECSEI 2019), p. 43 (2019)
18. Ting, X.W., Jun, Y.G.: An improved K-means algorithm based on kurtosis test. In: Proceedings of 2019 3rd International Conference on Artificial Intelligence, Automation and Control Technologies (AIACT 2019), pp. 241–248. IOP Publishing (2019)
19. MacQueen, J., et al.: Some methods for classification and analysis of multivariate obser-vations. In: Proceedings of the Fifth Berkeley Symposium on Mathematical Statistics and Probability, vol. 1, pp. 281–297. Oakland, CA (1967)
20. Kaufman, L., Rousseeuw, P.J.: Finding Groups in Data: An Introduction to Cluster Analysis, vol. 344. Wiley, Hoboken (2009)
21. Wang, Z., Zhou, W., Li, G.: Anomaly detection by using streaming K-means and batch K-means. In: 2020 5th IEEE International Conference on Big Data Analytics (ICBDA), pp. 11–17 (2020). https://doi.org/10.1109/ICBDA49040.2020.9101212
22. Ville, O.: Clustering enhancement for a token-based recommender. In: CIKM Workshops (2018)
23. Huang, H., et al.: K-means hybrid iterative clustering based on memory transfer sailfish optimization. J. Shanghai Jiaotong Univ. 1–12 (2021). https://doi.org/10.16183/j.cnki.jsjtu.2021.292
24. Fränti, P., Sieranoja, S.: K-means properties on six clustering benchmark datasets. Appl. Intell. **48**(12), 4743–4759 (2018). https://doi.org/10.1007/s10489-018-1238-7
25. Li, Y., Zhang, Y., Tang, Q., Huang, W., Jiang, Y., Xia, S.T.: t-k-means: A ROBUST AND STABLE k-means VARIANT. In: ICASSP 2021 - 2021 IEEE International Conference on

Acoustics, Speech, and Signal Processing (ICASSP), pp. 3120–3124 (2021). https://doi.org/10.1109/ICASSP39728.2021.9414687

26. Olukanmi, P.O., Twala, B.: K-means-sharp: modified centroid update for outlier-robust k-means clustering. In: 2017 Pattern Recognition Association of South Africa and Robotics and Mechatronics (PRASA-RobMech), pp. 14–19 (2017). https://doi.org/10.1109/RoboMech.2017.8261116

27. Geoffrey, J.M., Kaye, E.B.: Mixture models: inference and applications to clustering. Appl. Stat. **38**(2) (1988)

28. Yoder, J., Priebe, C.E.: Semi-supervised K-means+. J. Stat. Comput. Simul. **3** (2016)

29. Lee, M.: Non-alternating stochastic K-means based on the probabilistic representation of solution space. Electron. Lett. **55**, 605–607 (2019)

30. Maliheh, H.S., Reza, T.: Parallelization of Kmeans++ using CUDA. CoRR (2019)

31. Hussain, S.F., Haris, M.: A k-means based co-clustering (kCC) algorithm for sparse, high dimensional data. Expert Syst. Appl. **118**, 20–34 (2019)

32. Yuan, M., Xu, Z., Li, C.Y.: Multiple linear regression analysis of platform route pricing based on entropy method and Kmeans. J. Innov. Soc. Sci. Res. **7**(7) (2020)

Social Network and Group Behavior

Inductive Matrix Completion Based on Graph Attention

Zhou Zhou, Yuxing Zong, Zhongtao Yue, and Shimin Cai(✉)

University of Electronic Science and Technology of China, Chengdu 611731, Sichuan, China
shimincai@uestc.edu.cn

Abstract. We propose an inductive matrix completion model based on graph attention (IGAT-MC) for the rating prediction recommendation task. IGAT-MC is inductive through enclosing subgraph extraction and node labeling, which makes it can be generalized to predict user/item ratings that do not appear during the training process. More importantly, we use the graph attention mechanism to improve the rating prediction performance of IGAT-MC, and focus on more important user/item interactions for message passing. Based on the MovieLens-100K, the effectiveness of IGAT-MC is verified based on the evaluation of RMSE. By comparing with several mainstream methods, IGAT-MC surpasses some of the mainstream methods and shows competitive performance.

Keywords: Matrix completion · Graph attention · Recommendation · Graph neural network · Deep learning

1 Introduction

With the emergence of large amounts of graph data, numbers of studies on graph neural network (GNN) have emerged in recent years. Among these deep learning algorithms, GNNs have achieved advanced performance on semi-supervised node classification [1], network embedding [2], graph classification [3], link prediction [4], etc. We view the interaction data in the matrix completion task for the rating prediction recommendation as a bipartite graph [5]. And, we apply GNN to compute the bipartite graph embedding, which aims to represent a graph as low dimensional vectors to predict scores while preserving the graph structure [6].

The matrix completion task is an alternative issue in the recommendation field and has been applied for the rating prediction recommendation. Most matrix completion methods are transductive, which suggests that they aren't able to generalize to nodes that do not appear in the training phase and additional information that can bring extra gain in the testing phase (or that can be learned from its feature distribution). Alternatively, we propose an inductive matrix completion model based on graph attention (IGAT-MC) for the rating prediction recommendation. IGAT-MC is made inductive by one-hop enclosing subgraph extraction and node labeling, which makes the model more applicable to real application scenarios. And graph convolutional neural networks (GCNNs) in recommendation models usually treat user or item information equally for

X. Meng et al. (Eds.): BDSC 2022, CCIS 1640, pp. 159–166, 2022.
https://doi.org/10.1007/978-981-19-7532-5_10

neighborhood information aggregation, without distinguishing the importance of different neighboring information. Thus, we use the attention mechanism to improve the effectiveness of rating prediction and reduce the root mean square error (RMSE) based on the experimental datasets. The experimental results suggest that IGAT-MC surpasses some of the mainstream methods and shows competitive performance.

2   Related Works

The method based on GNN has the advantage of processing structural data and exploring structural information [7]. The development of convolutional neural network (CNN) promotes the rise of GNNs, and GNNs can be briefly divided into four typical frameworks [8]:

(1) GCNN [9]: GCNNs obtain the first-order feature decomposition of the approximate Laplacian graph which iteratively aggregates the information from the neighbors.
(2) GraphSage [2]: It samples fixed-size neighborhoods for each node and proposes averaging, summation, and maximum pooling aggregator operations.
(3) GAT [10]: The graph attention network (GAT) uses the attention mechanism to distinguish the contribution of neighbors, and updates the vector of each node by attention-weighted information aggregation.
(4) GGNN [11]: The gated graph sequence neural network (GGNN) is a typical recursive GNN method that uses selected pass recursive units in the update step.

In the field of matrix completion in recommendation, Berg et al. [12] proposed GC-MC, which uses GNN to aggregate neighborhood information to obtain node-level embeddings. He et al. [13] proposed LightGCN which is a simplifying and powering GCN for recommendation. Zhang et al. [14] proposed IG-MC, which can make the matrix complementation task inductive by enclosing subgraph extraction. Schlichtkrull et al. [15] used the recurrent graph convolutional network (RGCN) to consider the effects of different rating types for achieving better prediction results.

Attention, which has recently been used in deep learning, is an important brain-inspired function [16]. Veličković et al. [10] proposed GAT, which implements weighted neighborhood aggregation on neighbors by learning the weights of neighbors. Busbridge et al. [17] proposed RGAT. It assumes that different transformation matrices should be used for messaging with different edge types and use attention coefficients as weights in message passing. Wang et al. [18] proposed KGAT, using knowledge graph (KG) combined with GAT to make better recommendations for users. Yang et al. [19] proposed a hierarchical attention graph convolutional network in the heterogeneous knowledge graph.

3   Inductive Graph-Attention Based Matrix Completion

3.1   One-Hop Enclosing Subgraph Extraction and Node Labeling

The first subsection is the one-hop enclosing subgraph extraction and node labeling, and we adopt the implementation of IG-MC [14]. In the graph, the target user is denoted by

u and the target item is denoted by v. We extract a new subgraph that includes the items that have been rated by the user u and the users who are rated by the target item v as well as the target user u and target item v. We will feed the extracted one-hop enclosing subgraph to GNN and train the GNN model. Then, in the testing phase, for each test pair, we predict the ratings on the extracted enclosing subgraph. We need to remove the target edge to be predicted in the enclosing subgraph after extracting the training one-hop enclosing subgraph.

After the one-hop enclosing subgraph extraction, an integer label needs to be generated for each node in each subgraph. The purpose of the node labeling is to feed to GNN as the initial feature. First, the target user is tagged with 0 and the target item is tagged with 1. The user node is tagged with 2 if it has an edge with the target item in the first-hop enclosing subgraph, and the item node is tagged with 3 if it has an edge with the target user in the first-hop enclosing subgraph. The one-hot encoding of these node tags is regarded as the initial node feature of the subgraph.

Some methods use the one-hot encoding of nodes as the initial input features of nodes, which are unable to generalize to nodes beyond the serial number range. Thus, it is a transductive model and cannot be generalized to nodes that are not visible during the training phase. The one-hop enclosing extraction and node labeling methods make our model inductive.

3.2 Graph Neural Network Architecture

The second subsection is to train a multilayer GNN model based on graph attention in the one-hop enclosing subgraph we extract before. Our GNN model consists of three parts, an attention-based messaging passing layer, a pooling layer, and a multilayer perceptron layer. Figure 1 shows the overall network architecture of IGAT-MC.

In the attention-based messaging passing layer, different edge types should convey different information, and for each edge type, an intermediate feature transformation should be performed using the learnable weight matrix. We refer to RGAT and make some changes in calculating the attention factor as our final GNN's message passing layer. Specifically, the node embedding aggregated neighborhood information for embedding updates is as follows :

$$x_i^{l+1} = \sigma \left(\sum_{r \in \mathcal{R}} \sum_{j \in \mathcal{N}_i^{(r)}} \alpha_{i,j}^{l(r)} W^{l(r)} x_j^l \right) \tag{1}$$

where x_i^l is the node i's feature vector at layer l, $\alpha_{i,j}^{l(r)}$ is the attention coefficient of the layer l under edge type r, $W^{l(r)}$ is a learnable parameter matrix of the layer l under edge type r. $\mathcal{R}$ denotes all values for the edge type r $\mathcal{N}_i^{(r)}$ and denotes neighbor nodes of node i under edge type r. σ denotes the activation function. Herein, we use tanh function.

Next, we describe the calculation of the attention factor $\alpha_{i,j}^{l(r)}$. Before that, we generate the query vector and key vector of nodes:

$$q_i^{l(r)} = d_i^{l(r)} Q^{l(r)}, \ k_i^{l(r)} = d_i^{l(r)} K^{l(r)}, \tag{2}$$

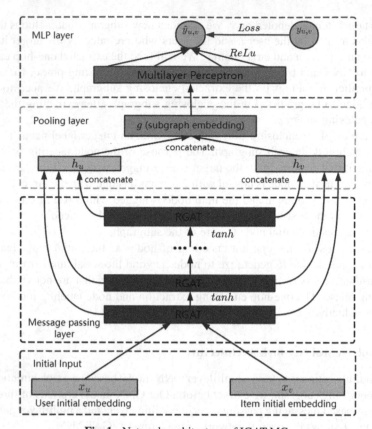

Fig. 1. Network architecture of IGAT-MC.

where $q_i^{l(r)}$ denotes the query vector of the node at the l layer under edge type r, and $k_i^{l(r)}$ denotes the key vector of the node at the l layer under edge type r. $d_i^{l(r)} = W^{l(r)}x_j^l$ denotes the transformed node feature vector. $Q^{l(r)}$ and $K^{l(r)}$ are learnable parameter matrices, and v_r is a learnable parameter vector. The calculation method is as follows:

$$E_{i,j}^{l(r)} = \text{LeakyReLu}\left(v_r^T \cdot \left(q_i^{l(r)} + k_j^{l(r)}\right)\right). \tag{3}$$

In the following, we normalize $E_{i,j}^{l(r)}$ to obtain the attention coefficient $\alpha_{i,j}^{l(r)}$ as follows:

$$\alpha_{i,j}^{l(r)} = \frac{\exp\left(E_{i,j}^{l(r)}\right)}{\sum\limits_{r'\in\mathcal{R}}\sum\limits_{k\in\mathcal{N}_i^{(r')}}\exp\left(E_{i,k}^{l(r')}\right)}, \quad \forall i: \sum_{r\in\mathcal{R}}\sum_{j\in\mathcal{N}_i^{(r)}}\alpha_{i,j}^{l(r)} = 1. \tag{4}$$

Then, in the pooling layer, we pool the hidden vectors of the output of each layer of the message passing layer into the embedding vector at the one-hop enclosing subgraph. The final representation of the node i:

$$h_i = \text{concat}(x_i^1, x_i^2, ..., x_i^L), \tag{5}$$

and the target user node embedding and the target item node embedding in the same one-hop enclosing subgraph are concatenated into the embedding of the subgraph as follows:

$$g = \text{concat}(h_u, h_v), \tag{6}$$

where h_u denotes the embedding of the user and h_v denotes the embedding of the item, and g denotes the final embedding of the subgraph.

Finally, in the multilayer perceptron layer, we use a multilayer perceptron g as input to output the prediction rating. $\hat{r}$ denotes the final prediction rating, which is calculated as:

$$\hat{r} = w^T \sigma(Wg), \tag{7}$$

where W w and are parameters of the multilayer perceptron, and σ denotes the activation function. Herein, we use ReLU function.

3.3 Model Training

In the model training phase, the loss function is mean square error (MSE):

$$\mathcal{L} = \frac{1}{|\{(u, v)|\Omega_{u,v} = 1\}|} \sum_{(u,v):\Omega_{u,v}=1} \left(R_{u,v} - \hat{R}_{u,v} \right)^2, \tag{8}$$

where $R_{u,v}$ denotes the observed rating and $\hat{R}_{u,v}$ denotes the predicted rating. Ω is a mask matrix that contains only 0 or 1 values to represent the ratings that exist.

4 Experiment and Result

We perform the testing experiments of rating prediction based on the benchmark dataset, MovieLens-100K [20]. We use its official partition u1.base (80% of the dataset) and u1.test (20% of the dataset) as the training set and testing set.

The hyperparameters of IGAT-MC are adjusted according to the cross-validation results. The one-hop closed subgraph is extracted, and the message-passing layer uses a 4-layer RGAT network with an output dimension being 32 for each layer, and the layers are connected by the tanh. The subgraph embedding dimension of the input to the final fully connected neural network is 256, and this subgraph embedding is obtained by concatenating a 128-dimensional user node embedding with a 128-dimensional item node embedding. The fully connected neural network layer has 128 hidden layer units and uses the ReLU nonlinear activation function. We train the model using the Adam optimizer. And we set the batch size to 32 and the learning rate to 0.001. We set the number of training epochs to be 80.

We compare our IGAT-MC with matrix completion (MC) [5], inductive matrix completion (IMC) [21], GMC [22], GRALS [23], RGCNN [24], F-EAE [25] and PinSage [26]. These algorithms are divided into two types according to whether they are inductive, and some of them (e.g., IMC, GMC, CRALS, RGCNN, PinSage) integrates with

Table 1. RMSE on MovieLens-100K datasets.

Model	Inductive	RMSE
MC	no	0.973
GMC	no	0.996
IMC	no	1.653
GRALS	no	0.945
RGCNN	no	0.929
F-EAE	yes	1.142
PinSage	yes	0.920
IGAT-MC (ours)	yes	**0.910**

the additional information of the content in MovieLens-100K. The RMSE is adopted to evaluate the rating prediction performance.

The results are averaged over 10 testing experiments, which are presented in Table 1. We can see that the value of RMSE obtained from IGAT-MC is the lowest in comparison with those obtained from other algorithms. It also suggests that the inductive learning and the additional information of the content play an important role in the rating prediction performance. For example, for these algorithms based on inductive learning, they present relatively lower values of RMSE, and the additional information of the content further reduces the value of RMSE (e.g., PinSage).

We also do ablation experiments on the size of the introduced v-vectors and the matched Q, K matrix. These experiments are with the ablation of the size of the learnable parameter v_r (related to v-vectors) and the sizes of Q, K matrix are adaptively matched to v_r. Thus, we mainly consider the changes of v_r. First, we present the baseline of RMSE, which doesn't use the learning matrix, then increase the size of v_r from 4 to 128. Table 2 shows the ablation experiments results. We can see that the value of RMSE is greatly reduced when the size of v_r only increases to 8. Nevertheless, when the size of v_r is above 8, the effectiveness of IGAT-MC isn't improved greatly, but increases training time significantly. The results of ablation experiments suggest that the sizes of v-vectors and the matched Q, K matrix are greatly important for IGAT-MC.

Table 2. RMSE results for different v-vector sizes on MovieLens-100K

Model	RMSE
IGAT-MC (original)	0.945
IGAT-MC (size = 4)	0.940
IGAT-MC (size = 8)	0.912
IGAT-MC (size = 16)	0.911
IGAT-MC (size = 32)	0.911
IGAT-MC (size = 64)	0.911
IGAT-MC (size = 128)	0.910

5 Conclusion

We propose an inductive graph-attention-based matrix completion model (i.e., IGAT-MC) and it is able to predict user/item ratings that are not seen during the training process (as long as there is an interaction between them). We also improve the effectiveness of IGAT-MC by focusing on the more important user/item interactions for messaging, which reduces the RMSE of the rating prediction to improve the recommendation performance. The recommendation model proposed in this paper is compared with several advanced recommendation models on the benchmark dataset and the experimental results are analyzed. Additionally, we will introduce the additional information of the content for IGAT-MC to improve the rating prediction performance in the future work.

Acknowledgments. This work is supported by the Ministry of Education of Humanities and Social Science Project under Grant No. 21JZD055.

References

1. Kipf, T N., Welling, M.: Semi-supervised classification with graph convolutional networks. arXiv preprint arXiv:1609.02907 (2016)
2. Hamilton, W., Ying, Z., Leskovec, J.: Inductive representation learning on large graphs. In: Advances in Neural Information Processing Systems, vol. 30 (2017)
3. Zhang, M., Cui, Z., Neumann, M., et al.: An end-to-end deep learning architecture for graph classification. In: Proceedings of the Thirty-Second AAAI conference on Artificial Intelligence, pp. 4438–4445 (2018)
4. Zhang, M., Chen, Y.: Link prediction based on graph neural networks. In: Advances in Neural Information Processing Systems, vol. 31 (2018)
5. Candès, E.J., Recht, B.: Exact matrix completion via convex optimization. Found. Comput. Math. **9**(6), 717–772 (2009)
6. Cai, H., Zheng, V.W., Chang, K.C.C.: A comprehensive survey of graph embedding: problems, techniques, and applications. IEEE Trans. Knowl. Data Eng. **30**(9), 1616–1637 (2018)
7. Gao, C., Wang, X., He, X., et al.: Graph neural networks for recommender system. In: Proceedings of the Fifteenth ACM International Conference on Web Search and Data Mining, pp. 1623–1625 (2022)

8. Wu, S., Sun, F., Zhang, W., et al.: Graph neural networks in recommender systems: a survey. arXiv preprint arXiv:2011.02260 (2020)
9. Pei, H., Wei, B., Chang, K., et al.: Geom-GCN: geometric graph convolutional networks. arXiv preprint arXiv:2002.05287 (2020)
10. Veličković, P., Cucurull, G., Casanova, A., et al.: Graph attention networks. arXiv preprint arXiv:1710.10903 (2017)
11. Li, Y., Zemel, R., Brockschmidt, M., et al.: Gated graph sequence neural networks. arXiv preprint arXiv:1511.05493 (2015)
12. Berg, R., Kipf, T N., Welling, M.: Graph convolutional matrix completion. arXiv preprint arXiv:1706.02263 (2017)
13. He, X., Deng, K., Wang, X., et al.: Lightgcn: simplifying and powering graph convolution network for recommendation. In: Proceedings of the 43rd International ACM SIGIR Conference on Research and Development in Information Retrieval, pp. 639–648 (2020)
14. Zhang, M., Chen, Y.: Inductive matrix completion based on graph neural networks. arXiv preprint arXiv:1904.12058 (2019)
15. chlichtkrull, M., Kipf, T.N., Bloem, P., van den Berg, R., Titov, I., Welling, M.. Modeling Relational Data with Graph Convolutional Networks. In: Gangemi,A., et al.: The Semantic Web. ESWC 2018. Lecture Notes in Computer Science, vol 10843, pp.593–607 Springer, Cham. (2018). https://doi.org/10.1007/978-3-319-93417-4_38
16. Lee, J.B., Rossi, R.A., Kim, S., et al.: Attention models in graphs: A survey. ACM Trans. Knowl. Discov. Data **13**(6), 1–25 (2019)
17. Busbridge, D., Sherburn, D., Cavallo, P., et al.: Relational graph attention networks. arXiv preprint arXiv:1904.05811 (2019)
18. Wang, X., He, X., Cao, Y., et al.: KGAT: knowledge graph attention network for recommendation. In: Proceedings of the 25th ACM SIGKDD International Conference on Knowledge Discovery & Data Mining, pp. 950–958 (2019)
19. Yang, Z., Dong, S.: HAGERec: hierarchical attention graph convolutional network incorporating knowledge graph for explainable recommendation. Knowl.-Based Syst. **204**, 106194 (2020)
20. Miller, B N., Albert, I., Lam, S K., et al.: Movielens unplugged: experiences with an occasionally connected recommender system. In: Proceedings of the 8th International Conference on Intelligent User Interfaces, pp. 263–266 (2003)
21. Jain, P., Dhillon, I S.: Provable inductive matrix completion. arXiv preprint arXiv:1306.0626 (2013)
22. Kalofolias, V., Bresson, X., Bronstein, M., et al.: Matrix completion on graphs. arXiv preprint arXiv:1408.1717 (2014)
23. Rao, N., Yu, H F., Ravikumar, P K., et al.: Collaborative filtering with graph information: consistency and scalable methods. In: Advances in Neural Information Processing Systems, vol. 28 (2015)
24. Hartford, J., Graham, D., Leyton-Brown, K., et al.: Deep models of interactions across sets. In: International Conference on Machine Learning, pp. 1909–1918 (2018)
25. Monti, F., Bronstein, M., Bresson, X.: Geometric matrix completion with recurrent multigraph neural networks. In: Advances in Neural Information Processing Systems, vol. 30 (2017)
26. Ying, R., He, R., Chen, K., et al.: Graph convolutional neural networks for web-scale recommender systems. In: Proceedings of the 24th ACM SIGKDD International Conference on Knowledge Discovery & Data Mining, pp. 974–983 (2018)

Identifying Spammers by Completing the Ratings of Low-Degree Users

Guo-Hua Li[1(✉)], Jun Wu[1], and Hong-Liang Sun[1,2(✉)]

[1] Key Lab of E-commerce in JiangSu Province,
Nanjing University of Finance and Economics, Nanjing 210023, China
1120201143@stu.nufe.edu.cn, hlsun84@mail.ustc.edu.cn
[2] University of Nottingham, Ningbo 315100, China

Abstract. Along with the rapid development of e-commerce, a large number of spammers disrupt the fair order of the e-commerce platform. The false ratings rated by these spammers do not match the quality of items, confusing the boundaries of good and bad items and seriously endangering the real interests of merchants and normal users. To eliminate the malicious influence caused by these spammers, many effective spamming detection algorithms are proposed in e-commerce platforms. However, these algorithms are ineffective in judging how trustworthy a user with insufficient rating data. In order to address this issue, we take inspiration from traditional recommender systems by completing the missing ratings of low-degree users to improve the efficiency of spamming detection algorithms when approaching those users. User similarity is used in this paper to predict the missing ratings of users. A novel reputation ranking method IOR_LU is proposed. We then test our improvements compared with DR, IGR, and IOR. Experimental results on three typical data sets suggest that our method combined with IOR has improved by at least 9.68%, 3.29%, and 0.21% in dealing with malicious spammers, respectively. As for results on detecting random spammers, our method improves by a least 5.06%, 21.12% and 4.46%, respectively.

Keywords: Fraud detection · Spamming attacks · Rating prediction · User similarity · E-commerce

1 Introduction

The reputation of individuals plays an instrumental role in building a healthy e-commerce ecosystem on the Internet [1–5]. This makes it crucial to assess the reputation of users. So many e-commerce platforms (including Taobao, JD.com, Amazon, etc.) have implemented online rating systems that allow users to rate their shopping experiences. Similarly, e-commerce platforms can assign reputation index to users based on their ratings. However, a few dishonest businesses disturb the fair operation of online ecosystems [6,7]. Due to low ratings resulting from poor quality items, they cannot convince consumers to buy. So they hire

X. Meng et al. (Eds.): BDSC 2022, CCIS 1640, pp. 167–179, 2022.
https://doi.org/10.1007/978-981-19-7532-5_11

spammers to fraudulently increase their own products' ratings [8–10]. These practices often mislead consumers and diminish their shopping experience, as well as their trust in the platform. In the long run, such consumers will become less loyal to the platform and ultimately switch to other platforms. Thus, it is critical to reduce the impact of malicious spammers on e-commerce platforms [11,12].

In response to these concerns, scholars have proposed a variety of methods so far [13,14]. Those methods will be roughly introduced in the following. Early CR (Correlation-based Ranking) [15] and IR (Iterative Refinement Ranking) [16] algorithm considered users whose ratings significantly overlap with the majority of others as reliable and their ratings contributed much to the quality of items. User reputation is then assigned on the basis of the difference between user's rating scores and the corresponding item's quality. Just a short while later, Liao et al. introduced a process called reputation redistribution to enhance the importance of highly prestigious users [17]. Gao et al. proposed GR (Group-based Ranking) [18], which classified users into groups with different reliability and users from groups with high reliability had higher reputation values. Later, it was optimized to IGR (Iterative Group based Ranking) [19] by iteratively update the user's reputation value, which further scaled up the detection performance. DR (Deviation-based Ranking) [20] assumed that user rating obeys the Gaussian distribution and each user receives a reputation index based on how well quality classification is accurate. Wu et al. proposed BR [21], whose core idea is to consider that user ratings obeyed beta distribution. Later by eliminating the rating bias responsible for reducing the fairness of rating systems, they improved it to IBR [22]. Not long before, according to Sun's research that reliable users' ratings followed the pattern of peak distribution, while rating of spammers does not show some obvious patterns [23]. Other exciting hypotheses exist as well. The work by Lv et al. provided a thorough review many noteworthy applications and approaches of reputation-based ranking methods [24], which is highly recommended to read.

However, due to the common existence of the long tail phenomenon, user rating data is very sparse. In most cases, the above-mentioned methods cannot effectively determine whether a low-degree user is a malicious spammer or not. For this reason, we attempt to fill in the rating data of low-degree users as a framework to effectively alleviate the extreme sparsity of rating data. Initially, we calculate the similarity between users by Pearson correlation coefficient, and then predict users' missing ratings from their neighbors' ratings of items. After completing many experiments, we find that our method significantly outperforms DR [20], IGR [19] and IOR [23] on the three classical data sets *Movielens*, *Netfilx*, and *Movielens_100* when detecting spammers. In terms of detecting malicious spammers, our algorithm achieves an improvement from 9.68% to 159% than DR [20], from 3.29% to 107% than IGR [19], and from 0.21% to 1.60% than IOR [19]. In detecting random spammers, it improves respectively 5.06%–43.57%, 21.12%–292% and 4.46%–440%.

As for the remainder of the paper, it is organized as follows: The second part lists the related preliminary knowledge. The third part describes the method of this article in detail. In the fourth part, we present the data used in this article followed by introduction of two evaluation metrics for the spamming detection method. In the next section, we present the results and analysis of our experiment. In the last part, we provide a brief summary of our findings and a glimpse of our future plans.

2 Preliminaries

In this section, we will first present the network as well as the bipartite graph. Then we list the symbolic representation of some technical terms in rating networks.

2.1 Network

A network is composed of nodes and links connecting these nodes, which represents objects and their interconnections [25,26]. A network $G(V, E)$ can be seen as a set containing, where V suggests a set whose elements we call vertices, and E is usually a set of paired vertices called edges. A network can generally be divided into two kinds: (i) directed network: Edges in A directed graph or digraph all have orientations; (ii) undirected network: Each edge has no orientation.

2.2 Rating Network

The rating network can be seen as a user-object bipartite graph with weights. In the mathematical field of graph theory, a bipartite divides vertices into two independent and disjoint sets, that is every edge connects a vertex between two sets of nodes. Vertex sets are usually called the parts of the graph. Equivalently, a bipartite graph usually does not include any odd-length cycles.

Rating system is generally modeled as a bipartite network $G = \{U, O, R\}$ among which $U = \{u_i \mid i \in \{1, 2, ..., m\}\}$ and $O = \{o_\alpha | \alpha \in \{1, 2, ..., n\}\}$ represent a set of users and items respectively [12]. There are interactions between users and items where ratings are merely given by users to items. Here ratings are denoted by $R = \{r_{i\alpha} \mid i \in \{1, 2, ..., m\}, \alpha \in \{1, 2, ..., n\}\}$ illustrating that a group of rating scores $r_{i\alpha}$ that user i gives to object α. Therefore n is the number of objects set in the data sets. Similarly, U_α means the user set that have already rated the object o_α.

3 Methodology

In the e-commerce world, users and items grow exponentially. However, items rated by users usually could not exceed 1% of the total number of items [27], so the user rating data is rather sparse. In most current reputation-based methods, some users are even filtered out in the data pre-processing stage due to incomplete rating information, which causes rating data more sparse. We refer to those users whose rating times below a particular threshold collectively as low-degree users. In $Movielens$, 80 is the threshold, in $Movielens\_100$ it is 50, and in $Netflix$ it is 20. Under such circumstance, the traditional spamming detection algorithm will be compromised in accuracy. Despite being the best algorithm for detecting spammers at present, IOR is no exception.

Algorithm 1: Identifying Spammers By Completing The Ratings Of Low-degree Users

---

Input: $rating\ data\ set : R$; threshold of similar neighbours: θ; threshold of
　　　　low-degree spammer: Ω; length of spammer list: L
Output: $filled\ rating\ data\ set : R'$; spammer set U and U';

1 // Initialization
2 $R' \leftarrow R$;
3 **for** $user\ u_1\ in\ R$ **do**
4 　　**for** $user\ u\ in\ R\ (u_1\ not\ included)$ **do**
5 　　　　Compute $sim(u_1, u)$ from Eq.1;
6 　　　　**if** $sim(u_1, u) > \theta$ **then**
7 　　　　　　Add u to u_1's neighbour N_{u1};

8 　　**for** $l = 1, \ldots, \Omega_{(R)} - degree_{(u_1)}$ **do**
9 　　　　Select a item o without being rated by u_1 randomly;
10 　　　　Calculate the predicted rating value $pred(u_1, o)$ of user u_1 to item o
　　　　　from Eq.2;
11 　　　　Update R' with $\{u_1, o, pred(u_1, o)\}$;

12 Calculate user reputation scores via $\{IOR, IOR\_LU\}$ in R and R', respectively;
13 Obtain the top-L users as spammers by sorting users based on their reputation scores.
14 Output the spammer set U(in R) and U'(in R').

To alleviate the reduced accuracy of spam detection resulting from the extreme sparse of user rating data, we decide to complete the ratings of low-degree users based on user similarity. Specifically, as a first step, we use the Pearson Correlation Coefficient to compute the similarity between users and complete the rating data of low-degree users. This approach can alleviate the extreme sparsity of the ratings data on which our framework is based. Our framework can then be combined with any existing spammer detection methods. In this paper we combine it with IOR as a solution for completing low-degree users' ratings on IOR and detecting spam, which can be be abbreviated as IOR_LU. Experimental results conducted on three benchmark data sets demonstrate that IOR_LU outperforms much better than other methods in detecting spammers. Next, we will introduce the main concepts of IOR and IOR_LU, respectively.

3.1 Iterative Optimization Ranking (IOR)

A key feature of the Iterative Optimization Ranking (IOR) [23] is its ability to distinguish between normal users and spammers depending on their rating patterns. It involves iterative optimization and updating. It postulates that normal users will form a unique distribution of ratings based on their knowledge backgrounds, shopping experiences, etc., while spammers' ratings won't appear to have any pattern. Since ratings rated by normal users represent the true quality of the goods and have a specific distribution pattern. IOR defines a variable expected divergence D and a parameter ε which reflects the variation between real quality of the product and user ratings to measure the peak distribution of user ratings.

3.2 Completing the Ratings of Low-degree Users on IOR (IOR_LU)

To alleviate the extreme sparsity of the rating data sets, completing the ratings of each low-degree users is an easy and effective practice. Traditional recommendation systems assume that user preferences hardly change over time. If users shared similar tastes in the past, it is likely that they will hold similar tastes in the future [28]. Hence, we can predict users' missing ratings via the rating behavior of their similar users. We use the Pearson correlation coefficient to measure user similarity in this paper. Suppose user u_1's rating matrix is extremely sparse, and we need to fill in his/her missing ratings. Specifically, we first need to calculate u_1's similarity with other users and get the nearest neighbors set N_{u_1} of u_1. Next we use ratings given by users from N_{u_1} to an item to predict u_1's missing rating of the corresponding unrated item until u_1's rating matrix becomes not significantly sparse. Finally we combine the filled data set with IOR to detect spammers. Experimental results demonstrate the effectiveness of our method to solve the shortcomings of IOR under extreme sparse rating data and generally improve the effect of spam detection. The whole process of IOR_LU is illustrated in Algorithm 1. Generally, our framework involves the following three parts:

Measuring Similarity Between Users. There are various methods to measure inter-user similarity, including the following three methods [27]: (i) Pearson correlation coefficient; (ii) cosine similarity; (iii) modified cosine similarity. In this paper, we adopt the Pearson correlation coefficient to be the indicator of the similarity of users. Pearson coefficient is insensitive to absolute values, which can avoid user rating preference's effect on classifying similar users [29,30]. It is commonly used to describe the tendency of two sets of linear data to move together. Its value changes from -1 to 1, where -1 shows robust negative correlation and 1 presents intense positive correlation. When the linear relationship between two variables increases simultaneously, it implies that they are positively correlated and the correlation coefficient is greater than 0. The correlation coefficient less than 0 means that they are negatively correlated, i.e., when one variable increases and the other decreases. In general, if the Pearson correlation coefficient between two users is greater than 0, we can consider them to be similar. Similarity based on Pearson correlation coefficient of two users in shown in Eq. 1, mathematically reads:

$$sim(u_1, u_2) = \frac{\sum_{o \in O} (r_{u_1,o} - \overline{r_{u_1}})(r_{u_2,o} - \overline{r_{u_2}})}{\sqrt{\sum_{o \in O} (r_{u_1,o} - \overline{r_{u_1}})^2} \sqrt{\sum_{o \in O} (r_{u_2,o} - \overline{r_{u_2}})^2}} \tag{1}$$

where u_1 and u_2 are two different users, o indicates the item, $r_{u_1,o}$ indicates the rating given by user u_1 to item o, $\overline{r_{u_1}}$ is the mean rating of u_1, $sim(u_1, u_2)$ reflects the similarity between u_1 and u_2.

It is crucial to select neighbors that are akin to the target user. If selected neighbors are not identical to target user, we will get an inaccurate rating prediction. Herlocker et al. first introduced user similarity adjustment parameter and neighbor selection threshold θ, and experimentally demonstrated the improvements by introducing these parameters [31,32]. Therefore, we adopt the parameter θ to optimize the selection process of neighbors. The value of θ determines the number of similar neighbors, and a user will be regarded as similar to the target user only when their similarity exceeds the threshold θ. Therefore, it is useful to define the neighbor set N_{u_1} which consists of users whose Pearson correlation coefficient with user u_1 is no less than θ. N_{u_1} can be expressed as $\{u \mid sim(u, u_1) > \theta, u \in R \text{ and } u \neq u_1\}$. It is worth noting that a user cannot belong to his own neighbor set.

Making Predictions. Once nearest neighbors of target user u_1 is obtained by Pearson correlation coefficient, our next step is to predict user's missing ratings. Let the set of nearest neighbors of user u_1 be denoted by N_{u_1}, then the predicted rating $pred(u_1, o)$ of user u_1 for item o can be obtained from Eq. 2.

$$pred(u_1, o) = \overline{r_{u_1}} + \frac{\sum_{u_2 \in N_{u_1}} sim(u_1, u_2) * (r_{u_2,o} - \overline{r_{u_2}})}{\sum_{u_2 \in N_{u_1}} sim(u_1, u_2)} \tag{2}$$

where $pred(u_1, o)$ is the predicted rating of user u_1 to item o, N_{u_1} is the set consisting of similar users of u_1.

Identifying Spammers. As a solution to detect spammers under sparse rating data, we propose a novel framework based on user similarity to complete the rating data of low-degree users. We then combine it with existing reputation-based ranking methods (take IOR, for example), that is IOR_LU. The general process of IOR_LU to detect spammers can be summarized into the following steps. First we predict the missing ratings of low-degree users by Pearson correlation coefficient. Afterward, we extend the predicted rating information to the original dataset to alleviate the sparsity, which is the foundation of our framework. Finally, we combine the framework with IOR to detect spammers. Experimental results conducted on real data sets demonstrate that IOR_LU works well to identify both malicious and random spammers of low degree.

4 Data and Metric

4.1 Rating Data Set

We use the datasets *Movielens*, *Movielens_100*[1] and *Netflix*[2] to test the performance of spamming detection algorithms. Movielens created and maintained by the GroupLens research group at the University of Minnesota, features information on movie ratings, movie attributes, and movie tags. *Movielens* and *Netflix* have a range of ratings (scores from 1 to 5, with higher scores indicating that users deem the movie is better). *Movielens_100* has a rating range from 1 to 10. The network structure of three data sets can be found in Table 1.

Table 1. The principal information of *MovieLens* and *Netflix* data sets, where m indicates number of users, n means the number of objects, l indicates the rating times of users, and $s = l/mn$ reflects data sparsity.

DataName	m	n	l	s
Movielens	943	1682	100000	0.06305
Movielens_100	7120	130462	1048575	0.00113
Netflix	5000	17768	3496614	0.03936

4.2 Generating Artificial Spammers

To evaluate the objective performance of spamming detection methods, we select a random subset of users within the data sets, and intentionally substitute their rating for distorted ratings. We then calculate their reputation values using the ranking method as mentioned before.

A spammer can be either intentionally malicious or random. Extremely malicious spammers tend to rate objects with the highest or lowest rating, resulting in an excessive increase or decrease in object quality. Random spammers are those who rate objects at random. In this experiment, we select d users at random and change their rating matrix based on two criteria: (i) malicious users: the ratings of such users are changed to integers 1 or 5 (ii) random users: the ratings of such users will be changed to a random integer from 1 to 5 with the same probability. we always repeat N times of experiments to deal with users who are randomly selected. As each selection is made, we will restore user ratings and remove artificial spammers.

4.3 Evaluation Metric

To assess the effectiveness of above methods, we adopt two widely used metrics: Recall and AUC (area under the curve).

---

[1] Movielens, please refer to https://grouplens.org/datasets/movielens/.
[2] Netflix, please refer to https://pan.baidu.com/s/1t2fjFYXxyCwdqjRCg65ErA.

Recall. Recall is a ranking-based metric for detecting spammers, which measures how many malicious users can be identified in the top L ranking list. A higher Recall value is indicative of a higher accuracy rate. To calculate the value of Recall, we first need to calculate the users' reputation value and sort them in an ascending order. Then, we pick out the top L users with the lowest reputation value and the value of Recall is equal to the proportion of the number of artificial spammers counted in the top L users. Recall is calculated as shown in Eq. 3.

$$R(L) = \frac{d'(L)}{d} \tag{3}$$

where $R(L)$ means the recall value, d indicates the number of users randomly selected to be assigned distortion ratings; $d'(L)$ is the number of spammers that detected in the top L ranking list.

AUC. The AUC value indicates the probability that a randomly selected normal user has a higher reputation than a randomly selected spammer. It reflects the performance of a sorted ranking list. It's value changes from 0 to 1. In general, the algorithm performs better when the value is higher. The value of AUC is calculated as in Eq. 4.

$$AUC = \frac{N' + 0.5N''}{N} \tag{4}$$

where N indicates the number of comparison time, N' refers to the number of times the reputation value of the randomly selected spammer is lower than the corresponding value of the normal user in N comparisons, and N'' means the number of times they have the same reputation value.

5   Experimental Results

In this section, we compare our method with DR [20], IGR [19] and IOR [23] in terms of Recall and AUC. We conduct an experimental study on three real data sets to assess both random spammers and malicious spammers. In our first experiment, we set $d = 50$ and let L vary between 0 and 250 to calculate the Recall value. In the second experiment, we let L equal d and p vary from 0.05 to 0.30, and calculate Recall and AUC separately under each p.

5.1   Effectiveness

We first calculate the Recall values by the introduced methods when L changes. As shown in Fig. 1, three methods after being combined with our framework have improvements both for detecting malicious and random spammers. As shown in panel (a)–(c), our method we take IOR_LU as example has much improvement over both DR and IGR in detecting malicious spammers. However, the effect is only slightly higher than IOR, since the IOR algorithm is almost optimal in detecting malicious spammers. Compared with DR, IGR, and

IOR, the improvement vector for our method on three data sets is respectively [9.68%, 159%, 674%], [3.29%, 107%, 3.90%], and [0.21%, 1.60%, 0.63%]. It is clear from our results that our algorithm improves much under the more spare data set. In Panel (d)–(f), our method detects random spammers with a large improvement compared to the other three methods. This means that our method works better at detecting random spammers.

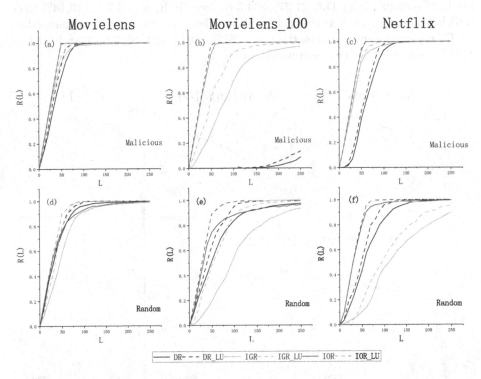

Fig. 1. The Recall scores of DR, IGR and IOR compared with their variants from our framework. Recall changes with the value of L. The number of spammers d is set to 50 and L changes from 0 to 250 increasing by 10 every time. The experiment was repeated 100 times and averaged to obtain the final results.

5.2   Robustness

In this section, we test the robustness of our method by increasing the number of spammers. We want to see if our method works well if a large number of spammers present. Here $p = d/m$ is the indicator of the ratio of spammers to all users. P changes from 0 to 0.25 by each step with the length 0.01. To avoid losing generality, we set the length of the ranking list L be always the same to the number of spammers d.

From Fig. 2 and Fig. 3, we can see the value of Recall of three methods combined with our framework have improved to some extent. Next, we will compare IOR_LU with the other three methods. When detecting malicious spammers, our method improves by 16.82%–23.76% over DR, 22.60%–23.34% over IGR, and 0.47%–1.22% over IOR on the Recall; as for AUC, our method improves by 0.97%–5.19%, 4.84%–63.05% and 0.003%–0.04% compared to the above three methods, respectively. In terms of identifying random spammers, we can improve by 4.61%–16.40% over DR, 21.97%–64.59% over IGR, and 3.11%–13.14% over IOR when using Recall as the metric; When the evaluation metric is changed to AUC, we can improve our method by 0.81%–1.01%, 0.91%–3.05% and 0.13%–1.31% respectively over the previous methods.

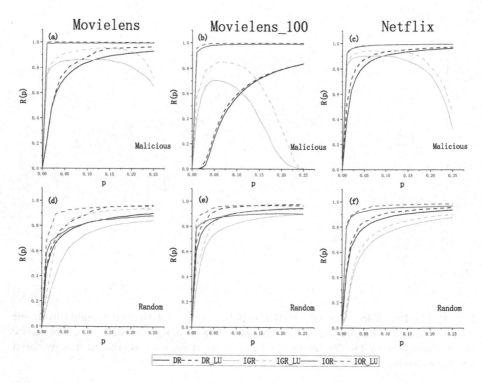

Fig. 2. The Recall scores of DR, IGR and IOR compared with their variants from our framework. Recall changes with the same proportion of p in three data sets. p increases by 0.01 every time with step ranging from 0.05 to 0.25. The experiment was repeated 100 times and averaged to obtain the final results.

6   Conclusion and Discussion

In this paper, we make a preliminary exploration of tackling spamming detection issues under sparse rating data. We propose a framework by completing low-degree users' rating data based on user similarity and later apply it on IOR, which is proved to be more effective in identifying spammers of low degree. To complete the missing ratings of low-degree users, we investigate the potential relationship between users by way of Pearson correlation coefficient. Then, combining it with different spam detection methods, we propose a more satisfactory framework which can further exploit the better performance in detecting spammers. Experimental results on three data sets indicate that our framework has acceptable results for detecting both malicious and random spammers.

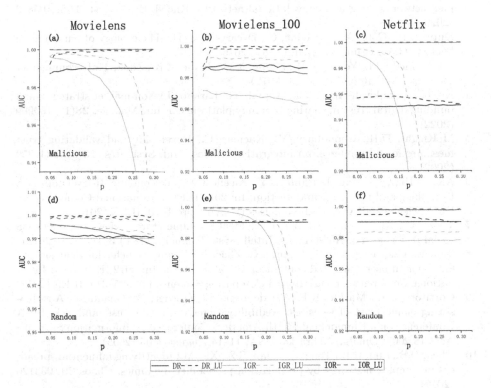

Fig. 3. The AUC scores of DR, IGR and IOR compared with their variants from our framework. The parameter p ranges from 0.05 to 0.3 with the step length 0.01. The experiment was repeated 100 times and averaged to obtain the final results.

We have also recognized the limitations and vulnerability of our method. Since the performance of our method depends on the accurate prediction of user ratings. Once user preferences change, ratings predicted by the Pearson correlation coefficient may differ significantly from missing ratings, which can adversely affect our ability to detect spammers. For this reason in the future, we intend to mine information with timestamps in combination with convolutional networks to make more accurate predictions of users' missing ratings.

Acknowledgment. This work has supported by the National Natural Science Foundation of China, including Grant Nos. 71901115, 71871109, 61673085 and 61803266. It is also supported by Young Scholar Programme from NUFE (NosSHLXW19001), International Cooperation Programme of JiangSu Province (BZ2020008) and Guangdong Province Natural Science Foundation (Grant Nos. 2019A1515011173).

References

1. Yu, E.Y., Wang, Y.P., Fu, Y., Chen, D., Xie, M.: Identifying critical nodes in complex networks via graph convolutional networks. Knowl.-Based Syst. **198**, 105893 (2020)
2. Dupont, B., Côté, A.M., Savine, C., Décary-Hétu, D.: The ecology of trust among hackers. Glob. Crime **17**(2), 129–151 (2016)
3. Lü, L., Medo, M., Yeung, C.H., Zhang, Y.C., Zhang, Z.K., Zhou, T.: Recommender systems. Phys. Rep. **519**, 1–49 (2012)
4. Ko, G., Amankwah-Amoah, J., Appiah, G., Larimo, J.: Non-market strategies and building digital trust in sharing economy platforms. J. Int. Manage. **28**(1), 100909 (2022)
5. McKnight, D.H., Choudhury, V., Kacmar, C.: Developing and validating trust measures for e-commerce: an integrative typology. Inf. Syst. Res. **13**(3), 334–359 (2002)
6. Xie, S., Hu, Q., Zhang, J., Philip, S.Y.: An effective and economic BI-level approach to ranking and rating spam detection. In: 2015 IEEE International Conference on Data Science and Advanced Analytics (DSAA), pp. 1–10. IEEE (2015)
7. Wang, G., Xie, S., Liu, B., Yu, P.S.: Identify online store review spammers via social review graph. ACM Trans. Intell. Syst. Technol. (TIST) **3**(4), 1–21 (2012)
8. Tan, E., Guo, L., Chen, S., Zhang, X., Zhao, Y.: Spammer behavior analysis and detection in user generated content on social networks. In: 2012 IEEE 32nd International Conference on Distributed Computing Systems, pp. 305–314. IEEE (2012)
9. Corritore, C.L., Marble, R.P., Wiedenbeck, S., Kracher, B., Chandran, A.: Measuring online trust of websites: credibility, perceived ease of use, and risk. In: A Conference on a Human Scale. 11th Americas Conference on Information Systems, AMCIS 2005, Omaha, Nebraska, USA, 11–14 August 2005 (2005)
10. Chen, D.B., Sun, H.L., Tang, Q., Tian, S.Z., Xie, M.: Identifying influential spreaders in complex networks by propagation probability dynamics. Chaos **29**, 033120 (2019)
11. Ling, G., Lyu, M.R., King, I.: Ratings meet reviews, a combined approach to recommend. RecSys 2014. - In: Proceedings of the 8th ACM Conference on Recommender Systems, pp. 105–112 (2014)
12. Sun, H.L., Chng, E., Garibaldi, J.M., Simon, S., Chen, D.B.: A fast community detection method in bipartite networks by distance dynamics. Phys. A **496**, 108–120 (2018)
13. Goyal, P., Ferrara, E.: Graph embedding techniques, applications, and performance: a survey. Knowl.-Based Syst. **151**(JUL.1), 78–94 (2017)
14. Khosravifar, B., Bentahar, J., Gomrokchi, M., Alam, R.: CRM: an efficient trust and reputation model for agent computing. Knowl.-Based Syst. **30**, 1–16 (2012)
15. Zhou, Y., Lei, T., Zhou, T.: A robust ranking algorithm to spamming. Europhys. Lett. (epl) **94**, 48002 (2010)
16. Laureti, P., Moret, L., Zhang, Y.C., Yu, Y.K.: Information filtering via iterative refinement. EPL (Europhysics Letters) **75**, 1006 (2007)

17. Liao, H., Zeng, A., Xiao, R., Ren, Z.M., Chen, D.B., Zhang, Y.C.: Ranking reputation and quality in online rating systems. PLoS ONE 9(5), e97146 (2014)
18. Gao, J., Dong, Y.W., Shang, M.S., Cai, S.M., Zhou, T.: Group-based ranking method for online rating systems with spamming attacks. EPL (Europhysics Letters) 110, 28003 (2015)
19. Gao, J., Zhou, T.: Evaluating user reputation in online rating systems via an iterative group-based ranking method physica A: Statist. Mech. Appl. 473, 546–560 (2015)
20. Lee, D., Lee, M., Kim, B.: Deviation-based spam-filtering method via stochastic approach. EPL (Europhysics Letters) 121, 68004 (2018)
21. Wu, Y.Y., Guo, Q., Liu, J.G., Zhang, Y.C.: Effect of the initial configuration for user-object reputation systems. Physica A: Stat. Mech. Appl. 502, 288–294 (2018)
22. Wu, L., Ren, Z., Ren, X.L., Zhang, J., Lü, L.: Eliminating the effect of rating bias on reputation systems. Complexity 2018 (2018)
23. Sun, H.L., Liang, K.P., Liao, H., Chen, D.B.: Evaluating user reputation of online rating systems by rating statistical patterns. Knowl.-Based Syst. 219, 106895 (2021)
24. Lü, L., Chen, D., Ren, X.L., Zhang, Q.M., Zhang, Y.C., Zhou, T.: Vital nodes identification in complex networks. Phys. Rep. 650, 1–63 (2016)
25. Biggs, N., Lloyd, E.K., Wilson, R.J.: Graph Theory Oxford, pp. 1736–1936. University Press, Oxford (1986)
26. Asratian, A.S., Denley, T.M., Häggkvist, R.: Bipartite Graphs and their Applications, vol. 131. Cambridge University Press, Cambridge (1998)
27. Sarwar, B., Karypis, G., Konstan, J., Riedl, J.: Item-based collaborative filtering recommendation algorithms. In: Proceedings of the 10th International Conference on World Wide Web, pp. 285–295 (2001)
28. Breese, J.S., Heckerman, D., Kadie, C.: Empirical analysis of predictive algorithms for collaborative filtering. arXiv preprint arXiv:1301.7363 (2013)
29. Jiang, Y., Liu, J., Tang, M., Liu, X.: An effective web service recommendation method based on personalized collaborative filtering. In: 2011 IEEE International Conference on Web Services, pp. 211–218. IEEE (2011)
30. Tkalcic, M., Kunaver, M., Tasic, J., Košir, A.: Personality based user similarity measure for a collaborative recommender system. In: Proceedings of the 5th Workshop on Emotion in Human-Computer Interaction-Real world challenges, pp. 30–37 (2009)
31. Herlocker, J., Konstan, J.A., Riedl, J.: An empirical analysis of design choices in neighborhood-based collaborative filtering algorithms. Inform. Retrieval 5(4), 287–310 (2002)
32. Herlocker, J.L., Konstan, J.A., Terveen, L.G., Riedl, J.T.: Evaluating collaborative filtering recommender systems. ACM Trans. Inform. Syst. (TOIS) 22(1), 5–53 (2004)

Predicting Upvotes and Downvotes in Location-Based Social Networks Using Machine Learning

Jianxi Zhang, Jinyan Zhu, Tianzheng Meng, Chenfan Zhuang, and Yang Chen[✉]

School of Computer Science, Fudan University, Shanghai 200433, China
{jianxizhang18,jinyanzhu19,chenyang}@fudan.edu.cn,
tianzhengmeng@hotmail.com, zhuangchenfan@gmail.com

Abstract. Nowadays, Online Social Networks (OSNs) have become indispensable spaces for people to express their opinions. In order to evaluate comments, tips, answers or posts, most OSNs design "upvote" or "like" buttons, and some of them provide "downvote" or "dislike" buttons as well. While there are some existing works making predictions related to upvote, downvote prediction has never been systematically explored in OSNs before. However, downvote is just as meaningful and informative as upvote, representing opposite voices. In this paper, we focus on predicting both numbers of downvotes and upvotes together on Foursquare, a leading location-based social network (LBSN). Our work has three main contributions. Firstly, by unprecedentedly viewing downvotes and upvotes together from a holistic prospective, we discern features that are effective to the differentiation of both downvote and upvote prediction. Secondly, by making use of structural hole theory and information theory, we propose a robust model that can be used for both downvote and upvote prediction. To the best of our knowledge, we are the first to predict number of downvotes in OSNs. Finally, we complete a thorough prediction performance and feature importance analysis. Our predictions of downvotes and upvotes using XGBoost model achieve AUC scores of 0.99 and 0.98, separately. In other words, our approach not only fills the gap of downvote prediction, but also increases the prediction performance of upvote prediction in OSNs.

Keywords: Location-based social networks (LBSNs) · Machine learning · Social graph analysis · Structural hole theory · Downvote prediction

1 Introduction

Online Social Networks (OSNs) [14] are widely used for communication and connection between people. It is one of the biggest uses of the Internet nowadays. Different types of OSNs include Blog [1] such as Facebook, Twitter, and Tumblr; discussion forum such as Quora, Reddit and Zhihu; as well as location-based social network (LBSN) [21] such as Foursquare [6], Yelp [18], and Dianping [11]. One of the key features of these OSNs is "upvote", which is more commonly called "like". Upvote has multiple uses in OSNs, including expressing preferences and trending content. While most OSNs provide upvote or like function [8], the "downvote" or "dislike" function [13], which may result in negative emotions, also reflects a user's opinion from another angle. Blogs like Facebook and Twitter, which focus on sharing content, only have upvote function, for the reason that downvote would reduce people's willingness to share [8]. Other OSNs, such as Foursquare [6], Quora and Reddit, use downvote to manifest comprehensive viewpoints. While there are many existing works about upvote, such as predicting popularity of Reddit post [10], and predicting answer quality on generic social Q&A sites [17], downvote is often overlooked. Nonetheless, sometimes conclusions extracted from upvote would be extremely misleading if ignoring downvote. For example, a viewpoint with a lot of upvotes does not guarantee correctness, for it may be controversial if it has a large amount of downvotes too. Hence, only combining upvote with downvote could ensure us to get a panorama of the community's attitudes toward a certain post.

Our work mainly focuses on Foursquare, one of the most popular LBSNs. Foursquare has two key functions: User interaction and point of interest (POI) recommendation [28]. Through user-generated content (UGC) called tips, other users could understand POIs from those who have been there. Based on this, Foursquare allows publishers to upvote or downvote tips, which may affect the credibility of tips significantly. Also, according to [7], Foursquare was considering adding downvote to tips as a feature in tip ranking algorithm, making downvote prediction on Foursquare even more useful. It allows Foursquare to detect negative emotions on a tip in advance, and adjust tips ranking dynamically.

In this paper, we focus on the problem of predicting both upvotes and downvotes in LBSNs. We crawl a Foursquare dataset and then build a supervised machine learning-based model for the prediction. In addition to conventional features related to tip publisher, venue and tip context, we leverage structural hole theory [19] and information theory to extract some unique features to further enhance the prediction performance. We have made the following three key contributions. First, we extract a series of features according to the Foursquare dataset, and conduct a data-driven study to show how they could distinguish between upvote/downvote tips and ordinary tips[1]. A set of features related to descriptive information, venue, and tip context has been chosen, including the number of tips posted by the publisher, the number of friends or followers of the tip publisher, the number of unique visitors at the venue, length of tip context, etc. Second, we build a machine learning model for the upvote/downvote prediction. Besides conventional features, we adopt both structural hole theory and information theory to enhance the prediction. The entropy of countries and venue categories that the publisher has visited and the effective size have been selected as new features for the model, and they play an important role in making the prediction more accurate.

---

[1] Here an ordinary tip denotes a tip without any upvote and downvote.

Finally, applying our model to downvote prediction, XGBoost [5] model shows an AUC score of 0.99. When using the same model on upvote prediction, the achieved AUC score is 0.98. Compared with the current baseline [27], which has a low precision of about 0.5 for SVM model, our SVM model in upvote prediction outperforms it with a precision of 0.74. Also, our feature importance analysis indicates that features related with venues are the most critical to the performance in general. More specifically, country entropy is in the dominant place of downvote prediction, while the outcome of upvote prediction is driven by a more diversified feature set.

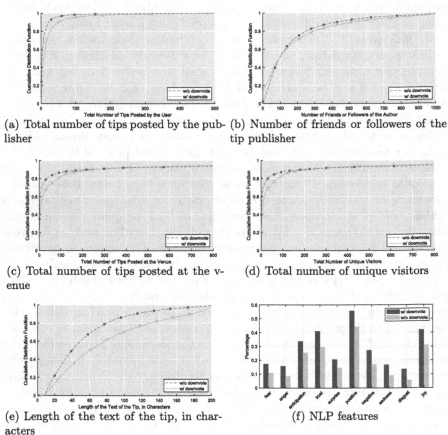

(a) Total number of tips posted by the publisher

(b) Number of friends or followers of the tip publisher

(c) Total number of tips posted at the venue

(d) Total number of unique visitors

(e) Length of the text of the tip, in characters

(f) NLP features

Fig. 1. Feature differences between downvoted and non-downvoted tips.

2   Data Collection and Conventional Feature Analysis

In this section, we will firstly describe our dataset in Sect. 2.1, and then examine some conventional features to distinguish between upvote/downvote tips and ordinary tips in Sect. 2.2.

2.1 Dataset

We crawled our dataset from January 15th, 2021, using Foursquare API and a distributed Python crawler developed by us. After selecting a popular tip publisher as the starting point, we managed to use BFS algorithm to fetch 1.6 million entries, and each entry contains all the information related to a user, i.e., basic user profile, his/her posted tips (tip content, venue, number of upvotes and downvotes), and a friend list. Because of the adoption of BFS algorithm, the whole dataset represents a subnetwork of Foursquare. Therefore, for any given tip, we can extract the information of its publisher, venue, and the tip publisher's ego network.

2.2 Analysis of Conventional Features

Normally, it takes a period of time for tips to gain upvotes and downvotes. Therefore, we examine a set of conventional features to distinguish between upvote/downvote tips and ordinary tips.

By observing the dataset, it is natural to generate the idea that whether a tip will be upvote or downvote is mainly affected by three domains of factors, i.e., descriptive information of tip publishers, venue information, and tip content information:

- `Descriptive information`: since descriptive information is a compelling exposure of the publishers' historical behavior, we extract some common statistics such as *"number of tips posted," "the number of venues where tips were posted."*
- `Venue`: One unique character of LBSN is that every tip is associated with a venue, such as a bar, a restaurant, or a scene. Therefore, the popularity of the venue will have a significant impact on the tip's vote number. To reflect the influence of venue, we select the following features, i.e., *"number of tips posted at the venue," "number of upvotes received by tips posted at the venue," "number of unique visitors at the venue,"* and *"venue category defined by Foursquare."*
- `Tip context`: the tip content is also relevant to the numbers of upvotes and downvotes it received. For example, the information density, the attitude, and the correctness will all give the readers positive or negative feelings, and then further lead to the vote behavior. Here, we mainly use NLP measurements, such as LIWC [23] and NRC Emotion Lexicon [22]. The open-source tool used is named lexica[2].

To catch a glimpse of whether these features are distinct when applying to tips with and without upvote/downvote, we select two representative features from each of the three feature categories, and visualize their distributions as shown in Fig. 1. Specifically, for sentiment analyzing, since the lexica library provides 10 types of sentiments and emotions including *negative, positive, anger, anticipation, disgust, fear, joy, sadness, surprise, trust*, we use all of them and simply

---

[2] https://github.com/AbdulSaleh/lexica.

use a binary statistic of 0 or 1 to indicate whether the text includes the words of certain type of sentiment or emotion. In general, it is satisfying that all these selected features are discriminative to our predicting target. Features extracted from downvoted tips, the red line of Fig. 1, are validated to be more "active" in all kinds of criteria. More concretely, downvoted tips, as well as publishers and venues associated with them, are more likely to possess more posted tips, more friends or followers, more unique visitors, longer text, and stronger emotions. It can be assumed that such characteristics could lead to higher attention paid on the tips. Given the fact that only a small fraction of tips on Foursquare have downvote, it is reasonable that high attention of tips within the community lays the foundation of gaining downvote. The same feature analysis is also conducted on upvoting scenario generating similar outputs. Therefore, it is natural to leverage these features to further build a supervised machine learning classifier to uncover upvote/downvote tips.

3   System Design and Implementation

In this section, we propose a robust machine learning classifier with newly added features, which can be applied to both upvote and downvote prediction, as shown in Fig. 2. Section 3.1 provides an overview for the design and basic workflow of our system. Later, Sect. 3.2 and 3.3 introduce the two categories of newly added features, i.e., entropy and effective size, and demonstrate their effectiveness, separately. Finally, Sect. 3.4 describes the details of model construction and the differences between upvote and downvote prediction.

3.1   Overview

As shown in Fig. 2, our model has a feature list with four different types. Except for the conventional features mentioned in Sect. 2.2, we also add some sophisticated and meaningful features, entropy and effective size, to feature list, which will be elaborated in the following subsections. With sampled dataset divided into training set and test set, we could extract feature list of the training set and feed it into upvote/downvote classifiers. The classifiers are different supervised machine learning models, and each of them makes predictions for whether a tip will be upvoted/downvoted. After the classifiers are successfully trained, we evaluate their performance on the test set. Also, it is worth mentioning that the technologies such as location spoofing [30], would not weaken our results. This is because our model does not contain locations of those users who conduct upvote/downvote.

3.2   Entropy

In this subsection, we introduce entropy, a concept derived from information theory, to our feature list. Both country entropy and category entropy are used as the features. For the country entropy of a publisher, it is an indicator of the

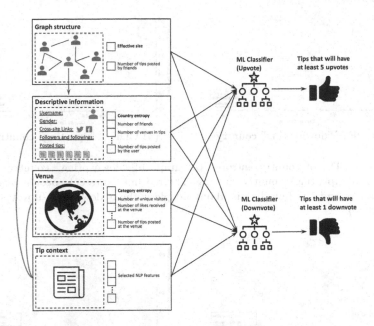

Fig. 2. The prediction model of a Foursquare tip's upvote and downvote

number of different countries and regions the publisher has visited. In detail, the "upvoting" entropy only includes the locations of those upvoted tips, while the "downvoting" entropy collects the places of tips with downvotes. Similarly, the category entropy defines the degree of difference of the tips' category. We also distinguish the "upvoting" and "downvoting" situation for the category entropy.

We calculate the entropy according to its definition. Using the country entropy as the example, the algorithm needs the probability of each country (P_{cnty}) to get the result. In the "upvoting" situation, $P_{upvoting_{cnty}}$ is defined as the ratio of the number of upvoted tips showing the country as location to the total number of tips, as shown in Eq. (1):

$$P_{upvoting_{cnty}} = \frac{number(upvoting_{cnty})}{number(upvoting_{tips})} \tag{1}$$

Then as in Eq. (2), for each publisher p, we can get the entropy using the following equation:

$$Entropy(upvoting_p) = \sum_{upvoting_{cnty}} P_{upvoting_{cnty}} \times log(P_{upvoting_{cnty}}) \tag{2}$$

Then we can get the other three entropy metrics – "downvoting" country entropy, "upvoting" category entropy and "downvoting" category entropy – in the same way.

Figure 3(a) shows the cumulative distribution function (CDF) of "downvoting" country entropy of all the Foursquare tip publishers. We can see that over

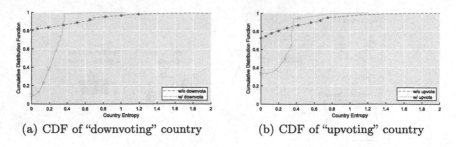

(a) CDF of "downvoting" country   (b) CDF of "upvoting" country

Fig. 3. The CDF of country entropy: (a) graph of "downvoting" country entropy; (b) graph of "upvoting" country entropy. The red line represents people with down-votes/upvotes and the blue line is about people without downvotes/upvotes. (Color figure online)

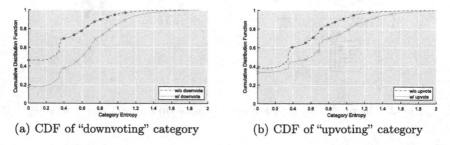

(a) CDF of "downvoting" category   (b) CDF of "upvoting" category

Fig. 4. The CDF of category entropy: (a) graph of "downvoting" category entropy; (b) graph of "upvoting" category entropy. The red line represents people with down-votes/upvotes and the blue line is about people without downvotes/upvotes. (Color figure online)

80% of the publishers without being downvoted have an entropy of 0, which means they always label themselves as in the same place. For those whose tips are downvoted, on the contrary, the entropy varies for different publishers. Only about 10% of these publishers have an entropy of 0 and the range of 0 to 0.4 almost includes all the publishers we sampled. This indicates that people tend to visit more than 1 but still limited places. Things are similar for "upvoting" country entropy (Fig. 3(b)), except that this time about 70% of the publishers without upvotes receive the entropy of 0 and more than 30% of those with upvotes have the "0" entropy.

When we look at the category entropy (Fig. 4(a)), it shows that for publishers without downvotes, those whose entropies are 0 cover more than 40% of the total number while the percentage is about 10% for publishers with downvotes. The distribution of the category entropy is similar in both situations. However, for a certain entropy, the number of publishers with downvotes is less than the number of publishers without them. This indicates people with downvotes are having a higher entropy in general. As shown in Fig. 4(b), the percentage of people is always lower for publishers with upvotes than for those without them.

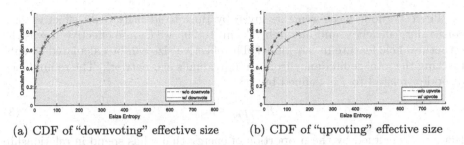

(a) CDF of "downvoting" effective size   (b) CDF of "upvoting" effective size

Fig. 5. The CDF of effective size: (a) graph of "downvoting" effective size; (b) graph of "upvoting" effective size. The red line represents people with downvotes/upvotes and the blue line is about people without downvotes/upvotes. (Color figure online)

Compared with the "downvoting" situation, the entropy for "upvoting" is more diverse.

The "downvoting" situation and the "upvoting" situation can both be explained with the fact that people prefer those who like to travel around or share different things of life and may be attracted to give their comments. Besides, people who are influential on the social platform are more likely to make controversial remarks, thus receiving more upvotes and downvotes. To understand the difference between "downvoting" and "upvoting", we notice that compared with giving upvotes, publishers are more cautious when giving downvotes, so the range of people being downvoted are smaller than the one of those with upvotes, which means a greater difference with general situation in entropy distribution. Therefore, as can be seen in Fig. 3 and Fig. 4, the two entropy metrics have a greater effect on "downvoting".

3.3 Effective Size

Another newly-added feature is effective size. By adding effective size originated from the structural hole theory [19], we add another aspect to our feature list: graph structure. As graph structure is relevant to the information inflow and outflow to certain tips, it is likely to be useful for predictions. The effective size is a quantitative measure of the non-redundancy size of an individual's ego network. Defined by Burt [4], the effective size is used as one of the four measurements to identify structural hole spanners (SHS) in a social network. In social networks, the connections between people form small groups in the large community. According to the structural hole theory, the unconnected parts between the groups form structural holes, and individuals who occupy the holes are defined as SHS. Being an SHS, an individual has advantages of both information and control. Information advantage means that one can access information from different sources, and because of those distinct information, one can be more influential between groups. Thus, it is meaningful to examine the upvotes and downvotes of SHS and non-SHS publishers.

There are four measurements given by Burt to identify SHS: effective size, constraint, efficiency, and hierarchy. As in [16,29], we choose effective size as the structural hole feature in our model. The effective size can be calculated by subtracting the total redundancy from an individual's ego-network. The redundancy of node i related to j is defined by

$$R = p_{iq} - m_{jq}. \tag{3}$$

Here, p_{iq} is defined by the proportion of energy that i has spend in relationship with q, and m_{jq} is given by j's interaction with q over j's strongest relationship among all the users.

Then, we can calculate the total redundancy of i's ego-network by summing up all of q's redundancy in the network.

Thus, the definition of effective size is as follows:

$$\sum_j \left[1 - \sum_q p_{iq} m_{jq} \right], q \neq i, j \tag{4}$$

There is also a simpler approach given by Borgatti [2], in which the redundancy is given by

$$R = \frac{2t}{n}, \tag{5}$$

where t is the number of the total non-ego ties in the ego-network, and n is the number of total non-ego nodes. Thus, we have the equation for effective size as follows:

$$n - \frac{2t}{n} \tag{6}$$

We build the ego-network graphs of 1.6 million users from Foursquare, and calculate the effective size of each of them using EasyGraph[3]. Then, as it is shown in Fig. 5, we calculate the cumulative distribution function (CDF) of the effective size of publishers with and without upvotes, and with and without downvotes from 10,000 random samples.

Figure 5(a) shows the CDF of "downvoting" effective size of the Foursquare publishers, and Fig. 5(b) shows the CDF of "upvoting" effective size. In Fig. 5(a), under the same cumulative probability, the "downvoting" effective size is larger than the "upvoting" effective size. For example, 80% of publishers without downvotes have the effective size around 90, and those with downvotes have the effective size around 120. To explain the result, we may refer to the definition of effective size. As we mentioned above, effective size measures the redundancy of an ego network, and higher effective size represents lower redundancy. Publishers with high effective size are more likely to receive and release more nonredundant information, and be more influential. Thus, they are more likely to get more attention, and receive downvotes. Similarly in Fig. 5(b), the effective size of publishers with upvotes is higher than the effective size of publishers without

---

[3] https://easy-graph.github.io/.

upvotes. We also notice that the difference is larger in Fig. 5(b) than in Fig. 5(a). 80% of publishers with and without upvotes have the effective size of 200 and 90, compared to the effective size of 120 and 90 in "downvoting". This can be explained by the fact that publishers with more non-redundant information are more likely to post more valuable and recognized content than controversial content. Thus, the impact of effective size in upvoting is more significant than downvoting.

3.4   Model Construction

Our downvote and upvote prediction have similar feature lists and models. However, there are some subtle differences between them, so we firstly discuss the process of downvote prediction. As discussed in Sect. 2, we extracted and applied 52 features. In our study, we randomly select 10,000 tips as our training set and 2,000 tips as test set. We restrict that one publisher can only have at most one tip in the training or test set. Also, tips with 0 downvote are recognized as negative instances and tips with 1 or more downvotes are recognized as positive instances. Thus, we convert this predicting process into a binary classification problem.

Then, we predict upvotes using the same model constructing methods, except for some adjustments of features and classifying method: (1) we remove the total number of "likes" received by previous tips of the publisher, assuming that previous upvoting number would have a strong correlation with the incoming one, and thus should not be involved in this model; (2) we reset the boundary of positive and negative outputs to 5, which means only tips with 5 or more upvotes are recognized as positive instances, and others are regarded as negative.

Both downvote and upvote prediction leverages a supervised machine learning-based classifier. To begin with, we feed selected data to prevailing machine learning algorithms, including Decision Tree (DT) [24], Support Vector Machine (SVM) [12], Naive Bayes (NB) [9], Random Forest (RF) [3], and XGBoost [5] algorithms. To achieve the best performance, we apply a grid search method to every algorithm to find the best fitting parameters, as shown in Table 1.

4   Evaluation of Prediction Performance

4.1   Performance Evaluation

In this subsection, we use four classical metrics to evaluate the classifier, i.e., precision, recall, F1-score, and AUC. To define these four metrics, we use 4 parameters TP, FP, TN, and FN, representing true positive, false positive, true negative, and false negative respectively. Besides AUC, whose meaning is the area under the ROC curve, the definitions are as follows:

$$Precision = \frac{TP}{TP + FP} \qquad (7)$$

$$Recall = \frac{TP}{TP + FN} \tag{8}$$

$$F1 - Score = \frac{2 \times Precision \times Recall}{Precision + Recall} \tag{9}$$

Since our sampled dataset is well balanced, we use macro averaged precision, recall, and F1 score to evaluate the models. Thus, all the precision, recall, and F1 score mentioned in this paper are the macro averaged values of the two classes. As shown in Table 1, XGBoost achieves the best performance in downvote prediction, and it has an F1-score of 0.96 and an AUC of 0.99. Also, we notice that all three tree-based machine learning models perform well, whereas other models like SVM and NB show unsatisfactory performances. In Foursquare, the vast majority of tips do not have downvote at all, and other tips often have only 1 downvote, leading us to generate the previous idea that downvote number is nearly unpredictable at Foursquare because limited downvoting quantity means a higher stake of randomness. Nevertheless, our predicting result is encouraging that we actually can still predict the downvoting number with high credibility.

As shown in Table 2, XGBoost keeps performing the best out of 6 machine learning models in upvote prediction, with an AUC score of 0.98. Compared to downvote prediction, tree-based models (XGBoost, RF, and DT) keep showing their robustness, while other models (SVMr, SVMp, and NB) improve significantly both in precision and recall. This finding is likely due to the fact that upvoted tips are much more commonplace than downvoted tips, so the linkage between inputs and outputs is more straightforward for these rudimentary models to capture and then classify. The SVM model, with novel features added, has a precision of 0.74, a recall of 0.73, and an AUC value of 0.81, which significantly outperforms the current prediction method with a precision of about 0.5 [27].

Table 1. Prediction of Downvotes

Model	Parameter	Precision	Recall	F1	AUC
XGBoost	n_estimators = 50, learning_rate = 0.3, max_depth = 8, subsample = 1	0.96	0.96	0.96	0.99
RF	n_estimators = 50, Max depth = 11	0.93	0.93	0.93	0.97
DT	Min samples leaf = 1, Max depth = 5	0.92	0.92	0.92	0.97
SVMr	degree = 1, gamma = 0.0001, C = 100	0.70	0.70	0.70	0.77
NB	-	0.70	0.61	0.57	0.74

4.2 Feature Importance Analysis

To tell how different kinds of features contribute to the final prediction, we manage to remove features related to upvotes (not necessary in upvote prediction), user, venue, and content, separately, and then run the machine learning model again. Here, we use DT model to evaluate the importance of different feature categories, as shown in Table 3 and Table 4.

Table 2. Prediction of Upvotes

Model	Parameter	Precision	Recall	F1	AUC
XGBoost	n_estimators = 100, learning_rate = 0.3, max_depth = 10, subsample = 1	0.93	0.93	0.93	0.98
RF	n_estimators = 100, Max depth = 11	0.92	0.92	0.92	0.97
DT	Min samples leaf = 1, Max depth = 8	0.91	0.91	0.91	0.95
SVMr	degree = 1, gamma = 0.0001, C = 50	0.74	0.73	0.73	0.81
NB	–	0.73	0.69	0.67	0.79

Table 3. Prediction of Downvotes after Removing Certain Features

Features	Precision	Recall	F1	AUC
all	0.92	0.92	0.92	0.97
w/o like	0.86	0.84	0.84	0.87
w/o user	0.89	0.88	0.88	0.95
w/o venue	0.71	0.70	0.70	0.77
w/o content	0.86	0.84	0.84	0.90

In our selected features, there are 8 features that is about upvotes, i.e., (1) total number, median, average and standard deviation of upvotes received by previous tips of the publisher; (2) total number, median, average and standard deviation of upvotes received by tips posted at the venue. These features are worth studying because they possibly reveal the correlation between upvote and downvote. Therefore, Table 3 manifests the predicting results after ignoring these features, as well as removing features of user, venue, and content, separately. The AUC score using complete dataset and DT is 0.97, and it decreases the most to 0.77 after ignoring features of venue, suggesting that venue-related features are the most important to downvote prediction. If removing upvoting features, usage data features, and tip context features separately, the AUC would be 0.87, 0.95, and 0.90, indicating that these features are useful but not critical. In Table 4, with AUC score dropping from 0.95 to 0.77 after removing venue-related features, venue continues to demonstrate its position as the most influential fac-

Table 4. Prediction of Upvotes after Removing Certain Features

Features	Precision	Recall	F1	AUC
all	0.91	0.91	0.91	0.95
w/o user	0.90	0.90	0.90	0.95
w/o venue	0.70	0.70	0.70	0.77
w/o content	0.91	0.91	0.91	0.95

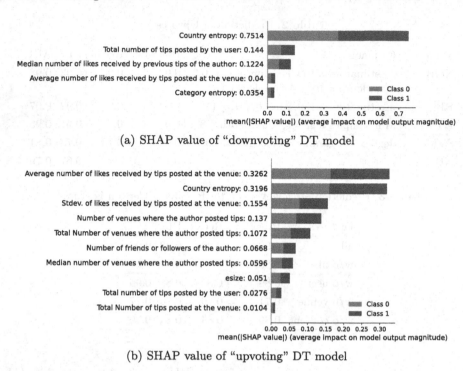

(a) SHAP value of "downvoting" DT model

(b) SHAP value of "upvoting" DT model

Fig. 6. The features with highest SHAP values: (a) features with top 5 highest SHAP values in upvote prediction; (b) features with top 10 highest SHAP values in downvote prediction.

tor in upvoting scenario. Thus, as an LBSN, Foursquare tips' downvotes are greatly affected by their locations: some hot spots might naturally get more attention along with a higher chance of getting downvoted and upvoted. Meanwhile, whether the tip publisher or venue has a large quantity of previous upvotes does not drastically change the possibility of incoming downvotes.

Furthermore, we manage to make our model more interpretable via SHAP (SHapley Additive exPlanations), a widely used framework proposed by Lundberg et al [20], and help explain outputs of machine learning models. Specifically, the algorithm generates one SHAP value for every feature of all the samples, and that value represents the positive or negative effect brought to the outputs by the particular feature. To evaluate the importance of every feature, we calculate and aggregate the mean absolute SHAP value of features of all the samples, as shown in Fig. 6(a) and Fig. 6(b). In downvote prediction, we recognize that country entropy is the dominant feature, and it has a SHAP value of 0.75. This finding matches our previous analysis of country entropy in Sect. 3.2: About 80% tips without downvote whose publishers' country entropy is 0; yet the number is only approximate 10% when referring to those downvoted tips. Also, we can observe that in Fig. 6(a), features ranked 1st, 4th, and 5th are venue-related, corresponding our previous results that venue-related features play a critical role in downvote prediction. In Fig. 6(b), compared with downvote prediction, upvote prediction is more of an output generated from mixed features and contributed by them more evenly. Specifically, top 10 influential features include country entropy, number of "likes" received by tips posted at the venue, and some features about network structure. It is worth mentioning that the new features we add, i.e., entropy and effective size, are validated to contain wealth of information, and play significant roles in our model according to SHAP value. Also, we notice that there are 125 features used in the baseline approach [27]. In contrast, we only use 52 features and achieve a better performance. This also confirms that our newly-added features are more effective.

5 Related Work

Previous works on upvotes and tip popularity prediction adopt different methods, including machine learning methods and methods combined with NLP features. Vasconcelos et al. [27] studied the upvotes of Foursquare from three aspects. They crawled data of 13 million users. First, they predicted the popularity of the tip at the time it was posted, using all previous data. Second, they predicted the popularity evolution of tips in a certain period after it was posted. Third, they built and evaluated models on different specializations including city-based and category-based models. On predicting upvotes of a tip at the time it was posted, they set the boundary of non-upvote to lower than 5 upvotes, which is the same as our setting. Under such setups, they reached a satisfying recall of about 0.8, but the precision of around 0.5 remains to be improved.

Kasper et al. [15] conducted research on key features of review helpfulness on Metacritic, a video game reviews website. By defining helpfulness of a review as its upvotes divided by the sum of upvotes and downvotes, they found out that helpfulness is correlated with the score given by the review. Then, they built prediction models for helpfulness, and achieved up to the F1 score of 0.64, using only text-related features. Scellato and Mascolo [25] analyzed the pattern of user activities of an LBSN. They showed that the number of check-ins and the number of places per publisher followed a log-normal distribution. Also, they showed that due to the difference between the system's restrictions on checking-in new locations and adding new friends, the distributions of friends and check-ins/places varied.

There are studies on predicting upvotes on LBSNs studying different platforms. Li et al. [17] did a research on predicting answer quality on ResearchGate (RG). They used two groups of characteristics: those could be obtained directly from the web content, and those were generated by post-processing. They sampled 1128 posts in 107 question threads, used Naive Bayes, SVM and multiple regression models for prediction, and reached a highest accuracy of 0.62. Segall and Zamoshchin [26] conducted a study on predicting Reddit post popularity. Their dataset contains a random sampling of 2 million posts from Reddit. They used Naive Bayes, SVM, and linear regression to predict, and used an NLP approach called stemming to decrease the feature set. Overall, ResearchGate and Reddit both provide a downvote option, yet none of the previous work makes predictions about it.

6 Conclusion

In this paper, we undertake predictions of Foursquare tips' upvotes (outperforms previous results of the baseline [27]) and downvotes (the first prediction on OSN's downvotes to our acknowledgement) and on our selected dataset of all crawled 1.6 million Foursquare users' data. Firstly, we establish a comprehensive feature list and conduct analysis about key features. In addition, to build a supervised machine learning-based prediction, we further introduce novel features such as geographical and categorical entropy (information theory), effective size (structural hole theory), and NLP features of tips. Furthermore, we conduct a data-driven analysis on our model and we can see satisfying outcomes. Our XGBoost model shows an AUC value of 0.99 in downvote prediction and 0.98 in upvote prediction. Given the fact that our prediction is quite accurate, social networking service providers can leverage it to improve user satisfaction by adjusting recommending weight dynamically and promptly. Lastly, we dive deeper to calculate the contribution of different features by removing some of them and using SHAP value. It turns out that the venue-related features of the tip and the publisher are the most influential to upvotes and downvotes, whereas the tip content itself and the publisher's social network are not as crucial as we thought. This is largely because Foursquare is an LBSN, and publishers' information flow is mostly decided by venues. Our findings are helpful to both LBSN service providers and users. Besides, Foursquare is a place for people to comment on city venues, and therefore we believe that our work can be extended to a wider range of comment-based OSNs, such as hotel evaluation like Booking.com, answer evaluation like Quora, and movie evaluation like Rotten Tomatoes.

Acknowledgments. This work is sponsored by National Natural Science Foundation of China (No. 62072115, No. 71731004, No. 61602122). Jinyan Zhu and Tianzheng Meng have equal contribution.

References

1. Ali-Hasan, N., Adamic, L.A.: Expressing social relationships on the blog through links and comments. In: Proceedings of AAAI ICWSM (2007)
2. Borgatti, S.P.: Structural holes: unpacking Burt's redundancy measures. Connections **20**(1), 35–38 (1997)
3. Breiman, L.: Random forests. Mach. Learn. **45**(1), 5–32 (2001)
4. Burt, R.S.: Structural Holes. Harvard University Press, Cambridge (1992)
5. Chen, T., Guestrin, C.: XGBoost: a scalable tree boosting system. In: Proceedings of ACM KDD, pp. 785–794 (2016)

6. Chen, Y., Hu, J., Xiao, Y., Li, X., Hui, P.: Understanding the user behavior of Foursquare: a data-driven study on a global scale. IEEE Trans. Comput. Soc. Syst. **7**(4), 1019–1032 (2020)
7. Cruz, E., Kapicioglu, B.: Tip Ranker: A ML Approach to Ranking Short Reviews. In: RecSys Posters (2016)
8. Eranti, V., Lonkila, M.: The social significance of the Facebook Like button. First Monday 20 (2015)
9. Friedman, N., Geiger, D., Goldszmidt, M.: Bayesian network classifiers. Mach. Learn. **29**(2), 131–163 (1997)
10. Glenski, M., Weninger, T.: Predicting user-interactions on reddit. In: Proceedings of the 2017 IEEE/ACM International Conference on Advances in Social Networks Analysis and Mining 2017, pp. 609–612 (2017)
11. Gong, Q., et al.: DeepScan: exploiting deep learning for malicious account detection in location-based social networks. IEEE Commun. Mag. **56**(11), 21–27 (2018)
12. Hearst, M., Dumais, S., Osuna, E., Platt, J., Scholkopf, B.: Support vector machines. IEEE Intell. Syst. Appl. **13**(4), 18–28 (1998)
13. Davis, J.L., Graham, T.: Emotional consequences and attention rewards: the social effects of ratings on Reddit. Inform. Commun. Soc. **24**(5), 649–666 (2021)
14. Jin, L., Chen, Y., Wang, T., Hui, P., Vasilakos, A.V.: Understanding user behavior in online social networks: a survey. IEEE Commun. Mag. **51**(9), 144–150 (2013)
15. Kasper, P., Koncar, P., Santos, T., Gütl, C.: On the role of score, genre and text in helpfulness of video game reviews on metacritic. In: Proceeding of 6th SNAMS, pp. 75–82. IEEE (2019)
16. Kwon, Y.D., Mogavi, R.H., Haq, E.U., Kwon, Y., Ma, X., Hui, P.: Effects of Ego Networks and Communities on Self-Disclosure in an Online Social Network. In: Proceedings of ASONAM (2019)
17. Li, L., He, D., Jeng, W., Goodwin, S., Zhang, C.: Answer quality characteristics and prediction on an academic Q&A Site: a case study on ResearchGate. In: Proceedings of WWW, pp. 1453–1458 (2015)
18. Li, W., et al.: DeepPick: a deep learning approach to unveil outstanding users with public attainable features. IEEE Trans. Knowl. Data Eng. (2022)
19. Lin, Z., Zhang, Y., Gong, Q., Chen, Y., Oksanen, A., Ding, A.Y.: Structural hole theory in social network analysis: a review. IEEE Trans. Comput. Soc. Syst. **9**(3), 724–739 (2022)
20. Lundberg, S.M., Lee, S.I.: A Unified approach to interpreting model predictions. In: Proceedings of NIPS (2017)
21. Luo, H., Guo, B., Wang, Z., Feng, Y., et al.: Friendship prediction based on the fusion of topology and geographical features in LBSN. In: Proceedings of HPCC & EUC, pp. 2224–2230. IEEE (2013)
22. Mohammad, S.M., Turney, P.D.: NRC emotion lexicon. Nat. Res. Council, Canada **2**, 234 (2013)
23. Pennebaker, J.W., Francis, M.E., Booth, R.J.: Linguistic inquiry and word count: LIWC 2001. Mahwah, NJ: Lawrence Erlbaum Associates (2001)
24. Quinlan, J.R.: C4.5: programs for machine learning. Morgan Kaufmann Publishers, Inc. (1993)
25. Scellato, S., Mascolo, C.: Measuring user activity on an online location-based social network. In: Proceedings of INFOCOM Workshops, pp. 918–923. IEEE (2011)
26. Segall, J., Zamoshchin, A.: Predicting reddit post popularity (2012)
27. Vasconcelos, M., Almeida, J.M., Gonçalves, M.A.: Predicting the popularity of micro-reviews: a foursquare case study. Inform. Sci. **325**, 355–374 (2015)

28. Ye, M., Yin, P., Lee, W.C., Lee, D.L.: Exploiting geographical influence for collaborative point-of-interest recommendation. In: Proceedings of ACM SIGIR, pp. 325–334 (2011)
29. Ying, Q.F., Chiu, D.M., Zhang, X.: Diversity of a user's friend circle in OSNs and its use for profiling. In: Proceeding of SocInfo (2018)
30. Zhao, B., Sui, D.Z.: True lies in geospatial big data: detecting location spoofing in social media. Ann. GIS **23**(1), 1–14 (2017)

How Does Participation Experience in Collective Behavior Contribute to Participation Willingness: A Survey of Migrant Workers in China

Meng Cai[1]([✉]) [iD], Han Luo[1] [iD], Xiao Meng[2] [iD], and Haifeng Du[3] [iD]

[1] School of Humanities and Social Sciences, Xi'an Jiaotong University, Xi'an 710049, China
mengcai@mail.xjtu.edu.cn
[2] School of Journalism and New Media, Xi'an Jiaotong University, Xi'an 710049, China
[3] School of Public Policy and Administration, Xi'an Jiaotong University, Xi'an 710049, China

Abstract. Aiming at investigating the "repetitive dilemma" of collective behavior and the conditions under which participation experience affects willingness to participate. Based on a survey of migrant workers from Shenzhen in China, this study constructs a mediated moderating model, focusing on the moderating role of social networks in the relationship and the mediating role of institutional support. The results show that collective behavior participation experience has a significant positive predictive effect on willingness to participate. Institutional support has a significant negative predictive effect on willingness to participate in collective behavior. Social networks negatively moderate the relationship between collective behavior participation experience and institutional support, while positively moderating the relationship between institutional support and willingness to participate in collective behavior. The relationship between collective behavior participation experience and willingness to participate was negatively moderated by social networks through the indirect effect of institutional support. The results of the study have implications for exploring the repetition and formation conditions of collective behavior and guiding the group of migrant workers to reasonably express their willingness to participate in group demands.

Keywords: Collective behavior · Social network · Institutional support · Migrant workers · Repetitive dilemma

1 Introduction

China today is in an important social transition period, where some social conflicts and social issues, such as economic reforms and land acquisition and resettlement, have triggered many social events, and some collective protest behaviors, such as demonstrations, strikes, illegal occupations of public places, protests, and vandalism, seriously threaten China's social stability [1]. In the context of the new crown epidemic, complex collective behaviors such as collective actions against the epidemic have emerged again at the grassroots level [2]. As an important factor affecting social stability and solidarity, collective behavior is a common governance challenge faced by governments at all levels. Therefore, reasonable and appropriate handling of collective behavior is conducive to regulating the relationship between various social groups and maintaining social stability and unity.

In the existing studies, collective behavior is more often assumed to be any action taken by members of the same group in a political context to achieve group goals and improve group status based on objective conditions [3]. Related studies have mostly started from the psychosocial dimension, emphasizing the subjective perception factors that shape the willingness to participate in collective behavior [4]. For example, some researchers focus on the role of trust and risk perception in climate change-related collective behavior [5]. Becker & Tausch [6] constructs three important antecedents for the formation of willingness to participate in collective behavior based on social deprivation theory and social identity theory: anger at perceived injustice, social identification, and beliefs about group efficacy. In addition, some objective factors that can influence should not be ignored. On the one hand, the size, composition, and structural location of the network can have an impact on the formation of collective behavior, and in some cases, additional network connections can reduce participation in collective behavior [7]. A previous study noted that people on the edges of social networks are able to generate collective action, while mobilization efforts at the core lead to a decrease in protest [8]. On the other hand, the policy context of collective behavior influences the level of political participation, with low levels of service provision generating high levels of collective behavior [9]. When the level of government trust is high, an alternative option for collective behavior is to draw support from institutional structures.

However, with the rapid development of the economy, the accumulated social conflicts formed by inadequate resources and distribution imbalances are increasingly intensified and more likely to trigger repetitive collective behavior. Under the influence of external factors, collective behavior is characterized as short-term, rapid, and repetitive [3]. Only a small number of studies have focused on the possibility that past experiences may influence future participation in collective behavior [10]. Under the influence of past experiences, individuals who have experienced collective behavior participation are more likely to consider similar ways of dealing with the dilemma of inequity and relative deprivation, i.e., engaging in collective behavior again. Moreover, existing researches on the mechanisms of transformation between historical participation experiences and willingness to participation in future collective behavior are still at an initial stage and have not yet considered the role of social networks and external institutional support external factors.

The above-mentioned research gaps indicate that in order to further investigate the formation paths of willingness to collective behavior, it is necessary to adopt collective behavior participation experiences as explanatory variables from the perspective of social network analysis. In view of this, this study focuses on the relationship between collective behavior participation experience and willingness to participate, and clarifies the mechanisms of institutional support and social networks' roles in it. Specifically, based on the resource mobilization theory, the social network of migrant workers in Shenzhen is incorporated into the research framework as a moderating variable through an actual survey of migrant workers in Shenzhen. Based on the theory of planned behavior, the institutional support is introduced as a mediating variable to examine the interaction of network characteristics as well as the role of institutional support in the social network in influencing the willingness to participate in collective behavior. The model is designed to examine the interaction effect of network characteristics and the role of institutional support in influencing the relationship between collective behavior participation experience and willingness to participate.

2 Literature Review and Research Hypotheses

2.1 Planned Behavior and Resource Mobilization

The Planned behavior Theory (TPB). Collective behavior, as a classical problem in social science research, has not been short of theoretical explanatory perspectives. However, among the studies of collective behavior that take the behavior-will relationship as the starting point, the theory of planned behavior has received much attention. In fact, the theory of planned behavior has been widely used to explain the antecedents of behavioral will formation, arguing that attitudes toward behavior, subjective norms, and perceived behavioral control jointly lead to the formation of behavioral will [11], where attitudes are defined as individuals' positive or negative evaluations of a particular behavior. A positive attitude encourages individuals to act accordingly. Subjective norms are defined as the social pressure exerted on an individual to participation in a particular behavior, and each individual tends to conform to the expectations or views of certain important people. That is, the approval or disapproval of someone important to the individual will affect the individual's judgment of the intention of the action [12]. Perceived behavioral control is another important variable that influences individuals' behavioral intentions, and is the degree of difficulty individuals perceive in performing particular behaviors. If individuals have sufficient opportunities, resources, time, knowledge, and skills to carry out specific behaviors, then individuals may be able to be more confident about the results of behaviors, thus promoting the implementation of behaviors.

The Resource Mobilization Theory (RMT). However, collective behavior is not a behavior under isolated individuals, but a product of the mobilization of network resources and group agglomeration. The resource mobilization theory (RMT) is a classic theory for studying collective behavior, which can provide explanations for objective factors that influence collective behavior. Resource mobilization theory emphasizes that the existence of individual attitudes is not sufficient to explain why social movements emerge. Instead, resource mobilization theory proposes that the transition from condition to action depends on the availability of resources in the opportunities for collective action to occur [13]. It is through the mobilization of their social network resources that participants in collective behavior participation in social movements such as protests as a way to achieve organizational goals [14]. According to resource mobilization theory, the use of social networks to recruit members and acquire resources can help collective behavior [15]. Studies have shown that people are more likely to contribute to a collective behavior when the collective behavior is initiated by friends, colleagues, or fellow countrymen who are related to the respondent [16]. Parents' past and present involvement even predicted children's protest participation [17]. Network scale, as an important factor for contacting others and accessing resources, is related to the likelihood that collective behavior can achieve a specific goal and plays an important role in the formation of willingness to collective behavior.

2.2 Research Hypotheses

The Effect of Collective Behavior Participation Experience. Actors' experience of collective behavior participation is an important factor in studying future willingness to participation in collective behavior. Collective behaviors are unstable, characterized by rapid and unexpected changes in intensity, type, and goals, and are somewhat repetitive [18]. When faced with a dilemma caused by a sense of inequity, actors tend to deal with it in different ways. One is through institutional support, seeking help from the government, administrative office workers, etc., and the other is through non-institutional support, seeking help from relatives, friends, colleagues, and fellow countrymen.

When the help brought by institutional support resolves the dispute and conflict and compensates for the loss of benefits, the anger of the harmed group will often be appeased and mediation will be successful, otherwise, mediation will fail and the anger of group members will rise high, driving the formation of social mobilization [19]. When institutions fail, individuals are more likely to engage in protests, strikes, petitions, and other radical collective actions with the support of non-institutions. According to the theory of planned behavior, individuals who have experienced collective behaviors are more likely to choose behaviors actions in the future. On the one hand, they are more likely to form useless stereotypes about the administrative system, and will be more inclined to seek non-institutional support out of a negative attitudinal evaluation of institutional support. On the other hand, the experience of social protest activities will prompt actors to have sufficient expectations of the cost-benefit outcomes of collective action, face lower pressure in choosing the way of collective behavior, and have a higher degree of perceived behavioral control over collective behavior, which makes them inclined to participate in protest activities again through non-institutional support. Also, the collective behavior participation experience makes it easier for actors to receive recognition and support from other group members when they are willing to e participation in collective behavior again.

Therefore, according to the theory of planned behavior, actors who have experienced collective behavior participation tend to be more inclined to participation in collective behaviors such as protest activities again when faced with the dilemma of unfairness formation due to the influence of past participation experiences. Based on this study, the following hypothesis is proposed:

H1: Collective behavior participation experience can effectively promote the formation of willingness to participate in collective behavior.

The Effect of Institutional Support. Although non-institutional support is an important way for actors to seek help when facing unfair dilemmas institutional support sought by actors is also an integral and important part of the field of collective behavior research. While institutions are generally defined as regulations and norms set by policymakers, institutional support refers to support from government departments and policies that constrain or support actors' social behavior. When an actor first faces a dilemma, the actor may seek institutional support more actively because of the trust in the system, and according to the rights and obligations clearly defined by the governmental agencies in order to solve the problem they face [20].

Seeking institutional support and participating in collective behavior are alternatives. As mentioned earlier, institutional support in this study refers to the process by which actors, when faced with a dilemma caused by injustice, are able to properly deal with the problem, defend their rights, and protect their legitimate interests through relevant policy documents issued by the government or by seeking appropriate help from government agencies. The theory of planned behavior suggests that attitudes predict individual behavior in different contexts [21], and that actors who are able to solve problems with the help of institutional support inevitably lose interest in participating in collective behavior. Previous research has also pointed to cultural differences in the mobilization of collective behavior [22], and in China's long-standing governmental tradition, seeking help from the government is the primary option for actors to solve problems, followed by protest and other forms of collective behavior. The political and legal constraints imposed by authoritarian regimes can make it difficult for ordinary citizens to have a voice, and public participation in legislation has enforcement gaps that make it difficult for the public to gain support from the system, thus leading to an increase in protests [23].

Therefore, actors with institutional support will be more inclined to reflect their problems to formal organizations such as government agencies and communities when faced with dilemmas. If actors are helped by institutional support and consider it valuable and beneficial to solve problems, they will hold positive attitudes and will be more inclined to engage in behaviors such as voting in elections and reflecting problems to government agencies. At the same time, actors will be less willing to participate in collective behaviors such as petitions and protest activities. Therefore, this study proposes the following hypothesis:

H2: Institutional support can effectively weaken the formation of willingness to participate in collective behaviors.

The Moderating Role of Social Networks. Resource mobilization theory also suggests that characteristics such as the structure and size of social networks have a positive effect on the formation of willingness to engage in collective behavior [24]. For example, it is widely believed that participants in collective behavior are mobilized through pre-existing social ties and that factors such as the size of actors' social ties determine the degree of mobilization. Previous research has found that mobilization by social networks is important for sustained political participation, and that participation in one protest during a political movement increases attendance at subsequent protests, provided that a sufficient portion of an individual's social network is motivated to participate in the initial protest [25]. The size of the social network thus becomes an important factor influencing the experience of collective behavior participation and generating willingness to participate in collective behaviour.

More specifically, actors with larger network scales differ in their collective action patterns compared to those with smaller sizes [26]. Under the influence of low levels of social network scale, actors are more likely to seek institutional support, because, at low levels of social network scale, it is difficult for actors to mobilize sufficient resources to support collective behaviors to achieve their goals, increasing the pressure on actors to participate in collective behaviors [27]. In contrast, actors at high levels of social network scale have a greater ability to mobilize participation and have access to a larger number of other actors who have the willingness to participate in collective behavior. Groups composed of actors at high levels of network scale are more diverse in type and size, and also have a broader and more diverse range of forms of expression in collective behavioral participation [28]. More importantly, a high level of social network scale may reduce the price that individuals have to pay for participating in collective behavior. As the Chinese idiom goes, "The law fails when there are many lawbreakers". When acting in groups, individuals may receive less legal punishment. Actors with high levels of social network scale may be more likely to seek non-institutional support than institutional support, facilitating the willingness to engage in collective behaviour.

However, it is important to note that the effect of social networks is indirect, because collective behavior is an alternative solution when institutional support cannot be realized. To be specific, in the first half of the pathway of the influence of collective behavior participation experience on institutional support, actors with collective behavior participation experience, if their social network mobilization ability is low, their collective behavior is less likely to succeed, and they are more inclined to seek institutional support. However, actors in high-level social networks without collective behavior participation experience may be less willing to seek institutional support due to their ability to mobilize higher social network resources. In the second half of the path of the influence of institutional support on the willingness to engage in collective behavior, the more dependent the actors in low-level social networks are on institutional support, the less likely they are to form the willingness to engage in collective behavior, while the actors in high-level social networks are more likely to form the willingness to engage in collective behavior even though they are more dependent on institutional support. Based on this, this study proposes the hypothesis.

H3: Social networks negatively affect the relationship between collective behavioral engagement experiences and institutional support.

H4: Social networks positively influence the relationship between institutional support and willingness to engage in collective behavior.

The Mediating Role of Institutional Support. The formation of collective behavior has its institutional causes [29]. According to the theory of planned behavior, attitudes toward behavior, subjective norms, and perceived behavioral control jointly lead to the formation of behavioral intentions. On the one hand, individual participation in social protests may be caused by institutional inequities [30], so actors who have experienced collective behavioral participation such as social protests tend to have negative attitudinal evaluations of formal organizational sectors such as government agencies and are not inclined to seek institutional support when faced with a dilemma, while low levels of institutional support make actors more inclined to form again new willingness to engage in collective behavior. On the other hand, according to the theory of planned behavior, the higher the actor's perceived subjective norms, i.e., the higher the recognition from important people, the more likely he or she is to engage in a certain behavior, while individuals with low levels of institutional support are more likely to receive high levels of support from informal relationships such as relatives, friends, and hometowns. In addition, if actors have relevant experiences of collective behavior participation and possess relevant experience and knowledge, the stronger the perceived control behavior of actors, the easier it is to form a willingness to participate in collective behaviour.

Based on the above analysis, institutional support may mediate the relationship between collective behavior participation experience and the willingness to participate in collective behavior, and social network plays a moderating role. First, individuals with collective behavior participation experience may not be inclined to seek institutional support. At the same time, actors of different social network levels have different abilities to organize and mobilize collective behavior, which makes them tend to adopt different institutional support when facing the experience of participating in collective behavior. Then, institutional support affects the formation of willingness to participate in collective behavior to a great extent. Meanwhile, actors with different social network levels face different resistance when they abandon institutional support and seek collective behavior instead. Therefore, we argue that the moderating role of social networks in collective behavior participation experience and willingness to participate can be realized through the indirect effect of institutional support. This study proposes the following hypothesis. The moderated mediation model proposed is shown in Fig. 1.

H5: Social networks negatively moderate the relationship between collective behavior participation experience and willingness to participate through the mediating effect of institutional support.

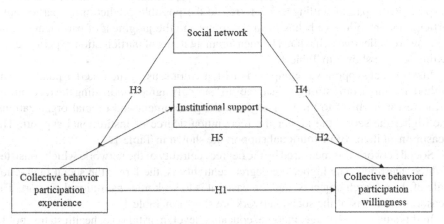

Fig. 1. Theoretical model.

3   Methodology

3.1   Data

Considering that in cities with rapid economic development, migrant workers are more likely to encounter difficulties caused by the sense of injustice, this study adopted the method of questionnaire survey to obtain data. In this study, 3 factories in Pingshan New District, Shenzhen city, Guangdong Province were randomly selected, and non-local migrant workers in the factories were selected as the research objects by the combination of quota sampling and collective sampling. A total of 600 questionnaires were collected, of which 433 were effective, with an effective recovery of 72.17%.

In the effective sample, there were 200 males, accounting for 46.2%, and 232 females, accounting for 53.6%. The age group was mainly 21–40 years old, accounting for 64.9%; 44 people were 20 years old and below, accounting for 10.2%; 86 people were 41–50 years old, accounting for 19.9%; 18 people were 51–60 years old, accounting for 4.2%; and 4 people were over 60 years old, accounting for 0.9%. The health status of "good" and "very good" was the most, 173 and 144, respectively, accounting for 40.0% and 33.3%. There were 250 married people and 171 unmarried people, accounting for 57.7% and 39.5%, respectively. The political status was mainly for the masses, 353 in total, accounting for 81.5%. The education level was mainly in junior high school, 234, accounting for 54%. A total of 151 people, accounting for 35%, had junior high school education or above.

3.2 Variables

The collective behavior of migrant workers was divided into collective behavior participation experience and collective behavior participation willingness. Participation experience referred to whether the respondents have participated in collective behavior in the past. Participation willingness referred to the possible prediction of participants' participation in collective behavior in the future and the judgment of participants' attitude toward collective behavior. The measurement items of participation experience and willingness are shown in Table 1.

Institutional support was composed of 14 questions, using the Likert 5-point scoring method, ranging from "strongly disagree" to "strongly agree", indicating the recognition of the research object to the support from the government and official organizations. The higher the score, the higher the recognition degree of institutional support. The measurement items of institutional support are shown in Table 1.

Social network was measured by the degree centrality of the network, which consisted of three questions. The higher the degree centrality is, the larger the social interaction scale of the research object is, and the easier it is to seek non-institutional support. The measurement items of the social network are shown in Table 1.

In this study, gender, age, income, education level, marital type, health status, political status, and job satisfaction were used as control variables for the regression equation. Among them, job satisfaction referred to the degree of job satisfaction of the research object as a group of migrant workers in different places. The level of job satisfaction affected the generation of participation willingness. Individuals with higher job satisfaction were more likely to participate in positive behaviors under the guidance of positive emotions, which reduced the possibility of forming the willingness to participate in collective behaviors [31]. Therefore, this study controlled the job satisfaction by the Likert 5-point scoring method.

Table 1. Measurement items of main variables.

Variable	Measurement items
Dependent variable	
Participation willingness	If necessary, will you participate in petition/collective signature petition activities later?
	If necessary, will you take part in strikes, collective protests, and collective wage collection activities later?
Independent variable	
Participation experience	Have you participated in petition/collective signature petition activities in the past?
	Have you participated in strikes, collective protests, collective wage collection, and other activities in the past?
Mediator variable	
Institutional support	Do you agree with the good service attitude of the workers in charge of migrant workers in Shenzhen?
	Do you agree or disagree with the opinion that the workers in charge of migrant workers in Shenzhen are not competent enough?
	Do you agree that the working environment and service facilities for migrant workers in Shenzhen are very good?
	Do you agree that the procedures for migrant workers in Shenzhen are clear and standardized?
	Do you agree with the complicated procedures for migrant workers in Shenzhen?
	Do you agree or disagree with the statement that Shenzhen's charges for migrant workers are reasonable?
	Do you agree or disagree with the following statement? Social organizations and social work volunteers help me a lot in my work and life?
	Do you agree or disagree? I find it easier for migrant workers to get things done in Shenzhen than expected
	Do you agree or disagree? I believe the starting point of the migrant workers in Shenzhen is to serve them
	Do you agree or disagree? I am willing to turn to the relevant departments of Shenzhen city for help when I meet with difficulties or unfair treatment
	Do you agree or disagree? If there is an opportunity, I would like to put forward my opinions and suggestions to Shenzhen on improving the work of migrant workers in cities

(continued)

Table 1. (*continued*)

Variable	Measurement items
	Do you agree or disagree? I think Shenzhen has an equal service attitude
	Do you agree that Shenzhen provides equal service processes and procedures for migrant workers, which are no different from local workers?
	Do you agree or disagree? I think Shenzhen provides equal employment information and opportunities for migrant workers, no different from local people
Moderator variable	
Social network	How many family members or relatives do you have in Shenzhen?
	How many fellow villagers do you know in Shenzhen?
	How many friends, colleagues, and acquaintances do you have in Shenzhen besides the first two categories?

4 Results

4.1 Common Method Deviation Biases

In the questionnaire survey, the same data source or control environment often leads to artificial co-variation, resulting in systematic errors in the results [32]. In this paper, the research not only adopted the methods of reverse scoring of some variables and anonymous filling in the questionnaire design to reduce the influence caused by common method biases, but also adopted the Harman single-factor test and confirmatory analysis method to test the collected data [33].

Harman single-factor test showed that there were 8 factors with characteristic roots greater than 1, and the maximum factor variance explanation rate was 18.207% (less than 40%). Therefore, there were no serious common deviation biases. In addition, AMOS 26.0 was used to conduct confirmatory factor analysis on the questionnaire items, and the results showed that $x^2/df = 8.55$, CFI $= 0.50$, GFI $= 0.77$, AGFI $= 0.71$, NFI $= 0.47$, RMSEA $= 0.13$, indicating poor model fitting degree. Therefore, there was no serious problem of common method biases in this study.

4.2 Descriptive Statistical Analysis

Before the analysis, we conducted a preliminary test on the relationship between participation experience and willingness of collective behavior. We divided the relationship between participation experience and willingness into four types and conducted a descriptive analysis. The four types are: having participation experience and having participation willingness, having participation experience but not having participation willingness, not having participation experience but having participation willingness and not having participation experience and not having participation willingness. Analysis of the relationship between participation experience and willingness of collective behavior is shown in Table 2.

As can be seen from Table 2, among the respondents who have no experience of participating in collective behavior, those who have no participation willingness account for 85.38%, and those who have participation willingness account for 14.62%. However, when the respondents had participated in collective behavior in the past, the proportion of respondents who had no participation willingness decreased to 69.23%, and the proportion of respondents who had formed participation willingness increased to 30.77%. The Chi-square test showed a significant relationship between them ($p < 0.001$). Collective behavior participation experience has a positive influence on participation willingness.

Through the analysis of the relationship between the participation experience and willingness of collective behavior, we found that it was not necessarily the respondents who have participated in collective behavior that would have the willingness to participate in collective behavior. More than half of the respondents who had participated in collective behavior did not form the participation willingness. However, nearly 15% of respondents who had no experience of participating in collective behavior will form the participation willingness. The relationship between the two confirmed that the influence of participation experience on participation willingness of collective behavior was not necessarily direct, but more likely there was an intermediate mechanism or other influencing factors. Specifically, there were effective conditions for the influence of collective behavior participation experience on participation willingness. It provided a premise for us to further use the conditional process model to test the influence of collective behavior participation experience on participation willingness.

Table 2. Analysis of the relationship between experience and willingness

Collective behavior participation experience		Collective behavior participation willingness	
		NO	YES
No	Count	181	31
	Row percentage	85.38%	14.62%
YES	Count	153	68
	Row percentage	69.23%	30.77%
χ^2	15.96**		
Cramér's V	0.1922		

Sample size was 433; $^+ p < 0.1$, $^* p < 0.05$, $^{**} p < 0.01$.
Source: Authors' data.

The descriptive statistics and correlation analysis results of major variables are shown in Table 3. As can be seen from Table 3, the correlation coefficient between participation experience and willingness of collective behavior was 0.161, $p < 0.010$, indicating a significant positive correlation. H1 was preliminarily supported. Secondly, the correlation coefficient between institutional support and participation willingness was -0.133, $p < 0.050$, indicating a significant negative correlation. H2 was preliminarily supported.

Table 3. Description analysis and correlation test of main variables.

Variables	M	SD	1	2	3	4
1. Participation experience	0.14	0.27	1			
2. Participation willingness	0.37	0.41	0.161^{**}	1		
3. Institutional support	2.59	0.38	0.002	-0.133^{*}	1	
4. Social network	57.48	67.68	-0.029	0.026	-0.023	1

4.3 Hypothesis Testing

Based on existing studies [34], we controlled variables such as gender, age, income, political status, and education level, and standardized the main variables. Hierarchical regression and Process were used to test the mediated moderator model with the willingness to participate in collective behavior as the dependent variable. The results are shown in Table 4 and Table 5.

In Table 4, model 1 shows the regression results of control variables on willingness to participate in collective behavior, model 2 examines the influence of participation experience on willingness, and model 3 examines the influence of institutional support on participation willingness. The results of model 2 show that the regression coefficient of participation experience on willingness is 0.188, $p < 0.010$, indicating that there is a significant positive relationship between participation experience and willingness. Therefore, the participation experience of collective behavior could effectively promote the formation of participation willingness. H1 was supported. The results of model 3 show that the regression coefficient between institutional support and participation willingness is -0.362, $p < 0.050$, indicating that there is a significant negative correlation between institutional support and participation willingness. Therefore, institutional support could effectively weaken the formation of participation willingness. H2 was supported.

The test results of the moderating effect of social networks are shown in Table 5. Model 4 shows the influence of control variables on institutional support. Based on model 4, model 5 examines the influence of collective behavior participation experience and social networks on institutional support. Based on model 5, the interaction term between participation experience and social network was added in model 6 to test the moderating effect of social networks on the relationship between participation experience and institutional support. Model 7 shows the regression results of control variables on participation willingness. Model 8 examines the influence of institutional support and social network on participation willingness. Based on model 8, the interaction term of institutional support and social networks was added to model 9 to test the moderating effect of social networks on the relationship between institutional support and participation willingness. The results of model 6 show that the interaction terms between participation

Table 4. Main effect test results.

	Dependent variable: participation willingness		
	Model 1	Model 2	Model 3
Independent variable			
Participation experience		.188**	
Mediator variable			
Institutional support			−.362*
Moderator variable			
Social network		.024	.014
Control variables			
Male	.289*	.245*	.316*
Age	−.016*	−.014*	−.018+
Income	.275	.342+	.518*
Married	.136	.085	−.003
Health	.042	.048	.037
Political identity			
League member	.289+	.273+	.389*
Communist	.096	.076	.373
Democrats	−.731	−.944	−.482
Education level			
Highschool	−.240*	−.219+	−.302*
Junior college or above	−.206	−.112	−.383
Job satisfaction	.072	−.001	.091
R^2	.055*	.085**	.102*

Source: Authors' data.

experience and social network have a significant negative impact on institutional support ($\beta = -0.458, p < 0.010$). Social networks had a moderating effect on participation experience and institutional support. H3 was supported. The results of model 9 show that the interaction terms of social network and institutional support have a significant positive impact on participation willingness ($\beta = 0.196, p < 0.050$). Therefore, social networks had a moderating effect on institutional support and participation willingness. H4 was supported.

To test hypothesis 5, model 1 in Process was used to test the moderating effect of social networks between the independent variable and dependent variable. The regression coefficient of interaction terms between participation experience and social network to participation willingness was 0.128, $p = 0.038 < 0.050$. Therefore, social networks had a moderating effect on participation experience and willingness. The results of model 6 show that the regression coefficient of interaction terms between participation experience and social network to institutional support was $-0.326, p < 0.050$. The results of model 9 show that the regression coefficient of interaction terms between social networks and institutional support on participation willingness was $0.192, p < 0.050$. Therefore, the moderating effect of social networks on participation experience and willingness was mediated by institutional support. H5 was supported.

Table 5. Test results of the mediated moderator model.

	Institutional support			Participation willingness		
	Model 4	Model 5	Model 6	Model 7	Model 8	Model 9
Main effect						
Participation experience		.032	−.090			.179$^+$
Institutional support					−.137*	−.105
Social network		.000	−0.078		.014	.092
Mediator effect						
Participation experience × Social network			−.458**			
Institutional support × Social network						.196*
Control variables						
Male	.007	−.005	−.029	.289**	.316*	.289$^+$
Age	.021*	.021*	.020**	−.016*	−.018$^+$	−.018 +
Income	−.250	−.267	−.300	.275	.518*	.592*
Married	−.363$^+$	−.359$^+$	−.351$^+$	.136	−.003	.018
Health	.024	.021	.013	.042	.037	.049
Political identity						
League member	.301$^+$	.302$^+$	.281	.289$^+$	.389*	.382*
Communist	.420	.413	.491	.096	.373	.279
Democrats	.960	.958	1.832*	−.731	−.482	−1.015
Education level						
Highschool	−.262$^+$	−.262$^+$	−.274$^+$	−.240*	−.302*	−.302*
Junior college or above	−.231	−.197	−.219	−.206	−.383	−.424
Job satisfaction	−.162	−.169	−.164	.034	.091	.056
R^2	.071$^+$	.072	.105**	.055*	.089*	.129**

Source: Authors' data.

In addition, based on existing studies [35], this paper drew graphs of the moderating effect of social networks by adding and subtracting one standard deviation from the mean, to display the moderating effect more intuitively. The moderating effect of social networks on participation experience and institutional support is shown in Fig. 2, while the moderating effect of social networks on institutional support and participation willingness is shown in Fig. 3. In Fig. 2, when the level of social network is low, participation experience of collective behavior has a significant positive impact on institutional support (Simple slope $= 0.261, t = 2.253, p = 0.025 < 0.100$). When the level of social network is high, the negative effect of collective behavior participation experience on institutional support is strong and significant (Simple slope $= -0.584, t = -2.583, p = 0.010 < 0.100$). In Fig. 3, when the level of social network is high, institutional support has a strong and significant positive impact on the willingness to participate in collective behavior (Simple slope $= 0.501, t = 2.115, p = 0.036 < 0.100$). When the level of social networks is low, the negative effect of institutional support on participation willingness is not significant (Simple slope $= -0.049, t = -0.416, p > 0.100$). Therefore, H3 and H4 were further supported.

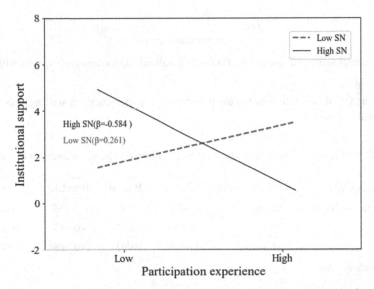

Fig. 2. Moderating effect of social networks on participation experience and institutional support.

To test the mediating effect of social networks at two stages, the Process program was used in this study, and the Bootstrap method was used to perform 5000 times putting back sampling to estimate the indirect effect value of social networks and the confidence interval of indirect effect value at high and low levels. The test results are shown in Table 6. As can be seen from Table 6, when the level of social network is high, the indirect effect value is -0.063, the standard error is 0.093, 95% confidence interval is $[-0.288, 0.088]$, including 0. When the level of social network is low, the indirect effect value of institutional support is -0.067, the standard error is 0.040, 95% confidence interval is $[-0.166, -0.011]$, excluding 0. Institutional support played a significant mediating role. The results showed that there were both moderating and mediating variables in the model of the influence of participation experience on the willingness to participate in collective behavior, and the moderating variable plays a role at least partly through the mediating variable. Specifically, social networks can negatively moderate the

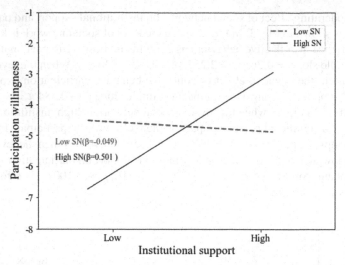

Fig. 3. Moderating effect of social networks on institutional support and participation willingness.

indirect impact of collective behavior participation experience on willingness through institutional support.

Table 6. Test results of mediating effect at the level of moderating variables in two stages.

Dependent variable	Social network	Effect	BootSE	BootLLCI	BootULCI
Participation willingness	M-1SD	−0.067	0.040	−0.166	−0.011
	M	0.009	0.015	−0.012	0.047
	M + 1SD	−0.063	0.093	−0.288	0.088

Source: Authors' data.

4.4 Robustness Test

Considering that the scale of the network cannot fully reflect the social network of respondents, the variable in the socio-centric network is included in the analysis for the robustness test. The method of social network analysis is divided into two basic trends. One is the egocentric network, which studies the relationship between individuals and other individuals. The other is the socio-centric network that focuses on the relationships of all members within the group. The former is mainly used to analyze the social ties between individuals, while the latter is commonly used to analyze the network structure within groups [36, 37]. The above measurement of the degree centrality of social networks is mainly based on the individual level to measure the connection among individual members. However, the relationship between individual members is insufficient in reflecting the overall characteristics, so the degree centrality in the socio-centric network is introduced to measure.

In the selection of specific variables, this paper chose the network of work connection as the replacement variable. First of all, the work network was relatively common and did not involve personal privacy. At the same time, there were many relationships among members in the work network, which could meet the needs of empirical research. Secondly, the work network had the dual properties of formal network and informal network and was highly representative. In the working environment, a formal network was formed among colleagues to ensure the normal operation of work. When outside the work environment, colleagues formed informal networks in their daily communication [38]. Finally, the work network was also important support for migrant workers to deal with conflicts and disputes in the city and form the willingness to participate in collective behavior [39]. Therefore, the work network in the socio-centric network was selected to replace the original network variable. In the process of data collection, the work network was obtained mainly through cluster sampling, and the relationship was symmetrized.

In this study, the work network collected was directed, and the degree centrality can be divided into indegree and outdegree. Among them, indegree represents the degree of attention of an individual. The higher the indegree, the stronger the attraction of an individual in the group. The outdegree indicates the enthusiasm of the individual. The higher the outdegree, the more active the individual is in the group. Compared with the network scale represented by social network data in the egocentric network, the indegree of the work network can not only reflect the characteristics of interaction scale in the socio-centric network but also reflect the differences in group status and prestige. Individuals of different statuses and prestige have different ways to deal with conflicts and solve problems. Contrary to the social network in the egocentric network, when faced with conflict and injustice, individuals with higher prestige are more inclined to mobilize resources to solve problems through institutional support without resorting to coerciveness [40]. It reduces the possibility of forming a willingness to participate in collective behavior. To supplement the research, the indegree of the work network was selected as the moderator variable.

Firstly, model 1 in Process was used to test the moderating effect of social networks between the independent variable and the dependent variable. The regression coefficient of the interaction terms between the independent variable and the work network to the dependent variable was $-0.121, p = 0.039$. The moderating effect of work network on participation experience and willingness of collective behavior was verified. The results of Table 7 show that the regression coefficient of the interaction terms between the participation experience of collective behavior and the work network on institutional support is 0.151, and there is a significant positive impact ($p < 0.050$), which meets the research expectation. In addition, the regression coefficient of interaction terms between the work network and institutional support on the participation willingness is 0.084, and the positive impact is also significant ($p < 0.100$). Therefore, the moderating effect of the work network on participation experience and willingness of collective behavior was mediated by institutional support.

The results showed that the mediated moderator model was verified by replacing the social network variable with the socio-centric network of work connection. In addition, the direction and significance of the influence were in line with the research expectations. Therefore, the robustness test was passed.

Table 7. Results of the robustness test.

	Institutional support	Participation willingness
Main effect		
Participation experience	.035	.061
Institutional support		−.149*
Work connection network	−.032	−.071
Mediator effect		
Participation experience × Work connection network	.151*	
Institutional support × Work connection network		.084+
Control variables		
Male	.041	.268+
Age	.020*	−.020*
Income	−.203	.678**
Married	−.374+	.060
Health	.028	.042
Political identity		
League member	.307+	.364*
Communist	.476	.327
Democrats	−1.050*	−.687
Education level		
Highschool	−.278+	−.278+
Junior college or above	−.231	.380
Job satisfaction	−.149	.069
R^2	.088**	.120**

Source: Authors' data.

Secondly, the method of propensity score matching was used to further verify the robustness of the analysis results. To control the difference more effectively between the two groups (whether the respondents have participated in collective behavior), this study adopted the PSM method to estimate the influence of collective behavior participation experience on the formation of willingness to participate [41]. First, the nearest neighbor matching method was used to estimate the robustness, and then the radius matching method and the kernel matching method were used to test the robustness. The results show that the value of ATT is 0.2960 with the nearest neighbor matching method, and is significant at 1% level. At the same time, the results of the radius matching method and the kernel matching method were consistent with the nearest neighbor matching method. Therefore, the robustness test was passed.

Finally, considering possible missing variables is also one of the commonly used methods for robustness testing [41]. In addition to considering some attribute characteristics of the respondents (such as age, income, education level, etc.), there may also be some missing variables that affect participation willingness, such as the social experience of migrant agricultural workers [42], the confidence that group conflicts can safeguard their interests [43], and the trust in the local government agencies and personnel [44]. Specifically, social experience determines whether the respondents can quickly integrate into the local life circle and affects the difficulty of working in different places. The expectation of group conflict participation can better reflect the respondents' confidence and expectation of participating in collective behavior. The lower the confidence, the lower the willingness to engage in collective behavior. The degree of trust in the local government institutions and personnel also plays an important role in the formation of the participation willingness and is also the choice of the process of safeguarding rights. When the above variables were included in the analysis, the results showed that the significance and value of the test coefficients did not change significantly, indicating that the omitted variables had little influence on the formation of participation willingness.

5   Conclusion

In this study, the methods of hierarchical regression and Bootstrap were used to construct a mediated moderator model with the social network as the moderating variable and institutional support as the mediating variable under the theoretical support. First, the study explores the influence of collective behavior participation experience on willingness and confirms the influence relationship between behavior and willingness. At the same time, the research also explores the important factors influencing the formation of participation willingness, from the perspective of institutional support.

Secondly, with the social network as the moderating variable, this study examines how participation experience affects the formation of participation willingness through the social network. Finally, with institutional support as the mediating variable, the study further analyzes how social networks play a role under the influence of institutional support. The research results not only enrich the research on collective behavior and provide a new perspective for collective behavior research but also provide helpful intervention measures for government departments to promote the effective governance of collective behavior. The specific results are shown below.

First, the study found that collective behavior participation experience can promote the re-formation of participation willingness, and institutional support has a weakening effect on willingness to participate in collective behavior. H1 and H2 were supported. As a part of individual experience, collective behavior participation experience inevitably has an impact on individual cognition and psychology. It makes the individual have better adaptability when facing the collective behavior and can reduce psychological resistance. On the other hand, the characteristics of rapid and unexpected changes in collective behavior can also help individuals achieve their goals in the shortest possible time, which confirms the repetitive characteristic of collective behavior. However, when respondents believe that institutional support is valuable and conducive to solving problems, respondents are more inclined to achieve their goals through institutional support in consideration of risk avoidance. The research is the verification of planned behavior theory and enriches the existing research.

Secondly, the results showed that social networks positively moderated the relationship between participation experience and willingness. At the same time, the social network also played a moderating role in the two pathways of participation experience and institutional support, institutional support, and participation willingness. H3 and H4 were supported. On the one hand, this means that the scale of the network can have a great impact on the willingness of respondents to seek institutional support. On the other hand, the scale of the network can also moderate the degree of influence of institutional support on participation willingness. When the scale of the network is at a high level, respondents can obtain support from the informal network or obtain institutional support from the formal network to solve problems. However, when the network scale is at a low level, institutional support is often the only channel for respondents to obtain support. At the same time, institutional support is also an important factor affecting the willingness to participate in collective behavior. The more institutional support, the lower the possibility of forming the willingness to participate in collective behavior. Therefore, it is particularly important to establish sound grassroots service measures to provide institutional support and help for migrant workers, especially for respondents at a lower level of the network scale, which can effectively reduce the possibility of forming collective behaviors.

Finally, we found that institutional support mediated the moderating effect of the social network, and the indirect effect on the relationship between participation experience and willingness would decrease with the increase of social network level. Compared with respondents who have a high level of the social network, respondents with participation experience of collective behavior are more likely to seek institutional support when the social network is at a low level. At the same time, when institutional support was lacking, respondents were more likely to form the willingness to participate in collective behavior. H5 was supported. When there is a high level of the social network, respondents have stronger organizational mobilization ability and are more inclined to seek non-institutional support under the influence of the participation experience of collective behavior. Moreover, the effect intensity of institutional support is reduced. On the contrary, when there is a low level of the social network, respondents are more inclined to seek institutional support when network resources are limited. Without sufficient institutional support, it is easy to generate the willingness to participate in collective behavior and form a higher effect intensity. The findings further explain how the moderating effect of the social network influences the formation of participation willingness. Relevant findings are of great significance for the government to adopt appropriate governance behaviors to reduce the occurrence of collective behaviors.

There are also some limitations in this paper, which need to be improved in the future. First, cross-sectional data are difficult to reveal temporal causality. In the future, the causal relationship will be further studied in combination with panel data. Secondly, the research on the inertia mechanism of collective behavior is insufficient, and the problems of efficiency and cognition in the formation of collective behavior cannot be further explored. In the future, the research will further explore the important factors affecting collective behavior more comprehensively. Finally, the collective behavior discussed by the research is only the collective behavior under a negative state such as protest. In the future, the research will combine different types of collective behavior for further analysis.

Acknowledgments. The research presented here was supported by the "Young Talent Support Plan" of Shaanxi Province, the Natural Science Basic Research Program of Shaanxi [Grant No. 2022JM-397], Xi'an Social Science Planning Fund [Grant No. 22LW78], and the Fundamental Research Funds for the Central Universities [Grant No. SK2022005].

Compliance of Ethical Standard Statement. The authors declare that they have no conflict of interest. All procedures performed in studies involving human participants were in accordance with the ethical standards of the institutional and/or national research committee and with the 1964 Helsinki declaration and its later amendments or comparable ethical standards. This article does not contain any studies with animals performed by the authors.

Informed Consent. Informed consent was obtained from all individual participants included in the study.

Disclosure Statement. The authors declare that they have no conflict of interest.

References

1. Guo, X., Tu, W.: Corruption tolerance and its influencing factors—the case of China's civil servants. J. Chin. Govern. **2**, 307–328 (2017). https://doi.org/10.1080/23812346.2017.134 2897
2. Yang, L., Ren, Y.: Moral obligation, public leadership, and collective action for epidemic prevention and control: evidence from the corona virus disease 2019 (COVID-19) emergency. Int. J. Environ. Res. Public Health **17**, 2731 (2020). https://doi.org/10.3390/ijerph17082731
3. Wright, S.C.: The next generation of collective action research. J. Soc. Issues **65**, 859–879 (2009)
4. Van Zomeren, M.: Building a Tower of Babel? Integrating core motivations and features of social structure into the political psychology of political action. Polit. Psychol. **37**, 87–114 (2016)
5. Smith, E.K., Mayer, A.: A social trap for the climate? Collective action, trust and climate change risk perception in 35 countries. Glob. Environ. Chang. **49**, 140–153 (2018)
6. Becker, J.C., Tausch, N.: A dynamic model of engagement in normative and non-normative collective action: psychological antecedents, consequences, and barriers. Eur. Rev. Soc. Psychol. **26**, 43–92 (2015)
7. Siegel, D.A.: Social networks and collective action. Am. J. Polit. Sci. **53**, 122–138 (2009)
8. Steinert-Threlkeld, Z.C.: Spontaneous collective action: peripheral mobilization during the Arab spring. Am. Polit. Sci. Rev. **111**, 379–403 (2017). https://doi.org/10.1017/S00030554 16000769
9. Hern, E.: In the gap the state left: Policy feedback, collective behavior, and political participation in Zambia. Stud. Comp. Int. Dev. **52**, 510–531 (2017)
10. Wilkins, D.J., Livingstone, A.G., Levine, M.: All click, no action? Online action, efficacy perceptions, and prior experience combine to affect future collective action. Comput. Hum. Behav. **91**, 97–105 (2019). https://doi.org/10.1016/j.chb.2018.09.007

11. Ajzen, I.: From intentions to actions: a theory of planned behavior. In: Kuhl, J., Beckmann, J. (eds.) Action Control, pp. 11–39. Springer, Heidelberg (1985). https://doi.org/10.1007/978-3-642-69746-3_2

12. Chen, M.-F., Tung, P.-J.: Developing an extended theory of planned behavior model to predict consumers' intention to visit green hotels. Int. J. Hosp. Manag. **36**, 221–230 (2014)

13. Yan, G., Pegoraro, A., Watanabe, N.M.: Student-athletes' organization of activism at the university of missouri: resource mobilization on Twitter. J. Sport Manag. **32**, 24–37 (2018). https://doi.org/10.1123/jsm.2017-0031

14. Hassan Abdullah, F.: Resource mobilization theory: political movement in Egypt. IAU Int. J. Soc. Sci. **8**, 1–12 (2018)

15. McCarthy, J.D.: Social movements and networks: relational approaches to collective action (review). Soc. Forces **83**, 1289–1290 (2005)

16. Takács, K., Janky, B., Flache, A.: Collective action and network change. Soc. Netw. **30**, 177–189 (2008)

17. González, R., et al.: The role of family in the intergenerational transmission of collective action. Soc. Psychol. Pers. Sci. **12**, 856–867 (2021)

18. Louis, W., Thomas, E., McGarty, C., Lizzio-Wilson, M., Amiot, C., Moghaddam, F.: The volatility of collective action: theoretical analysis and empirical data. Polit. Psychol. **41**, 35–74 (2020)

19. Tausch, N., Becker, J.C.: Emotional reactions to success and failure of collective action as predictors of future action intentions: a longitudinal investigation in the context of student protests in Germany. Br. J. Soc. Psychol. **52**, 525–542 (2013). https://doi.org/10.1111/j.2044-8309.2012.02109.x

20. Scott, W.R.: Institutions and Organizations: Ideas, Interests, and Identities. SAGE Publications (2013)

21. Webb, D., Soutar, G.N., Mazzarol, T., Saldaris, P.: Self-determination theory and consumer behavioural change: evidence from a household energy-saving behaviour study. J. Environ. Psychol. **35**, 59–66 (2013)

22. Odağ, Ö., Uluğ, Ö.M., Kanık, B., Maganić, M.M.: Exploring the context-sensitivity of collective action motivations and the mobilizing role of social media: a comparative interview study with activists in Germany and Turkey. Polit. Psychol. (2022). https://doi.org/10.1111/pops.12836

23. Hensengerth, O., Lu, Y.: Emerging environmental multi-level governance in China? Environmental protests, public participation and local institution-building. Public Policy Adm. **34**, 121–143 (2019). https://doi.org/10.1177/0952076717753279

24. McClurg, S.D.: Indirect mobilization: the social consequences of party contacts in an election campaign. Am. Polit. Res. **32**, 406–443 (2004)

25. Bursztyn, L., Cantoni, D., Yang, D.Y., Yuchtman, N., Zhang, Y.J.: Persistent political engagement: social interactions and the dynamics of protest movements. Am. Econ. Rev.: Insights **3**, 233–250 (2021). https://doi.org/10.1257/aeri.20200261

26. Oliver, P., Marwell, G., Teixeira, R.: A theory of the critical mass. I. Interdependence, group heterogeneity, and the production of collective action. Am. J. Sociol. **91**, 522–556 (1985)

27. Rivera, M.T., Soderstrom, S.B., Uzzi, B.: Dynamics of dyads in social networks: assortative, relational, and proximity mechanisms. Ann. Rev. Sociol. **36**, 91–115 (2010)

28. Marwell, G., Oliver, P.E., Prahl, R.: Social networks and collective action: a theory of the critical mass. III. Am. J. Sociol. **94**, 502–534 (1988)

29. Liu, L., de Jong, M.: The institutional causes of environmental protests in China: a perspective from common pool resource management. J. Chin. Govern. **2**, 460–477 (2017). https://doi.org/10.1080/23812346.2017.1354432

30. Yang, J., Zhang, C., Liu, K.: Income inequality and civil disorder: evidence from China. J. Contemp. China **29**, 680–697 (2020)

31. De Clercq, D., Haq, I.U., Azeem, M.U.: Why happy employees help: How meaningfulness, collectivism, and support transform job satisfaction into helping behaviours. Pers. Rev. **48**(4), 1001–1021 (2019)
32. Chang, S.-J., Van Witteloostuijn, A., Eden, L.: From the editors: common method variance in international business research (2010)
33. Wu, G., Zheng, J., Zhao, X., Zuo, J.: How does strength of ties influence project performance in Chinese megaprojects? A conflict-based perspective. Int. J. Conflict Manag. **31**(5), 753–780 (2020)
34. Liu, B., Xiao, J., Li, L., Wu, G.: Do citizen participation programs help citizens feel satisfied with urban redevelopment policy in China? J. Chin. Govern. **7**(3), 341–371 (2021)
35. Aiken, L.S., West, S.G., Reno, R.R.: Multiple Regression: Testing and Interpreting Interactions. Sage (1991)
36. Chung, K.K., Hossain, L., Davis, J.: Exploring sociocentric and egocentric approaches for social network analysis. In: Proceedings of the 2nd International Conference on Knowledge Management in Asia Pacific, pp. 1–8 (2005)
37. Marsden, P.V.: Egocentric and sociocentric measures of network centrality. Soc. Netw. **24**, 407–422 (2002)
38. Cai, M., Wang, W., Cui, Y., Stanley, H.E.: Multiplex network analysis of employee performance and employee social relationships. Phys. A **490**, 1–12 (2018)
39. Wei, W., Gao, W.: Positive or negative? The role of native place enclave in the conflicts between migrant workers and their employers. Int. J. Conflict Manag. **29**(5), 570–590 (2018)
40. Offord, M., Gill, R., Kendal, J.: The effects of prestige on collective performance and information flow in a strictly hierarchical institution. Palgrave Commun. **5**, 1–11 (2019)
41. Huang, J., Huang, Y., Wu, K.: Tenure of office, political rotation and the prevention and control of the COVID-19 epidemic in China. J. Chin. Govern. 1–26 (2022)
42. Jingkun, N., Jingjing, W., Nan, Z., Haifeng, D.: Collective action inertia of immigrant peasant. J. Northwest A&F Univ. (Soc. Sci. Edn.) **17**, 84–94 (2017)
43. Goncalo, J.A., Polman, E., Maslach, C.: Can confidence come too soon? Collective efficacy, conflict and group performance over time. Organ. Behav. Hum. Decis. Process. **113**, 13–24 (2010)
44. Hu, R.: Farmers' petition and erosion of political trust in government. Sociol. Stud. **3**, 39–55 (2007)

Research on Network Invulnerability and Its Application on AS-Level Internet Topology

Lu Zhang[1,2], Jiaqi Nie[1,2], Songtao Peng[1,2], and Xincheng Shu[1,2,3(✉)]

[1] Institute of Cyberspace Security, Zhejiang University of Technology,
Hangzhou 310023, China
sxc.shuxincheng@foxmail.com
[2] College of Information Engineering, Zhejiang University of Technology,
Hangzhou 310023, China
[3] Department of Electrical Engineering, City University of Hong Kong,
Hong Kong 999077, China

Abstract. With the development of complex network theory, network invulnerability has become a hot topic of research. Facing the limitations of most studies to determine the importance of nodes through a single perspective only, we propose the neighbor influence index, which considers the impact of multi-hop neighbors with attributes fusion. Moreover, we introduce node attributes into our method and propose a node importance evaluation method based on multi-attributes. Finally, we conduct vulnerability analysis experiments on five real datasets to verify the validity of our method. Specially, we apply the method to autonomous systems (AS) Internet networks for different countries, which is of great significance to developing network security.

Keywords: Complex networks · Multi-attribute combination · Node importance · Network invulnerability · Internet topology

1 Introduction

Many complex systems in nature and human society can be represented as different complex networks, which have attracted a great deal of research attention in decades. Within this broad field, the investigation of network invulnerability is one of the most important and meaningful directions [16, 22], of which purpose is to find the key nodes that play an important role in transmitting information between several nodes of the network structure. For example, in 2021, the Korean telecommunications company's wired and wireless network services, which rank first and second in the market share of Korean wired network and mobile communication, were suddenly interrupted. This event caused a nationwide network outage of at least 40 min in South Korea, and many business systems of enterprises could not operate. After the analysis, it was found that accidents were often caused by small disturbances and faults in several key nodes, resulting in jumping or blocking of local lines in the system, and then producing cascading effects that spread to the entire system, and finally led to the global paralysis of the system. Therefore, the study of network invulnerability is of great importance in practical scenarios.

Typically, critical nodes in a network are often tied to the importance of the node. Due to the pervasiveness of the key node identification algorithms, they have been applied to different scenarios such as social networks [1,5], power grids [12,21], epidemics [4,19], computer networks [3,8], etc. In general, the importance of a node is usually measured based on local and global network structural information [13]. Classical nodal importance metrics include degree centrality, closeness centrality [17], betweenness centrality [6], k-shell decomposition [11] and Katz centrality [10], etc. While the above approaches have considered local or global structural information, it is limited to determining the importance of nodes through a single perspective only [18]. Therefore, based on the existing centrality index, we propose an influence ranking algorithm of aggregated neighbors, which takes the node's first-order and second-order neighbors as the influence factors with different coefficients of attention. Furthermore, the properties of the nodes themselves determine the status of the nodes in a scenario-specific network, such as AS-level Internet topology [20]. Therefore, in the Internet domain, we have coupled network topology information with node properties to uncover a more consistent approach that delves into the invulnerability of Internet networks for different countries. This method provides theoretical guidance for the efficient protection of critical nodes in large-scale AS-level networks and prevents devastating damage to the network when the nodes are attacked.

This paper is organized as follows. In Sect. 2, we introduce the extended threshold model by considering the positive feedback mechanism. In Sect. 3, we present the metrics for assessing the importance of network nodes. In Sect. 4, we analyze the numerical results under varying model parameters and network topologies. We summarize in Sect. 5.

2 Theory

2.1 Node Importance Indicators

In this section, we summarize the basic node importance metrics, which provide the theoretical basis for our follow-up, and their detailed definitions are as follows.

Definition 1. *Degree Centrality DC.* *The more neighbor nodes around the characteristic node of degree centrality, the greater the influence of that node. The formula is as follows:*

$$DC(v_i) = \frac{d(v_i)}{N-1} \tag{1}$$

where N is the total number of nodes and $d(v_i)$ denotes the degree of v_i. In practical applications, each node has a different impact. Degree centrality describes the direct impact of v_i. A greater degree means that the node is more important.

Definition 2. Closeness Centrality CC. *Closeness centrality uses the proximity of a node to other nodes in the network to characterize its level of importance. In a connected network of network size N, the closeness centrality of a node v_i is calculated as:*

$$CC(v_i) = \frac{N-1}{\sum_{j \neq i} d_{ij}} \qquad (2)$$

where d_{ij} is the shortest path length between v_i and v_j.

Definition 3. Katz Centrality. *Katz centrality assumes that the importance of a node is positively related to the degree of connectivity between the node and other nodes in the network, so the importance of nodes is calculated by designing certain weights for paths of different lengths The Katz centrality of node v_i in a network is defined as:*

$$\text{Katz}(v_i) = \sum_{k=1}^{\infty} \sum_{j=1}^{N} \alpha^k \left(A^k \right)_{ij} \qquad (3)$$

where A is the adjacency matrix and α is a contribution parameter taking values between 0 and 1, and k represents the contribution of a path of length k to the degree of connectivity of node v_i.

Definition 4. K-shell Decomposition. *The network topology is decomposed into many layers based on the degree, and nodes in the inner layers are considered to have higher importance. The specific decomposition rule is: when the kth layer is decomposed, all nodes in the topology with a degree not greater than k are removed, and the degree of the remaining nodes is updated continuously during the removal process. The k-shell decomposition method can analyze the hierarchical structure of the network better. It has the advantage of low computational complexity and can be used for large-scale networks.*

Definition 5. Eigenvector centrality EC. *The eigenvector centrality of a node is determined by the number and importance of neighbor nodes. The relationship for topological node importance is as follows.*

$$EC(v_i) = c \sum_{j=1}^{n} a_{ij} x_j \qquad (4)$$

where c is a proportional constant, $x = [x_1, x_2, ..., x_n]_T$, When x reaches steady state after multiple iterations, it can be written as $x = cAx$, where c is a proportional constant, a i j if and only if i is connected to j, otherwise 0, and x is the eigenvector corresponding to the eigenvalue of matrix A.

Definition 6. Betweenness centrality BC. *Betweenness centrality considers that the more the shortest paths through a node, the more important the node.*

Therefore, it precisely identifies those hub nodes in the network that can improve the efficiency of information transmission.

$$BC\left(v_i\right) = \sum_{j,k \neq i} \frac{g_{jk}\left(v_i\right)}{g_{jk}} \tag{5}$$

where g_{jk} denotes the number of shortest paths between nodes j and k, and $g_{jk}(i)$ denotes the number of shortest paths between nodes j and k through node i.

2.2   Neighbor Influence-based Node Ranking

This part will introduce our node importance algorithm based on the influence of neighbors in detail. The core idea of our method is that the effect of neighbors also determines the importance of nodes to a certain extent, but its influence will decrease with the increase of distance. The detailed implementation process of the algorithm is shown below.

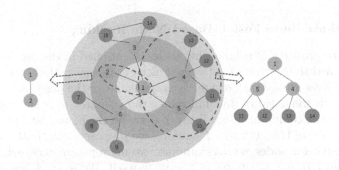

Fig. 1. Node neighborhood relationship diagram.

Given a network G in which a node v_i is randomly connected to any one of its neighbors, its degree represents all possible connections. We define the inverse of the degree as the contribution probability $P(v_i)$ of node v_i.

$$P\left(v_i\right) = \frac{1}{d\left(v_i\right)} \tag{6}$$

where the degree $d(v_i)$ of v_i is used as an indicator of its impact.

Then, the sum of the inverse of the degrees of all neighbors of a node in a given network G is called the clustering efficiency and is defined as follows:

$$E\left(v_i\right) = \sum_{v_j \in \eta(v_i)} \frac{1}{d\left(v_j\right)} \tag{7}$$

where $\eta(v_i)$ is the set of neighbour nodes.

In combination with the above, we propose $NI(v_j)$, neighbor node influence, which reflects the influence of a node depending on its surroundings. Considering the complexity of the algorithm, we focus only on the two-order structure outside target node, and the neighbor node influence can be obtained from the contribution of the nearest and next-nearest neighbor nodes and is defined as follows:

$$NI(v_i) = \sum_{j=1}^{k} P(v_j) \cdot BC(v_i) \sum_{j=1}^{k} \left[DC(v_j) + BC(v_j) \sum_{q=1}^{Q} DC(v_q) \right] \quad (8)$$

where k is the set of nearest neighbor nodes of the node, and Q is the set of second nearest neighbor nodes of the node. As shown in Fig. 1, the neighbours of node 1 are 2, 3, 4, 5, 6; the sub-neighbours are 7, 8, 9, 10, 11, 12, 13, 14, 15. The higher the number of neighbors of a node and the lower the degree of network topology overlap between neighbors, the less likely it is that the node's role in network structure and function will be replaced by other nodes, and the higher the importance of the node.

2.3   Multi-attribute Fusion-Based Node Ranking

The influence property of neighboring nodes, mentioned in the previous section, is more inclined to the view of network structure. However, the attributes of the nodes themselves are somewhat directly responsible for the position and function of the nodes in the network, including how they connect to other nodes, which nodes reduce the communication distance between them, and how they enhance the connectivity of the network. Therefore, we propose a multi-attribute fusion influence metric for nodes, which examines two main parameters: neighbor node influence and internal attributes of the node itself. We have elaborated on the neighboring node influence in the previous subsection. In this section, we will focus on the internal attributes of the node itself.

In this paper, we apply our method to the AS-level Internet topology. The Internet topology at the AS-level is typically modelled using a complex network where each node is an AS and each link represents a business relationship between two ASes [9,14,15]. These relationships reflect who pays when traffic is exchanged between ASes and are critical to the proper functioning of Internet systems [7]. AS relationships have typically been categorized into three types: (1) C2P, (2) P2P, and (3) S2S. Customers in a C2P relationship pay the provider to access the Internet, and the other two types, P2P and S2S, are generally settlement-free, meaning each party of the P2P and S2S relationship exchanges no money and prefers a win-win partnership.

Understanding of AS relationship is vital to the technical research and economic exchanges of the inter-domain structure of the Internet. We use the AS relationship dataset provided by the CAIDA website[1], from which we can get

---

[1] https://www.caida.org/catalog/datasets/as-relationships/.

the number of providers, customers, and siblings of each AS and use the customer value of each node as the node property of this AS. Because from the business point of view, the more customers owned, the more the node has more communication resources in the network, i.e., it has a stronger communication capability [2].

The combined attributes of node v_i, mul(v_i), are expressed as a weighted sum:

$$mul(v_i) = \mu_1 NI(v_i) + \mu_2 OI(v_i) \tag{9}$$

where μ_1 is the weight of the influence of neighbouring nodes and μ_2 is the weight of the node's attributes, and μ_1, μ_2 take values in the range (0.5, 5).

3   Evaluation Metrics

Many researchers have proposed indicators to measure the connectivity of networks under attack. In this paper, the network core scale S and the connectivity component C are used to study the splitting process of the network in the event of an attack. Referring to its definition, we define the following evaluation metrics for network invulnerability analysis. Given a network $G = \{V, E\}$, where V represents the node set of the network, E represents the link set, and G contains N nodes and M links. Remove r nodes from the network to get the network $G^r = \{V^r, E^r\}$.

Definition 7. The Network Core Size S. *The ratio of the maximum connectivity component size in G^r to the initial network size is defined as the core size of G^r. It measures the maintenance of the connectivity of the core portion of the network during an attack.*

$$S(r) = \frac{\max\{|V_1^r|, |V_2^r|, \ldots, |V_R^r|\}}{|V|} \tag{10}$$

Definition 8. The Network Connectivity Component C. *The network connected component C is the number of all connected subgraphs in G^r.*

$$C(r) = number\, G^r \tag{11}$$

The purpose of finding the connectivity component is to determine whether another vertex in the graph can be reached from one vertex in the graph, i.e., whether there is a path reachable between any two vertices in the network.

4   Experiment

4.1   Datasets

Network vulnerability experiments based on the neighbour influence node ranking algorithm were conducted on our six datasets. The statistics information is shown in Table 1. Specifically, AS20000102 is the undirected network of AS-level Internet. As in Fig. 2, we offer the topology of the four networks. Email network and AS20000102 network are not shown here due to a large number of nodes.

Table 1. Statistics of seven real-world networks and two synthetic networks: node number $|N|$, edge number $|E|$, the values of the diameter δ for all networks, maximum degree K_{max}, the average degree $\langle K \rangle$, and clustering coefficient $\langle C_c \rangle$.

	ARPANET	Jazz	Infectious	Email	Air_traffic	AS20000102
$|N|$	21	198	410	1133	1226	6474
$|E|$	26	2742	2765	5451	2615	13895
δ	3	6	9	3	17	9
K_{max}	4	100	50	71	20	1,459
$\langle K \rangle$	2.48	27.70	13.49	9.00	4.27	4.29
$\langle C_c \rangle$	0.0714	0.5203	0.4558	0.2202	0.0639	0.0096

4.2   Structure-Based Evaluation Experiments

We used BC, CC, DC, EC, and the proposed method NI to conduct experiments on six different size datasets of ARPANET, Jazz, Infectious, Email, Air_traffic, and AS20000102, respectively. The ranking results of the five algorithms were compared and analyzed based on these six real networks. In addition, a certain percentage of the top-ranked nodes were removed from the original network to simulate the change in network size when the network was deliberately attacked to evaluate the feasibility of each ranking algorithm.

According to the node ranking, the following experiments were designed to remove nodes from the network, one node at a time. The termination condition of the experiment is to fragment the network to the extent that the core size in the network does not exceed 20% of the original topological network. As a result, the fragmentation curve is obtained as shown in Fig. 3, where the x-axis is the number of removed nodes, and the y-axis is the proportion of the core size in the network to the whole network.

Table 2 shows the experimental results for six data sets under different methods. In the networks ARPANET, Jazz, Infectious, and Air_traffic, our method performs the best, i.e., the fewest nodes are removed, and the network has more or the most connected components after fragmentation. In the Email network, our method removes the same number of nodes as the DC method. The difference is that the proposed method in this paper makes the network break up more. Finally, in the AS network, the DC method performs the best, and the CC and EC methods perform poorly.

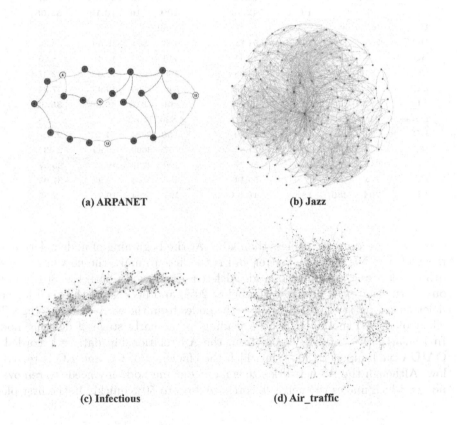

(a) ARPANET   (b) Jazz

(c) Infectious   (d) Air_traffic

Fig. 2. Real networks with different topological characteristics: (a) ARPANET; (b) Jazz; (c) Infectious; (d) Air_traffic.

As shown in Fig. 3(a), our method excels in the ARPANET network, where our method and the BC method disrupt the network to a core size below 60% when two nodes are removed, and the network core size drops to less than 20% when nine nodes are removed. In Fig. 3(b), the NI method is the first to make the network size drop to 20% at a later stage. As in Fig. 3(c), at first, all methods proceed similarly because the degree values of the nodes are similar in the Jazz network. However, these methods show individual differences when the network

Table 2. Experimental results of six data sets in different methods: number of deleted nodes Del, number of connected components C(r), network core size ratio S(r), deletion rate Del rate, and the five methods are DC, BC, CC, EC, NI.

	Del	C(r)	S(r) (%)	Del rate (%)	Del	C(r)	S(r) (%)	Del rate (%)
Datasets	ARPANET				Jazz			
DC	14	3	19.05	66.67	133	17	19.70	67.17
BC	10	5	19.05	47.62	112	18	16.16	56.57
CC	13	4	19.05	61.90	112	13	19.19	56.57
EC	16	2	19.05	76.19	141	13	19.70	71.21
NI	**9**	**6**	**19.05**	**42.86**	**109**	**16**	**16.16**	**55.05**
Datasets	Infectious				Email			
DC	225	37	19.02	54.88	400	281	19.59	35.30
BC	178	39	12.93	43.41	440	330	15.45	38.83
CC	184	20	19.51	44.88	480	264	16.06	42.37
EC	291	19	20.00	70.98	542	264	19.95	47.84
NI	**167**	**30**	**18.54**	**40.37**	**400**	**310**	**19.86**	**35.30**
Datasets	Air_traffic				AS20000102			
DC	206	292	18.68	16.80	**156**	**3758**	**17.21**	**2.41**
BC	268	303	19.66	21.86	157	3699	19.99	2.43
CC	647	167	19.33	52.77	2290	2263	19.57	35.37
EC	725	108	19.98	59.14	2457	2146	19.93	37.95
NI	**204**	**280**	**18.68**	**16.64**	191	3864	19.97	2.95

core size is decomposed to less than 40%. At the beginning of node deletion, our method, i.e., NI, performs better and is the first to make the network core size drop to 20% as the number of nodes deleted increases. In both Fig. 3(d) and (e), our methods are the first to reach below 20%, and because of the need for node deletion comparison, we can analyze the nodes from the early deletion stage. The effect of the NI method has been leading in the early stage of deleting nodes. In Fig. 3(f), the network comes from the AS relationship dataset recorded by CAIDA on January 2, 2000, in which the efficiency of CC and EC is relatively low. Although the AS network size is large, our method only needs to remove 70 nodes, which makes the network core size drop to 50% quickly in the first place.

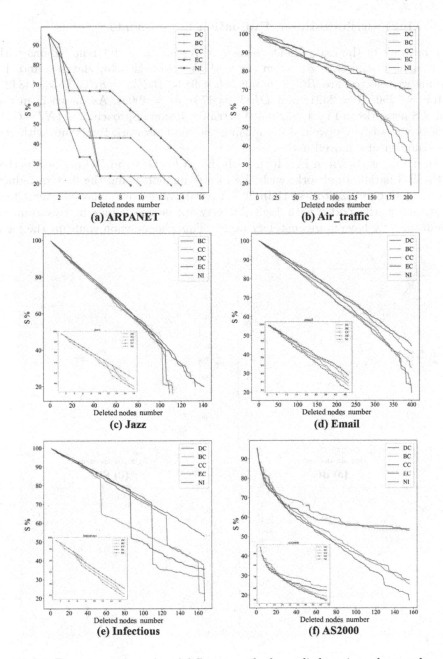

Fig. 3. Experimental results of different methods applied to six real networks.

4.3   Multi-attribute-Based Evaluation Experiments

The network in the experiment consists of AS nodes in different regions with relationships between nodes from the CAIDA AS-relationship dataset, and the regions we selected are $BG(V = 608, M = 984)$, $BR(V = 8193, M = 44842)$, $CA(V = 1250, M = 2421)$ and $DE(V = 1797, M = 4902)$. As shown from the four AS networks in Fig. 4, our multi-attribute fusion approach, i.e., $(NI + OI)$, performs consistently well, decomposing the most network fragments with the least number of removed nodes.

In detail, as shown in Fig. 4(a), both the $(NI + OI)$ and DC perform better in the BG national network, with the former method being the first to reduce the network core size to less than 20% when 13 nodes are removed. According to statistics, the nodes with high AS network degree values in this country simultaneously have more customer nodes. This phenomenon confirms the view

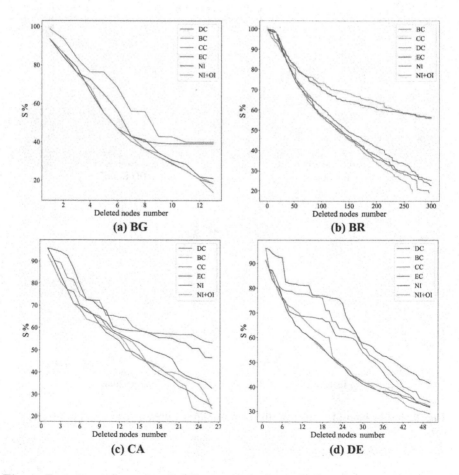

Fig. 4. Experimental results of different methods applied to four national-level AS networks: (a) Bulgaria, (b) Brazil, (c) Canada, and (d) Germany.

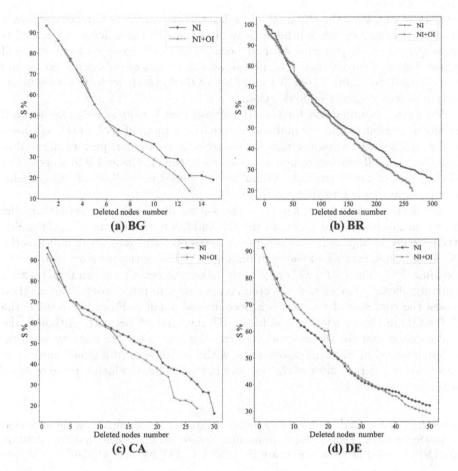

Fig. 5. Comparison of experimental results of NI and ($NI+OI$) methods in AS network data from four countries.

that the node's own attributes are also a major importance assessment feature. Moreover, in Fig. 4(b), the advantage of our method is that the number of deleted nodes is the least among all methods when the results are obtained when the network is disconnected by less than 40%. Our proposed method has a more significant impact on network fragmentation when fewer nodes are removed. However, the degree centrality (DC) effect is slightly ahead of our method as the number of deleted nodes increases. After analyzing the network structure, the AS links in BR countries have rich club characteristics with significant differences in node degrees. Figure 4(c) shows that our structural attribute, i.e., (NI), performs consistently better when the network jumbo slicing ratio reaches 60% or higher. On the other hand, the multi-attribute fusion approach is the first to achieve a network fragmentation of 80% or less, which is more in line with the actual situation when an entire network is deliberately attacked. In the DE national network of Fig. 4(d), the DC method makes the network core size decline slowly when the number of deletion nodes is greater than 10 when degree centrality is no longer the most powerful method because although some nodes have small degree values, their neighbouring nodes, as well as sub-neighbouring nodes, are more critical. In addition, our NI and $(NI+OI)$ methods perform better in the early and late stages of node deletion.

We show a comparison for the NI method that considers only the network structure attributes and the multi-attribute fusion method $(NI+OI)$, as shown in Fig. 5. The latter shows significant progress, in particular, performing well in removing a small number of nodes as well as in the middle and late stages. The effectiveness of multi-attribute fusion for influential node discovery in domain-specific networks is intuitively verified.

Similarly, Table 3 shows the experimental results for the AS network in the four countries mentioned above. In the BG and CA national networks, the multi-attribute fusion approach in this paper removes the same number of nodes as the DC approach according to the requirement of reducing the network core size to less than 20%. The $(NI+OI)$ approach makes the network decomposed with a more significant number of connected components, in other words, this method makes the core size of the network decomposed smaller. From the results, the $(NI+OI)$ method performs best in the BR national AS network. Although the final result is that the DC method performs the best in the DE country network, as our analysis of Fig. 4(d) above says, with the removal of a small number of nodes, we can disrupt most of the network in that country, which is more relevant to the actual situation.

Table 3. Experimental results of four different national AS networks:number of deleted nodes Del, number of connected components C(r), network core size ratio S(r), deletion rate Del rate, and he six methods are DC, BC, CC, EC, NI, and NI+OI.

	Del	C(r)	S(r) (%)	Del rate (%)	Del	C(r)	S(r) (%)	Del rate (%)
Datasets	BG				BR			
DC	13	399	18.39	2.15	296	4125	18.98	3.61
BC	13	399	18.39	2.15	337	4383	19.70	4.11
CC	32	349	18.88	5.29	864	3930	19.81	10.55
EC	136	293	15.44	22.48	1684	3832	19.98	20.55
NI	15	403	18.56	2.48	358	4400	19.97	4.37
NI+OI	**13**	**400**	**13.79**	**2.15**	**266**	**4150**	**19.72**	**3.25**
Datasets	CA				DE			
DC	27	743	15.04	2.16	**58**	**999**	**19.53**	**3.23**
BC	29	772	19.04	2.32	77	1117	15.53	4.28
CC	124	691	14.48	9.92	100	1000	19.64	5.56
EC	186	759	11.92	14.88	88	1007	15.30	4.90
NI	30	778	16.16	2.40	65	1055	19.19	3.62
NI+OI	**27**	**758**	**18.64**	**2.16**	63	1096	19.19	3.51

5 Conclusion

By evaluating the importance of nodes, we can strengthen key nodes in the network design and deployment stage to reduce the possibility of network failure, or analyze the communication network with known topology, which can shorten the maintenance time of the network. For the research on the regional invulnerability of the Internet, we first focus solely on the network structure and propose a node ranking method that focuses on neighbours' influence to overcome local attributes' limitations. We have carried out in vulnerability experiments on many networks in different fields, proving our method's effectiveness and superiority. Innovatively, based on structural attributes, we introduce node attributes and a multi-attribute node sorting method, which makes our performance further in network vulnerability testing. Based on the multi-attribute method, we study the invulnerability of AS-level networks in different countries, make an in-depth analysis combined with the network topology, and find that other network structures have extra resistance to attacks. This research provides good guidance for the security protection of network infrastructure.

Acknowledgment. The authors would like to thank all the members of the IVSN Research Group, Zhejiang University of Technology for the valuable discussions about the ideas and technical details presented in this paper.

References

1. Akritidis, L., Katsaros, D., Bozanis, P.: Identifying the productive and influential bloggers in a community. IEEE Trans. Syst. Man Cybern. Part C Appl. Rev. **41**(5), 759–764 (2011)
2. Carisimo, E., Selmo, C., Alvarez-Hamelin, J.I., Dhamdhere, A.: Studying the evolution of content providers in the internet core. In: 2018 Network Traffic Measurement and Analysis Conference (TMA), pp. 1–8. IEEE (2018)
3. Carmi, S., Havlin, S., Kirkpatrick, S., Shavitt, Y., Shir, E.: A model of internet topology using K-shell decomposition. Proc. Natl. Acad. Sci. **104**(27), 11150–11154 (2007)
4. Comin, C.H., da Fontoura Costa, L.: Identifying the starting point of a spreading process in complex networks. Phys. Rev. E **84**(5), 056105 (2011)
5. De Arruda, G.F., Barbieri, A.L., Rodriguez, P.M., Rodrigues, F.A., Moreno, Y., da Fontoura Costa, L.: Role of centrality for the identification of influential spreaders in complex networks. Phys. Rev. E **90**(3), 032812 (2014)
6. Freeman, L.C.: A set of measures of centrality based on betweenness. Sociometry **40**, 35–41 (1977)
7. Giotsas, V., Luckie, M., Huffaker, B., Claffy, K.: Inferring complex as relationships. In: Proceedings of the 2014 Conference on Internet Measurement Conference, pp. 23–30 (2014)
8. Gregori, E., Improta, A., Lenzini, L., Orsini, C.: The impact of IXPs on the AS-level topology structure of the internet. Comput. Commun. **34**(1), 68–82 (2011)
9. Jin, Y., Scott, C., Dhamdhere, A., Giotsas, V., Krishnamurthy, A., Shenker, S.: Stable and practical {AS} relationship inference with {ProbLink}. In: 16th USENIX Symposium on Networked Systems Design and Implementation (NSDI 2019), pp. 581–598 (2019)

10. Katz, L.: A new status index derived from sociometric analysis. Psychometrika **18**(1), 39–43 (1953). https://doi.org/10.1007/BF02289026
11. Kitsak, M., et al.: Identification of influential spreaders in complex networks. Nat. Phys. **6**(11), 888–893 (2010)
12. Liu, B., Li, Z., Chen, X., Huang, Y., Liu, X.: Recognition and vulnerability analysis of key nodes in power grid based on complex network centrality. IEEE Trans. Circ. Syst. II Express Briefs **65**(3), 346–350 (2017)
13. Lü, L., Chen, D., Ren, X.L., Zhang, Q.M., Zhang, Y.C., Zhou, T.: Vital nodes identification in complex networks. Phys. Rep. **650**, 1–63 (2016)
14. Peng, S., et al.: A multi-view framework for BGP anomaly detection via graph attention network. Comput. Netw. **214**, 109129 (2022)
15. Peng, S., Shu, X., Ruan, Z., Huang, Z., Xuan, Q.: Inferring multiple relationships between ASes using graph convolutional network. arXiv preprint arXiv:2107.13504 (2021)
16. Peng, X., Yao, H., Du, J., Wang, Z., Ding, C.: Invulnerability of scale-free network against critical node failures based on a renewed cascading failure model. Phys. A: Stat. Mech. Appl. **421**, 69–77 (2015)
17. Sabidussi, G.: The centrality index of a graph. Psychometrika **31**(4), 581–603 (1966). https://doi.org/10.1007/BF02289527
18. Salavati, C., Abdollahpouri, A., Manbari, Z.: Ranking nodes in complex networks based on local structure and improving closeness centrality. Neurocomputing **336**, 36–45 (2019)
19. Shah, D., Zaman, T.: Rumors in a network: who's the culprit? IEEE Trans. Inf. Theory **57**(8), 5163–5181 (2011)
20. Siganos, G., Faloutsos, M., Faloutsos, P., Faloutsos, C.: Power laws and the AS-level internet topology. IEEE/ACM Trans. Netw. **11**(4), 514–524 (2003)
21. Wenli, F., Zhigang, L., Ping, H., Shengwei, M.: Cascading failure model in power grids using the complex network theory. IET Gener. Transm. Distrib. **10**(15), 3940–3949 (2016)
22. Yunming, W., Si, C., Chengsheng, P., Bo, C.: Measure of invulnerability for command and control network based on mission link. Inf. Sci. **426**, 148–159 (2018)

Digital Society and Public Security

FedDFA: Dual-Factor Aggregation for Federated Driver Distraction Detection

Hang Gao and Yi Liu[✉]

Institute of Public Safety Research, Department of Engineering Physics,
Tsinghua University, Beijing 100084, China
gaohang@mail.tsinghua.edu.cn, liuyi@tsinghua.edu.cn

Abstract. This paper proposes FedDFA (Federated Dual-Factor Aggregation), an effective aggregation strategy for the application of federated learning in the field of vision-based driver distraction detection task. We argue that simply treating this task as an image recognition task is not enough. Image characteristics are further explored in this paper and we found that the driver's diversity is an important factor. Based on the image characteristic analysis, FedDFA is introduced, which calculates the aggregation weights based on the number of images and that of drivers on each client for better parameter aggregation during federated learning. Extensive experiments are conducted and experimental results show that FedDFA achieves satisfactory performance.

Keywords: Federated learning · Driver distraction detection ·
Intelligent transportation · Public safety · Computer vision

1 Introduction

Driver distractions, such as talking on the phone, operating the radio, and drinking while driving, have become the main causes of traffic accidents and seriously endangered public safety. Therefore, many researchers pay attention to detecting driver distractions. Benefitting from the development of deep learning, most of the recent works are vision-based, i.e., building a neural network for analyzing in-vehicle surveillance videos to detect distractions. Convolutional neural networks (CNNs) are the most widely-adopted architecture [4,8,11,16] because it has been proved to be suitable for image analysis. As the vision transformer (ViT) yields unusually brilliant results, the choice between CNNs and ViT for driver distraction detection has been studied [9], and results show that ViT has no obvious advantages and CNNs should be given priority. Besides, two hot issues have attracted the spotlight, the first one is the overfitting brought by the limitation of the dataset. Several data augmentation schemes [3,13] have been proposed to reduce overfitting. The second one is the real-time requirement. Some recent work [5,14] has been devoted to design lightweight CNNs for real-time driver distraction detection. In summary, the driver distraction detection technology is developing fast, however, the above researches ignore a social problem: data privacy.

Generally, training a neural network requires collecting a large amount of data to a computation center, which is called centralized training. However, in the field of driver distraction detection, videos and images contain driver's privacy. Centralized training means that the driver's privacy will be leaked to the computing center. Similar problems exist in many field of social computing, therefore, how to train a neural network under the premise of preserving privacy has become a hot issue.

Recently, federated learning [12] has been proposed for privacy-preserving learning. It is a decentralized training strategy. Two kinds of roles, a server and multiple clients, train a global neural network collaboratively. Specifically, federated learning consists of multiple communication rounds. At each round, the server first sends initial parameters to each client. Then, to preserve data privacy, each client loads the received parameters to its local network and trains with its local data, and trained parameters are sent to the server. Finally, the server aggregates the received parameters and sends the aggregated parameters back to the clients to start the next round. It can be seen that the local data stored on each client do not need to be uploaded, therefore, privacy can be preserved. Some scholars have studied the application of federated learning in the field of driver drowsiness detection [18], which is also vision-based, and proved that the federated learning achieves satisfactory performance compared with centralized learning meanwhile protecting data privacy. In the above scheme, the driver drowsiness detection task is simply regarded as an image recognition task. It does make sense. However, in-vehicle images, including images used for detecting drivers' drowsiness and distractions, have their characteristics (see Sect. 3). Classical federated learning does not take this into account. We argue that when federated learning is applied to a specific field, the characteristics of that field must be fully considered so that effective federated learning can be achieved.

This paper proposes federated dual-factor aggregation (FedDFA), an effective aggregation algorithm for the application of federated learning in the field of driver distraction detection. The impact of data characteristics on the performance of the trained model is explored, and it can be found that the driver's diversity is an important factor. FedDFA is designed to calculate weights based on both the number of images and the number of drivers in the training set to achieve better aggregation. Experimental results show that the performance of FedDFA is satisfactory.

In summary, the main contributions of this paper are as follows:

- We explore the image characteristics, and the analysis proves that the driver's diversity in the training set is an important factor for the performance of the trained model.
- A novel federated dual-factor aggregation (FedDFA) algorithm is proposed, which utilize two factors to calculate aggregation weights to achieve better aggregation.

– Extensive experiments are conducted, and experimental results show that the proposed FedDFA achieves satisfactory performance.

2   Related Work

2.1   Vision-Based Driver Distraction Detection

So far, many vision-based driver distraction detection schemes have been proposed. Among them, the first public dataset for driver distraction identification is released and a deep learning-based scheme is proposed [4]. The proposed scheme that consists of face and hand localizations, and skin segmentation shows great performance. Similarly, a two-stage scheme [16] is proposed to localize key points of the driver and feed the extracted features into a recurrent neural network. Moreover, a hybrid approach [11] proposes to integrate spatial and spectral features into a deep neural network, and it achieves the state-of-the-art performance. Besides, based on the idea of the capsule network, a CapsNet-based approach [8] is proposed.

To reduce overfitting, a class based data augmentation is proposed [3]. For a specific distraction class, key regions of the images are first extracted, and these regions are randomly interchanged between different images of the same class. A combination data augmentation scheme is proposed [13], which consists of skin segmentation, facial blurring, and classical augmentation techniques. Results show that it has great promise.

To meet real-time requirements, a lightweight MobileVGG [2] is proposed. MobileVGG contains only 2.2M parameters and achieves 34 FPS, the performance of MobileVGG is also satisfactory. A drowsiness and distraction detection system [5], which is based on face detection, is designed for compact mobile devices is proposed. Although the performance of the system is slightly lower than InceptionV3 and VGG16, considering the system achieves higher FPS and lower memory space requirement, it has great potential in practical application.

It can be seen that vision-based driver distraction detection schemes show outstanding performance, however, most of them are centralized training, and driver's privacy is ignored.

2.2   Federated Learning

Federated learning [12] has attracted a lot of attention since it can be used to train a neural network under the premise of privacy protection. FedAvg [12] is the most well-known aggregation algorithm. At each round, it performs a weighted summation of the trained parameters on different clients to obtain global parameters. Aggregation weights are calculated based on the number of data stored on each client. Let us take the t-th communication round as an example, the aggregation can be formulated as follow:

$$
\begin{aligned}
w_{t+1} &= \sum_{k=1}^{K} \frac{n_k}{n} w_{t+1}^k \\
&= \sum_{k=1}^{K} \frac{n_k}{n} (w_t - \eta g_t^k) \\
&= \sum_{k=1}^{K} \frac{n_k}{n} w_t - \sum_{k=1}^{K} \frac{n_k}{n} \eta g_t^k \\
&= w_t - \eta \sum_{k=1}^{K} \frac{n_k}{n} g_t^k
\end{aligned}
\tag{1}
$$

where w_t is the initial parameters for the t-th communication round, and each client adopted w_t as the initial parameters. η is the learning rate, and g_t^k is the average gradient on the k-th client at t-th round. n_k is the amount of data on k-th client and $n = \sum_{k=1}^{K} n_k$. It can be seen that based on this computation mode, FedAvg allows all clients to update global parameters cooperatively, so that the model can be trained iteratively. Meanwhile, data used for training can be stored locally, which is helpful to avoid the risk of privacy disclosure. From the perspective of privacy protection, this is superior to existing centralized training.

Federated learning has shown great application potential in many fields, such as smart cities [7,10], smart healthcare [1,15] and public safety [6]. In the field of human factors related intelligent transportation, federated learning has been studied for vision-based driver drowsiness detection [18]. To apply federated learning effectively, we argue that the characteristics of different fields should be carefully considered.

3   Pre-experiments

Most existing researches regard vision-based driver distraction detection as an image recognition task. However, previous study [4] have shown that there is a performance gap between two data set configuration: split-by-random and split-by-driver. Split-by-random means that the collected images are divided into training set, validation set, and test set randomly, and each driver's images are contained in three sets. Split-by-driver is a more realistic setup [4] because during the model training stage, it is impossible to predict the drivers that may be encountered in the future. Therefore, follow the split-by-driver configuration, each driver's data is contained in only one set, which means drivers in the training set, validation set and test set are not overlap.

As reported in [4], the trained InceptionV3 achieves an accuracy of 95.17% on the split-by-random data set and that of 90.068% on split-by-driver data set. The most intuitive difference between the two configurations is whether the trained model has ever seen the driver described by the testing image during the training phase. Therefore, we argue that the driver's diversity is an important factor for the performance of a trained model for vision-based driver distraction detection. To support our instinct, some experiments are conducted. We fix the number of images in the training set, and changed the number of drivers to construct several training sets. Then, models are trained on different training sets and evaluated on the same testing set. Experiments in this section are conducted on the State Farm data set (details are shown in Sect. 5.1). Four training sets

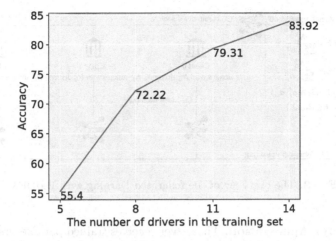

Fig. 1. Performance of models trained on different training set.

are constructed. Each of them contains 5,000 images yet numbers of drivers are different. The testing set contains 8,409 images with 12 drivers. Results are shown in Fig. 1. It can be seen that as the number of drivers in the training set increases, the performance of the trained model also increases significantly. Therefore, our intuition is supported: driver's diversity is noteworthy in the field of vision-based driver distraction detection.

4 Method

4.1 Problem Definition

There are K enterprises expect to jointly build a model for driver distraction detection and each of them owns a labeled dataset. Let N_I^k denotes the number of training images stored on the k-th client, and N_D^k denotes the number of drivers in the training set on the k-th client, where $k \in \{1, 2, ..., K\}$. For date privacy-preserving consideration, all enterprises agreed to adopt the federated learning framework to train a neural network. The goal is to train a global model which benefits from abundant data sources from all enterprises.

4.2 Overview

Figure 2 shows the overview of the federated learning framework with the proposed FedDFA.

It is an iterative training process which consists of multiple communication rounds. At each round, there are four steps:

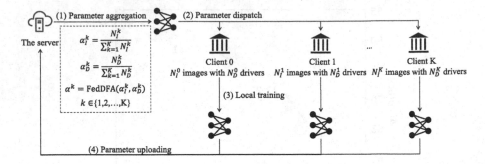

Fig. 2. The overview of the federated learning with FedDFA.

- **Parameter Aggregation.** The server receives trained parameters from each client, and aggregate them following FedDFA.
- **Parameter Dispatch.** The aggregated parameters are dispatched to each client.
- **Local Training.** Each client loads the received parameters to its local network, and trains the network with its local training set.
- **Parameter Uploading.** After local training, trained parameters are uploaded to the server. The server conduct parameter aggregation and start the next round.

4.3   Federated Dual-Factor Aggregation

As illustrated in Sect. 3, the performance of a trained neural network for driver distraction detection is not only affected by the number of images in the training set, but also the number of drivers. The classical FedAvg calculates the aggregation weights based on the number of images owned by each client, this ignores the factor about drivers. Although FedAvg follows the standard gradient descent algorithms, however, some studies [17] that focus on aggregation algorithm show that more factors should be considered during aggregation. Therefore, we propose an intuitive improvement strategy to calculate aggregation weights based on two factors, i.e., the number of images and that of drivers on each client. The core principle is that if a client has more images about more drivers, it should be assigned a higher weight for aggregation.

To calculate aggregation weights based on two factors, firstly, two factor-specific weights are calculated according to the number of images and that of drivers respectively. Formally:

$$
\begin{aligned}
\alpha_I^k &= \frac{n_I^k}{\sum_{k=1}^{K} n_I^k} \\
\alpha_D^k &= \frac{n_D^k}{\sum_{k=1}^{K} n_D^k}
\end{aligned}
\tag{2}
$$

where α_I^k and α_I^k is the weight calculated by the number of images and that calculated by the number of drivers for the k-th client. Then, We investigate the following two strategies to obtain the aggregation weight.

Average. In this strategy, the average of α_I^k and α_I^k is obtained as the aggregation weight. That is to say, the contribution of the two factors is regard as the same. Formally:

$$\alpha^k = 0.5 \times \alpha_I^k + 0.5 \times \alpha_D^k \tag{3}$$

where α^k is the aggregation weight for the k-th client. It is undeniable that the weighted summation may be a more effective method, i.e., $\alpha^k = \beta \times \alpha_I^k + (1 - \beta) \times \alpha_D^k$. However, the weighted summation means that β will be treated as a hyperparameter, this requires a lot of effort to tune β and the cost is too high in the actual scenario. Therefore, we simply assign the same weight to α_I^k and α_D^k.

Product. In this strategy, the product of α_I^k and α_D^k is obtained, and all products of K clients are normalize as the aggregation weights. Formally:

$$\alpha^k = \frac{(\alpha_I^k \times \alpha_D^k)}{\sum_{k=1}^{K}(\alpha_I^k \times \alpha_D^k)} \tag{4}$$

where α^k is the aggregation weight for the k-th client.

The choice between Average and Product is treated as a hyperparameter. Algorithm 1 shows the pseudo-code of FedDFA. Note that when each client has the same number of drivers, the proposed FedDFA is equivalent to the FedAvg. Besides, it is obvious that FedDFA is a static aggregation strategy, which means the aggregation weights can be calculated and fixed before training rather than changing during training like other dynamic aggregation strategies [17]. We will explore a combination of static and dynamic aggregation strategies to achieve effective and efficient federated learning in future work. In this paper, we focus on proving the validity of the factor of driver's diversity and the effectiveness of FedDFA.

5   Experiments

In this section, datasets used in this paper are first introduced. Then, experimental settings are introduced in detail. Finally, experimental results are analyzed.

5.1   Datasets

The proposed FedDFA is evaluated on two widely-studied datasets: the State Farm Distracted Driver Detection (State Farm for short) dataset[1], and the AUC Distracted Driver V2 (AUC for short) dataset [4]. Both of them contains 10 distracted driving behaviors, including safe driving, text right, phone right, text

---

[1] https://www.kaggle.com/competitions/state-farm-distracted-driver-detection.

Algorithm 1. FedDFA. K is the number of selected clients and k is the index of k-th client, D_k is the training set owned by the k-th client, E is the local epoch, B is the local batch size, η is the learning rate. N_I^k denotes the number of images and N_D^k denotes that of drivers on k-th client.

Server executes:
  initialize w_0
  for each round $t = 1, 2, \ldots$ **do**
    $S_t \leftarrow$ (random set of K clients)
    for each client $k \in S_t$ **in parallel do**
      $w_{t+1}^k \leftarrow \text{ClientUpdate}(k, w_t)$
    end for
    $\alpha_I^k = \dfrac{N_I^k}{\sum_{k=1}^K N_I^k}$
    $\alpha_D^k = \dfrac{N_D^k}{\sum_{k=1}^K N_D^k}$
    $\alpha^k = \text{FedDFA}(\alpha_I^k, \alpha_D^k)$ // *Average or Product*
    $w_{t+1} \leftarrow \sum_{k=1}^K \alpha^k w_{t+1}^k$
  end for

ClientUpdate(k, w)**:**
  $\mathcal{B} \leftarrow$ (split D_k into batches of size B)
  for each local epoch i from 1 to E **do**
    for batch $b \in \mathcal{B}$ **do**
      $w \leftarrow w - \eta(w; b)$
    end for
  end for
  return w to server

---

left, phone left, adjusting radio, drinking, reaching behind, hair or makeup, and talking to passenger.

The state farm dataset contains 22,437 images with 26 drivers. Driver IDs in State Farm dataset are provided therefore it is easy to construct datasets that simulate specific data distributions. In this paper, 5 clients are assumed and statistics of constructed state farm training sets following the split-by-driver configuration are shown in Table 1. In D0,D1 and D2, data distributions of specific scenarios are simulated. In D3 and D4, drivers are random selected to form datasets to evaluate the generalization of FedDFA. For evaluation, 3,642 images with 6 drivers are selected as testing set.

The AUC dataset contains 44 drivers and 14,478 images. There is a split-by-driver AUC dataset where 12,555 images of 38 drivers in the training set and 1,923 images of 6 drivers in the test set. The AUC dataset is a more challenging dataset because the test set contains more factors in addition to driver's diversity, including cars, lighting conditions, and driving conditions [4]. We manually annotate the driver ID of each image and the constructed AUC training sets following the split-by-driver configuration are shown in Table 1.

Table 1. Statistics of State Farm training sets and AUC training sets used in this paper. Statistics in each box refers to (the number of drivers/the number of images).

Training sets	Statistics				
	Client 0	Client 1	Client 2	Client 3	Client 4
State Farm D0	1/1000	2/1000	3/1000	4/1000	10/100
State Farm D1	1/1000	2/1000	3/1000	4/1000	10/1000
State Farm D2	1/1000	2/500	3/333	4/250	10/100
State Farm D3	2/2470	5/5545	2/1796	4/3381	7/5590
State Farm D4	3/3696	3/3308	1/1011	4/3519	9/7248
AUC D0	4/1000	5/1000	6/1000	7/1000	16/100
AUC D1	4/1000	5/1000	6/1000	7/1000	16/1000
AUC D2	4/1000	5/800	6/600	7/400	16/200
AUC D3	3/966	5/1862	11/4260	7/2042	12/1600
AUC D4	10/3736	3/1141	5/1844	10/2409	10/1600

5.2 Comparison Method

This paper proposes a novel factor to improve the aggregation algorithm in federated learning framework for driver distraction detection, therefore, experiments aim to demonstrate the efficiency of the new factor. For fairness considerations, FedAvg [12], which is also a static aggregation algorithm, is taken as the compared method for experiments. Follow FedAvg, the aggregation weights are calculated based on the number of images in the training set on each client. Formally:

$$\alpha^k = \frac{n_I^k}{\sum_{k=1}^{K} n_I^k} \tag{5}$$

where n_I^k is the number of images in the training set on the k-th client.

5.3 Implementation Details

Models in this paper are implemented with PyTorch (version 1.11.0), and torchvision (version 0.12.0), and trained on one Tesla P100 GPU. The MobileNetV2 [14] is adopted as the target global network, and parameters pre-trained on ImageNet is taken as the initial parameters for the first communication round. The SGD optimizer with learning rate of 0.01 is adopted for training. Mini-batch is taken to train the models, and the batch size is set to 32. The local epoch is set to 1. During training, parameters of the batch normalization layers in MobileNetV2 are frozen. All results reported in this section are the average of at least 3 runs.

5.4 Experimental Analysis

The Effectiveness of FedDFA. Experimental results are reported in Table 2, the following conclusions can be drawn:

Table 2. Accuracy of models trained on different training sets. Best results are in bold type.

Training sets	FedAvg	FedDFA
State Farm D0	80.34	**84.18**
State Farm D1	84.07	**88.31**
State Farm D2	77.50	**82.13**
State Farm D3	87.42	**88.61**
State Farm D4	**88.58**	88.48
AUC D0	55.28	**62.32**
AUC D1	72.51	**75.74**
AUC D2	58.87	**65.55**
AUC D3	71.49	**76.13**
AUC D4	68.95	**72.09**

- **Driver's diversity is noteworthy in federated learning.** In D0, client 5 owns the least images, however, these images describe the behavior of 10 drivers, which is the largest number of drivers among all clients. As shown in both State Farm D0 row and AUC D0 row, FedDFA performs better than FedAvg, which shows that driver's diversity is noteworthy for the application of federated learning in the field of driver distraction detection.

  Moreover, D1 is a more realistic setup: every enterprise tries to make equal contributions to the agreed federated learning, i.e., no matter how many drivers the enterprise employs, the number of images collected by each client is the same. As shown in State Farm D1 row, FedDFA outperforms FedAvg by 4.24% in terms of accuracy. This also illustrates the importance of the factor of driver's diversity. Results on AUC D1 row show the same conclusion. D2 is another setup that every enterprise tries to make equal contributions to the agreed federated learning: if an enterprise cannot find enough drivers, it will collect more images about limited drivers for training. In this case, FedDFA outperforms FedAvg significantly on both State Farm D2 and AUC D2.

- **The effectiveness and generalization ability of FedDFA is satisfactory.** Results in D0, D1, and D2 rows illustrate the effectiveness of FedDFA. Besides, results on State Farm D3, AUC D3, and AUC D4 show that the proposed FedDFA achieves the best performance. These prove that the effectiveness and generalization ability of the proposed FedDFA is satisfactory, and indicate that taking the number of drivers in the training set as a factor for calculating aggregation weights is crucial for better federated learning performance in the field of vision-based driver distraction detection. Although the performance of FedDFA shows in State Farm D4 is slightly worse than FedAvg, considering other experimental results, the factor of driver's diversity still worth further exploration for the application of federated learning in the field of driver distraction detection.

Table 3. Ablation study. Experiments are conducted on AUC training sets. Best results are in bold type.

Aggregation method	AUC D0	AUC D1	AUC D2	AUC D3	AUC D4
FedDFA	**62.32**	**75.74**	65.55	**76.13**	**72.09**
Removing the number of images	61.89	75.74	**67.36**	69.56	70.46
Removing the number of drivers	55.28	72.51	58.87	71.49	68.95

Ablation Analysis. This section aims to demonstrate the relative effectiveness of two factors introduced in FedDFA. We remove one factor at a time and observe how that factor affects the performance of the model. We evaluate two different configurations. In (1), the number of images is removed. In (2), the number of drivers is removed, which is equal to FedAvg. Experiments are conducted on AUC training sets.

As shown in Table 3, removing the number of drivers significantly decreases the performance, which reveals that the driver's diversity plays a crucial role in FedDFA. Furthermore, in most cases, removing the number of drivers causes greater performance degradation, which indicates that the driver's diversity contributes more to the performance than the number of images does. It is noteworthy that results on AUC D2 show that removing the number images achieves the best performance, which indicates that he number of images has a negative effect on model performance. We argue that a possible explanation is that the number of images mislead the aggregation weights, so that the weights can not reasonably express the quality of models on different clients. However, results on AUC D2 still support the view that driver's diversity is a crucial factor for better performance. We will conduct in-depth research about this phenomenon in the future work.

Visualization. To further investigate the inner workings of FedDFA, we visualize the curves of test set accuracy vs. communication rounds on AUC training sets. As shown in Fig. 3, except for AUC D0, FedDFA achieves better performance with fewer communication rounds than that of FedAvg. Overall, the communication cost of FedDFA is acceptable, this is friendly for practical application scenarios.

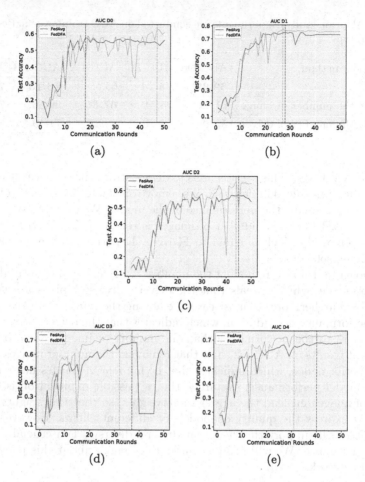

(a)

(b)

(c)

(d)

(e)

Fig. 3. Test set accuracy vs. communication rounds on AUC training sets. The dotted line marks the communication round that the model reaches the best performance.

6   Discussion and Conclusion

This paper explores the characteristics of images used for vision-based driver distraction detection and their effects on the performance of the trained model. We find that besides the number of images in the training set, the number of drivers in the training set is equally important. Based on this fact, FedDFA is introduced, which calculates aggregation weights based on the number of images and that of drivers owned by each client. Extensive experiments illustrate that the proposed FedDFA shows satisfactory performance. In the era that privacy should be paid more and more attention, FedDFA can provide a valuable reference for the application of federated learning in the field of human factors related intelligent transportation, and further, the field of human factors related social computing, such as personalized education.

Acknowledgments. Funded by National Key R&D Program of China (No. 2021YFC3001500) and National Natural Science Foundation of China (No.72174102).

References

1. Baghersalimi, S., Teijeiro, T., Atienza, D., Aminifar, A.: Personalized real-time federated learning for epileptic seizure detection. IEEE J. Biomed. Health Inform. **26**, 898–909 (2021)
2. Baheti, B., Talbar, S., Gajre, S.: Towards computationally efficient and realtime distracted driver detection with mobilevgg network. IEEE Trans. Intell. Veh. **5**(4), 565–574 (2020)
3. Cronje, J., Engelbrecht, A.P.: Training convolutional neural networks with class based data augmentation for detecting distracted drivers. In: Proceedings of the 9th International Conference on Computer and Automation Engineering, pp. 126–130 (2017)
4. Eraqi, H.M., Abouelnaga, Y., Saad, M.H., Moustafa, M.N.: Driver distraction identification with an ensemble of convolutional neural networks. vol. 2019. Hindawi (2019)
5. Flores-Monroy, J., Nakano-Miyatake, M., Perez-Meana, H., Escamilla-Hernandez, E., Sanchez-Perez, G.: A CNN-based driver's drowsiness and distraction detection system. In: Vergara-Villegas, O.O., Cruz-Sánchez, V.G., Sossa-Azuela, J.H., Carrasco-Ochoa, J.A., Martínez-Trinidad, J.F., Olvera-López, J.A. (eds.) Pattern Recognition. MCPR 2022. Lecture Notes in Computer Science Mexican Conference on Pattern Recognition, vol. 13264, pp. 83–93. Springer (2022). https://doi.org/10.1007/978-3-031-07750-0_8
6. Gao, H., Liu, Y.: Fedurr: a federated transfer learning framework for multi-department collaborative urban risk recognition. In: Proceedings of the 7th ACM SIGSPATIAL International Workshop Emergency Management Using GIS, pp. 1–5 (2021)
7. Gao, Y., Liu, L., Zheng, X., Zhang, C., Ma, H.: Federated sensing: edge-cloud elastic collaborative learning for intelligent sensing. IEEE Internet Things J. **8**(14), 11100–11111 (2021)
8. Jain, D.K., Jain, R., Lan, X., Upadhyay, Y., Thareja, A.: Driver distraction detection using capsule network. Neural Comput. Appl. **33**(11), 6183–6196 (2021)
9. Koay, H.V., Chuah, J.H., Chow, C.O.: Convolutional neural network or vision transformer? benchmarking various machine learning models for distracted driver detection. In: TENCON 2021–2021 IEEE Region 10 Conference (TENCON), pp. 417–422. IEEE (2021)
10. Liu, Y., Nie, J., Li, X., Ahmed, S.H., Lim, W.Y.B., Miao, C.: Federated learning in the sky: Aerial-ground air quality sensing framework with UAV swarms. IEEE Internet Things J. **8**(12), 9827–9837 (2020)
11. Mase, J.M., Chapman, P., Figueredo, G.P., Torres, M.T.: A hybrid deep learning approach for driver distraction detection. In: 2020 International Conference on Information and Communication Technology Convergence (ICTC), pp. 1–6. IEEE (2020)
12. McMahan, B., Moore, E., Ramage, D., Hampson, S., Arcas, B.A.: Communication-efficient learning of deep networks from decentralized data. In: Artificial intelligence and statistics, pp. 1273–1282. PMLR (2017)

13. Mofid, N., Bayrooti, J., Ravi, S.: Keep your ai-es on the road: tackling distracted driver detection with convolutional neural networks and targeted data augmentation. arXiv preprint arXiv:2006.10955 (2020)
14. Sandler, M., Howard, A., Zhu, M., Zhmoginov, A., Chen, L.C.: Mobilenetv 2: inverted residuals and linear bottlenecks. In: Proceedings of the IEEE conference on computer vision and pattern recognition, pp. 4510–4520 (2018)
15. Wang, Q., Zhou, Y.: Fedspl: federated self-paced learning for privacy-preserving disease diagnosis. Briefings Bioinf. **23**(1), bbab498 (2022)
16. Weyers, P., Schiebener, D., Kummert, A.: Action and object interaction recognition for driver activity classification. In: 2019 IEEE Intelligent Transportation Systems Conference (ITSC), pp. 4336–4341. IEEE (2019)
17. Yeganeh, Y., Farshad, A., Navab, N., Albarqouni, S.: Inverse distance aggregation for federated learning with non-IID data. In: Albarqouni, S., et al. (eds.) DART/DCL -2020. LNCS, vol. 12444, pp. 150–159. Springer, Cham (2020). https://doi.org/10.1007/978-3-030-60548-3_15
18. Zafar, A., Prehofer, C., Cheng, C.H.: Federated learning for driver status monitoring. In: 2021 IEEE International Intelligent Transportation Systems Conference (ITSC), pp. 1463–1469. IEEE (2021)

Defense of Signal Modulation Classification Attack Based on GAN

Jiawei Zhu[1], Yuhang Liu[2,3(✉)], Dongwei Xu[2,3], Hao Yang[2,3], Qi Xuan[2,3], and Shunling Wang[1]

[1] Science and Technology on Communication Information Security Control Laboratory, Jiaxing 314033, China
[2] Institute of Cyberspace Security, Zhejiang University of Technology, Hangzhou 310023, China
2112103266@zjut.edu.cn
[3] College of Information Engineering, Zhejiang University of Technology, Hangzhou 310023, China

Abstract. Although deep learning has been broadly used in all kinds of domains and has also achieved very good performance, it is obvious that deep learning is very vulnerable to be attacked shown by extensive researches (e.g. even a very small perturbation is added to the raw signal data, the result of the modulation classification of the signal by the deep neural network will be wrong), which will cause serious consequences. Thus, it is necessary to find some ways to defense this attack. As a new deep learning model in recent years, Generative Adversarial Network (GAN) has been applied to the field of radio communication, which can encrypt the signal data, so as to ensure the reliable transmission of the signal. In this paper, a defense method against signal modulation classification attack based on GAN is developed, which is used to utilize generator to reconstruct the signal sample to improve the classification accuracy of the model, while the defense ability of the model against adversarial samples is improved. It has been shown that the method achieved good results in experiments.

Keywords: Deep learning · Generative Adversarial Network · Signal modulation classification · Adversarial samples defense

1 Introduction

With the powerful ability of learning and inference, deep learning has now been broadly used in all kinds of domains of AI, such as natural language processing (NLP), autonomous driving, image recognition, biomedical, etc. Deep learning can use a large neural network to effectively extract data features and excavate potential connections between data, with strong feature learning capabilities and feature expression capabilities. At present, deep learning is also becoming increasingly broadly used in the domain of radio communication (e.g. the signal modulation types can be classified according to the cyclo-stationary characteristics or spectral characteristics of the signal. And also DL can be used for radio parameter adaptive decisions and tuning and optimize the target selection radio parameters according to the current channel quality and user needs etc.).

X. Meng et al. (Eds.): BDSC 2022, CCIS 1640, pp. 251–259, 2022.
https://doi.org/10.1007/978-981-19-7532-5_16

There are following advantages applying DL to the signal modulation classification: first, it is convenient to obtain a large amount of data from the communication environment for DL to learn; second, DL is famous for its powerful ability to extract features instead of manual selection; and last, convolutional neural networks (CNN) can reduce data parameters by using convolutional layers instead of fully connected layers [1]. However, DL is very vulnerable to be attacked. Szegedy et al. [2] recently has found that DL model is easily to be deceived by adversarial examples designed by humans. They add an invisible small perturbation to the data samples, the CNN classifier will change its predictions to be wrong with high confidence, which means that if there is an adversary transmitting perturbations to our communication network, our receiver classifier will not classify the signals received correctly. Thus, it is necessary to find some ways to defense this attack.

As a new deep learning model in recent years, Generative Adversarial Network (GAN) [3] has made a breakthrough in the field of image. GAN can be used to realize the migration of picture style or realize face transformation and picture writing. In addition to the image field, GAN is also applied in the field of radio communication, enabling encryption of signal data to ensure reliable transmission of the signal.

In this paper, a defense method against signal modulation classification attack based on GAN is presented, which is used to utilize generator to reconstruct the signal sample to improve the classification accuracy of the model, so as to improve the performance of defense of the model against samples. A certain proportion of raw signal samples and adversarial samples is contained in the signal samples reconstructed using the generator, while all as raw signal samples or all as adversarial samples is also accepted. The method presented here aims to improve the performance of defense of the model, so the signal samples should contain large or all adversarial samples with only small or no raw signal samples.

The contribution of this paper is as follows: the method of this paper uses the raw signal data to train the GAN with the raw network data, so that the parameter distribution in the generate network G^* conforms to the raw signal data; and then the signal samples are reconstructed by G^*, which conform to the distribution of the raw signal data; and finally the noise in the adversarial sample is removed and classification accuracy of the classification model is improved.

2 Related Work

Since 2006, the concept of artificial neural networks with deep learning has been proposed by Professor Hinton et al. [4]. Its excellent ability to learn has received wide attention. Deep learning learns the data sample characteristics by training the data and then performs excellent performance of classification or regression tasks, enabling it to be applied to all aspects.

With the powerful ability of learning and inference of the DL, researchers have begun to apply it in the field of classification of modulated signal. Timothy J et al. proposed an algorithm based on Convolutional Neural Networks (CNN) [5], by which good results were achieved with 74% accuracy at high signal to noise ratio; Yanlun Wu et al. proposed a CNN_LSTM algorithm [6], by modifying the full-connected layer to a long short-term memory network of the convolutional neural network, and the data volume was reduced to 10% with more than 80% accuracy; Rajendran et al. proposed to directly use LSTM for signal modulation recognition [7], and when Multilayer LSTM was also stacked, the experiments showed 90% accuracy when SNR > 5 dB.

Since deep learning is highly vulnerable, the proposal of defense methods against attacks becomes necessary. In light of the vulnerability and robustness of the model, the concept of adversarial samples is proposed by Christian Szegedy [8]. Adversarial samples are carefully designed by the attacker to add small perturbations, which enable the model to output artificial results with high confidence. Based on this, scholars proposed adversarial defense methods based on adversarial samples. Data cleaning [9] is a common method of defense, and the defense effect is achieved through cleaning up the malicious data(e.g. a defense against spam detection systems, as mentioned by Nelson B [10]).There are also methods to improve defense ability by enhancing algorithm robustness (e.g. Bagging(bootstrap aggregating)、 RSM(random subspace method), Antidote [11–13] etc.). In addition to screening for malicious data, there are methods that constantly add adversarial samples to the training data to enhance the robustness of the model, which can effectively solve model overfitting, but Moosavi Dezfooli's study shows that new adversarial attack samples present can deceive the network again [14].

3 Our Work

In this paper, a defense method based on the GAN for signal modulation classification attack is proposed. First, the GAN is built according to the signal dataset, trained until the network reaches Nash equilibrium or the set maximum number of iterations; then, the signal samples are reconstructed by using the generator G^* in the trained GAN and finally the reconstructed samples are input into the raw model to test its classification accuracy.

The method this paper used is shown in Fig. 1. According to the radio signal data, an appropriate GAN will be built, which mainly contains two parts. The first part is generator G, which mainly utilize the input random noise to generate artificial signal. The second part is discriminator D which mainly judge whether the signal is a real signal or an artificial signal generated by G. The goal of generator G is generating the most "true" signal to deceive the discriminator D. And the discriminator D is used to correctly identify the signal is a real signal or an artificial signal generated by the generator G with as high as possible accuracy. The two models are always competing during mutual training. After the GAN has been trained completely, the signal samples will be reconstructed with R times random retrain using the generator G. Since the raw signal samples are used to train the GAN, the parameter distribution of the generator G complies with the raw signal samples. Therefore, the reconstructed samples using the generator G also fit the raw signal samples, thus the adversarial samples are eliminated from the signal sample and the classification accuracy of the model will be improved.

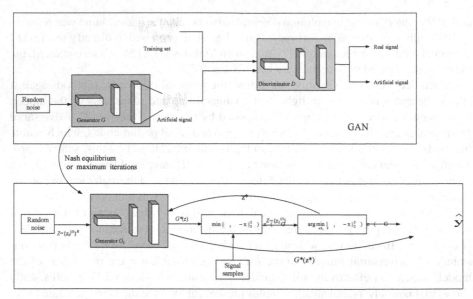

Fig. 1. Schematic diagram of the defense methods based on generative adversarial network.

3.1 Model

According to the signal dataset, then the GAN shown in Fig. 2 is constructed, where the generator G is shown in Fig. 2 (a).It contains a fully-connected layer, three deconvolutional layers, and one convolutional layer. The mathematical representation of the fully-connected layer is given as:

$$z^{(i)} = w^T x^{(i)} + b^{(i)} \tag{1}$$

where $z^{(i)}$ is the linear computation of the neurons; w^T is the neuronal weight matrix; $x^{(i)}$ represents the feature vector, and $b^{(i)}$ represents the bias.

The mathematical representation of the deconvolutional layer is as follows:

$$H_{out} = (H_{in} - 1)stride - 2padding + kernel\_size \tag{2}$$

$$W_{out} = (W_{in} - 1)stride - 2padding + kernel\_size \tag{3}$$

In summary, the H_{out} is the width of the deconvolutional layer output; the W_{out} is the length of the deconvolutional layer output; the H_{in} is the width of the input deconvolutional layer; the W_{in} is the length of the input deconvolutional layer; the $stride$ is the convolutional step length; the $padding$ complements the number of layers of 0 for each edge of the input, and the $kernel\_size$ is the convolutional kernel size.

The discriminator D is shown in Fig. 2(b), containing three convolutional layers and two fully-connected layers. The following equation shows this process.

$$H_{out} = (H_{in} + 2padding - kernel\_size)/stride + 1 \tag{4}$$

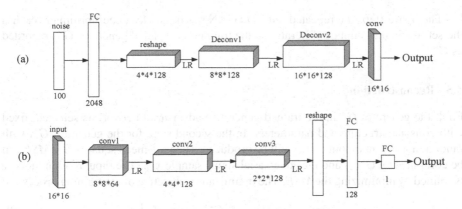

Fig. 2. Structure of the generative adversarial network.

$$W_{out} = (W_{in} + 2padding - kernel\_size)/stride + 1 \qquad (5)$$

where the H_{out} is the width of the deconvolutional layer output; the W_{out} is the length of the deconvolutional layer output; the H_{in} is the width of the input deconvolutional layer; the W_{in} is the length of the input deconvolutional layer; the *padding* complements the number of layers of 0 for each edge of the input and the stride is the convolutional step length, the *kernel_size* is the convolutional kernel size.

3.2 Training

First, the generator of the GAN is fixed, and the random noise z is input into the generator G, the output $G(z)$ is get. Then the $G(z)$ and the raw signal x_{ori} which means signal without attack are input to the discriminator D, and we calculates cross entropy loss of the output of the discriminator D with the confidence 0 or 1. And the parameters of the discriminator D is trained by minimizing the loss function, where the confidence of the artificial signal $G(z)$ generated by the generator G is 0 and the confidence of the raw signal G is 1. The optimization objective of the training process is:

$$\max_{D} V(D, G) = E_{x \sim P_{data(x_{ori})}}\big[\log D(x)\big] + E_{z \sim P_z(z)}\big[\log(1 - D(G(z)))\big] \qquad (6)$$

where the $D(\cdot)$ represents the output of the discriminator D; the $G(\cdot)$ represents the output of the generator G; the x_{ori} indicates the raw signal; the z indicates random noise; the $x \sim P_{data(x_{ori})}$ represents that x is sampled from the raw signal x_{ori}; the $z \sim P_z(z)$ represents z sampled from random noise and the $E(\cdot)$ represents expectations.

Then we fix the discriminator D of the GAN, the random noise z is input into the generator G. Then we obtain the output $G(z)$, which is input of the discriminator D. The cross-entropy loss is calculated between the output of D and $G(z)$, and the parameters of the generator G is trained by minimizing the loss function. The optimization objective of the training process is:

$$\min_{G} V(D, G) = E_{z \sim P_z(z)}\big[\log(1 - D(G(z)))\big] \qquad (7)$$

The above steps are repeated until the GAN reaches a Nash equilibrium or reaches the set maximum number of iterations, the training-completed generator G is recorded as G^*.

3.3   Reconstruction

First, the generator G^* in the trained generative adversarial network is selected, fixed with constant structure and parameters. In the second step, for the generator G^*, with random noise z, an output $G^*(z)$ will be produced. Then the mean square error MSE can be computed by $G^*(z)$ and the adversarial signal sample x_{sig}. The input random noise z is trained by minimizing the MSE. The optimization objective of the training process is:

$$\min_z E_{x \sim P_{data(x_{sig})}} \left[\left\| G^*(z) - x_{sig} \right\|_2 \right] \qquad (8)$$

Among these, $G^*(z)$ represents the generator G^* obtained after training described above; x_{sig} represents signal sample; $x \sim P_{data(x_{sig})}$ represents x is sampled from signal sample and $E(\cdot)$ is expectation.

The second step is repeated until the MSE is less than the set threshold, or the maximum number is reached iterations L:

$$E_{x \sim P_{data(x_{sig})}} \left[\left\| G^*(z) - x_{sig} \right\|_2 \leq \theta \right] \qquad (9)$$

where θ is a constant ($\theta > 0$).

The second and third steps were repeated for the R times random retrain signal which is used to reconstruct samples, and the z^* with the lowest error in the reconstruction was selected:

$$z^* = \arg \min_{z \in z_R} \left\| G^*(z) - x_{sig} \right\|_2^2 \qquad (10)$$

Finally, the defense performance test was conducted, and the raw signal sample x_{ori} and the reconstructed sample $G^*(z^*)$ were respectively input into the submodel to test its classification accuracy.

4   Experiment

4.1   Data Selection

The experiment selected the RML2016.10a signal dataset generated by simulation, and there are 11 modulation categories as follows contained in the dataset: BFSK, BPSK, 8PSK, QPSK, 16QAM, 64QAM, WBFM, PAM4, AM-DSB, CPFSK and AM-SSB. The SNR for each category was evenly distributed from 20 to 18 dB. Every sample is an IQ electromagnetic signal, and the sampling rate for per sample is 128. We selected electromagnetic signal samples with a signal-to-noise ratio above 10 db from the training set species, and the number of samples for the experiments was 44,000.

4.2 Experiment Setup

When building a GAN, the input dimension of the random noise z in the generator G is 100*1. And it contains a fully-connected layer, the neurons number of which of is 2048. And there are 2 deconvolutional layers, the step length of all the two layers is 1. All the convolutional kernel are sized with [5, 5, 128] with step length 1. The activation functions are all "Leaky Relu", which contains 1 convolutional layer. And the step length of the convolutional layer is 1. The convolutional kernel size [1, 5]. The discriminator D contains 3 convolutional layers, and the step lengths of all the three layers are 1, the activation functions are all "Leaky Relu", the convolutional kernel size in the first convolutional layer is [5, 5, 64]; the second convolutional layer has a convolutional kernel sized [5, 5, 128]; the convolutional kernel size in the third convolutional layer is [2, 2, 128], containing 2 fully-connected layers. The number of neurons in the first fully-connected layer is 128; the number of neurons in the second fully-connected layer was 1, as the output of the discriminator. The mathematical expression of the "Leaky Relu" is:

$$y_i = \begin{cases} x_i, x_i \geq 0 \\ \frac{x_i}{a_i}, x_i \leq 0 \end{cases} \tag{11}$$

In this paper, $a_i = 2$. During adversarial training, the maximum iterations was set as 20000.

For signal sample reconstruction, the selected random restarts R is 20 and the maximum number of iterations L was 800. The selected loss function is: Root Mean Squared Error ($RMSE$), and the expression of the loss function is:

$$minRMSE = \sqrt{\frac{1}{N}\sum_{i=1}^{N}(x_i^{sig} - \hat{x}_i)^2} \tag{12}$$

where x_i^{sig} is the signal sample, and $\hat{x}_i$ is the reconstructed sample which means defensed signal.

4.3 Result

In the result analysis, we use the signal data of SNR with more than 10 dB. In order to test its defense performance, we choose 1D_ResNet [15] as the classification model, and use the raw signal without attack to train the 1D_ResNet model. Then we test the accuracy of the classifier using adversarial samples, and the attack methods used to generate adversarial samples are PGD attack, DeepFool attack and JSMA attack [16–18]. Vincent et al. had introduced a denoising method based on AutoEncoder called Denoising AutoEncoder(DAE) [19], which is selected as the baseline contrast with our method. As seen from Table 1, the metrics is classification accuracy, with all attack, the accuracy of our defense method is higher than DAE, which shows that this method has better defense capability.

Table 1. Defense performance under different attack.

Attack	Without attack	Without defense	DAE	Our
PGD	91.24%	0.00%	67.49%	**75.68%**
DeepFool	91.24%	0.15%	78.68%	**81.69%**
JSMA	91.24%	1.95%	74.60%	**78.61%**

5 Conclusion

We know that although deep learning has been broadly used in all kinds of domains and has also achieved very good performance, a large number of researches show that deep learning is vulnerable to attack, we can add perturbations to achieve accurate control misclassification category. The deep learning model classification accuracy will be greatly reduced, which pose great danger to radio safe transmission. This paper proposes a defense method based on GAN, which generates network reconstructed signal samples to improve the classification accuracy of the model, and thus improve the defense ability against adversarial samples. From the experiments, the defense method has good performances.

Acknowledgments. This work was supported by the National Natural Science Foundation of China under Grants U21B2001 and the Key R&D Programs of Zhejiang under Grant 2022C01018.

References

1. Long, J., Shelhamer, E., Darrell, T.: Fully convolutional networks for semantic segmentation. In: Proceedings of the IEEE Conference on Computer Vision and Pattern Recognition, pp. 3431–3440 (2015)
2. Szegedy, C., et al.: Intriguing properties of neural networks. arXiv preprint. arXiv:1312.6199 (2013)
3. Goodfellow, I., et al.: Generative adversarial nets. In: Advances in Neural Information Processing Systems, vol. 27 (2014)
4. Hinton, G.E., Osindero, S., Teh, Y.W.: A fast learning algorithm for deep belief nets. Neural Comput. **18**(7), 1527–1554 (2006)
5. O'Shea, T., West, N.: Radio machine learning dataset generation with gnuradio. In: Proceedings of the GNU Radio Conference, vol. 1, no, 1 (2016). https://pubs.gnuradio.org/index.ph/p/gron/article/view/11
6. Wu, Y., Li, X., Fang, J.: A deep learning approach for modulation recognition via exploiting temporal correlations. In: 2018 IEEE 19th International Workshop on Signal Processing Advances in Wireless Communications (SPAWC), pp. 1–5. IEEE (2018)
7. Rajendran, S., Meert, W., Giustiniano, D., Lenders, V., Pollin, S.: Deep learning models for wireless signal classification with distributed low-cost spectrum sensors. IEEE Trans. Cogn. Commun. Netw. **4**(3), 433–445 (2018)
8. Goodfellow, I.J., Shlens, J., Szegedy, C.: Explaining and harnessing adversarial examples. arXiv preprint. arXiv:1412.6572 (2014)

9. Huang, L., Joseph, A.D., Nelson, B., Rubinstein, B.I., Tygar, J.D.: Adversarial machine learning. In: Proceedings of the 4th ACM Workshop on Security and Artificial Intelligence, pp. 43–58 (2011)
10. Nelson, B., et al.: Misleading learners: co-opting your spam filter. In: Machine learning in cyber trust, pp. 17–51. Springer, Boston (2009). https://doi.org/10.1007/978-0-387-887 35-7_2
11. Rubinstein, B.I., et al.: Antidote: understanding and defending against poisoning of anomaly detectors. In: Proceedings of the 9th ACM SIGCOMM Conference on Internet Measurement, pp. 1–14 (2009)
12. Biggio, B., Fumera, G., Roli, F.: Multiple classifier systems for robust classifier design in adversarial environments. Int. J. Mach. Learn. Cybern. 1(1), 27–41 (2010)
13. Biggio, B., Corona, I., Fumera, G., Giacinto, G., Roli, F.: Bagging classifiers for fighting poisoning attacks in adversarial classification tasks. In: Sansone, C., Kittler, J., Roli, F. (eds) International Work-Shop on Multiple Classifier Systems, pp. 350–359. Springer, Berlin (2011). https://doi.org/10.1007/978-3-642-21557-5_37
14. Moosavi-Dezfooli, S.M., Fawzi, A., Fawzi, O., Frossard, P.: Universal adversarial perturbations. In: Proceedings of the IEEE Conference on Computer Vision and Pattern Recognition, pp. 1765–1773 (2017)
15. O'Shea, T.J., Roy, T., Clancy, T.C.: Over-the-air deep learning based radio signal classification. IEEE J. Sel. Top. Sign. Process. 12(1), 168–179 (2018)
16. Madry, A., Makelov, A., Schmidt, L., Tsipras, D., Vladu, A.: Towards deep learning models resistant to adversarial attacks. arXiv preprint. arXiv:1706.06083 (2017)
17. Moosavi-Dezfooli, S.M., Fawzi, A., Frossard, P.: Deepfool: a simple and accurate method to fool deep neural networks. In: Proceedings of the IEEE Conference on Computer Vision and Pattern Recognition, pp. 2574–2582 (2016)
18. Papernot, N., McDaniel, P., Jha, S., Fredrikson, M., Celik, Z.B., Swami, A.: The limitations of deep learning in adversarial settings. In: 2016 IEEE European sym-posium on security and privacy (EuroS&P), pp. 372–387. IEEE (2016)
19. Vincent, P., Larochelle, H., Lajoie, I., Bengio, Y., Manzagol, P.A., Bottou, L.: Stacked denoising autoencoders: learning useful representations in a deep network with a local denoising criterion. J. Mach. Learn. Res. 11(12), 3371–3408 (2010)

Dual-Channel Early Warning Framework for Ethereum Ponzi Schemes

Jie Jin[1,2], Jiajun Zhou[1,2(✉)], Chengxiang Jin[1,2], Shanqing Yu[1,2], Ziwan Zheng[5], and Qi Xuan[1,2,3,4]

[1] Institute of Cyberspace Security, Zhejiang University of Technology, Hangzhou 310023, China
jjzhou@zjut.edu.cn
[2] College of Information Engineering, Zhejiang University of Technology, Hangzhou 310023, China
[3] The PCL Research Center of Networks and Communications, Peng Cheng Laboratory, Shenzhen 518000, China
[4] The Utron Technology Company Limited, Hangzhou 310056, China
[5] Zhejiang Police College, Hangzhou 310053, China

Abstract. Blockchain technology supports the generation and record of transactions, and maintains the fairness and openness of the cryptocurrency system. However, many fraudsters utilize smart contracts to create fraudulent Ponzi schemes for profiting on Ethereum, which seriously affects financial security. Most existing Ponzi scheme detection techniques suffer from two major restricted problems: the lack of motivation for temporal early warning and failure to fuse multi-source information finally cause the lagging and unsatisfactory performance of Ethereum Ponzi scheme detection. In this paper, we propose a dual-channel early warning framework for Ethereum Ponzi schemes, named *Ponzi-Warning*, which performs feature extraction and fusion on both code and transaction levels. Moreover, we represent a temporal evolution augmentation strategy for generating transaction graph sequences, which can effectively increase the data scale and introduce temporal information. Comprehensive experiments on our Ponzi scheme datasets demonstrate the effectiveness and timeliness of our framework for detecting the Ponzi contract accounts.

Keywords: Ethereum · Ponzi scheme detection · Graph classification · Early warning

1 Introduction

Ponzi scheme [1] is a traditional financial fraud that lures investors into investing by promising high returns, and pays profits to earlier investors with funds from more recent investors, convincing them that the profits came from legitimate business activity. Traditional Ponzi schemes generally share similar characteristics that deserve high vigilance of the investors: 1) Suspiciously high investment returns with little or no risk; 2) Overly consistent returns; 3) Secretive or complex strategies [2]. However, with the rapid development of Blockchain technique and its widespread adoption in the field of digital cryptocurrencies, these traditional Ponzi fraud has also infected the digital finance world. Fraudsters combine Ponzi schemes with blockchain technology (i.e., Smart Contracts) to create a new form of fraud — the smart Ponzi scheme. In Ethereum, the fraudsters create and deploy fraudulent Ponzi contracts, and advertise them as high-return investments, finally swindle money without offline publicity by spreading Ponzi contract addresses to victims in any way such as emails, chat groups, web links, apps, etc. Although the Ponzi contract code with complex logic is incomprehensible to investors, it is still trusted because of the openness, transparency and immutability characteristics of blockchain technique. According to a report published by the Cryptoanalysis, a cryptocurrency investigation and risk analysis company, Ponzi schemes, fraudulent ICOs and other forms of fraud are on the rise, causing at least $725 million in losses so far. As a result, financial security has become a top priority in the blockchain ecosystem [3].

Existing Ponzi scheme detection methods in Ethereum mainly concentrate on manual feature engineering and graph representation learning. The former mainly combines traditional machine learning methods and manual features (i.e. statistical and structural features) of accounts to detect Ponzi contracts. The statistical features can be code-level [4,5] or transaction-level [6] while the structural features can be behavior patterns [7,8]. The latter generally constructs Ethereum transaction graphs and utilizes graph representation learning techniques to capture implicit features. The transaction graphs generally consist of account nodes and transaction edges, while the graph representation learning methods can be random walk [9,10] and graph neural network [11]. However, there are still two major restricted problems on existing research of Ponzi detection:

- **Lack of motivation for temporal early warning.** The existing methods utilize the last transaction records to detect Ponzi contracts from the moment the fraud has occurred, i.e., following a hindsight perspective, instead of taking temporal information of account behaviors into consideration, which results in failure to detect the occurrence of Ponzi schemes and impose sanctions in a timely manner.
- **Failure to fuse multi-source information.** Multi-source information such as contract codes and transaction records is available for Ponzi detection. However, existing methods usually use a single type of features, or simply concatenate multi-source features for Ponzi detection, without adaptive processing and organic fusion.

To address the above problems, in this paper, we propose Dual-channel Early Warning Framework (*Ponzi-Warning*) for detecting the Ethereum Ponzi scheme. We first collect and collate all current known Ethereum Ponzi scheme data involving contract addresses and corresponding labels from different blockchain platforms, yielding an Ethereum Ponzi Scheme Dataset. Then we propose a Temporal Evaluation Augmentation strategy for generating transaction graph sequences that reserve temporal transaction information of contract accounts.

Finally, we design a dual-channel early warning framework that fuses multi-source information and consists of a code-aware channel and transaction-aware channel. The code-aware channel can extract contract opcode features via an MLP model, and the transaction-aware channel can capture the structural transaction behavior features via arbitrary GNN models. The output of the two channels will be concatenated and fed into the classifiers to identify Ponzi contracts. Extensive experiments are conducted on real-world datasets to verify the effectiveness of *Ponzi-Warning*.

This work has the following contributions:

- We collect and collate all current known Ethereum Ponzi scheme data involving contract addresses and corresponding labels from different blockchain platforms, yielding an Ethereum Ponzi Scheme Dataset.
- We propose a temporal evolution augmentation (*TEAug*) strategy for generating transaction graphs of different scales, which can alleviate the data scarcity and imbalance to some extent without using fake data generation techniques.
- We propose a dual-channel early warning framework (*Ponzi-Warning*) for Ponzi schemes, which can extract and fuse code-level and transaction-level features from raw data, further achieving powerful and timely early warning for Ponzi schemes on Ethereum.

The rest of the paper is organized as follows. The related work of Ponzi scheme detection is presented in Sect. 2. The proposed *Ponzi-Warning* framework is detailedly described in Sect. 3. The experimental results and discussion are presented in Sect. 4. We conclude our work in Sect. 5.

2   Related Work

Ponzi schemes in Ethereum not only retain the characteristics of traditional Ponzi schemes, but also make use of smart contracts.

For a newly created contract, there is no transaction record related to it on the blockchain platforms, so we can only judge its legitimacy by using the characteristics of contract codes, that is, to detect whether it is a Ponzi contract. Bartoletti et al. [4] pioneered an Ethereum Ponzi scheme detection method, where they first classified Ponzi schemes into four categories (i.e. tree, chain, waterfall and permission transfer) based on the logic of the contract source code, and further detect Ponzi schemes by using Levenshtein distance to measure the similarity between bytecodes. Lou et al. [5] converted bytecodes into single-channel images and used a convolutional neural network for image recognition to achieve Ponzi scheme detection.

Once the contract is deployed, the transaction record related to it will be generated once the contract is called. In this case, the transaction features can also serve to detect whether it is a Ponzi contract. Jung et al. [6] extracted transaction features from the transaction records of different time periods and combined with the opcode features, finally inputting them to different machine learning classifiers for Ponzi detection. Hu et al. [12] used the transaction records to analyze the investment and return features, and trained LSTM models with the contract transaction data for future Ponzi scheme detection.

In the final stage of a Ponzi scheme, the complete transaction history is available. At this point, most of the work is to combine the complete transaction features with the code features for Ponzi scheme detection. Chen et al. [13,14] used machine learning methods to identify Ponzi contracts by analyzing account features and opcode features. Zhang et al. [15] considered bytecode features on top of existing features, again detected by the LightGBM model.

3 Methodology

To be clear, the Ponzi scheme studied in this paper is a blockchain financial fraud generated by the Ponzi contract deployed on the Ethereum platform to attract external investment, excluding the Ponzi scheme that uses email, social media and other means to defraud under the guise of spreading the concept of "blockchain".

Table 1. Statastics of the Ethereum Ponzi contract addresses we collected.

Ponzi address	Num.	Feature		Transaction Num.		
		Code	Trans.	Min.	Max.	≥ 100
Code (only)	68	√		0	0	0
Code & Trans	230	√	√	1	105005	75
All	298			1	105005	75

Table 2. Statastics of the Ethereum Ponzi scheme dataset.

Contract address	Num.	Feature		Transaction Num.		
		Code	Trans.	Min.	Max.	≥ 100
Ponzi	75	√	√	103	105005	75 (100%)
Non-Ponzi	325	√	√	100	11761	325 (100%)
All	400	√	√	100	105005	400

3.1 Data Collection

Since the known Ponzi schemes published by different platforms are not completely consistent, we collect and collate all current known Ethereum Ponzi scheme data involving contract addresses and corresponding labels from different platforms such as Etherscan[1], XBlock[2] and Google Cloud[3], as shown in Table 1. Moreover, we consider Ponzi detection as a classification problem, so we select an additional part (325) of normal contract accounts with transaction records as negative samples, and combine them with all Ponzi contract accounts with transaction records (75), yielding an **Ethereum Ponzi Scheme Dataset** (**Eth-Ponzi Dataset**, symbolized as D here), see Table 2. Formally, we represent the dataset as $D = \{(a_i, y_i)\}$, where y_i is the identity label reflecting whether the account a_i is a Ponzi account (1 for Ponzi, 0 for non-Ponzi).

---

[1] https://cn.etherscan.com/.
[2] http://xblock.pro/.
[3] http://goo.gl/CvdxBp.

3.2   Micro Transaction Graph

The fraudulent behavior of Ponzi schemes is mainly manifested in the interactions between the central Ponzi contract and the surrounding investor accounts. Hence for a target contract account a, we can construct a contract-centric micro transaction graph using all the transaction records related to this account, yielding $g = (a, V, E(t), \mathbf{x}^c, \mathbf{X}^t, y)$, where node set V consists of accounts involved in these transactions, edge set $E(t)$ consists of related transactions with timestamp. Note that the node set V consists of the target contract account(CA) a, externally owned accounts(EOA) participating in the transactions, and other possible contract accounts. The CA is controlled by the smart contract code, but the EOA is not, so we use $\mathbf{x}^c$ to represent the code features of the target CA a, and $\mathbf{X}^t$ to represent the transaction features of all accounts. The code features are 76-dimensional vectors consisting of the frequency of different opcodes, and the transaction features are 15-dimensional manual features that are consistent with [8].

3.3   Temporal Evolution Augmentation of Transaction Graph

As we concern above, existing Ponzi detection methods follow hindsight and utilize the last transaction records (i.e. the full transaction graph) to detect Ponzi schemes, which fails to provide timely warning and sanctions for such financial risks. In this paper, we propose a **T**emporal **E**volution **Aug**mentation (*TEAug*) strategy for transaction graph with the following purposes: 1) Ponzi schemes on Ethereum begin with the creation and deployment of Ponzi contracts, experience interactions with surrounding investors, and end with the scammer running away with the money or being detected, which is a temporal evolution process. We use *TEAug* to highlight the micro transaction states of Ponzi contracts in different life cycles. 2) The number of known Ethereum Ponzi schemes is small (several hundred), and direct training with existing data can easily lead to overfitting and low generalization of detection models. We consider *TEAug* as a data augmentation strategy and increase the scale of trainable data.

For each CA in Eth-Ponzi Dataset, we can construct corresponding micro transaction graph, finally yielding a graph set $D_g = \{g_i \mid \forall a_i \in D\}$. During *TEAug*, we perform data augmentation on each transaction graph g_i based on a fixed-scale growth of the number of transactions over time (parameterized by Δn_t), as illustrated in Fig. 1. Formally, for a transaction graph g_i, *TEAug* generates a series of transaction subgraphs of different scales based on transaction timestamps:

$$\{g_i^1, g_i^2, \cdots, g_i^m\} \leftarrow \mathsf{TEAug}\,(g_i, \Delta n_t, m)\,,$$
$$\text{where} \quad g_i^k \subseteq g_i \text{ and } y(g_i^k) = y(g_i) \text{ and } |E_i^{k+1}(t)| = |E_i^k(t)| + \Delta n_t. \tag{1}$$

Note that each augmented transaction graph g_i^k is actually the subgraph of g_i and has the same label. After *TEAug*, we obtain a larger transaction graph dataset with 4000 samples.

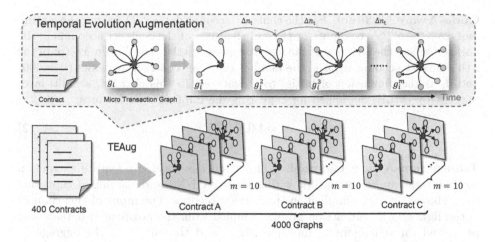

Fig. 1. Illustration of temporal evolution augmentation for Ethereum Ponzi scheme dataset.

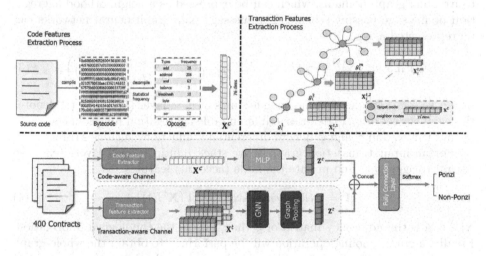

Fig. 2. Illustration of dual-channel early warning model for Ethereum Ponzi schemes

3.4   Dual-Channel Early Warning Model

In this section, we present a dual-channel early warning model for Ethereum Ponzi schemes, named *Ponzi-Warning*, which focuses on both the contract code and transaction behavior for detecting the occurrence of Ponzi schemes in Ethereum. As illustrated in Fig. 2, this model mainly consists of two channels: the code-aware channel and the transaction-aware channel. The former characterizes the code-level features of contract accounts and can take effect at any time after the smart contract is created, and the latter characterizes the transaction behavior patterns of contract accounts and will only take effect after the smart contracts are called and transaction records are generated.

Code-Aware Channel. For the contract account dataset D, we use the feature matrix $\mathbf{X}^c \in \mathbb{R}^{n \times f_c}$ to represent the code features of the contract accounts in the dataset, where the i-th row of the matrix represents the code feature vector of the i-th contract account a_i, n is the number of target contract accounts ($n = 400$) and f_c is the dimension of initial code features. In this channel, a multi-layer perceptron (MLP) is applied for capturing the implicit code features:

$$\mathbf{Z}^c = \mathsf{MLP}\left(\mathbf{X}^c\right). \tag{2}$$

Transaction-Aware Channel. This channel is a generic feature extraction module that can be compatible with arbitrary GNN layers, aiming at capturing the behavior features implicit in transaction records. The input of this channel is the lightweight transaction graphs sampled from the augmented dataset and processed through merging multiple edges, and the output is the aggregated graph features $\mathbf{Z}^t$.

Formally, graph neural networks (GNN) generalize the convolution operator to irregular graph domains, which can be expressed as a neighborhood aggregation or message passing scheme. The message pass graph neural networks can be represented as:

$$\mathsf{GNNLayer}: \quad \mathbf{x}_i^{(k)} = \gamma^{(k)}\left(\mathbf{x}_i^{(k-1)}, \square_{j \in \mathcal{N}(i)} \phi^{(k)}\left(\mathbf{x}_i^{(k-1)}, \mathbf{x}_j^{(k-1)}\right)\right), \tag{3}$$

where $\mathbf{x}_i^{(k-1)} \in \mathbb{R}^F$ denotes the node features of v_i in layer $(k-1)$, $\mathcal{N}(i)$ denotes the neighbor set of v_i, $\square$ denotes a differentiable aggregation function, e.g., sum, mean or max, and γ and ϕ denote differentiable functions such as MLPs.

For an input transaction graph g, we stack multiple GNN layers (e.g. two layers) to aggregate and update the node (account) features:

$$\mathbf{H}^t = \mathsf{GNNLayer2}\left(\mathsf{GNNLayer1}\left(\mathbf{X}^t, A\right)\right), \tag{4}$$

where A is the adjacency matrix of g that reflects the topological information. Finally, a graph pooling operation will be performed to obtain the whole-graph representation that reflects the graph-level account behavior pattern features:

$$\mathbf{z}^t = \mathsf{GraphPoolingLayer}\left(\mathbf{H}^t\right). \tag{5}$$

Dual-Channel Joint for Prediction. The code features output by the code-aware channel and the pattern features output by the transaction-aware channel will be combined through a concatenation operation, and input into a fully connected layer for Ponzi detection:

$$\mathbf{Z} = \mathsf{Concat}\left(\mathbf{Z}^c, \mathbf{Z}^t\right), \tag{6}$$

$$\hat{Y} = \mathsf{Softmax}\left(\mathsf{MLP}\left(\mathbf{Z}\right)\right). \tag{7}$$

where $\hat{Y}$ is the set of predicted labels.

4   Experiments

In this section, we perform empirical evaluations to demonstrate the effectiveness of the proposed *Ponzi-Warning* framework, answering the following research questions:

- **RQ1**: How effective and timely is the proposed *Ponzi-Warning* framework for detecting Ponzi schemes in Ethereum?
- **RQ2**: How do code and transaction features affect Ponzi scheme detection?
- **RQ3**: What is the appropriate transaction threshold in our framework for reporting Ponzi schemes?
- **RQ3**: How does the backbone model affect Ponzi scheme detection?

4.1   Data Setting

As we can see from Table 1, 22.82% of the Ponzi contracts have no transaction records and 52.01% of the Ponzi contracts have transaction records of no more than 100. We filter these contracts with transaction records of less than 100, and use the remaining Ponzi contracts as well as additionally sampled normal contracts, as shown in Table 2, to evaluate our proposed model.

We split dataset D into training, validation and testing sets with a proportion of $D_{train} : D_{val} : D_{test} = 256 : 64 : 80$. We perform *TEAug* in the three parts:

$$D_{train}^{aug} = \bigcup_{g_i \in D_{train}} \{g_i^1, g_i^2, \cdots, g_i^m\} \leftarrow \text{TEAug}\,(D_{train}, \Delta n_t, m)\,,$$

$$D_{val}^{aug} = \bigcup_{g_i \in D_{val}} \{g_i^1, g_i^2, \cdots, g_i^m\} \leftarrow \text{TEAug}\,(D_{val}, \Delta n_t, m)\,, \qquad (8)$$

$$D_{test}^{aug-i} = \{g_1^i, g_2^i, \cdots, g_{|D_{test}|}^i\}, i \in \{1, 2, \cdots, m\} \leftarrow \text{TEAug}\,(D_{test}, \Delta n_t, m)\,.$$

Note that we mix augmented samples of all scales (1 to m) to form the augmented training set D_{train}^{aug}. for D_{val}, we take augmented samples of all scales to validate our model performance to find the best model parameters. As for D_{test}, we mix all augmented samples of the same scale to form the augmented training set at that scale, finally yielding m augmented validation sets and augmented testing sets, respectively.

4.2   Baselines

Manual feature engineering relies on high-performance downstream classifiers to achieve good task performance, so we use three ensemble learning models, XGBoost classifier (XGB), Random forest classifier (RFC) and AdaBoost classifier (ADA), to directly learn the function mapping manual features to account identity. Meanwhile, since we emphasize the high compatibility of the transaction-aware channel, we use five GNN models for evaluation, namely GCN [11], GAT [16], ASAPooling [17], SAGPooling [18,19] and GlobalAttentionNet(GLAN) [20].

Table 3. Statistics of augmented datasets (after lightweight) of different scales. $avg.|V|$ and $avg.|E|$ are the average numbers of nodes and edges, respectively.

Scale ($m = 10, \Delta n_t = 10$)		$avg.|V|$	$avg.|E|$	**Proportion**
i	$|E_i^k(t)|$			
1	10	6.76	6.52	
2	20	11.08	11.35	
3	30	15.12	15.89	
4	40	19.11	20.34	
5	50	23.09	24.74	75:325
6	60	27.01	29.13	
7	70	30.89	33.50	
8	80	34.72	37.76	
9	90	38.45	41.91	
10	100	42.12	46.06	

4.3 Experiment Setting

For the hyperparameter in *TEAug*, we set the scale growth (Δn_t) as 10, and set the augmentation number (m) as 10. Our model is implemented based on the Pytorch-geometric[4]. For all methods, the random seed is set as 0, the hidden dimension of each channel is searched from $[16, 32, 64, 128]$, the graph pooling operation is chosen from [MaxPooling, MeanPooling, SumPooling], and the transaction-aware channel is implemented using 2-layer GNN. In addition, all parameters of the model are initialized using a Gaussian distribution with a mean and standard deviation of 0 and 0.1, respectively. And the batch size and L2 penalty are set to 200 and 10^{-5}, respectively, and a negative log-likelihood loss function is used. The Adam optimizer is used to optimize these parameters, where the initial learning rate and the dropout rate are set to 0.01 and 0.1, respectively.

We use D_{train}^{aug} for model training, and validate and test our model using corresponding augmented sets with different scales. We repeat the experiments five times and report the average F1-score at different stages of the temporal transaction evolution.

4.4 Evaluation on Ponzi Detection (RQ1)

To answer **RQ1**, we evaluate the performance of all the methods in the task of Ponzi scheme detection on Ethereum. Table 4 reports the detection results, from which we can obtain the following **Obs**ervations.

(1) *Obs.1. Both code and transaction features play an important role in Ponzi detection, and our framework achieves the best performance.* Overall, our framework outperforms all the other compared

---

[4] https://github.com/pyg-team/pytorch_geometric.

Table 4. Performance comparison results w.r.t. F1-score on Ethereum Ponzi scheme dataset.

Method			Feature		Scale									
Name	Channel-1	Channel-2	Code	Trans.	1	2	3	4	5	6	7	8	9	10
Code-aware	MLP	×	✓		0.8908	0.8908	0.8908	0.8908	0.8908	0.8908	0.8908	0.8908	0.8908	0.8908
Trans-aware	×	GCN		✓	0.8283	0.8582	0.8685	0.8604	0.8627	0.8713	0.8880	0.8858	0.8831	0.8980
Ours	No MLP	GCN	✓	✓	0.8740	0.8794	0.8928	0.9056	0.9021	0.9019	0.9077	0.9167	0.9169	0.9164
Ours	MLP	GCN	✓	✓	**0.9054**	**0.9077**	**0.9077**	**0.9100**	**0.9100**	**0.9100**	**0.9124**	<u>**0.9171**</u>	**0.9171**	**0.9171**
Trans-aware	×	GAT		✓	0.8596	0.8659	0.8685	0.8625	0.8627	0.8841	0.8892	0.8863	0.8938	0.8989
Ours	No MLP	GAT	✓	✓	0.8802	0.8864	0.8962	0.8946	0.9026	0.9017	0.8976	0.901	0.9093	0.9093
Ours	MLP	GAT	✓	✓	**0.9012**	**0.9016**	**0.9038**	**0.9065**	**0.9134**	**0.918**	**0.9228**	**0.9228**	**0.9202**	<u>**0.9230**</u>
Trans-aware	×	SAGPooling		✓	0.8569	0.8888	0.8869	0.8894	0.9007	0.9119	0.9120	0.9137	0.9170	0.9154
Ours	No MLP	SAGPooling	✓	✓	0.8869	0.9017	0.9094	0.9164	0.9164	0.9161	0.9244	0.9177	0.9232	0.9233
Ours	MLP	SAGPooling	✓	✓	**0.9040**	**0.9041**	**0.9092**	**0.9212**	**0.9186**	**0.9261**	**0.9288**	**0.9288**	**0.9288**	<u>**0.9311**</u>
Trans-aware	×	ASAPooling		✓	0.8452	0.8783	0.8774	0.8915	0.9075	0.9064	0.9034	0.9119	0.9119	0.9119
Ours	No MLP	ASAPooling	✓	✓	0.8940	0.9054	0.9000	0.9178	0.9199	0.9196	0.9199	0.9231	0.9231	0.9184
Ours	MLP	ASAPooling	✓	✓	**0.9233**	**0.9239**	**0.9239**	**0.9239**	**0.9239**	<u>**0.9239**</u>	**0.9239**	**0.9239**	**0.9239**	<u>**0.9245**</u>
Trans-aware	×	GLAN		✓	0.8478	0.8647	0.8937	0.9016	0.8908	0.9038	0.9109	0.9146	0.9017	0.9182
Ours	No MLP	GLAN	✓	✓	0.8857	0.9025	0.8946	0.9114	0.9009	0.9082	0.9154	0.9185	0.9186	0.9187
Ours	MLP	GLAN	✓	✓	**0.9164**	**0.9118**	**0.9182**	**0.9182**	**0.9182**	**0.9204**	<u>**0.9280**</u>	**0.9280**	**0.9280**	**0.9280**

frameworks by a significant margin. When compared with the "code-aware" method that only uses code features and MLP model for Ponzi detection, our *Ponzi-Warning* achieves 0.74% ~ 4.03% average relative improvement. When compared with the "transaction-aware" method that only uses transaction graph and GNN model for Ponzi detection, our *Ponzi-Warning* achieves 0.98% ~ 2.41% average relative improvement. These phenomena suggest that both the smart contract code and account transaction behavior can expose the information related to account identity.

(2) ***Obs.2. Our framework enables timely early warning of Ponzi schemes.*** The transaction graph is constructed based on the transaction records with timestamp information. During *TEAug*, we only generate the transaction graphs by using transaction records no more than 100, i.e., yielding small-scale transaction graphs. A smaller-scale transaction graph (with Scale ID $i \leq 10$) shows a less active time of the central contract account. Our method achieves high and stable detection performance on small-scale transaction graphs, indicating that our *Ponzi-Warning* can achieve timely early warning of Ponzi schemes.

4.5 Single Channel Analysis (RQ2)

To answer **RQ2**, we analyze the performance of each channel independently and obtain the following **Obs**ervations.

(1) ***Obs.3. The characteristics of the code carry the purpose of the contract creation.*** Code features accompany the entire life cycle of a contract account, and we can use code features to perform Ponzi detection at the initial stage of contract creation. From Table 4, we can observe that using only code features has achieved detection accuracy up to 89%, far surpassing the method of using transaction features in the early stages, indicating that

Table 5. The top 5 most important opcode features of Ponzi and non-Ponzi contracts.

Comparison	Opcode	Explanation	Proportion
Ponzi : non-Ponzi	returndatasize	Size of the last returndata	207.13
	returndatacopy	Copy the returned data	59.22
	codesize	Length of the contract	6.21
	gaslimit	Block gas limit of the current block	2.53
	smod	int256 modulo	1.97
non-Ponzi : Ponzi	delegatecall	Calling another contract's method using the current contract's store	17.31
	create2	Create a subcontract using a defined address	14.31
	byte	Return (u)int256 x the i-th byte starting from the highest byte	5.31
	difficulty	Difficulty of the current block	4.62
	sar	int256 right shift	3.92

there is a strong correlation between the characteristics of the contract code and the legitimacy of the contract account. We list the top 5 most important opcodes of Ponzi and non-Ponzi contracts according to the feature importance analysis of RFC, as shown in Table 5. We observe that Ponzi contracts involve more "returndata" opcodes and will make plenty of judgments about the "returndata". On the contrary, non-Ponzi contracts involve more "delegatecall" and "create" opcodes, which suggests that normal contracts would have a large number of methods to call other contracts, while the nature of Ponzi schemes is to attempt to carry out as much fraud as possible in one contract.

(2) ***Obs.4. The characteristics of the transaction records expose the purpose of the contract creation over time.*** Transaction features can only be available after transaction has occurred. From Table 3, we can observe that with few transaction records (with Scale ID $i = 1$), the transaction-aware channel achieves poor detection performance. And the performance of this channel is greatly improved as the size of the transaction graph increases, indicating that more transaction records can expose more account purpose, thereby improving the Ponzi detection. Furthermore, we find that transaction-aware channel can achieve a higher performance limit than code-aware channel, which inspires us to perform dynamic detection for better early warning.

4.6 Threshold of Reporting Ponzi Schemes (RQ3)

To answer **RQ3**, we further analyze the performance curve in Fig. 3 in terms of detection accuracy and timeliness. The two types of curves (GNNs and our framework) all show a certain upward trend, in which the former shows a poor initial performance and a large increase, while the latter shows a power initial performance and a stable and small increase. In our framework, the high initial performance benefits from the blessing of the code channel, and the subsequent

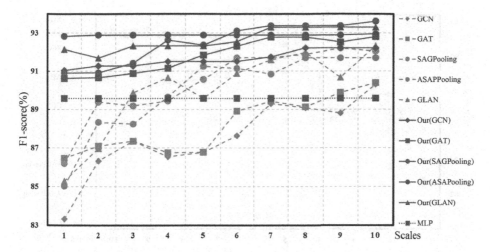

Fig. 3. Performance comparison between our framework and the ordinary graph neural network methods under different scales of transactions.

increase benefits from the temporal evolution of the transaction. We further observe that in most cases, the performance curves rise first, reach the critical point when the Scale ID equals to 7, and then gradually stabilize. So we reasonably consider 70 (with Scale ID $i = 7$) as the appropriate transaction threshold for reporting Ponzi schemes.

4.7 Ablation Study

To answer **RQ4**, we perform an ablation study by removing or replacing the backbone models in the two channels. As shown in Fig. 4 and 5, the corresponding observation results have the following aspects:

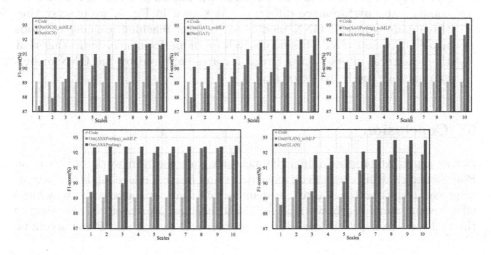

Fig. 4. Performance comparison between code-aware channels with and without MLP.

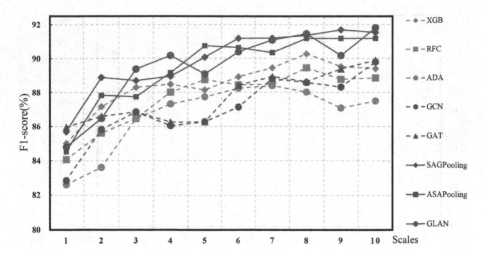

Fig. 5. Performance comparison between GNNs and machine learning methods under different transaction scales in the case of transaction-only features.

(1) **Obs.5. Further feature extraction on initial opcode features benefits Ponzi detection.** We first remove the backbone model (MLP) in the code-aware channel, and directly concatenate the unprocessed initial code features and the output of the transaction-aware channel, yielding the comparison graph Our(GNN)_noMLP. As shown in Fig. 4, we observe that Our(GNN) always outperforms Our(GNN)_noMLP across all scales, suggesting that implicit information extracted from initial code features can significantly improve the Ponzi detection. This phenomenon encourages us to further design more powerful backbone models in the code-aware channel.

(2) **Obs.6. Powerful GNN models can capture the account interaction behavior benefitting Ponzi detection.** We replace the backbone model (GNN) in the transaction-aware channel with machine learning models, and compare the performance difference. As shown in Fig. 5, we observe that three more powerful GNN models outperform machine learning methods while GCN and GAT obtain relatively poor performance, indicating that the structural interaction behavior features captured by the GNN models can improve the Ponzi detection.

5   Conclusion

In this paper, we propose a dual-channel early warning framework for Ethereum Ponzi schemes, which can effectively extract and fuse code-level and transaction-level features. Experimental results demonstrate that our framework can achieve effective and timely early warning for Ponzi schemes. Moreover, we also analyze the code and transaction level differences between normal and Ponzi accounts.

In the future work, we will consider designing a more powerful code-aware channel and replacing the transaction-aware channel with a dynamic graph neural network model for better Ponzi detection.

Acknowledgments. This work was partially supported by the National Key R&D Program of China under Grant 2020YFB1006104, by the Key R&D Programs of Zhejiang under Grants 2022C01018 and 2021C01117, by the National Natural Science Foundation of China under Grant 61973273 and 62103374, and by the Zhejiang Provincial Natural Science Foundation of China under Grant LR19F030001, and by Basic Public Welfare Research Project of Zhejiang Province Grant LGF20F020016 and Open Project of the Key Laboratory of Public Security Informatization Application Based on Big Data Architecture Grant 2020DSJSYS003.

References

1. Frankel, T.: The Ponzi Scheme Puzzle: A History and Analysis of Con Artists and Victims. Oxford University Press, London (2012)
2. Springer, M.: The Politics of Ponzi Schemes: History, Theory, and Policy. Routledge, Milton Park (2020)
3. Morris, D.Z.: The rise of cryptocurrency ponzi schemes. The Atlantic, vol. 31 (2017)
4. Bartoletti, M., Carta, S., Cimoli, T., Saia, R.: Dissecting ponzi schemes on ethereum: identification, analysis, and impact. Futur. Gener. Comput. Syst. **102**, 259–277 (2020)
5. Lou, Y., Zhang, Y., Chen, S.: Ponzi contracts detection based on improved convolutional neural network. In: 2020 IEEE International Conference on Services Computing (SCC), pp. 353–360. IEEE (2020)
6. Jung, E., Le Tilly, M., Gehani, A., Ge, Y.: Data mining-based ethereum fraud detection. In: 2019 IEEE International Conference on Blockchain (Blockchain), pp. 266–273. IEEE (2019)
7. Zhou, J., Hu, C., Chi, J., Wu, J., Shen, M., Xuan, Q.: Behavior-aware account de-anonymization on ethereum interaction graph. arXiv preprint. arXiv:2203.09360 (2022)
8. Jin, C., Jin, J., Zhou, J., Wu, J., Xuan, Q.: Heterogeneous feature augmentation for ponzi detection in ethereum. arXiv preprint. arXiv:2204.08916 (2022)
9. Perozzi, B., Al-Rfou, R., Skiena, S.: Deepwalk: online learning of social representations. In: Proceedings of the 20th ACM SIGKDD International Conference on Knowledge Discovery and Data Mining, pp. 701–710 (2014)
10. Grover, A., Leskovec, J.: node2vec: scalable feature learning for networks. In: Proceedings of the 22nd ACM SIGKDD International Conference on Knowledge Discovery and Data Mining, pp. 855–864 (2016)
11. Kipf, T.N., Welling, M.: Semi-supervised classification with graph convolutional networks. arXiv preprint. arXiv:1609.02907 (2016)
12. Hu, T., et al.: Transaction-based classification and detection approach for Ethereum smart contract. Inf. Process. Manag. **58**(2), 102462 (2021)
13. Chen, W., Zheng, Z., Cui, J., Ngai, E., Zheng, P., Zhou, Y.: Detecting ponzi schemes on ethereum: towards healthier blockchain technology. In: Proceedings of the 2018 World Wide Web Conference, pp. 1409–1418 (2018)
14. Chen, W., Zheng, Z., Ngai, E.C.H., Zheng, P., Zhou, Y.: Exploiting blockchain data to detect smart ponzi schemes on ethereum. IEEE Access **7**, 37575–37586 (2019)

15. Zhang, Y., Yu, W., Li, Z., Raza, S., Cao, H.: Detecting ethereum ponzi schemes based on improved lightgbm algorithm. IEEE Trans. Comput. Soc. Syst. **9**(2), 624–637 (2021)
16. Veličković, P., Cucurull, G., Casanova, A., Romero, A., Lio, P., Bengio, Y.: Graph attention networks. arXiv preprint. arXiv:1710.10903 (2017)
17. Ranjan, E., Sanyal, S., Talukdar, P.: Asap: adaptive structure aware pooling for learning hierarchical graph representations. In: Proceedings of the AAAI Conference on Artificial Intelligence, vol. 34, pp. 5470–5477 (2020)
18. Lee, J., Lee, I., Kang, J.: Self-attention graph pooling. In: International Conference on Machine Learning, pp. 3734–3743. PMLR (2019)
19. Knyazev, B., Taylor, G.W., Amer, M.: Understanding attention and generalization in graph neural networks. In: Advances in Neural Information Processing Systems, vol. 32 (2019)
20. Li, Y., Tarlow, D., Brockschmidt, M., Zemel, R.: Gated graph sequence neural networks. arXiv preprint. arXiv:1511.05493 (2015)

Rumor Detection Based on the Temporal Sentiment

Chenbo Fu[1,2], Kang Chen[1,2], Xingyu Pan[1,2], Shanqing Yu[1,2], Jun Ni[3], and Yong Min[4,5(✉)]

[1] Institute of Cyberspace Security, Zhejiang University of Technology, Hangzhou 310023, China
[2] College of Information Engineering, Zhejiang University of Technology, Hangzhou 310023, China
[3] Hangzhou Zhongao Technology Company Limited, Hangzhou 310000, China
[4] Computational Communication Research Center, Beijing Normal University, Zhuhai 519087, China
[5] School of Journalism and Communication, Beijing Normal University, Beijing 100875, China
myong@bnu.edu.cn

Abstract. The development of social media has changed the way of information consumption by the public, and it has also shifted the spread of rumors from offline to online. The combined multiscale nature of rumors makes it challenging to develop an effective rumor detection method. This raises the fashion of multi-modal rumor detection. However, these multi-modal methods usually focus on explicit textual and visual features, ignoring the sentiment hidden in textual content, which expresses the individuals' opinions. Thus, we propose a rumor detection model based on temporal sentiment features in this work. Specifically, we first extract the temporal sentiment feature and text vectors from the text content in normalized reply series, then combine these two vectors as the microblog representation. After that, we apply RvNN to capture the comprehensive representation of the event. Finally, we adopt the multilayer perceptron neural network to detect rumors. The experiments on two real-world datasets, i.e., Weibo and RumourEval-2019, show that our method performs better than baseline methods. Moreover, the ablation study and the early rumor detection experiments show the effectiveness of our temporal sentiment feature. Our work supplements current rumor detection methods and highlights the important role of temporal sentiment features in rumor spreading.

Keywords: Rumor detection · Rumor spreading · Sentiment analyze · Temporal sentiment · Social network

1 Introduction

The development of social media has changed the way of information consumption by the public. However, the massive amount of information also brought many rumors [1,2]. Rumor is defined as information without official verification [3,4] and most rumors have a bad influence, for example, a lot of rumors emerged during the 2016 US election [5] and the period of the COVID-19 pandemic [6,7]. However, the cost of rumor detection is high, especially for the manual fact-checking methods [8]. And unfortunately, research has proven that humans are only a little better than random identification when facing rumors [9]. Therefore, it is necessary to develop effective rumor detection methods. Fortunately, with the continuous development of deep learning [10–14], more and more rumor detection methods have been proposed and used to detect rumors [15–19].

Most of the transitional rumor detection methods focus on textual features [20]. Recently, as social media develops, more features are investigated and integrated as the complex representation of the rumors [17,21], e.g., visual features. However, malicious users still can easily manipulate textual content and images through technology, e.g., deep fake and text generation, and human beings hard detect these generations [22–24]. Furthermore, compared to social media's textual and visual features, the propagation features are hard to manipulate by malicious users. Thus, more and more multi-modal detection models integrate the propagation feature into their methods [25–27].

Sentiments as a representation of people's psychological state [28] have also received increasing attention from researchers [29–36]. Most existing sentiment-based rumor detection methods treat sentiment as a supplement attribute of textual features [29,35] but ignore the sentiment change when the information spreads. Recent research finds that sentiment will change with the spreading of rumors, e.g., Davoudi et al. constructed and analyzed the sentiment network by connecting posts with similar sentiment scores, and found the event sentiment changes as rumor spreading [36].

To effectively capture the sentiment feature change as the rumor spreads, we propose the temporal sentiment feature, which encodes the sentiment of the text content and the normalized reply series. By integrating the temporal sentiment feature into the microblog representation, we propose a new model to detect rumors. Extensive experiments on the two real-world datasets, i.e., Weibo and RumourEval-2019, show that our proposed method performs better than the baselines. Moreover, the ablation study and early detection experiments prove the effectiveness of our temporal sentiment feature.

The main contributions of our work are summarized as follows:

- We propose the temporal sentiment feature, which can effectively capture the sentiment feature as information spreading.

- We propose a new multi-modal rumor detection method that includes the temporal sentiment feature. The results in two real-world datasets, i.e., the Weibo and RumourEval-2019, show that our proposed method performs better than the baseline methods, and the ablation study proves the effectiveness of our temporal sentiment feature.

The rest of this paper is organized as follows: Sect. 2 introduces related work, Sect. 3 presents the details of our method, and Sect. 4 gives detailed experimental steps, results, and discussions. Finally, we summarize our work in Sect. 5.

2   Related Work

2.1   Single-Modal Rumor Detection

The existing rumor detection methods can be roughly divided into single-modal and multi-modal methods. Single-modal methods mainly focus on one type of rumor feature, i.e., statistical and embedded features from text content [16,18,37], visual features from images [38,39] and propagation features from spreading networks or social networks [15,40]. For example, Bond et al. focused on the difference of rumors in semantic-level features in text content [37], such as the uncertainty words. Kaliyar et al. proposed the FakeBERT model to detect rumors, which mainly utilized the BERT to embed the text content of the microblogs [16]. For rumor detection based on visual features, Guarnera et al. modeled the convolutional generative process and extracted a set of local features utilizing the Expectation Maximization algorithm to detect the fake images [39]. Furthermore, Zhao et al. proposed a multi-attentional deepfake detection network that consisted of multiple spatial attention heads, visual feature enhancement blocks, and attention maps to find the fake images in rumors [38]. Moreover, Ma et al. proposed the PTK model to detect rumors which evaluated the similarities of propagation tree structures between rumors [40]. Bian et al. proposed the Bi-GCN model to explore the propagation and dispersion structures of rumors with top-down and bottom-up GCN [15].

2.2   Multi-modal Rumor Detection

However, single-modal methods can not capture the multi-media nature of social media. Thus, the single-modal methods are challenged by multi-media information and lead to low accuracy. Furthermore, the development of deep fake and text generation techniques makes malicious users can fool the rumor detection models easily [22–24]. For this reason, multi-modal methods are developed to capture the multi-information, e.g., combining the textual and visual features [17,21,41]. For example, Qian et al. proposed the HMCAN model, which used the ResNet to extract features of the image and used the BERT to extract features of text content [17]. Wang et al. proposed the EANN model, which used the Text-CNN to extract the feature of text content and the VGG-19 to extract the visual feature [21]. There are also many multi-modal methods based on the textual and user features. For example, Vo et al. proposed the MAC model, which combined the user information with the text content and used the attention mechanism to capture the feature of the source post and the replies [42]. Dou et al. combined the user engagement information and the text content to detect the rumors [43]. Furthermore, multi-modal methods also exist based on the propagation structure and text content. For example, Lu et al. proposed the GCAN model, which fused the text embedding and propagation representation to detect the rumors [19].

2.3   Rumor Detection Based on Sentiment Analyze

The sentiment is a latent textual feature hidden in the text content. It has been proven that sentiment is a vital feature for rumor detection [32,33,44]. Most previous sentiment based rumor detection methods focus on the sentiment in the source microblogs, such as Mackey et al. combined sentiment and the word embedding of source microblog [30]. Yang et al. proposed the TI-CNN model to extract the explicit and latent features of microblogs, where their explicit feature of the text included the sentiment [31]. Wang et al. proposed the SD-DTS-GRU model, which focused on the fine-grained sentiment of source microblogs [32]. There are also works focusing on the sentiment of both source microblogs and replies [29,35,45]. For example, Zhang et al. combined the publisher sentiment, social sentiment, and the sentiment gap as the dual emotion features with existing rumor detection methods to detect the rumors [29]. Guo et al. proposed the EFN model, which captured both sources' and replies' textual and sentimental features for rumor detection [45]. Recent research shows that the sentiment changes as the information spreads, and has a significant difference between rumor and non-rumor [46,47]. For this reason, Davoudi et al. proposed the DSS model, which captured the features of the sentiment network and propagation tree to detect rumors [36]. Inspired by the above works, we designed the temporal sentiment feature to detect rumors in this study.

3   Method

Our work focuses on rumor detection on social networks. The architecture of our model is illustrated in Fig. 1. As shown in Fig. 1, the architecture consists of three components, i.e., Microblog Representation, Comprehensive Representation and Rumor Classifier. First, we use Microblog Representation to represent one microblog of the event, then use the RvNN to catch the feature of microblog representation along the spreading path and get the Comprehensive Representation of the event. Finally, the Rumor Classifier is used to judge whether the event is a rumor.

3.1   Problem Statement

We denote the event-based dataset as $\mathcal{C} = \{C_1, C_2, ..., C_{|\mathcal{C}|}\}$, where $|\mathcal{C}|$ represents the number of event. Each event C_i is modeled as a tree structure $C_i = \langle V_i, E_i \rangle$ where i is the index of event. And $V_i = \{t_0^i, t_1^i, t_2^i, ..., t_{k_i-1}^i\}$ is the set of nodes, where k_i is the number of microblogs of event C_i, t_j^i is the microblogs of event C_i and the j is the index of microblog which are sorted by posting order. Because the source microblog must be the first microblog of the event C_i, so the j of the source microblog is 0 and we use t_0^i represents the source microblog of event C_i. $E_i = \{e_{st}^i | s, t = 0, ..., k_i - 1\}$ is the edge set of event C_i. For example, if t_m^i is the replay of t_n^i, where the t_n^i and t_m^i represent two microblogs in event C_i, there will have a direct edge $t_n^i \rightarrow t_m^i$, i.e., e_{nm}^i. The rumor detection task can

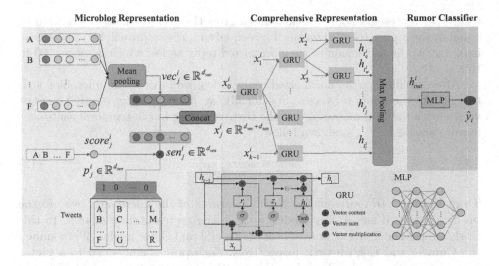

Fig. 1. The architecture of the proposed rumor detection model.

be defined as a classification problem, thus, our model outputs the $\hat{y}_i \in 0, 1$ to detect label of event C_i, where $y_i = 1$ and $y_i = 0$ denote the post is rumor and non-rumor, respectively.

3.2 Microblog Representation

Temporal Sentiment Feature. The sentiment as a representation of people's psychological state is hidden in the text content. In this work, we use the Baidu sentiment API[1] and the NLTK[2] to analyze the sentiment of the Chinese and English text, respectively. These sentiment analysis tools give a sentiment score $score^i_j$ of the text of microblog j in event i and range from -1 to 1, the score closer to 1, the more positive the text is.

To characterize the temporal features, we use a one-hot vector to encode the replies in the microblog in posting order. However, the number of responses to different social posts is heterogeneous and cannot be directly encoded, e.g., the dimension is different. Furthermore, the time interval between the two replies in the same event has a large variation, e.g., there are many replies in the early period and short time, accompanied by sporadic replies in the later period. Therefore, we need to normalize the length of the reply series, whose length is the number of posts. It should be noted that our reply series includes the source post. We use the following function to map the original one-hot vector to the normalized reply series $p^i_j \in \mathbb{R}^{d_{sen}}$:

$$p^i_j = [I(0 = \lfloor j \frac{d_{sen}}{k_i} \rfloor), I(1 = \lfloor j \frac{d_{sen}}{k_i} \rfloor), ..., I(d_{sen} - 1 = \lfloor j \frac{d_{sen}}{k_i} \rfloor)]^\top \quad (1)$$

---

[1] https://ai.baidu.com/tech/nlp_apply/sentiment_classify.
[2] https://www.nltk.org/.

where $\lfloor * \rfloor$ represents floor function which gives the greatest integer less than or equal to the input, $I(l = k)$ means if k is equal to l, the result will be 1, otherwise is 0. d_{sen} is the dimension of the normalized reply series, which is set as 100 in this study.

After calculating the normalized reply series, we incorporate microblog sentiment into the temporal vector. Specifically, we multiply the generated one-hot vector with the sentiment score of the text, resulting in the temporal sentiment feature $sen_j^i \in \mathbb{R}^{d_{sen}}$, as shown follow:

$$sen_j^i = score_j^i \cdot p_j^i \tag{2}$$

Text Vector. To represent the textual features of the microblogs, we use the pre-trained word embedding model to catch the representation of text. In this work, we use the Tencent word vector model [48] and Glove model [49] to embed the Chinese and English text, respectively. Each post is embedded to a vector sequence $[e_1, e_2, ..., e_l]$, where l is the length of the post, and $e_k \in \mathbb{R}^{d_{vec}}$ is the embedded vector obtained by the word embedding model, the d_{vec} is the dimension of the embedded vector, which is 200 in this study. To obtain the text vector, we add an meanpooling layer to catch the feature of the text. Finally, we can get the text vector $vec_j^i \in \mathbb{R}^{d_{vec}}$ as follow:

$$vec_j^i = Meanpooling(e_1, e_2, ..., e_l) \tag{3}$$

where $Meanpooling(*)$ represents the mean pooling layer, and vec_j^i represents the text vector representation of post j in event i.

Microblog Representation. After obtaining the text vector vec_j^i and the temporal sentiment feature sen_j^i, we concatenate the two vectors to obtain the microblog representation $x_j \in \mathbb{R}^{(d_{vec}+d_{sen})}$ as shown follow:

$$x_j^i = \begin{bmatrix} vec_j^i \\ sen_j^i \end{bmatrix} \tag{4}$$

3.3   Comprehensive Representation

In this study, we use RvNN to catch the feature of microblogs along the spreading path and get the comprehensive representation of the event. Furthermore, we use GRU as the hidden unit to recursively catch the features of the input microblog representation [50]. For the event C_i, the hidden state h_j^i of a node t_j^i can be computed by microblog representation x_j^i of node t_j^i and the hidden state of parent node $h_{P(t_j^i)}$, where $P(t_j^i)$ represents the parent node of t_j^i. Specifically, the process of RvNN can be formulated as follow:

$$h_{t_j^i} = GRU(x_j^i, h_{P(t_j^i)}) \tag{5}$$

where $GRU(*)$ represents the process of GRU. As the microblog spreads, a set of the hidden states $(h_{t_q^i}, h_{t_w^i}, ..., h_{t_l^i})$ is obtained, where t_q^i, t_w^i,...,t_l^i are the leaf nodes of V_i.

After obtaining the recursive representations of all leaf nodes, we add a max-pooling layer to obtain the comprehensive representation of event C_i:

$$h_{out}^i = Maxpooling(h_{t_q^i}, h_{t_w^i}, ..., h_{t_l^i}) \tag{6}$$

where $Maxpooling(*)$ represents the max pooling layer.

3.4 Rumor Classifier

We use a multi-layer neural network with Relu activation function as a rumor classifier to claim whether the source post is a rumor. The input is the comprehensive representation h_{out}^i of event C_i, and the output $\hat{y}_i$ is the detect label of event C_i. The process of MLP shows as follow:

$$\hat{y}_i = \sigma(W_1 \cdot Relu(W_2 \cdot Relu(W_3 \cdot h_{out}^i + b_3) + b_2) + b_1) \tag{7}$$

where $\hat{y}$ denotes prediction value, W_1, W_2, W_3, b_1, b_2 and b_3 denote the weight and bias of the MLP model, $Relu(*)$ is the Relu activation function and the $\sigma(*)$ is the Sigmoid activation function. Furthermore, the cross-entropy function is adopted as the loss function, as shown as follows:

$$\mathcal{L}_\Theta(y_i, \hat{y}_i) = -y_i * \log(\hat{y}_i) + (1 - y_i) * \log(1 - \hat{y}_i) \tag{8}$$

where y_i represents the label of sample C_i and the $\mathcal{L}_\Theta(y_i, \hat{y}_i)$ represents the loss of y_i and $\hat{y}_i$.

4   Experiments

4.1   Datasets

This work employs two public datasets, i.e., Weibo [51] and RumourEval-2019 [52], to evaluate our proposed and baseline methods. The Weibo dataset has 4609 events, with rumor and non-rumor labels. The dataset includes microblog content, social content and spatiotemporal information from Weibo. It should be noted that although the original Weibo dataset has 4664 events, our study focuses on the events which have no more than about 10000 microblogs. Thus, we only remain the 4609 events for the Weibo dataset.

The RumourEval-2019 dataset has 446 events, with rumor, non-rumor and unverified labels. The dataset includes microblog content, social content and spatiotemporal information from Twitter and Reddit. Since our goal is to identify the authenticity of rumors, thus, only the rumor and non-rumor labels remain (totaling 323 events). The statistical information of the two datasets is shown in Table 1.

Table 1. Statistics of the datasets.

Feature	Weibo	RumourEval-2019
Num of microblogs	2,002,060	6,085
Num of events	4,609	323
Num of rumors	2,274	138
Num of non-rumors	2,335	185

4.2 Baseline Models

This work compares six baseline models with our proposed model. The brief introduction to the baseline model is as follows:

- **BERT** [12]: BERT is a pre-trained language representation model with powerful performance.

- **BiGRU** [29]: BiGRU uses a bidirectional-GRU to catch the feature of content words in the microblogs and can detect rumors effectively.

- **Emotion Enhanced BiGRU (Emo-BiGRU)** [29]: The Emo-BiGRU is the BiGRU enhanced by the dual emotion features.

- **RNN** [51]: This method model the social context information of events as time series of variable length and classify the events with RNN.

- **RvNN** [25]: The RvNN uses the TF-IDF to represent the text content and use the RvNN to catch the feature of text content alone the propagation path.

- **BiGCN** [15]: Bi-GCN is a bi-directional graph model and uses the top-down GCN and the bottom-up GCN to catch the features of the spreading structures of microblogs.

Where the BERT, BiGRU, and Emo-BiGRU utilize the source posts and the remaining baseline methods (RNN, RvNN, and BiGCN) utilize both source posts and replies.

4.3 Experimental Settings

Two datasets are divided into the training set, validation set, and test set, where the ratios of these three sets in the two datasets are 3:1:1 in the Weibo dataset and 7:1:2 (remain the original division ratio) in the RumourEval-2019 dataset, respectively. Furthermore, our proposed model uses the Adam optimizer [53] with a learning rate of 0.005 and sets the hidden layer dimension as 128. For the BERT model, it uses Chinese BERT pre-trained with whole word masking [54] for the Chinese text in the Weibo dataset and the google pre-trained model [12] for the English text in the RumourEval-2019 dataset. Moreover, the BERT model use an MLP with Relu activation function to classify the events, where the dimension of the hidden layer is set as 256. For the other baseline models, we adopt the original parameters.

4.4   Evaluation Metrics

Our work commonly uses the accuracy, precision, recall, and macro-F1 score as the evaluation metrics to evaluate the model's performance. The details of the evaluation metrics are as follows:

$$Accuracy = \frac{TP + TN}{TP + TN + FN + FP} \tag{9}$$

$$Precision = \frac{TP}{TP + FP} \tag{10}$$

$$Recall = \frac{TP}{TP + FN} \tag{11}$$

$$F1 = \frac{2 \times Precision \times Recall}{Precision + Recall} \tag{12}$$

$$macro - F1 = \frac{F1_{rumor} + F1_{non-rumor}}{2} \tag{13}$$

where TP represents the number of true positives, TN represents the number of false negatives, FP represents the number of false positives, FN represents the number of false negatives, $F1_{rumor}$ represents the $F1$ score of rumor and $F1_{non-rumor}$ represents the $F1$ score of non-rumor.

4.5   Experimental Results

The experimental results of our proposed method and the baseline methods are shown in Table 2 and 3. Table 2 shows the results on the Weibo dataset. The results show that our proposed model achieves the best performance compared to the baseline models. Furthermore, the poorest performance of the RNN model may be because the RNN model simplifies the propagation structures and can not catch enough features from the content of the posts. Moreover, the Emo-BiGRU's better performance than the BiGRU model also shows the effectiveness of sentiment features. The excellent performance of the BERT model in capturing text representations makes the BERT model perform better than Emo-BiGRU and BiGRU. Finally, compared to the BERT, the better performance of RvNN and BiGCN shows the importance of the spreading structures in rumor detection, since the spreading structures are hard to be manipulated by malicious users.

Table 3 shows the experimental results on the RumourEval-2019 dataset. Compared to experiments on the Weibo dataset, the results on the RumourEval-2019 dataset are worse than that on the Weibo dataset. This may be caused by the sparse data and the low inter-annotator agreement of labels of the RumourEval-2019 dataset [55,56]. In Ref. [55] and Ref. [56], the authors pointed out that the rate of overall inter-annotator agreement is 63.7% which means that there are many conflicting or inconsistent labels and leading to worse performance.

Table 2. Rumor detection performance on the Weibo dataset.

Method	Accuracy	macro-F1	Rumor			Non-rumor		
			Precision	Recall	F1	Precision	Recall	F1
BERT	0.911	0.912	0.919	0.900	0.910	0.904	0.922	0.913
BiGRU	0.793	0.792	0.810	0.758	0.783	0.778	0.826	0.801
Emo-BiGRU	0.857	0.857	0.847	0.866	0.857	0.866	0.848	0.857
RNN	0.630	0.629	0.611	0.690	0.648	0.654	0.571	0.610
RvNN	0.919	0.919	0.938	0.895	0.916	0.902	0.942	0.921
BiGCN	0.921	0.677	0.675	0.690	0.676	0.679	0.689	0.678
Ours	**0.939**	**0.939**	**0.944**	**0.925**	**0.934**	**0.935**	**0.951**	**0.943**

Table 3. Rumor detection performance on the RumourEval-2019 dataset.

Method	Accuracy	macro-F1	Rumor			Non-rumor		
			Precision	Recall	F1	Precision	Recall	F1
BERT	0.509	0.526	**0.496**	0.475	0.478	0.565	0.594	0.573
BiGRU	0.423	0.421	0.486	0.425	0.453	0.361	0.419	0.388
Emo-BiGRU	0.423	0.423	0.484	0.375	0.423	0.375	0.484	0.423
RNN	0.408	0.282	0.418	**0.903**	0.517	0.250	0.025	0.046
RvNN	0.507	0.506	0.455	0.645	**0.533**	**0.593**	0.400	0.478
BiGCN	**0.600**	0.424	0.371	0.400	0.371	0.486	0.514	0.476
Ours	0.549	**0.534**	0.481	0.419	0.448	0.591	**0.650**	**0.619**

Nevertheless, our proposed approach still achieves the best macro-F1. Moreover, the performance of BiGCN demonstrates the robustness of the propagation structure features on different datasets, which helps the BiGCN get the best accuracy. Furthermore, the observed phenomenon of the better result in detecting the rumors and the worst result in detecting the non-rumors of RNN implies RNN is overfitting with limited data. Moreover, the Emo-BiGRU also can be observed that have a better result than BiGRU in macro-F1. The RvNN can use both the text content and the propagation structure, which helps RvNN perform better than Emo-BiGRU. The performance of BERT shows that BERT can effectively catch the features of the text content.

4.6 Discussions

Ablation Study. To further investigate the effectiveness of the key components of our proposed model, i.e., the temporal sentiment feature and the text vector, we additionally conduct an ablation study. In particular, we consider two types of ablations in our experiments: 1) *Ours w/o Text* that does not generate text vector in microblog representation, 2) *Ours w/o Sen* that does not generate the temporal sentiment feature in microblog representation. As the results are shown in Table 4, we observe that *Ours w/o Text* gets the poorest performance in the

Weibo dataset, implying the textual feature is more important than our temporal sentiment feature in detective the rumors in the Weibo dataset. Furthermore, *Ours w/o Sen* has worse performance than *Ours w/o Text* in the RumourEval-2019 dataset implies that the temporal sentiment feature is more important than the textual feature in the RumourEval-2019 dataset. Moreover, our proposed model with all key components has the best performance in both two datasets demonstrating the validity of the proposed microblog representation. The results also demonstrate that our temporal sentiment feature plays an important role in the sparse dataset, especially those with shallower reply depths, e.g., the RumourEval-2019 dataset.

Table 4. The results of ablation study.

Dataset	Metrics	w/o Text	w/o Sen	Ours
Weibo	*Accuracy*	0.855	0.926	**0.939**
	Precision	0.855	0.925	**0.939**
	Recall	0.854	0.925	**0.938**
	macro-F1	0.855	0.925	**0.939**
RumourEval-2019	*Accuracy*	0.493	0.493	**0.549**
	Precision	0.511	0.496	**0.536**
	Recall	0.510	0.496	**0.535**
	macro-F1	0.490	0.492	**0.534**

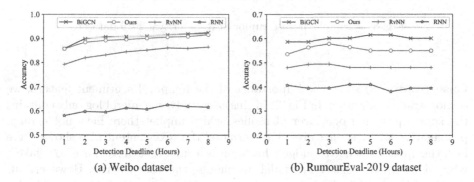

(a) Weibo dataset   (b) RumourEval-2019 dataset

Fig. 2. Early rumor detection accuracy of different methods on two datasets.

Early Rumor Detection. Early rumor detection is an important metric for evaluating the quality of the method in the early stage of information spread. Since the BERT, BiGRU and Emo-BiGRU mainly utilize the source post, early detection is meaningless for these methods. In this work, we compare our proposed method with the RNN, RvNN, and BiGCN in the Weibo and RumourEval-2019 datasets, as shown in Fig. 2. From Fig. 2, we can find that our proposed method reaches high accuracy at the early stage of the propagation. However, our model still performs worse than the BiGCN, which may be because the sentiment features do not appear significant in the early state of rumor spreading, especially for the situation when the propagation features are significant. We have experimented with the effective time of the temporal sentiment feature, and it shows that the temporal sentiment feature requires at least 17 h after source microblogs are posted.

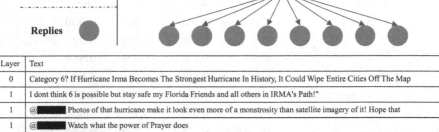

Layer	Text
0	Category 6? If Hurricane Irma Becomes The Strongest Hurricane In History, It Could Wipe Entire Cities Off The Map
1	I dont think 6 is possible but stay safe my Florida Friends and all others in IRMA's Path!"
1	@█████ Photos of that hurricane make it look even more of a monstrosity than satellite imagery of it! Hope that
1	@█████ Watch what the power of Prayer does
1	@█████ @█████ Pray to god the only chance you have
1	@█████ @█████ Dropping now, is Cat 3 Wed.
1	@█████ @█████ no such thing as category 6, but stay prepared, it's a dangerous storm and track is still unpredictable.
1	@█████ @█████ Get out of there people. Florida, South Carolina. Check on neighbors, give them a way to
1	@█████ @█████ I've never heard of a H6! No danger of it getting stronger as it crosses land, Although, it co

Fig. 3. A sample of false rumor in RumourEval-2019 dataset.

Case Study. To show the importance of the temporal sentiment feature, we demonstrate a case study in Fig. 3. In this case study, the microblog only contains the source post and one layer of replies, which implies there have not enough propagation structure features. Furthermore, the text content also shows there lack the direct evidence to judge whether it is a rumor, such as "false" or "fake", which leads to the *w/o Text* model misjudging this case as true. However, our proposed model with the temporal sentiment feature can correctly identify this case as a rumor, suggesting that the sentiment features do play an important role in the absence of textual and communication features.

5   Conclusion

Since the sentiment is a hidden feature and plays an important role in rumor spreading, this work proposes a rumor detection model based on temporal sentiment features. The experiments on two real datasets (the Weibo and RumourEval-2019) demonstrate that our proposed model has better performance than the baseline models, and the ablation study shows that our temporal sentiment feature is effective for rumor detection. However, our method performs worse than Bi-GCN in the early rumor detection. This may be because the temporal sentiment features focus on the long-term sentiment change as information spreads. In our future work, we will consider the importance of different replies to enhance early rumor detection performance. In conclusion, our work supplements current rumor detection methods and highlights that the proposed temporal sentiment feature can effectively capture the rumor in the propagation, especially when there are not enough propagation and text features.

Acknowledgements. This work was supported by the Zhejiang Fundamental Public Welfare Research Project under Grant (LGF21G010003 and LGF20F020016) and the National Natural Science Foundation of China under Grant (62103374).

References

1. Shao, C., Ciampaglia, G.L., Varol, O., Yang, K.C., Flammini, A., Menczer, F.: The spread of low-credibility content by social bots. Nature Commun. **9**(1), 4787 (2018)
2. Ruan, Z., Yu, B., Shu, X., Zhang, Q., Xuan, Q.: The impact of malicious nodes on the spreading of false information. Chaos: Interdisciplinary J. Nonlinear Sci. **30**(8), 083101 (2020)
3. Pendleton, S.C.: Rumor research revisited and expanded. Lang. Commun. **18**(1), 69–86 (1998)
4. Zubiaga, A., Aker, A., Bontcheva, K., Liakata, M., Procter, R.: Detection and resolution of rumours in social media: a survey. ACM Comput. Surv. **51**(2), 1–36 (2018)
5. Allcott, H., Gentzkow, M.: Social media and fake news in the 2016 election. J. Econ. Perspect. **31**(2), 211–36 (2017). May
6. Du, J., Dou, Y., Xia, C., Cui, L., Ma, J., Philip, S.Y.: Cross-lingual covid-19 fake news detection. In: Proceedings of the 16th International Conference on Data Mining Workshops, pp. 859–862. IEEE Computer Society, Los Alamitos (2021)
7. Cui, L., Lee, D.: CoAID: COVID-19 healthcare misinformation dataset. arXiv preprint. arXiv:2006.00885 (2020)
8. Hassan, N., Li, C., Tremayne, M.: Detecting check-worthy factual claims in presidential debates. In: Proceedings of the 24th International on Conference on Information and Knowledge Management, pp. 1835–1838. ACM, Atlanta (2015)
9. Rubin, V.L.: On deception and deception detection: content analysis of computer-mediated stated beliefs. In: Proceedings of the 73rd Annual Meeting on Navigating Streams in an Information Ecosystem, vol. 47, p. 10. ASIS, Pittsburgh (2010)
10. Mikolov, T., Chen, K., Corrado, G., Dean, J.: Efficient estimation of word representations in vector space. arXiv preprint. arXiv:1301.3781 (2013)
11. Vaswani, A.: Attention is all you need. In: Proceedings of the 31st International Conference on Neural Information Processing Systems, pp. 6000–6010. CAI, Long Beach (2017)

12. Devlin, J., Chang, M.W., Lee, K., Toutanova, K.: BERT: pre-training of deep bidirectional transformers for language understanding. arXiv preprint. arXiv:1810.04805 (2018)
13. Chenbo, F., Zheng, Y., Liu, Y., Xuan, Q., Chen, G.: NES-TL: network embedding similarity-based transfer learning. IEEE Trans. Netw. Sci. Eng. **7**(3), 1607–1618 (2020)
14. Chenbo, F., et al.: A novel spatiotemporal behavior-enabled random walk strategy on online social platforms. IEEE Trans. Comput. Soc. Syst. **9**(3), 807–817 (2022)
15. Bian, T.: Rumor detection on social media with bi-directional graph convolutional networks. arXiv preprint. arXiv:2001.06362 (2020)
16. Kaliyar, R.K., Goswami, A., Narang, P.: FakeBERT: fake news detection in social media with a bert-based deep learning approach. Multimedia Tools Appl. **80**(8), 11765–11788 (2021). https://doi.org/10.1007/s11042-020-10183-2
17. Qian, S., Wang, J., Hu, J., Fang, Q., Xu, C.: Hierarchical multi-modal contextual attention network for fake news detection. In: Proceedings of the 44th International Conference on Research and Development in Information Retrieval, pp. 153–162. ACM, New York (2021)
18. Qazi, M., Khan, M.U., Ali, M.: Detection of fake news using transformer model. In: Proceedings of the 3rd International Conference on Computing, Mathematics and Engineering Technologies, pp. 1–6. IEEE, Sukkur (2020)
19. Lu, Y.J., Li, C.T.: GCAN: graph-aware co-attention networks for explainable fake news detection on social media. In: Proceedings of the 58th Annual Meeting of the Association for Computational Linguistics, pp. 505–514. ACL (2020)
20. Feng, S., Banerjee, R., Choi, Y.: Syntactic stylometry for deception detection. In: Proceedings of the 50th Annual Meeting of the Association for Computational Linguistics, vol. 2, pp. 171–175. ACL, Jeju Island (2012)
21. Wang, Y.: EANN: event adversarial neural networks for multi-modal fake news detection. In: Proceedings of the 24th International Conference on Knowledge Discovery & Data Mining, pp. 849–857. ACM, East Lansing (2018)
22. Thies, J., Zollhöfer, M., Stamminger, M., Theobalt, C., Nießner, M.: Face2face: Real-time face capture and reenactment of RGB videos. Commun. ACM **62**(1), 96–104 (2018). Dec
23. Zhou, Z., Guan, H., Bhat, M.M., Hsu, J.: Fake news detection via nlp is vulnerable to adversarial attacks. arXiv preprint. arXiv:1901.09657 (2019)
24. Westerlund, M.: The emergence of deepfake technology: a review. Technol. Innov. Manag. Rev. **9**, 40–53 (2019)
25. Ma, J., Gao, W., Wong, K.F.: Rumor detection on Twitter with tree-structured recursive neural networks. In: Proceedings of the 56th Annual Meeting of the Association for Computational Linguistics, vol. 1, pp. 1980–1989. ACL, Melbourne (2018)
26. Wu, K., Yang, S., Zhu, K.Q.: False rumors detection on sina weibo by propagation structures. In: Proceedings of the 31st International Conference on Data Engineering, pp. 651–662. IEEE Computer Society, Los Alamitos (2015)
27. Zhiyuan, W., Pi, D., Chen, J., Xie, M., Cao, J.: Rumor detection based on propagation graph neural network with attention mechanism. Expert Syst. Appl. **158**, 113595 (2020)
28. Alonso, M.A., Vilares, D., Gómez-Rodríguez, C., Vilares, J.: Sentiment analysis for fake news detection. Electronics **10**(11), 1348 (2021)
29. Zhang, X., Cao, J., Li, X., Sheng, Q., Zhong, L., Shu, K.: Mining dual emotion for fake news detection. In: Proceedings of the 30th the Web Conference, pp. 3465–3476. ACM, Ljubljana (2021)

30. Mackey, A., Gauch, S., Labille, K.: Detecting fake news through emotion analysis. In: Proceedings of the 13th International Conference on Information, Process, and Knowledge Management, pp. 65–71. IARIA (2021)
31. Yang, Y., Zheng, L., Zhang, J., Cui, Q., Li, Z., Yu, P.S.: TI-CNN: convolutional neural networks for fake news detection. arXiv preprint. arXiv:1806.00749 (2018)
32. Wang, Z., Guo, Y., Wang, J., Li, Z., Tang, M.: Rumor events detection from chinese microblogs via sentiments enhancement. IEEE Access **7**, 103000–103018 (2019)
33. Ajao, O., Bhowmik, D., Zargari, S.: Sentiment aware fake news detection on online social networks. In: Proceedings of the 44th International Conference on Acoustics, Speech, and Signal Processing, pp. 2507–2511. IEEE, Brighton (2019)
34. Cui, L., Wang, S., Lee, D.: SAME: sentiment-aware multi-modal embedding for detecting fake news. In: Proceedings of the 4th International Conference on Advances in Social Networks Analysis and Mining, pp. 41–48. ACM, Vancouver (2019)
35. Wu, L., Rao, Y.: Adaptive interaction fusion networks for fake news detection. arXiv preprint. arXiv:2004.10009 (2020)
36. Davoudi, M., Moosavi, M.R., Sadreddini, M.H.: DSS: a hybrid deep model for fake news detection using propagation tree and stance network. Expert Syst. Appl. **198**, 116635 (2022)
37. Bond, G.: 'Lyin' Ted', 'Crooked Hillary', and 'Deceptive Donald': language of lies in the 2016 US presidential debates. Appl. Cogn. Psychol. **31**(6), 668–677 (2017)
38. Zhao, H., Zhou, W., Chen, D., Wei, T., Zhang, W., Yu, N.: Multi-attentional deepfake detection. In Proceedings of the 30st Conference on Computer Vision and Pattern Recognition, pp. 2185–2194. IEEE Computer Society, Los Alamitos (2021)
39. Guarnera, L., Giudice, O., Battiato, S.: Deepfake detection by analyzing convolutional traces. In: Proceedings of the 29th Conference on Computer Vision and Pattern Recognition Workshops, pp. 2841–2850. IEEE Computer Society, Los Alamitos (2020)
40. Ma, J., Gao, W., Wong, K.-F.: Detect rumors in microblog posts using propagation structure via kernel learning. In: Proceedings of the 55th Annual Meeting of the Association for Computational Linguistics, vol. 1, pp. 708–717. ACL, Vancouver (2017)
41. Li, B., Qian, Z., Li, P., Zhu, Q.: Multi-modal fusion network for rumor detection with texts and images. In: Þór Jónsson, B., et al. (eds.) MMM 2022. LNCS, vol. 13141, pp. 15–27. Springer, Cham (2022). https://doi.org/10.1007/978-3-030-98358-1_2
42. Vo, N., Lee, K.: Hierarchical multi-head attentive network for evidence-aware fake news detection. arXiv preprint. arXiv:2102.02680 (2021)
43. Dou, Y., Shu, K., Xia, C., Yu, P.S., Sun, L.: User preference-aware fake news detection. In: Proceedings of the 44th International Conference on Research and Development in Information Retrieval, pp. 2051–2055. ACM, Montreal (2021)
44. Wang, G., Tan, L., Shang, Z., Liu, H.: Multimodal dual emotion with fusion of visual sentiment for rumor detection. arXiv preprint. arXiv:2204.11515 (2022)
45. Guo, C., Cao, J., Zhang, X., Shu, K., Yu, M.: Exploiting emotions for fake news detection on social media. arXiv preprint. arXiv:1903.01728 (2019)
46. Guerini, M., Staiano, J.: Deep feelings: a massive cross-lingual study on the relation between emotions and virality. In: Proceedings of the 24th International Conference on World Wide Web, pp. 299–305. Association for Computing Machinery, New York (2015)

47. Pröllochs, N., Bär, D., Feuerriegel, S.: Emotions explain differences in the diffusion of true vs. false social media rumors. Sci. Rep. **11**(1), 1–12 (2021)
48. Song, Y., Shi, S., Li, J., Zhang, H.: Directional KKIP-Gram: explicitly distinguishing left and right context for word embeddings. In: Proceedings of the 16th Conference of the North American Chapter of the Association for Computational Linguistics: Human Language Technologies, vol. 2, pp. 175–180. ACL, New Orleans (2018)
49. Pennington, J., Socher, R., Manning, C.: GloVe: global vectors for word representation. In: Proceedings of the 19th Conference on Empirical Methods in Natural Language Processing, pp. 1532–1543. ACL, Doha (2014)
50. Cho, K.: Learning phrase representations using RNN encoder-decoder for statistical machine translation. arXiv preprint. arXiv:1406.1078 (2014)
51. Ma, J.: Detecting rumors from microblogs with recurrent neural networks. In: Proceedings of the 25th International Joint Conference on Artificial Intelligence, pp. 3818–3824. AAAI Press, New York (2016)
52. Gorrell, G., Bontcheva, K., Derczynski, L., Kochkina, E., Liakata, M., Zubiaga, A.: Rumoureval 2019: determining rumour veracity and support for rumours. arXiv preprint. arXiv:1809.06683 (2018)
53. Kingma, D.P., Ba, J.: Adam: a method for stochastic optimization. arXiv preprint. arXiv:1412.6980 (2014)
54. Cui, Y., Che, W., Liu, T., Qin, B., Yang, Z.: Pre-training with whole word masking for chinese bert. IEEE/ACM Trans. Audio Speech Lang. Process. **29**, 3504–3514 (2021)
55. Gorrell, G., et al.: SemEval-2019 task 7: RumourEval, determining rumour veracity and support for rumours. In: Proceedings of the 13th International Workshop on Semantic Evaluation, pp. 845–854. ACL, Minneapolis (2019)
56. Li, Q., Zhang, Q., Si, L.: eventAI at SemEval-2019 task 7: rumor detection on social media by exploiting content, user credibility and propagation information. In: Proceedings of the 13th International Workshop on Semantic Evaluation, pp. 855–859. ACL, Minneapolis (2019)

Research on Users' Trust in Customer Service Chatbots Based on Human-Computer Interaction

Yangyang Lv[1,6], Shuaibo Hu[2], Feng Liu[3,4,5,6(✉)] (iD), and Jiayin Qi[6(✉)]

[1] Shanghai University of International, Business and Economics, Shanghai 201620, China
[2] Shanghai Trusted Industrial Control Platform Co., LTD, Shanghai 200333, China
[3] Institute of AI for Education, East China Normal University, Shanghai 200062, China
lsttoy@163.com
[4] School of Computer Science and Technology, East China Normal University, Shanghai 200062, China
[5] Shanghai Key Laboratory of Mental Health and Psychological Crisis Intervention, School of Psychology and Cognitive Science, East China Normal University, Shanghai 200062, China
[6] Institute of Artificial Intelligence and Change Management, Shanghai University of International, Business and Economics, Shanghai 200336, China
ai@suibe.edu.cn

Abstract. As Human-Computer Interaction (HCI) moves towards deep collaboration, it is urgent to study users' trust in chatbots. This study takes customer service chatbots as an example. Firstly, literature review is conducted on the relevant research on users' trust in chatbots, and the value chain model of customer service chatbots is analyzed. Taking Taobaoxiaomi as the specific research object, we conducted in-depth interviews with 18 users, organized the interview data with value focused thinking method (VFT), constructed the users' trust model of customer service chatbots, and carried out an empirical test by questionnaire survey. The results show that professionalism, response speed and predictability have positive effects on users' trust in chatbots, while ease of use and human-likeness have no significant positive effects on users' trust. Besides, brand trust has a positive impact on users' trust in chatbots, risk perception negatively affects users' trust in chatbots, and human support has no significant negative effect on users' trust. Finally, privacy concerns have a moderating effect on environmental factors (brand trust, risk et al.). This study will deepen the understanding of human-computer trust and provide reference for the industry to improve chatbots and enhance users' trust.

Keywords: HCI · Computational affection · Artificial intelligence · Trust · Customer service chatbots · VFT

1 Introduction

Chatbots are software agents that interact with users through natural language conversations [1] and are seen as a promising customer service technology. Recent advances in artificial intelligence (AI) and machine learning, as well as the widespread adoption of messaging platforms, have prompted companies to explore chatbots as a complement to customer service [2]. According to a new report by Grand View Research, the global chatbots market is expected to reach $2.4857 billion by 2028 [3]. In addition, major platforms, such as Amazon, eBay, Facebook, Wechat, Jingdong and Taobao, have adopted chatbots for conversational commerce [4]. AI chatbots can provide unique business benefits [5]. They automate customer service and facilitate company-initiated communications. Chatbots are equipped with sophisticated speech recognition and natural language processing tools, enabling them to understand complex and subtle dialogue, and in a sympathy, and even humorous way to meet the requirements of the consumers [6]. Despite this potential benefit for vendors, one of the key challenges facing AI chatbots applications is customer response [7]. Human may be biased against chatbots, believing that they lack human emotion and empathy, and they are less credible in payment information and product recommendations (i.e., the Uncanny Valley theory and algorithm-based aversion proposed by Dietvorst et al. [8] and Kestenbaum[9]). In addition, some enterprises collect and use customer data illegally, resulting in the risk of user privacy disclosure [10].

Customer service is currently only an emerging application field of chatbots and has not yet achieved the expected general acceptance of customers [2]. From other technology areas, we know that users' trust is critical for the widespread adoption of new interactive solutions [11]. However, our understanding of users' trust in chatbots and the factors that influence this trust is very limited [2]. Therefore, it is of great theoretical and practical significance to study the users' trust construction of customer service chatbots.

2   Literature Review

There is a wide range of studies on trust, ranging from psychology, sociology to technology [11]. Therefore, there are many definitions of trust. Trust refers to one's dependence on another [12]. The relationship between people requires trust to make continuous interaction successful [13]. Trust is not only an important part of interpersonal communication but also an important part of the rapid development of the "human-machine" relationship [14]. Mayer et al. defined trust as a belief and will, emphasizing the risk of trust, the cause and effect of trust behavior [15]. They believe that "trust means that the trustor is willing to be in a vulnerable state influenced by the other party's behavior based on the expectation that the trustor will show an important behavior toward him or her, and it has nothing to do with the ability to monitor or control the other party" [15]. Rousseau et al. proposed an interdisciplinary definition of trust that reflects the commonality, believing that trust is based on the positive expectation of others' intentions or behaviors, while trusting (willing to take risks) is a psychological state that accepts vulnerability based on the positive expectation of another party's intentions or behaviors [16]. Mayer et al., and Rousseau et al., both emphasized the importance of the will of fragile states and the actions at stake [16], and did not limit the concept of trust to the interaction between people. The object of trust could be technology, including artificial intelligence [17].

Most of the existing studies on non-human trust focus on automated systems, and many foreign scholars have studied the trust in robot systems [2, 18–20], but the research on the trust in customer service chatbots is relatively new. While the study of trust in automated and robot systems provides a solid foundation for understanding users' trust in customer service chatbots to some extent, customer service chatbots are different from other forms of automation, and these differences will affect trust in ways that are not yet fully understood. This paper reviews the relevant literature on users' trust in customer service chatbots, and lists the influencing factors of trust, as shown in Table 1.

Table 1. Literature review on users' trust in chatbots.

Categories		Scholars	Influencing factors
External factors	Chatbots-related factors	Følstad et al. (2018) [2]	The quality of interpreting requests and suggestions, human likeness, self-presentation, professional image
		Nordheim (2018) [21]	Professionalism, quick response, human-likeness, lack of marketing
		Corritore et al. (2003) [11]	Professionalism, predictability, ease of use
		Ho and MacDorman (2010) [22]	Human-likeness
	Environment-related factors	Følstad et al. (2018) [2]	The brand of the chatbot provider, perceived privacy and security while using the chatbot, and overall perceived risk regarding the subject of the request
		Nordheim (2018) [21]	Brand, low risk, human support
		Corritore et al. (2003) [11]	Risk
	User-related factors	Nordheim (2018) [21]; McKnight et al. (2011) [23]	Trust in technology
		Corritore et al. (2003) [11]	Reputation

(*continued*)

Table 1. (*continued*)

Categories	Scholars	Influencing factors
Perceived factors	Corritore et al. (2003) [11]	Perceived ease of use, perceived reliability and perceived risk

According to the results of the above literature review, the influencing factors on users' trust in chatbots can be divided into three categories: factors related to chatbots, environment, and user [2, 11, 22, 23, 25]. Corritore et al. classified the above three influencing factors as external factors. Besides external factors, they also put forward perceived factors, including perceived ease of use, perceived reliability, and perceived risk [11].

Based on the above scholars on the research of the users' trust in chatbots, this paper puts forward the chatbots value chain, and analysis the main involving entities and their relations, thus confirming trust object. Then we conducted interviews with 18 users and made qualitative analysis of the influence factors of users' trust in chatbots using VFT methods. And a model of users' trust in customer service chatbots is established. Finally, we verified the model quantitatively by a questionnaire survey.

3   Interview Analysis Based on Value Focus Thinking

3.1   Value Focused Thinking

Due to the complexity of customer service systems containing chatbots, the factors that influence the users' trust in customer service chatbots are more complex. This paper uses value focused thinking (VFT) method to find out some of the key factors. This paper analyzes the forms of users' trust in online customer service chatbots, and establishes a users' trust model of online customer service chatbots.

Value focused thinking is a creative decision-making analysis method proposed by Keeney(1992), which is suitable for solving complex multi-objective problems requiring highly subjective decision-making based on the value goals of decision-makers and stakeholders [25]. This method firstly focuses on value rather than scheme, believing that value is the primary criterion to evaluate the satisfaction of any possible scheme, and then the scheme to realize value [26]. Value refers to the criteria for evaluating possible solutions or results, which are externalized by the way of goal recognition, while the goal is defined as a state that a person wants to achieve to a certain extent [27]. Value is the core connotation of VFT method, including economic value, personal value, social value, or other values [25]. The goals consist of three factors: decision background, subject, and general direction [28]. Keeney applied this method to the study of e-commerce and analyzed the consumer value of e-commerce by comparing the perceived value difference between online shopping and shopping through other channels [29]. Zhaohua Deng et al. studied consumer trust in mobile commerce by using VFT method [29]. The analytical steps of VFT method adopted in this paper are shown in Fig. 2 [29] (Fig. 1).

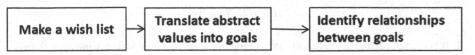

Fig. 1. The analytical steps of VFT method.

3.2 Interview Data Collection

According to the analysis steps of VFT method, the value of users should be directly inquired from users [29]. This paper takes the users' trust in online customer service chatbots as the target, and interviews 18 users of the shopping platform. These users are all college students and postgraduates with online shopping experience. Before the interview, we explained the purpose and general situation of the interview to each interviewee, and explained that the interview content would be recorded but without personal information, and it would only be used for this study and no other purposes. The interview in this study was conducted after the consent of the interviewee. This interview is mainly conducted through online meetings or voice calls. Taobaoxiaomi is taken as the main research object. And several major questions are asked for the interviewees to answer. The interview raw data is stored at the following address: https://github.com/Yangyangyounglv/chatbots-interview-record.git.

3.3 Analysis Steps

According to VFT method, the specific analysis steps are as follows.

Step 1. Make a list of all values. In order to obtain the value of users, we asked interviewees questions such as "What are the advantages of Taobaoxiaomi, Taobao's customer service chatbots? What are the advantages over human customer service?" "What are the shortcomings of Taobaoxiaomi? What are the disadvantages compared to human customer service?" "What do you think Taobao can do to repair or improve your trust in it?" "What future suggestions or assumptions do you have for Taobaoxiaomi?". We sorted out the answers of interviewees and obtained the value list, as shown in Table 2.

Table 2. Wish list.

1. It is convenient and quick to solve procedural problems; 2. Good software interface design, easy to operate common problems; 3. Relatively complete functions; 4. High security performance when it comes to payment; 5. Polite and patient; 6. Relieved the pressure of human customer service and coordinated human customer service; 7. The functions of voucher receiving center and evaluation management are quite useful; 8. Good question association function; 9. One-to-one precise service, fast and efficient; 10. Clear process and steps; 11. Professional; 12. Not competent when it comes to disputes with doubts and issues requiring communication and coordination between both parties; 13. Lack of intelligence, unable to solve personalized problems, limited database, blunt and repetitive answers; 14. No emotion, not close enough; 15. Insufficient authority to solve special problems; 16. Advanced functions with average performance in recommendation functions; 17. Can't understand what I'm asking; 18. It's harder to reach real human customer service; 19. After a long communication, I still find that I am not satisfied; 20. Not an information collator and content producer; 21. It may compromise personal privacy; 22. Customer service Xiaomi belongs to Taobao, so it's worthy to trust; 23. After all, it's just a robot. It can not complete the kind of human sensibility, understanding, and empathy;...

Step 2. Translate abstract values into goals. Three characteristics of goal in VFT method are decision context, subject, and decision of preference. For example, most interviewees believe that ensuring the professionalism of Taobaoxiaomi is the key factor influencing users' trust in online customer service chatbots. In this goal, the decision situation is related to chatbots, and the decision purpose is professional. The more professional the chatbots are, the more considerate and intelligent it is, the more users will trust the chatbots. Therefore, the decision maker's preference is the more considerate and intelligent situation. In this way, the abstract values in Table 3 are transformed into goals of the same format, as shown in Table 3.

Step 3: Identify relationships between goals. After the general formalization of goals in step 2, common goals with the same format were obtained, followed by the distinction between basic goals and means goals. Basic goals involve "goals that decision-makers attach importance to in a specific context", while means goals are "methods to achieve goals" [30]. In order to separate the basic goals and means goals to establish the relationship between them, our each goal was identified using a test called "why so important". Asking "why so important" will produce two possible responses. First, the goal is to focus on one of the fundamental causes of the situation, which also is the root of the decision, this is known as the basic goal. Another reaction is that a goal is important because it has an impact on other goals, which is called the means goal [31]. According to this method, the target is analyzed and the results obtained are shown in Table 4.

Table 3. General formalization of goals.

Decision context	Subject	Preference
Factors related to chatbots	Professionalism	Solve problems efficiently
	Response speed	Answer questions quickly
	Predictability	Provide expected results
	Ease of use	More convenient operation
	Human-likeness	Be emotional, polite and patient
Factors related to environment	Band trust	The service provider's brand is more reliable
	Risk	The using environment is safer
	Human support	Human customer service is always available
Factors related to users	privacy concerns	Sensitive personal information is protected
	Trust in technology	More willing to rely on technology

Table 4. Classify goals relation.

Goals categories	Main goals	Sub-goals
Means goals	Chatbots are more powerful	1. Professionalism; 2. Response speed; 3. Predictability; 4. Ease of use; 5. Human-likeness
	Environment is more reliable	1. Brand trust; 2. Risk; 3. Human support
	Users are more receptive to technology	1. Privacy concerns; 2. Trust in technology
Basic goal	Users' trust in Customer service chatbots maximization	Chatbots are more powerful
		Environment is more reliable
		Users are more receptive

3.4 Construction of Users' Trust Model for Customer Service Chatbots

According to the above analysis of customer service chatbots users' trust, there are three main factors influencing customer service chatbots users' trust, which are chatbots-related factors, environment-related factors and user-related factors. The specific forms of users' trust in customer service chatbots are more powerful chatbots, more reliable environment and users that more receptive. Based on the above analysis of the influencing factors of users' trust in customer service chatbots, this paper builds a model of users' trust in customer service chatbots, as shown in Fig. 2.

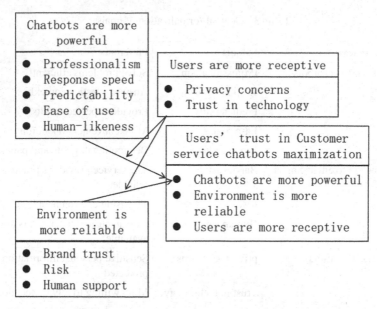

Fig. 2. The model of users' trust in customer service chatbots based on VFT.

4   The Questionnaire Survey

4.1   Hypothesis

Based on the theoretical model constructed by the interview, the following hypotheses are proposed:

H1. The professionalism of chatbots has a positive impact on users' trust in them.

H1a. Users' privacy concerns negatively moderates the positive relationship between chatbots' professionalism and users' trust.

H1b. Users' trust in technology positively moderates the positive relationship between chatbots' professionalism and users' trust.

H2. Chatbots' response speed has a positive impact on users' trust in chatbots.

H2a. Users' privacy concerns negatively moderates the positive relationship between chatbots' response speed and users' trust.

H2b. Users' trust in technology positively moderates the positive relationship between chatbots' response speed and users' trust.

H3. Chatbots' predictability has a positive impact on users' trust in chatbots.

H3a. Users' privacy concerns negatively moderates the positive relationship between chatbots' predictability and users' trust.

H3b. Users' trust in technology positively moderates the positive relationship between chatbots' predictability and users' trust.

H4. Chatbots' ease of use has a positive impact on users' trust in chatbots.

H4a. Users' privacy concerns negatively moderates the positive relationship between chatbots' ease of use and users' trust.

H4b. Users' trust in technology positively moderates the positive relationship between chatbots' ease of use and users' trust.

H5. Chatbots' human-likeness has a positive impact on users' trust in chatbots.

H5a. Users' privacy concerns negatively moderates the positive relationship between chatbots' human-likeness and users' trust.

H5b. Users' trust in technology positively moderates the positive relationship between chatbots' human-likeness and users' trust.

H6. Users' brand trust in chatbots providers has a positive impact on users' trust in chatbots.

H6a. Users' privacy concerns negatively moderates the positive relationship between users' trust in the chatbots provider and users' trust.

H6b. Users' trust in technology positively moderates the positive relationship between users' trust in the chatbots provider and users' trust.

H7. The risk of using a chatbot has a negative impact on users' trust in the chatbots.

H7a. Users' privacy concerns positively moderates the negative relationship between the risk of using a chatbot and users' trust.

H7b. Users' trust in technology negatively moderates the negative relationship between the risk of using chatbots and users' trust.

H8. Human support has a negative impact on users' trust in chatbots.

H8a. Users' privacy concerns positively moderates the negative relationship between human support and users' trust.

H8b. Users' trust in technology negatively moderates the negative relationship between human support and users' trust.

To sum up, further theoretical models are obtained by integrating various variables and their relations (see Fig. 3).

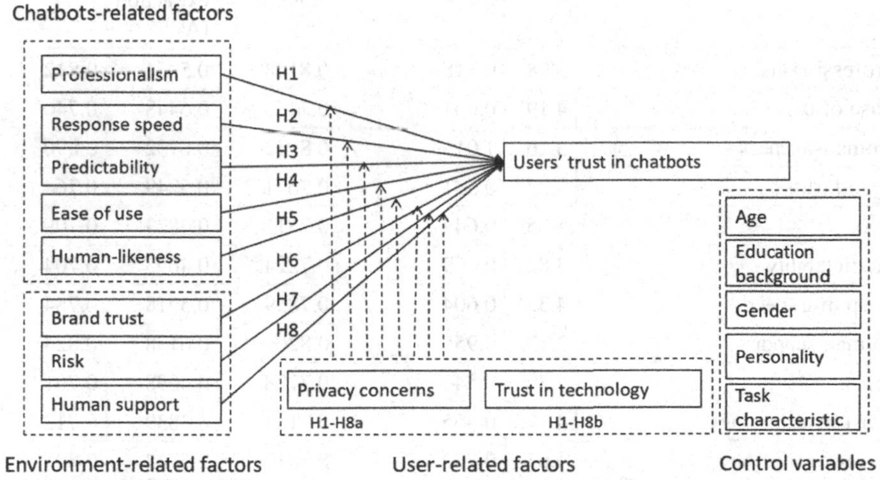

Fig. 3. The empirical test model of users' trust in customer service chatbots.

4.2 Questionnaire Data Collection

We collected data through a questionnaire survey, which lasted for two days from June 20, 2020 to June 21, 2020. Questionnaires were issued mainly through Credamo, an online data research platform. After the completion of the collection, the data were screened. And the person who adopted the questionnaire was rewarded with 2 yuan, while the person whose questionnaire was rejected was not rewarded. After the screening, the questionnaire was re-issued and repeated until 500 qualified samples were obtained. Samples were collected from Chongqing, Zhejiang, Shanghai, Yunnan, Tianjin, Shandong, Henan, Hebei, Shanxi, Sichuan, and Jiangsu provinces. During data screening, the questionnaires with the same answers to consecutive questions or contradictory answers to positive and negative questions were removed. A total of 592 questionnaires were collected, and finally, 500 were valid, with an effective rate of 84.46%.

4.3 Data Analysis

Before model verification, we performed skewness and kurtosis test, common method bias test on the data. After these test, the data from the formal questionnaire conform to the standard and can continue the following analysis. And the reliability and validity analysis results are showed in Table 5. Therefore, the structural model had good model fitness.

Table 5. The reliability and validity indexes of each variable.

Variables		Mean (M.)	Standard deviation(S.D.)	Composite reliability (CR)	Average variance extraction (AVE)	Cronbach's alpha
Professionalism		3.98	0.718	0.8148	0.5954	0.812
Ease of use		4.19	0.601	0.7453	0.6448	0.740
Human-likeness		3.26	1.01	0.8912	0.6732	0.890
Brand trust		4.37	0.531	0.7671	0.5249	0.764
Risk		1.85	0.647	0.7311	0.4823	0.709
Predictability		3.82	0.669	0.7224	0.4695	0.704
Response speed		4.33	0.604	0.7859	0.5518	0.784
Human support		3.17	0.955	0.8266	0.6138	0.824
Trust		4.30	0.544	0.7728	0.4698	0.761
Trust in technology		4.19	0.465	0.7133	0.3839	0.712
Privacy concerns		3.63	0.772	0.8017	0.5742	0.801
Personality	Extraversion	4.14	0.957	0.806	0.6873	0.792
	Conscientious-ness	4.54	0.810	0.5904	0.4254	0.564
	Openess	4.50	0.758	0.5679	0.4026	0.550

Regression analysis. Stepwise regression method is adopted to screen independent variables to ensure that the optimal model is finally obtained. Tolerance is close to 1, and variance inflation factor (VIF) is greater than 0. Therefore, there is no obvious colinearity problem in the model. After regression analysis, professionalism ($\beta = 0.351$, P < 0.001), risk ($\beta = -0.231$, P < 0.001), brand trust ($\beta = 0.211$, P < 0.001), speed of response ($\beta = 0.103$, P < 0.05), and predictability ($\beta = 0.103$, P < 0.05). H1, H2, H3, H6, and H7 are supported, while H4, H5, and H8 are not. The regression results are shown in Table 6.

Table 6. Model regression results.

Model	Normalization coefficient	t	Significance	Collinear statistics	
	Beta			Tolerance	VIF
(constant)		8.625	.000		
Professionalism	.351	7.423	.000	.455	2.198
Risk	−.231	−5.890	.000	.659	1.518
Band trust	.211	4.966	.000	.560	1.785
Response speed	.103	2.601	.010	.653	1.530
Predictability	.103	2.156	.032	.448	2.232

The results of model verification show that professionalism, response speed, and predictability of variables related to chatbots positively affect users' trust in chatbots. In variables related to environment, brand trust positively affects users' trust in chatbots, and risk negatively affects users' trust in chatbots. The professional regression coefficient is the largest, indicating that it has the greatest influence on trust. The coefficient of predictability and response speed is the smallest, which indicates that they have the least influence on trust.

Robustness test. In order to ensure the scientific nature and effectiveness of regression results, it is necessary to conduct robustness test for sample data, and use the whole sample and subsample (N = 500, after deleting ease-of-use, human-likeness and human support variables) to conduct input method regression test. Professional test results (whole sample: $\beta = 0.331$, P < 0.001; Subsample: $\beta = 0.351$, P < 0.001), risk (whole sample: $\beta = -0.226$, P < 0.001; Subsample: $\beta = 0.231$, P < 0.001), brand trust (whole sample: $\beta = 0.207$, P < 0.001; Subsample: $\beta = 0.211$, P < 0.001), response speed (whole sample: $\beta = 0.097$, P < 0.05; Subsample: $\beta = 0.103$, P < 0.05) and predictability (whole sample: $\beta = 0.114$, P < 0.05; Subsample: $\beta = 0.103$, P < 0.05) was significantly correlated with the dependent variable trust, and there was significant correlation between the two variables, such as human-likeness (whole sample: $\beta = -0.071$, P = 0.081), ease of use (whole sample: $\beta = 0.067$, P = 0.195), and human support (whole sample: $\beta = -0.027$, P = 0.422) was not significantly correlated with the dependent variable trust. In conclusion, it is consistent with the original results. Its robustness is proved.

Difference analysis. This part mainly uses the independent sample T-test and one-way variance analysis method to analyze whether there are significant differences between demographic variables of samples and task characteristics on trust. In this study, T-test of independent samples was used to analyze gender and task characteristics, and one-way ANOVA was used to analyze age, education background, and personality.

The results showed that there were no significant differences in task characteristics (P = 0.998 > 0.05), age (P = 0.849 > 0.05), education level (P = 0.922 > 0.05) and trust in chatbots. Gender, and personality (extraversion, conscientiousness, and openness) were significantly correlated with the level of trust in chatbots. There is a significant correlation between the users' gender and the level of trust between the user and the chatbots (P = 0.037 < 0.05), and the level of trust in males is higher than that in females.

The moderating effect analysis. H4, H5, and H8 fail, so we drop its assumptions, namely the adjustment effect test, and continue to test the assumptions of H1, H2, H3, H6, and H7, respectively test trust in technology and privacy concerns of professionalism, response speed, predictability, brand trust and risk the five variables and the moderation effect between users trust effect.

The results show that the moderating effect of trust in technology on all variables is not significant. The results of hypothesis verification in this study are summarized in Table 7, and the moderating effect of privacy concerns is shown in Fig. 4. Professionalism * trust in technology ($\beta = 0.041$, $P = 0.333$), response speed * trust in technology ($\beta = -0.064$, $P = 0.262$), predictability * Trust technology propensity ($\beta = -0.023$, $P = 0.660$), brand trust * trust in technology ($\beta = -0.052$, $P = 0.441$), risk * trust in technology ($\beta = 0.016$, $P = 0.784$), H1b, H2b, H3b, H6b, and H7b are not supported. Privacy concerns have moderating effects on environment-related factors, brand trust ($\beta = 0.097$, $P < 0.05$), and risk ($\beta = 0.104$, $P < 0.05$). H6a, and H7a are supported. As for chatbots related factors, professionalism ($\beta = 0.037$, $P = 0.303$), response speed ($\beta = 0.036$, $P = 0.347$), and the predictability ($\beta = -0.059$, $P = 0.103$) showed no moderating effect. H1a, H2a, and H3a are not supported.

5   Summary

5.1   Conclusions

It is found that the professionalism, response speed, and predictability of chatbots have a positive impact on users' trust in chatbots, which verifies the previous hypothesis.

Environment-related factors, brand trust, and risk are significantly correlated with users' trust in chatbots, in which brand trust is positively correlated and risk is negatively correlated, which verifies previous hypotheses. Human customer service and chatbots customer service are in a relatively independent position, so human support does not significantly change users' trust in chatbots customer service.

Although trust in technology can reflect the personal differences of users to a certain extent, our results showed that trust in technology is not a moderating variable.

The relationship between environmental factors (brand trust, risk, etc.) and trust is moderated by privacy concerns, while chatbot-related factors (professionalism, response

Table 7. Table of hypothesis verification results for the model.

Relationship	Supported or not	Moderating effect test	Supported or not
H1: Professionalism→ Trust	Yes	H1a	No
		H1b	
H2: Response speed→ Trust	Yes	H2a	No
		H2b	
H3: Predictability→ Trust	Yes	H3a	No
		H3b	
H4: Easy of use→ Trust	No	H4a	---
		H4b	
H5: Human-likeness→ Trust	No	H5a	---
		H5b	
H6: Brand trust→ Trust	Yes	H6a	Yes
		H6b	No
H7: Risk→ Trust	Yes	H7a	Yes
		H7b	No
H8: Human support→ Trust	No	H8a	---
		H8b	

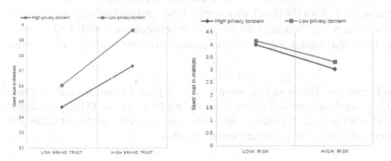

Fig. 4. The moderating effect of privacy concerns on brand trust (left) and risk (right).

speed, predictability, etc.) are not moderated by privacy concerns. Moreover, privacy concerns weaken the positive correlation between brand trust and chatbots trust, and enhance the negative correlation between risk and chatbots trust. In other words, enterprises need to increase the user privacy protection mechanism, establish clear and sufficient policy norms, and reduce users' privacy concerns. At the same time, the study found that for users with high privacy concerns, organizations should strive to improve environment-related factors rather than chatbot-related factors, which means improving brand management, improving users' trust in brands, or reducing users' perceived risks in using chatbots. But making chatbots more professional is a common approach for all users (high/low privacy concerns).

5.2 Contributions

In theory, this study further accumulates the knowledge of trust construction and promotion. At the same time, the interaction model between users and chatbots needs to take into account the trust factor, and the process of human-computer trust creating value for all parties in human-computer interaction as a whole.

In practice, the findings of this study can point out the improvement direction of chatbots, provide insights for improving users' trust in chatbots, and have practical guiding significance for the development of chatbots.

5.3 Limitations and Further Research

Distrust and trust are relatively independent and coexist with different constructs [32]. If we use Hertzberg's two-factor theory to divide factors into hygiene factors and motivators, and explore their correlation coefficients with trust and distrust, you might get some valuable research. Users' trust in chatbots should be measured from several angles, such as functional, helpful, and reliable, or cognitive versus affective.

The object of this study is Taobaoxiaomi, which can represent the current e-commerce field and other task-oriented chatbots. But there are chatbots in physical and virtual forms, task-oriented and non-task-oriented. Future chatbots already have better emotional interaction functions, such as Jingdongzhilian cloud intelligent emotional customer service. With the development of science and technology and the change of the scene, the influencing factors of the interaction between users and chatbots must change, and the theory and model construction of human-machine trust should be improved over time.

Acknowledgments. This work is supported by 2019, Digital Transformation in China and Germany: Strategies, Structures and Solutions for Ageing Societies, GZ 1570. Also supported by the Research Project of Shanghai Science and Technology Commission (No.20dz2260300) and The Fundamental Research Funds for the Central Universities.

References

1. Følstad, A., Brandtzæg, P., et al.: Chatbots and the New World of HCI. Interactions **24**(4), 38–42 (2017)
2. Følstad, A., Nordheim, C.B., Bjrkli, C.A.: What makes users trust a Chatbot for customer service? an exploratory interview study. In: The Fifth International Conference on Internet Science – INSCI 2018 (2018). https://doi.org/10.1007/978-3-030-01437-7_16
3. Grand View Research. Chatbot Market Size Worth $2,485.7 Million By 2028 I CAGR: 24.9%. https://www.grandviewresearch.com/press-release/global–chatbot—market, 2021–4/ 2021–5–29
4. Thompson, C.: May A.I. help you? New York Times (November 18). https://www.nytimes.com/interactive/2018/11/14/magazine/tech-design-ai-chatbot.html

5. Luo, X., Tong, S., Fang, Z., et al.: Frontiers: machines vs. humans: the impact of artificial intelligence Chatbot disclosure on customer purchases. Mark. Sci. **38**(6), 937--947 (2019)
6. Wilson, H.J., Daugherty, P.R., Morini-Bianzino, N.: The jobs that artificial intelligence will create. MIT Sloan Manage. Rev. **58**(4), 14 (2017)
7. Froehlich A. Pros and cons of chatbots in the IT helpdesk. Informationweek.com. https://www.informationweek.com/strategic-cio/it-strategy/pros-and-cons-of-chatbots-in-the-it-helpdesk/a/d-id/1332942. Accessed 18 Oct 2018
8. Dietvorst, B.J., Simmons, J.P., Massey, C.: Overcoming algorithm aversion: people will use imperfect algorithms if they can (even slightly) modify them. Manage. Sci. **64**(3), 1155–1170 (2018)
9. Kestenbaum, R.: Conversational commerce is where online shopping was 15 years ago —Can it also become ubiquitous? Forbes(June 27). https://www.forbes.com/sites/Richard%20Kestenbaum/2018/06/27/shopping-by-voice-is-small-now-but-it-has-huge-potential/?sh=40e52c907ba1
10. Evert, V., Zarouali, B., Poels, K.: Chatbot advertising effectiveness: when does the message get through? Comput. Hum. Behav. **98**, 150–157 (2019)
11. Corritore, C.L., Kracher, B., Wiedenbeck, S.: On-line trust: concepts, evolving themes, a model. Int. J. Hum. Comput. Stud. **58**(6), 737–758 (2003)
12. Rotter, J.B.: A new scale for the measurement of interpersonal trust. J. Pers. **35**(4), 651–665 (2010)
13. Arrow, K.E.: The Limits of Organization. Norton, Tempe (1974)
14. Baker, A.L., Phillips, E.K., Ullman, D., et al.: Toward an understanding of trust repair in human-robot interaction: current research and future directions. ACM Trans. Interact. Intell. Syst. **8**(4), 1–30 (2018)
15. Mayer, R.C., Davis, J.H., Schoorman, F.D.: An integrative model of organizational trust. Acad. Manag. Rev. **20**(3), 709–734 (1995)
16. Rousseau, D.M., Sitkin, S.B., Burt, R.S., et al.: Not so different after all: a cross-discipline view of trust. Acad. Manag. Rev. **23**(3), 393–404 (1998)
17. Glikson, E., Woolley, A.W.: Human trust in artificial intelligence: review of empirical research. Acad. Manag. Ann. **14**(2), 627–660 (2020)
18. Coeckel bergh, M.: Can we trust robots?. Ethics Inf. Technol. **14**(1), 53--60 (2012)
19. Desai, M., Stubbs, K., Steinfeld, A., et al.: Creating Trustworthy Robots: Lessons and Inspirations from Automated Systems (2009)
20. Hancock, P.A., Billings, D.R., Schaefer, K.E., et al.: A meta-analysis of factors affecting trust in human-robot interaction. Hum. Factors **53**(5), 517–527 (2011)
21. Nordheim, C.B.: Trust in Chatbots for customer service–findings from a questionnaire study (2018)
22. Ho, C.C., Macdorman, K.F.: Revisiting the uncanny valley theory: developing and validating an alternative to the godspeed indices. Comput. Hum. Behav. **26**(6), 1508–1518 (2010)
23. Mcknight, D.H., Carter, M., Thatcher, J.B., et al.: Trust in a specific technology: an investigation of its components and measures. ACM Trans. Manag. Inf. Syst. **2**(2), 12 (2011)
24. Bertinussen, N.C., Asbjrn, F., Alexander, B.C.: An initial model of trust in Chatbots for customer service—findings from a questionnaire study. Interact. Comput. **31**(3), 317—335 (2019)
25. Keeney, R.L.: Value-focused thinking : a path to creative decisionmaking (1992)
26. Keeney, R.L.: Creativity in MS/OR: value-focused thinking—creativity directed toward decision making. Interfaces **23**(3), 62–67 (1993)
27. Mcknight, D.H., Choudhury, V., Kacmar, C.: Developing and validating trust measures for e-commerce: an integrative typology. Inf. Syst. Res. **13**(3), 344–359 (2002)
28. Drevin, L., Kruger, H.A., Steyn, T.: Value-focused assessment of ICT security awareness in an academic environment. Comput. Secur. **26**(1), 36–43 (2007)

29. Deng, C.H., Lu, Y.B.: Research on VFT-based trust construction framework for mobile commerce. Sci. Technol. Manag. Res. **03**, 185–188 (2008)
30. Keeney, R.L.: Value-focused Thinking. Harvard University Press, Cambridge (1992)
31. Sheng, H., Nah, F.H., Siau, K.: Strategic implications of mobile technology: a case study using value-focused thinking. J. Strateg. Inf. Syst. **14**(3), 269–290 (2005)
32. Lin, H., et al.: An empirical study on the difference of influencing factors between trust and distrust in consumers' first online shopping. Mod. Inf. **35**(4), 5 (2015)

Digital Government and Public Big Data

Analysis of Influencing Factors of Birth Rate and Prediction of Policy Scenario

Heng Zhang[1], Zhanhui Sun[1](✉), Zhifei Wang[1], Qi Zhang[1], Rui Pan[1], and Shijia Cao[2]

[1] Department of Engineering Physics, Tsinghua University, Beijing 100084, China
zhsun@tsinghua.edu.cn
[2] Beijing GS Technology Co., Ltd., Beijing 100094, China

Abstract. The birth rates of China reaches a new low level in recent years. Current studies only focus on the influencing factors on birth rates, lacking a comprehensive consideration to construct an effective scenario prediction model. To establish the prediction model, firstly, this paper studied the birth rates from three dimensions, which consists of the marriage intention, fertility intention and the *Proportion of women of childbearing age*. Then, an indicator system is established as an assessment system. Second, the birth rate prediction model (BRPM) based on BP Neural Network (BPNN) is constructed that the accuracy was 91.486%. Third, three policy scenarios (positive, robust and negative) is set according to the trends of birth rate related to policies from 2021 to 2025. For positive scenario, the result is unsustainable and rarely feasible. The robust scenario is suitable for the current development status of China. The negative scenario is extremely dangerous and should be resolutely prevented. Thus, this paper gives suggestions from six aspects. As long as the *House price-income ratio* remains stable, the *Parenting cost* decreases at a rate of at least 5%, and the *Primary school teacher-student ratio* and *Number of beds per 1,000 people* increase at a rate of 5%, the birth rate will be in a more desirable position.

Keywords: Birth rate · Marriage intention · Fertility intention · BPNN · Scenario prediction

1 Introduction

Since the 21st century, the phenomenon of aging, fewer children and the trend of non marriage in China have been accelerating, which has a significant impact on society and the economy [1, 2]. In order to deal with many problems that may be caused by the reduction of the labor force, China promulgated "the universal two-child policy" in 2016 to adjust family planning, but it still has little effect. The birth rate of China in 2021 is 7.52‰, the lowest since the founding of new China. In May of the same year, the state implemented the "Three-child policy" and supporting measures [3].

There are many factors affecting the birth rate, including population, economic, social, policy and other dimensions [4]. Xu Kun et al. [5]evaluated the effectiveness of fertility policy by studying the relationship and empirical analysis between fertility

© The Author(s), under exclusive license to Springer Nature Singapore Pte Ltd. 2022
X. Meng et al. (Eds.): BDSC 2022, CCIS 1640, pp. 309–331, 2022.
https://doi.org/10.1007/978-981-19-7532-5_20

policy, socialization of fertility cost and birth rate; Su Liyun et al. [6] studied the birth rate in different regions of China by using statistical and test methods and found that there are significant regional differences, heterogeneity and spatial stratification in the birth rate of the Chinese population; Yang Bin and Ding Lijin [7] used the least square method to analyze the house price data of 31 administrative regions in China, and concluded that there was a negative correlation between house price and birth rates; Luca et al. [8] investigated the temporal and spatial evolution of birth rate and fertility rate in Italy under different geographical scales, the results show that the birth rate is related to the economic recession to a certain extent.

The method of studying the birth rate is to make descriptive statistics and regression analysis on the significance, robustness and the correlation of the birth rate by testing the indicator data, so as to determine the influence parameters of relevant variables. Wang Shu et al. [9] studied the internal role of children's education level and low fertility rate, and analyzed that they have a negative effect; Fang Huifen et al. [10] have studied and simulated the relationship between house prices and population in the Yangtze River Delta, and concluded that the rise of house prices has a significant inhibitory effect on fertility; Kato [11] explored the relationship between family policy reform and fertility in Japan, and the results show that low fertility was more related to the transformation of gender roles. Other scholars have conducted prediction research on population data. Guo et al. [12] made an accurate multi scenario prediction of the future population based on micro census data and local interpretation of global scenarios; Wang [13] used the time series prediction method to study the change trend of fertility and population birth rate in China.

Through the investigation, it is found that the current research focuses on the investigation of fertility, and there is little research on the birth rate. Therefore, it is particularly crucial to identify the factors influencing the birth rate and to establish a system of indicators. Section 2 aims to identify the influencing factors of the birth rate through screening and further put forward the indicator system. Section 3 trains BP neural network(BPNN) in combination with the indicator data and birth rate data at the provincial level to build a birth rate prediction model based on BPNN (BRPM-BPNN). Section 4 forecasts the relevant policy scenarios affecting the birth rate based on BRPM-BPNN model, and puts forward policy suggestions in line with the actual situation of China according to the scenario prediction analysis conclusions.

2   Birth Rate Evaluation Factor System

By analyzing the definition and calculation formula of the birth rate, the formula variables are expanded to obtain the three factors affecting the birth rate. Then based on the investigation of domestic and foreign literature, seven secondary indicators and seven tertiary indicators under the three primary indicators are determined.

2.1   Analysis of Influencing Factors of Birth Rate

The birth rate, also known as the crude birth rate, refers to the ratio of the average number of births per 1000 people in a certain period of time (usually within one year) [11]. The birth rate is calculated by the following formula:

$$Birth\,rate = \frac{Number\ of\ births}{Population} \times 1000\% \tag{1}$$

Fertility refers to the ratio of the number of people born in a certain period (usually within one year) to the number of women of childbearing age [12]. As we all know, the birth rate is closely related to the fertility rate. When the population base and population structure are stable, the higher the fertility rate, the higher the birth rate. However, the birth rate is more comprehensive than the fertility rate, which only reflects the fertility level of women of childbearing age, while the birth rate reflects the birth level of the total population, which is important to consider the demographic situation, especially the aging and childlessness in a comprehensive manner. Therefore, the birth rate formula is extended to:

$$Birth\,rate = \left(\frac{Number\ of\ births}{Number\ of\ women\ of\ childbearing\ age} \right)$$
$$\times \left(\frac{Number\ of\ women\ of\ childbearing\ age}{Population} \right) \times 1000\% \tag{2}$$

Under China's current legal and policy system, giving birth to children out of wedlock is an illegal act and social maintenance fees need to be punished. Therefore, it can be considered that the prerequisite for women of childbearing age to have children is marriage, so the prerequisite for marriage is included in the birth rate formula, which can be extended to:

$$Birth\,rate = \left(\frac{Number\ of\ births}{Number\ of\ married\ women\ of\ childbearing\ age} \right)$$
$$\times \left(\frac{Number\ of\ married\ women\ of\ childbearing\ age}{Number\ of\ women\ of\ childbearing\ age} \right)$$
$$\times \left(\frac{Number\ of\ women\ of\ childbearing\ age}{Population} \right) \times 1000\% \tag{3}$$

From the expanded birth rate formula, it can be seen that the birth rate is mainly composed of three parts: the fertility rate of married women of childbearing age, the marriage rate of women of childbearing age and the *Proportion of women of childbearing age*, which correspondingly reflects the three influencing factors of fertility intention, marriage intention and population structure. Therefore, this paper takes fertility intention, marriage intention and population structure as the primary indicators affecting the birth rate.

2.2 Analysis of Population Structure Factors

Population structure generally refers to the composition of the population, which refers to the overall division of the population into various components. This paper mainly considers the constituent factors affecting the birth rate, including gender and age [14]. The results of the seventh national census showed that among the national population, with female as the base 100, the gender ratio of the total population is 105.07. In addition, men have a longer reproductive cycle than women, so the *Proportion of women of childbearing age* has a key impact on the birth rate. The *Proportion of women of childbearing age* is estimated by formula.

$$P = \frac{N_1 \times R_1}{N_2 \times R_2} \tag{4}$$

where P is the *Proportion of women of childbearing age* in the administrative region, N_1 is the number of women of childbearing age in the country, N_2 is the national female population, R_1 is the regional female population, and R_2 is the total population in the region.

2.3 Analysis on Factors of Marriage Intention

China's marriage rate has declined for seven consecutive years since 2013, but the divorce rate is rising. In 2020, the national marriage rate was only 5.8%, and the divorce rate was as high as 3.1%. In recent years, the proportion of unmarried women aged 20–39 in China is as high as 25%–26%. All the data shows that young people's willingness to marry is declining (Fig. 1).

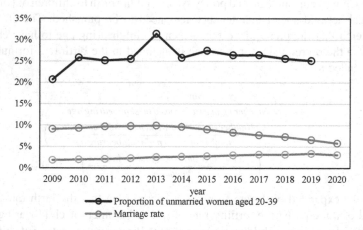

Fig. 1. China's marriage and divorce rates and the proportion of unmarried women.

Women's Rights. With the continuous improvement of women's education level and more equal employment opportunities in the labor market, women play an increasingly important role in the economy and society, so they also have enough ability to obtain labor income. The participation in labor also improves women's ideological independence and their requirements for self righteous. As a result contemporary women have reduced their intrinsic need for marriage. In this sense, the higher the level of women's rights, the lower the willingness to marry.

Ushma et al. [15] reviewed women's rights and several fertility related thematic studies. These studies evaluated the relationship between women's empowerment and fertility, and found that there are some positive links between women's rights and low fertility. Women's education level, women's income level, women's employment rate and other indicators can reflect women's rights. Song et al. [16] explained the reproductive behavior of people with different education levels and income levels and put forward the hypothesis that the fertility rate is negatively correlated with education level. Therefore, this paper selects *Female educational attainment* to represent women's rights, which is expressed by the proportion of women with college degree or above among the female population aged 6 and above.

Life Pressure. Life pressure makes many young people unbearable. High house prices and high consumption increase the life pressure of young people, and some people are afraid of marriage. Therefore, the greater the pressure of life, the lower the marriage intention. Wei et al. [17] showed that the rapid rise of house prices has exacerbated the life pressure of Chinese adults' housing burden.

House prices have an important impact on marriage decision-making. From 2000 to 2020, China's house prices increased by 412.32%, the marriage rate decreased by 13.43%, and the divorce rate increased by 222.92%. Young men and women marry to form a family, and housing is just needed. However, the reality is that house prices have increased and marriage costs have risen. However, young people have a weak economic foundation and cannot bear the huge combination costs brought by high house prices. This has led to the delay of marriage and greatly affected young people's marriage intention.

On the other hand, income is the basis of all expenditures. At present, the consumption ability of young people has been greatly improved, and the income level has become an important standard for mate selection. House purchase expenditure has become the most important expenditure of young families in China, accounting for a considerable part of disposable income. According to the 2021 new first tier cities residence report [18] released by the shell Research Institute, the household *House price-income ratio* in Shenzhen, Beijing and Shanghai reached 27.09, 25.14 and 22.28 respectively, which means that it will take more than 20 years for a family (calculated according to the data of the seventh census of 2.62 people / household) to spend all their income on house purchase, and the *House price-income ratio* will be greater for newlyweds. Therefore, from the perspective of house purchase pressure, the higher the *House price-income ratio*, the lower the marriage intention.

The *House price-income ratio* is measured by how many years a couple can afford to buy a 100-square-meter house, reflecting the ability of young couples to buy a house. Therefore, the definition of *House price-income ratio* in this paper is:

$$House\ price\ income\ ratio = \frac{100 \times Average\ selling\ price\ of\ residential\ commercial\ housing}{2 \times Per\ capita\ disposable\ income\ of\ all\ residents} \quad (5)$$

2.4 Analysis on Factors of Fertility Intention

Fertility intention has an important impact on fertility behavior [19]. At present, the fertility intention of Chinese residents is very low. The fertility intention surveyed in 2019 is only 75.4%, and the total fertility rate in 2020 is only 1.3 [20]. Traditionally, getting married and having children is like a natural thing, but now it seems that for many couples, having children is not a necessary option of marriage. At present, the main maintenance elements of marriage have been transformed into emotional and material factors, rather than the traditional family division of labor and inheritance.

Fertility Policy Index. China has formulated and formed a fertility policy since the 1950s and 1960s, and has practiced family planning since the 1980s, which has had an important impact on China's population development. The universal two-child policy and the three-child policy also have an important impact on the birth rate. Therefore, the impact of national fertility policy on fertility intention is very important. The looser the policy, the stronger the fertility intention. The *Fertility policy index* selected in this paper is a dynamic variable. The "One-child policy" is recorded as 0, "Single, two-child policy" is 1, "The universal two-child policy" is recorded as 2, "Three-child policy" is recorded as 3. According to the implementation of policy supporting measures, corresponding adjustments can be made on the basis of the benchmark index.

Parenting Cost. *Parenting cost* include two parts, one is consumer expenditure, including education expenditure and non education expenditure. Second, non consumer expenditure, including insurance expenditure, human relationship expenditure, donations, etc. According to the 2022 edition of the China Fertility cost report [21], the average cost of raising a child to the age of 18 in China is 485,000 RMB, which is 6.9 times the per capita GDP. The higher the *Parenting cost*, the greater the economic pressure on the family, and the lower the fertility intention of couples. The *Parenting cost* estimated in this report mainly refers to consumer expenditure.

Education Security Level. Miller et al. [22, 23] made a more in-depth analysis on the causes of reproductive motivation and found that in terms of specific shaping mechanism, the growth experience, adult experience and adult personality traits of children and adolescents will directly affect reproductive motivation. Therefore, the level of local education security directly affects the quality and cost of education. A higher level of education security is conducive to enhance the reproductive willingness of couples. This paper selects the *Primary school teacher-student ratio* to represent the level of education security.

Medical Security Level. Maira [24] found that, with the improvement of the health care level and human capital level, the role of birth insurance in promoting the birth rate is further enhanced after crossing the threshold. The higher the level of social and medical security, the lower the medical cost, and the higher the survival rate of infants. The *Number of beds per 1,000 people* is selected to represent the medical security level.

Women's Rights. With the development of China's economy, society and education, women's status is becoming higher and higher. The labor participation rate of women of childbearing age in China reached 60.5%, exceeding the world average of 51.6%. Many women find it difficult to balance their career and family directly. Due to the pursuit of career and ideological independence, as well as the importance of personal investment, it has occupied the investment in the family. The proportion of unpaid housework of women in China is 11.1%, which is lower than the world average of 12.5%. Therefore, women's professional labor has a negative impact on fertility intention. This paper selects *Female educational attainment* to represent women's rights.

Life Pressure. Zhang Xiayu [4] found through research that the level of house prices has an inhibitory effect on the birth rate. Specifically, the rapid rise of house prices mean greater pressure on survival. At the same time, the increase of housing expenditure will lead to the compression of *Parenting cost*s. People naturally delay the progress of childbirth and reduce their fertility intention. The pressure of buying a house is the main source of living pressure for young families. Therefore, under other conditions unchanged, the higher the house price level, the stronger the inhibition of fertility will be.

The income level of the family restricts the consumption expenditure of the family. Therefore, when making fertility decisions, the family must be based on the consideration of the family income level. When other conditions remain unchanged, the higher the family income level, the stronger the fertility will be. The current reality is that there is a negative correlation between income level and the birth rate. The birth rate in metropolitan areas is very low.

Therefore, the separate analysis of house price level and income level cannot fully reflect the impact of life pressure on the birth rate. This paper comprehensively considers the two and takes the *House price-income ratio* as a measurement index to reflect life pressure.

2.5 Construction of Evaluation Factor System

Based on the above analysis, this paper constructs an indicator system, including three primary indicators, seven secondary indicators and seven tertiary indicators from the three dimensions of population structure, marriage intention and fertility intention. Women's rights and life stress are common influencing factors for both marriage intention and fertility intention, and all indicators are considered together in the final indicator system to ensure that there is no duplication of tertiary indicators (Fig. 2).

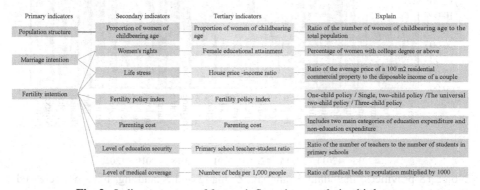

Fig. 2. Indicator system of factors influencing population birth rate.

3   Birth Rate Prediction Model Based on BPNN (BRPM-BPNN)

At present, the data of the National Statistical Yearbook in 2021 has not been published. Therefore, this paper obtains the statistical data of various administrative regions in the National Statistical Yearbook from 2013 to 2020 as the data of model training, verification and testing. The *Female educational attainment*, the *Proportion of women of childbearing age* and *Parenting cost* are calculated indirectly. The data in *Fertility policy index* is formed by investigating the implementation year of China's fertility policy and the implementation of supporting measures. And other indicator data can be obtained directly. Normalize the statistical data, train with MATLAB neural network toolbox, and build a birth rate prediction model based on BP neural network.

The national average *Parenting cost* is first estimated using average consumption data, for example, using 2019 consumption data results in an estimate of $485,000.Assuming that the proportion of the *Parenting cost* of residents in 31 provinces to the national average is the same as the proportion of per capita consumption expenditure, the average *Parenting cost* of children aged 0–17 in 31 provinces can be obtained.

3.1   Model Input Factor Description

In terms of birth rate, most administrative regions have experienced the process of first rising and then falling. Due to the continuous relaxation of fertility policy, especially the implementation of the comprehensive two-child policy in 2016, which released the fertility wishes of many families, the birth rate peaked around 2016 and 2017.

The range of birth rate in each province from 2013 to 2020 is between 5.36% and 17.89%. In order to improve the training effect of BP neural network model, the birth

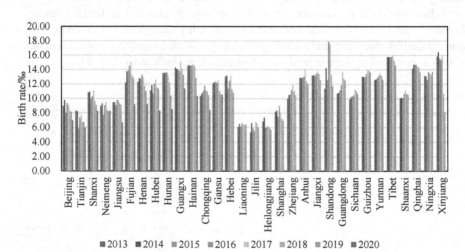

Note: 18 provinces, including Shanghai, Zhejiang and Shandong, have not released their birth rate data for 2020.

Fig. 3. China's birth rate data, 2013–2020.

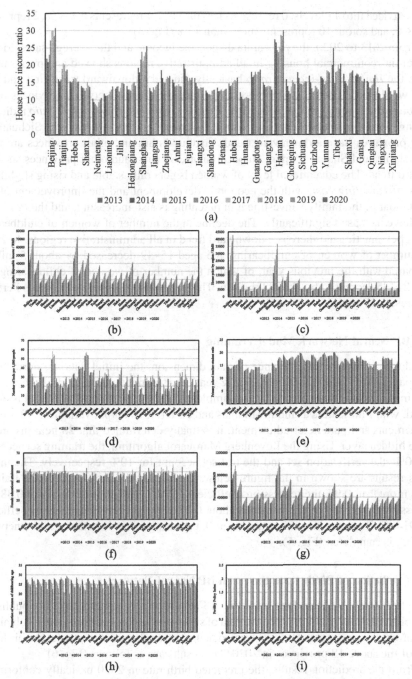

Fig. 4. Indicator data for 2013 to 2020(a) *House price-income ratio* (b) Per capita disposable income in all administrative regions (c) Average price of residential commercial properties (d) *Number of beds per 1,000 people* (e) *Primary school teacher-student ratio* (f) *Female educational attainment* (g) *Parenting cost* (h) *Proportion of women of childbearing age* (i) *Fertility policy index.*

rate is divided into 11 levels, 0 represents less than 6%, 1 represents 6%–7%, 2 represents 7%–8%, and so on, 10 represents more than 15% (Fig. 3).

From 2013 to 2020, the per capita disposable income and the average sales price of residential, commercial housing in all administrative regions showed an upward trend, while the *House price-income ratio* basically showed a downward trend first and then an upward trend. There are obvious changes and differences between provinces in the *Number of beds per 1,000 people* and the *Primary school teacher-student ratio* indicator. Beijing, Shanghai, Hebei, Zhejiang, Jiangxi, Henan, Guangxi, Chongqing, Sichuan and other provinces have a downward trend, Tianjin, Anhui and other provinces are basically stable, and Shanxi, Fujian, Hubei, Hainan, Shaanxi and other provinces show an upward trend. The educational level of women is generally stable and rising slightly. In terms of *Parenting cost*, with the economic development and the improvement of living standards, the family's investment in parenting is also increasing, and the *Parenting cost* have increased significantly. The decline in the number of women of childbearing age is pessimistic, and there is a downward trend in all administrative regions. In 2021, the number of women of childbearing age aged 15–49 decreased by about 5 million compared with the previous year, of which the number of women of childbearing age aged 21–35 decreased by about 3 million. This paper also summarizes China's Fertility Policies, see Fig. 4(i).

3.2   BP Neural Network Model Training

In order to eliminate the influence of data dimension, the initial data are normalized. This paper takes "administrative region & year" as a sample. After excluding the samples with missing data, there are 230 valid samples. The BP neural network model is established, with 7 indicators as input variables and birth rate as output variables. After many experiments and parameter adjustment, it is finally determined that 28 neurons are set in the hidden layer. Using the Levenberg Marquardt algorithm, the training set accounts for 80%, the verification set and the test set account for 10% respectively. The model trains results are shown in the figure below. The regression coefficient of the training set is more than 0.97, the regression coefficient of the verification set is about 0.88, the regression coefficient of the test set is about 0.71, and the overall regression coefficient is 0.91486. The error is concentrated near 0, the fitting effect is better, and the network training is completed (Fig. 5).

3.3   Prediction of Birth Rate Based on BP Neural Network

Shanghai, Zhejiang, Shandong and other 18 administrative regions have not published their birth rate data in 2020, while the data of seven evaluation indicators can be obtained. Therefore, this paper uses the constructed neural network model to predict the birth rate data of the above 18 provinces in 2020. The results are as follows (Fig. 6).

From the prediction results, the predicted birth rate in 2020 basically conforms to the change trend, and most of them are in a downward state, indicating that the model prediction is more in line with the reality and the effect is ideal. In particular, it is noted that the predicted values of Heilongjiang, Yunnan and Tibet have decreased significantly. The reason for this phenomenon may be that the population outflow of relevant provinces

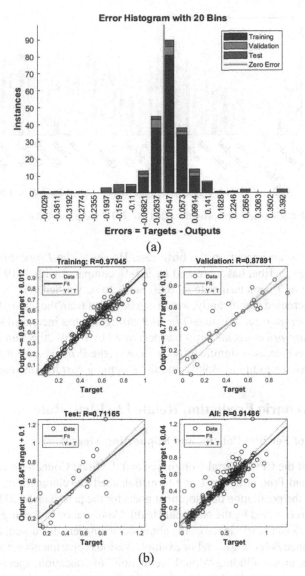

Fig. 5. BP Neural network training results (a) Error distribution (b) Regression coefficient.

is serious, resulting in sharp changes in population structure. Wang's study [13] found that the three northeastern provinces show that socio-economic problems are closely related to the decline of birth rate. For example, in 2020, the number of women of childbearing age in the permanent population of Heilongjiang decreased seriously, and the *Proportion of women of childbearing age* decreased by 29.66% compared with 2019; Yunnan is also mainly due to the *Proportion of women of childbearing age* decreased by 7.23% compared with 2019; The *House price-income ratio*, the *Number of beds per 1,000 people* and the *Primary school teacher-student ratio* in Tibet have adverse changes,

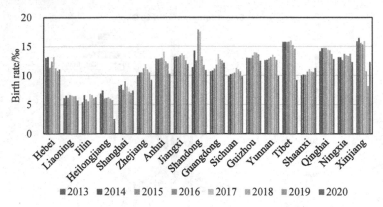

Fig. 6. Birth rates in selected provinces 2013 to 2019 and projected birth rates in 2020.

which have a certain impact on the birth rate. However, the *Proportion of women of childbearing age* in Tibet has increased by 9.58% compared with 2019. Therefore, the predicted value of Tibet's birth rate in 2020 needs to be verified. The forecast value of Xinjiang has increased significantly, which can be found from the factor data. Compared with 2019, the *Proportion of women of childbearing age* has increased significantly by 9.08%, the *House price-income ratio* has decreased by 6.76%, the *Number of beds per 1,000 people* has increased significantly by 75.69%, the *Primary school teacher-student ratio* has increased steadily by 4.95% and the *Parenting cost* has decreased by 5.92%.

4 Policy Scenario Prediction Related to Birth Rate

4.1 Analysis of Fertility Policies and Supporting Measures

The Decision of the CPC Central Committee and the State Council on Optimizing Fertility Policies and Promoting the Long-term Balanced Development of the Population clearly sets out the population development goals for the period up to 2025. Referring to the press conference held by the National Health Commission in Beijing on January 20, 2022, the progress and experience of the above decision were discussed, including some measures to reduce *Parenting cost*. For example, various departments actively introduced supporting measures, including "double reduction" of education, special deduction of infant care service fees under 3 years old individual income tax, and raising the standard of special family assistance. The scale of women of childbearing age has decreased significantly, and the years of education of relevant women have been prolonged, resulting in the delay of marriage and childbirth, which will affect the fertility level.

To sum up, the *Parenting cost* is further reduced. Under the "double reduction" and other policies, the cost of education can be further reduced, ranging from 5% to 10%; In terms of the teacher-student ratio, under the background of the COVID-19 epidemic, the teacher-student ratio may be further increased due to the stability of the teaching profession; As for women's education level, due to the increasing competitive pressure of employment, women will increase in their years of education. However, the proportion of women with college degree or above is generally stable. In terms of the *Proportion of women of childbearing age*, the number of women of childbearing age cannot be changed through policies and measures. Under the current trend, it is expected that the *Proportion of women of childbearing age* will decrease by 1.7% per year in the future. In terms of fertility policy, the three-child policy has been clearly implemented, which can meet the fertility needs of most couples. The policy supporting measures will affect the fertility intention to a greater extent, and there is a large room for adjustment in the relevant supporting measures and implementation. The change range of each factor in the three scenarios is determined with reference to the average value of the change rate in the past five years.

4.2   Scenario Design of Policies Related to Birth Rate

Select Scenario Analysis Samples. According to the indicator data of each administrative region in 2020, 31 administrative regions are clustered into 4 categories by using self organizing feature map (SOM) model. The clustering results are shown in the Fig. 7. Among them, Beijing and Shanghai are in the first category, Guangdong, Tianjin, Jiangsu, Zhejiang and Fujian are in the same category, Liaoning, Jilin, Heilongjiang, Shanxi, Inner Mongolia and Gansu are in the same category, and Shandong and other 18 administrative regions are in the same category. In order to facilitate the analysis of scenario prediction, Beijing, Guangdong, Shandong and Liaoning are selected as representative administrative regions for scenario prediction analysis.

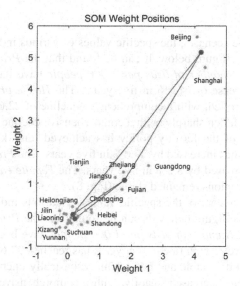

Fig. 7.   Clustering results for all provinces.

Scenario Design. The economic policy under the positive scenario is very optimistic and the fertility policy and supporting measures are actively and effectively implemented. The new marriage and childbearing culture have been deeply rooted in the hearts of the people, and the number of three children is increasing. Robust scenario with solid economic performance and gradual and orderly implementation of fertility policy and supporting measures, and residents have gradually begun to respond to the three-child policy issued by the state. In the negative scenario, the economic situation continues to be strict, the three-child policy and supporting measures have not been implemented as expected, and there are great challenges in the implementation. Residents' response to the national three-child policy is to correct and relatively negative (Table 1).

Table 1. Percentage changes per year in factors for three scenarios.

Factors	Positive scenario	Robust scenario	Negative scenario
House price-income ratio	−5%	0%	5%
Parenting cost	−10%	−5%	0%
Primary school teacher-student ratio	10%	5%	0%
Number of beds per 1,000 people	10%	5%	0%
Fertility policy index	5%	0%	−5%
Proportion of women of childbearing age	−1.7%	−1.7%	−1.7%
Female educational attainment	Unchanged	Unchanged	Unchanged

Under the positive scenario, the specific values of various indicators from 2021 to 2025 are shown in the figure below. It can be found that the *Primary school teacher-student ratio* and the *Number of beds per 1,000 people* have increased rapidly, with a comprehensive increase of 61.1% in five years. The *House price-income ratio* has been effectively controlled, with a comprehensive decline of 22.6% in five years. The cost of parenting has fallen sharply, with a comprehensive decline of 41% in five years. The implementation of the fertility policy has achieved remarkable results, and the *Fertility policy index* has increased by 27.6% in five years. The *Proportion of women of childbearing age* decreased by 8.2% in five years. The *Female educational attainment* in all administrative regions remained stable (Fig. 8).

Under the robust scenario, the specific values of various indicators from 2021 to 2025 are shown in the figure below. It can be found that the *Primary school teacher-student ratio* and the *Number of beds per 1,000 people* have been steadily improved, and the comprehensive growth rate in five years has reached 27.6%; The *House price-income ratio* is generally stable and has remained basically unchanged for five years; The *Parenting cost* has decreased steadily, with a comprehensive decline of 22.6% in five years; The fertility policy was steadily implemented, and the *Fertility policy index* remained at 3.0; The *Proportion of women of childbearing age* decreased by 8.2% in five years; The *Female educational attainment* in all administrative regions remained stable (Fig. 9).

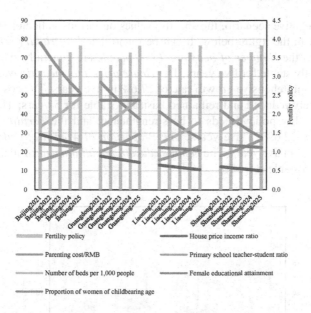

Fig. 8. Changes in the values of the indicators for the positive scenario.

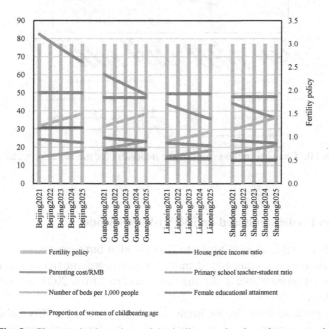

Fig. 9. Changes in the values of the indicators for the robust scenario.

Under the negative scenario, the specific values of various indicators from 2021 to 2025 are shown in the figure below. It can be found that the *Primary school teacher-student ratio* and the *Number of beds per 1,000 people* are generally stable, and have remained basically stable for five years; The *House price-income ratio* was poorly controlled, with a comprehensive growth rate of 27.6% in five years; The cost of parenting was not effectively reduced and remained basically stable for 5 years; The implementation of the fertility policy needs to be strengthened, and the *Fertility policy index* has decreased by 22.6% in five years; The *Proportion of women of childbearing age* decreased by 8.2% in five years; The *Female educational attainment* in all administrative regions remained stable (Fig. 10).

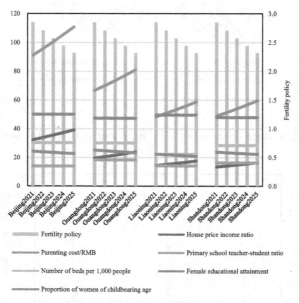

Fig. 10. Changes in the values of the indicators for the negative scenario.

4.3   Scenario Prediction Based on BRPM-BPNN Model

BRPM-BPNN model is used to predict the population birth rate under three scenarios. Beijing, Guangdong, Liaoning and Shandong are the representatives of scenario prediction. The population birth rate under the three scenarios from 2021 to 2025 is shown in the figure below.

Under the positive scenario, the implementation effect of Fertility Policies and supporting measures is very good. The birth rate in the four administrative regions has increased significantly, with an average annual growth rate of 16.88%–31.75%. By 2025, the birth rate can reach 15%–31%. Compared with 2020, by 2025, Liaoning will increase the most, with an increase of 296.97%, and the birth rate will reach 22.58%; The birth rate of Guangdong will increase 148.73%, and the birth rate will reach 30.18%; Shandong will increase 140.84%, and the birth rate will reach 26.31%; Beijing will increase 118.09%, and the birth rate will reach 15.22%.

Under the robust scenario, the fertility policy and supporting measures have been solidly promoted and steadily implemented. The birth rate in the four administrative regions has been effectively improved, with an average annual growth rate of 8.64%–18.01%. By 2025, the birth rate will reach 12%–21%. Compared with 2020, by 2025, Liaoning will also increase the most, with an increase of 128.87%, and the birth rate will reach 13.02%; Beijing will increase 84.93%, and the birth rate will reach 12.91%; Guangdong will increase 73.09%, and the birth rate will reach 21%; Shandong will increase 51.31%, and the birth rate will reach 16.53%.

Under the negative scenario, the implementation effect of fertility policy and supporting measures is poor, the incentive fertility strategy needs to be improved, and the birth rate changes in the four administrative regions are quite different. Among them, the birth rate in Guangdong still maintains an average annual growth rate of 8.02%, the birth rate in Shandong is relatively stable, declining slowly at an average annual growth rate of 1.1%, and the birth rate in Beijing and Liaoning has declined sharply. Compared with 2020, by 2025, Guangdong will increase by 47.05%, and the birth rate will reach 17.84%; The birth rate in Shandong fell by 5.39% and the birth rate will drop to 10.34%; Liaoning and Beijing have dropped to extremely low birth rates close to zero. The birth rate of Guangdong performs well under the three scenarios. The main reason is that Guangdong has a developed economy, attracts a large number of migrant population, has a younger population structure and a high *Proportion of women of childbearing age*. In addition, Guangdong has the regional characteristics of high fertility intention. Shandong has relatively strong resilience under the negative scenario because all influencing factors are at the national medium level and there are no exceptionally severe indicators, so the decline of birth rate will not be unusually obvious. In Liaoning and Beijing, the basis of birth rate is very low, and there are various extremely severe constraints. The *House price-income ratio* in Beijing ranks first in the country, and the *Proportion of women of childbearing age* in Liaoning is almost the bottom. Therefore, under the negative scenario, the continuous deterioration of relevant indicators will produce an obvious butterfly effect and reduce the birth rate to an unimaginable level (Fig. 11).

Comparative Analysis of Scenario Prediction in Four Types of Provinces. Considering the three scenarios, the optimistic degree of birth rate predicted in the four provinces is ranked as Guangdong, Shandong, Liaoning and Beijing. The class of provinces represented by Guangdong, under the three scenarios, the birth rate is at the highest level, which reflects that such provinces have good development potential and all indicators are developing well; The class of provinces represented by Shandong is accounting for the majority of the 31 provinces, representing the national average development level. Under the three scenarios, the birth rate level ranks second, with good toughness and easy policy regulation to improve the birth rate level. The class of provinces represented by Liaoning, the birth rate level ranks third in the three scenarios. The policy effect is the most prominent in the positive and stable scenarios, but the situation is severe in the negative scenario. Therefore, we must pay attention to such provinces and give appropriate policy preference; Beijing and Shanghai belong to the

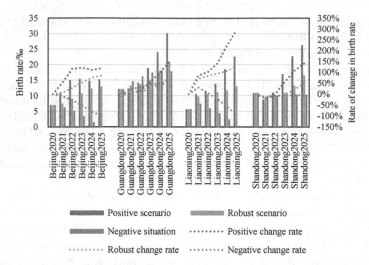

Fig. 11. Three scenario projection results.

same kind of provinces. The birth rate levels under the three scenarios are the lowest, and the positive and robust scenarios have good improvement effects. However, it is also found that the momentum in the later stage of the positive scenario is insufficient, and the robust scenario can be improved more stably, while the birth rate under the negative scenario is almost straight-line decline, and the situation is extremely severe. Therefore, Beijing and Shanghai should strive to solve the primary problem of high *House price-income ratio*, strive to prevent development in the negative scenario.

Comparative Analysis of Three Scenarios. In the positive scenario, through the implementation of positive and powerful fertility policies and the adoption of economic, social and cultural measures, we will vigorously break down the obstacles hindering the willingness to marry and have children, so that the birth rate will increase rapidly. However, if the policies and measures are too strong, there may be systemic problems that the economy and society cannot bear, and the way of rapid increase in the birth rate is unsustainable. In the long run, it will again lead to the pressure of rapid population growth. In the robust scenario, combined with China's overall national conditions and the specific reality of various administrative regions, steadily promote fertility policies and supporting measures, take appropriate policy means and incentive measures, reduce the pressure of young people on marriage and childbirth, and steadily improve their willingness to marry and childbirth, which can steadily increase the population birth rate, reach a reasonable level of population birth rate, alleviate the huge pressure of aging and fewer children in China, and provide a solid guarantee for the sustainable development of society. In the negative scenario, due to the severe obstacles of various problems, the poor implementation effect of fertility policies and supporting measures, various problems affecting young people's willingness to marry and have children have not been effectively solved and become more serious. The situation of population birth rate continues to deteriorate, resulting in the provinces with low birth rate falling to a very low level, and the birth rate of most provinces continues to decline along the current trend, Only Guangdong and other provinces with large population inflow can withstand the pressure of declining birth rate and maintain a certain growth rate of birth rate.

It is worth noting that although the statistical yearbook data of 2021 has not been released, 26 administrative regions have released the population data of 2021. Affected by the COVID-19 epidemic, the birth rate of each administrative region has basically maintained a downward trend. The birth rates of Beijing, Guangdong, Liaoning and Shandong are 6.35%, 9.35%, 4.71% and 7.38% respectively, while the predicted birth rates of 2021 under the negative scenario are 6.23%, 14.64%, 7.41% and 9.54% respectively, which shows that the situation of China's birth rate is very serious. Therefore, it is urgent to change young people's marriage and fertility intention, and alleviate the pressure of declining birth rate through policies and measures. We should resolutely prevent the continuous deterioration of negative scenarios.

Analysis of Main Indicators. The following figure shows the indicator values and birth rates for each scenario in 2025, of which the main indicators are now analyzed. The birth rates in the four administrative regions differ significantly in the three scenarios, correlating with the differences in certain main indicators. The following analyses are all based on negative scenario versus robust and positive scenarios within a single administrative region in 2025. The *Parenting cost* and house price income ratio increase significantly, and as a result, the life pressure of young people increases dramatically, thus seriously affecting their marriage intention and fertility intention.

In terms of social security, *Primary school teacher-student ratio* and *Number of beds per 1,000 people* plummet, representing a linear decline in the level of education security and medical security, and therefore the fertility intention in the negative scenario is greatly reduced.

In terms of *Fertility policy index*, the negative scenario is more unfavorable, as it directly reduces the fertility intention of couples of childbearing age, leading to a decrease in the birth rate.

It can be seen that the *Parenting cost, House price-income ratio, Primary school teacher-student ratio, Number of beds per 1,000 people,* and *Fertility policy index* all have important effects on the birth rate (Fig. 12).

4.4 Policy Recommendations

At present, China has issued a series of policies and measures such as the decision of the CPC Central Committee and the State Council on optimizing Fertility Policies and promoting long-term balanced development of the population. All parts of the country are also actively exploring specific implementation methods in line with the actual situation of the administrative region. For example, Panzhihua City, Sichuan Province pays 500 yuan per child per month to families with two or three children until the age of 3, and Zhejiang province gives childcare allowance to families with infants under the age of 3 Subsidies for childcare expenses, etc.

Based on the comparative analysis conclusion of scenario prediction of four types of provinces, this paper puts forward, two suggestions at the strategic level: first, we should

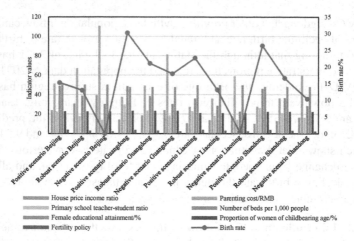

Fig. 12. Indicator values and birth rates for the four administrative regions under the three scenarios in 2025.

give full play to China's institutional advantages, coordinate the overall planning, Insisting on a national approach; Second, all provinces should implement policies, according to their own conditions, explore and implement differentiated and targeted policies and measures, and give priority to solving the primary contradiction.

Based on the comparative analysis conclusion of the three scenarios, combined with the current overall situation of China, the robust scenario is the most suitable to be adopted, and the policy effect is also in line with the expectation. This paper puts forward four robust policy suggestions at the tactical level: first, all parts of the country should actively implement the spirit of the decision, steadily explore and effectively promote the implementation of fertility policies and supporting measures in accordance with the central top-level design; Second, stabilize house prices and steady growth. We should implement policies, according to local conditions, and promote the virtuous cycle and healthy development of the real estate industry, strive to overcome the impact of the COVID-19 epidemic, promote economic growth, enhance residents' disposable income, and steadily reduce the *House price-income ratio*. We should adopt more people-friendly rental policies and measures to reduce the living pressure of young people; Third, strive to improve the service level of eugenics and child rearing, accelerate the construction of inclusive childcare service system, effectively reduce the cost of childbirth, parenting and education, innovate and explore the socialization mode of *Parenting cost* such as parenting insurance, and alleviate the parenting pressure of families; Fourth, effectively improve the level of protection of women's rights. In addition to the policies such as parental leave and parental subsidies that have been issued, we should also strive to create a social atmosphere and workplace atmosphere that respects women who raise children. Through the introduction of tax and fee reduction and other incentives for enterprises employing women workers, we should organically combine the interests of women of childbearing age, enterprises and society to effectively alleviate the contradiction between women's career development and marriage and childbirth.

5 Summary

By analyzing the calculation formula of population birth rate, this paper determines the influencing factors and establishes the indicator system of influencing factors on population birth rate. On this basis, combined with the actual indicator data and scenario prediction data, the BRPM-BPNN model is constructed. The prediction accuracy of the model is 91.486%, and the model training effect is very good.

In terms of prediction, 18 administrative regions such as Shanghai, Zhejiang and Shandong have not published their birth rate data in 2020. This paper forecasts the birth rate of these administrative regions in 2020 through BRPM-BPNN. The predicted values of Shanghai, Zhejiang, Shandong and Guangdong are 7.39%, 9.22%, 10.93% and 12.13% respectively. There is a huge rebound in Xinjiang, and the predicted value reaches 12.27%.

In terms of prediction, combined with the fertility policies and supporting measures issued in 2021, this paper analyzes and designs three development scenarios from 2021 to 2025. China's 31 administrative regions are grouped into four categories, with Beijing, Guangdong, Liaoning and Shandong as the representatives of various categories. Based on BRPM-BPNN model, this paper forecasts and analyzes the positive scenario, robust scenario and negative scenario respectively. Under the positive scenario, the birth rate will increase significantly, and the birth rate in all provinces will reach 15%–31% by 2025; Under the stable scenario, the birth rate will be effectively improved. By 2025, the birth rate in all provinces will reach 12%–21%; Under the negative scenario, there are great differences among provinces. By 2025, the birth rate in Beijing and Liaoning will drop to a very low level close to zero, that in Shandong will drop slightly to 10.34%, and that in Guangdong will still rise to 17.84%.

In terms of policy suggestions, the characteristics of various administrative regions are different. This paper puts forward, two suggestions at the strategic level: overall planning and implement policies according to local conditions. Among the three scenarios, the robust scenario is the most in line with China's reality, and the expected effect is relatively ideal. This paper puts forward four robust policy suggestions at the tactical level: actively and effectively implement the fertility policy and supporting measures, stabilize house prices and steady growth, effectively reduce *Parenting cost*, and effectively protect women's rights.

Finally, we should also note that the increase of uncertain factors caused by the COVID-19 epidemic makes the birth rate level face greater challenges and reduces the prediction accuracy of the model. If the indicator data and birth rate data of 2020 and 2021 are fully published and the data set training model is added, it will help BRPM-BPNN to predict the scenario more accurately.

Acknowledgments. This work was financed by the National Key R&D Program of China (2021YFC1523500).

References

1. Bi, W., et al.: A neural-network based forecast for aging population trend in China. PLoS ONE **26**(6), e0212772 (2004)

2. Zhang, X., Zhang, Y., Jia, G., Tang, M., Chen, G., Zhang, L.: Research Progress on low fertility in China: a literature review. Popul. Dev. **27**(06), 9–21 (2021)
3. Wang, J., Wang, G.: Research on low fertility willingness under China's three-child policy and its policy implications. J. Tsinghua Univ. (Philos. Soc. Sci. Edn.) **37**(02), 201–212 + 217 (2022). https://doi.org/10.13613/j.cnki.qhdz.3141
4. Zhang, X.: Study on macro influencing factors of China's birth rate. Anhui University of Finance and Economics (2021)
5. Xu, K., Hu, D., Liu, Y.: Fertility policy, cost socialization and birth rate. J. Guizhou Univ. Financ. Econ. (02), 69–78 (2022)
6. Su, L., Yu, H., Guo, W.: Study on regional differences in China's birth rate. J. Chongqing Univ. Technol. (Nat. Sci.) 1–6 (2022)
7. Yang, B., Ding, L.: The impact of rising house prices on China's birth rate – an empirical analysis based on provincial panel data. J. Southwest Petrol. Univ. (Soc. Sci. Edn.) **24**(02), 35–42 (2022)
8. Salvati, L., et al.: Spatial variability of total fertility rate and crude birth rate in a low-fertility country: patterns and trends in regional and local scale heterogeneity across Italy, 2002–2018. Appl. Geogr. (Sevenoaks) **124** (2020)
9. Wang, S., Meng, Y., Zhao, Q.: Low fertility rate, gender structure of compatriots and education level of children. Financ. Essays 1–13 (2022). https://doi.org/10.13762/j.cnki.cjlc.202203 03.001
10. Fang, H., Chen, J., Yuan, F., Gao, J.: The impact of urban house prices on fertility in China – an econometric analysis based on 41 cities in the Yangtze River Delta. Geogr. Res. **40**(09), 2426–2441 (2021)
11. Kato, T.: Associations of gender role attitudes with fertility intentions: a Japanese population-based study on single men and women of reproductive ages. Sex. Reprod. Healthc. **16**, 15–22 (2018)
12. Guo, A., et al.: Predicting the future chinese population using shared socioeconomic pathways, the sixth national population census, and a PDE model. Sustain. (Basel Switz.) **11**(13), 3686 (2019)
13. Wang, M.: A Retrospective and Predictive Study of Fertility Rates in China from 2003 to 2018. Heliyon **5**(3), e01460 (2019)
14. Wang, F., et al.: China's family planning policies and their labor market consequences. J. Popul. Econ. **30**(1), 31–68 (2016)
15. Upadhyay, U.D., Gipson, J.D., Prata, N.: Women's empowerment and fertility: a review of the literature. Soc. Sci. Med. **115**, 111–112 (2014)
16. Song, J., Kuang, Y.: An analysis on female education level, income and fertility rate in China. In: E3S Web of Conferences, vol. 251, p. 01088 (2021)
17. Wei, G., Zhu, H., Han, S., Chen, J., Shi, L.: Impact of house price growth on mental health: evidence from China. SSM – Popul. Health **13**, 100696 (2021)
18. Shell Research Institute 2021 new first tier cities residence report. 2021 new first tier Cities Summit, Beijing (2021)
19. Jiang, Q., Li, Y., Sánchez-Barricarte, J.J.: Fertility intention, son preference, and second childbirth: survey findings from Shaanxi Province of China. Soc. Indic. Res. **125**(3), 935–953 (2015). https://doi.org/10.1007/s11205-015-0875-z
20. Yang, S., et al.: China's fertility change: an analysis with multiple measures. Popul. Health Metrics **20**(1), 12 (2022)
21. Yuwa population research think tank China Fertility cost report 2022. Yuwa Population Research Official Account, Beijing (2022)
22. Miller, W.B.: Childbearing motivations, desires, and intentions: a theoretical framework. Genet. Soc. Gener. Psychol. Monogr. **120**(2), 223–258 (1994)

23. Miller, W.B.: Differences between fertility desires and intentions: implications for theory, research and policy. Vienna Yearbook Popul. Res. **9**, 75–98 (2011)
24. Maira, T., Chang, X.: Research on China's population birth rate and its influencing factors – an empirical analysis based on dynamic GMM model and threshold model. Price Theory Pract. (11), 53–56 (2019)

The Role of Positive Feedbacks in the Watts Model

Man Yang[1,2], Lina Zhang[1,2], Xincheng Shu[1,2,3], and Zhongyuan Ruan[1,2(✉)]

[1] Institute of Cyberspace Security, Zhejiang University of Technology,
Hangzhou 310023, China
zyruan@zjut.edu.cn
[2] College of Information Engineering, Zhejiang University of Technology,
Hangzhou 310023, China
[3] Department of Electrical Engineering, City University of Hong Kong,
Hong Kong 999077, China

Abstract. Watts model is a classic paradigm for studying social contagion phenomena. In prior research, the decision threshold of an individual is independent of its neighbors' states. In this paper, we extend the Watts model by introducing the positive-feedback mechanism. In our model, each adopter may give positive feedbacks with a certain probability. Correspondingly, the threshold of its susceptible neighbors will decrease by a small number. We perform extensive numerical simulations on synthetic networks and an empirical social network, and demonstrate that positive feedbacks could significantly facilitate the contagion process. Furthermore, we find that network heterogeneity plays a complex role in the cascading dynamics.

Keywords: Feedback mechanism · Threshold model · Social contagion · Complex networks · Information cascade

1 Introduction

In recent decades, modeling social contagion processes, such as the spread of misinformation [1, 2], norms, or innovations [3–5] in social networks has attracted a great deal of attention by researchers from various disciplines [6,7]. Different from the biological disease spreading processes [8–11], social contagion processes are usually characterized by complex contagion mechanisms, where node states are determined by multiple exposures of the neighbor nodes [12]. The threshold model which was first proposed in 1970s s [13,14], has been the predominant modeling framework used to study collective social behavior. In the threshold model, the susceptible individual becomes active only if the fraction of its active neighbors exceeds a certain threshold. This model captures the effect of peer pressure, which helps us to deeply understand some real spreading phenomena in society.

X. Meng et al. (Eds.): BDSC 2022, CCIS 1640, pp. 332–340, 2022.
https://doi.org/10.1007/978-981-19-7532-5_21

In 2002, Watts investigated the threshold model thoroughly by employing the network theory [15]. He considered a special case that there is only one single seed at the beginning of the dynamics. In this case, the complex dynamic problem turns into a static percolation problem that can be elegantly solved by a generating function approach. Watts demonstrated that the condition for a global cascade is that the component consisting of vulnerable nodes (defined as the nodes which will change state even if there is only one adopter neighbor) must percolate throughout the whole network. He then showed that there is a cascade window in the (ϕ, z) (ϕ is the average threshold and z is the average degree of the network) space in which a global cascade (occupying a macroscopic fraction of the network in the thermodynamic limit) can occur. Based on this pioneering work, researchers developed the model from different directions. For example, some researchers focused on how the underlying network structures may affect the cascading dynamics [16–20]. Others were concerned about the role of the initial seed size [21–23]. Besides, in recent years, a number of researchers incorporated some more realistic factors into the Watts model [24–26]. For instance, Huang et al. considered asymmetric individual interactions and introduces persuasion mechanisms in the threshold model [25]. Ruan et al. extended the threshold model by taking into account lurking nodes, who rarely interact with their neighbors [26].

These works all assume that the node threshold is fixed during the dynamics. However, this is not the case in reality. Empirical observations show that people often give feedbacks after they adopt a new product or an innovation [27]. In particular, if people give positive feedbacks, their friends are more prone to take the same behavior. In this paper, we modify the Watts model by considering the positive-feedback mechanism. Specifically, we assume the adopters may give positive feedbacks with a certain rate p, correspondingly, the threshold values of their susceptible neighbors will reduce by a small number δ. We investigate how the positive-feedback mechanism may affect the cascading dynamics on both synthetic and empirical networks.

This paper is organized as follows. In Sect. 2, we introduce the extended threshold model by considering the positive feedback mechanism. In Sect. 3, we present the numerical results on different network structures. We summarize in Sect. 4.

2   Model

Our model is defined as follows. We consider a network of N nodes. Each node in the network is in one of the three states: 0 (susceptible), 1^+ (adopter giving positive feedbacks), and 1^0 (adopter giving no feedbacks). We assign each node a threshold that will change with time. Specifically, the threshold of node i at time t is denoted by ϕ_t^i. For simplicity, we assume that all nodes have the same threshold ϕ_0 at $t = 0$. If a node gives positive feedbacks, each of its neighboring nodes will decrease the threshold by a small number $\delta > 0$ (called the feedback strength), indicating that it becomes more vulnerable to being infected. The algorithm is summarized as follows:

(i) Initially ($t = 0$), we randomly choose one node and let it be in the state 1^+. The remaining nodes are in state 0.

(ii) At each time step t, each node in state 0 will change to state 1^+ (1^0) with probability p ($1 - p$) if the threshold condition is satisfied, i.e., $\frac{m_t^i}{k_i} \geq \phi_t^i$, where k_i is the degree of node i, m_t^i is the number of the neighboring nodes in state 1^+ or 1^0 at time t. Nodes in sate 1^+ or 1^0 will keep in this state until the end of the dynamics.

(iii) At the meantime, each node updates its threshold according to the number of its neighboring nodes in state 1^+ (denoted by m^+): $\phi_t^i = \max(\phi_0 - m^+\delta, 0)$. Note that ϕ_t^i must be greater than or equal to 0.

(iv) Repeat steps (ii) and (iii) until no more nodes can be updated.

3   Simulation Results

We first focus on ER random networks which are constructed according to the following algorithm: M links are randomly placed between pairs of nodes selected with uniform probability. Correspondingly, the average degree is $z = 2M/N$. Note that this algorithm can result in an exact average degree z. All the simulation results presented here are obtained by taking the average on 10^4 different realizations. In the following, we will explore the effects of the average degree z, the probability p of an adopter giving positive feedbacks, and the feedback strength δ on the cascading dynamics on different network topologies. We focus on three different quantities: The final fraction of adopters ρ_∞ (including both the nodes in state 1^+ and 1^0), the final fraction of adopters giving positive feedbacks ρ_∞^+, and the final fraction of adopters giving no feedbacks ρ_∞^0.

Figure 1 (a) shows ρ_∞ as a function of average degree z for different values of p. Notice that $p = 0$ corresponds to the original Watts model. We see that ρ_∞ displays a non-monotonous change with the increase of z. In particular, we find there are two phase transition points in the dynamics, which have been well analyzed by Watts using the method of generating function. The physical picture is clear: When z is too small ($z < 1$), the underlying network is under percolation (no giant connected component exists). In such a case, no global cascade is possible since the contagion process is restricted to the network structure. While for large z, nodes are hard to fulfill the threshold condition, thus we again can not observe any global cascades. Introducing the positive feedback mechanism can notably facilitate the spreading process. We see that the range of z in which global cascades can occur increases as p grows. To investigate it in more detail, we further show how ρ_∞^+ and ρ_∞^0 change with z, respectively [see Fig. 1 (b) and (c)]. Evidently, ρ_∞^+ is significantly suppressed as p decreases, while the change in ρ_∞^0 as p decreases is much more intricate, which depends on the value of z.

To make it clear, we further plot ρ_∞, ρ_∞^+ and ρ_∞^0 as a function of p for different values of z, respectively, as shown in Fig. 2. Consider a specified pair of values of (z, ϕ_0) (for example, $z = 5$ and $\phi_0 = 0.2$) located near the center of the cascade window of the original Watts model, where the global cascades

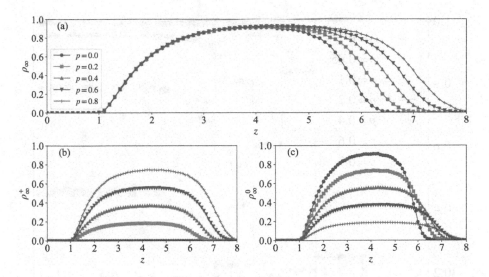

Fig. 1. (a) Fraction of final adopters ρ_∞, (b) fraction of final adopters with positive feedbacks ρ_∞^+, and (c) fraction of final adopters without any feedbacks ρ_∞^0 as a function of average degree z for different values of p in ER random networks. The simulation parameters are $N = 5000$, $\phi_0 = 0.2$, $\delta = 0.05$. All results are obtained over 10^4 realizations.

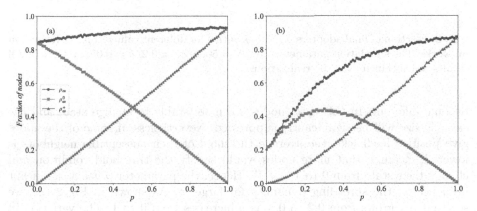

Fig. 2. ρ_∞, ρ_∞^+, and ρ_∞^0 as a function of p for different values of z in ER random networks. (a) $z = 5$, (b) $z = 6$. The simulation parameters are $N = 5000$, $\phi_0 = 0.2$, $\delta = 0.05$. All results are obtained over 10^4 realizations.

occur with high possibility. In this case, positive feedback (i.e., the parameter p) has little impact on the spreading dynamics [see the blue curve in Fig. 2 (a)].

As a result, the fraction of adopters giving positive feedbacks grows almost linearly as p increases [since $\rho_\infty^+ \approx p\rho_\infty$ and ρ_∞ remains unchanged at a high level, see the green curve in Fig. 2 (a)]. Correspondingly, ρ_∞^0 decreases almost linearly with p since $\rho_\infty^+ + \rho_\infty^0 = \rho_\infty$. Increasing z, however, makes the situation

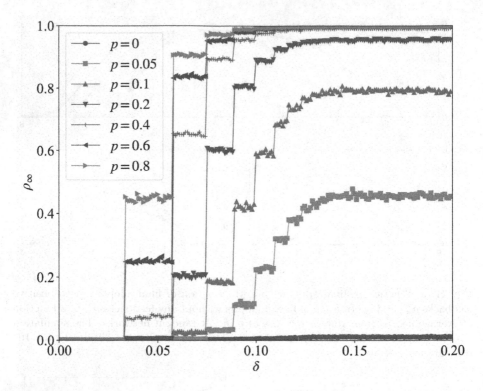

Fig. 3. Fraction of final adopters ρ_∞ varies with δ for different values of p in ER random networks. The simulation parameters are $N = 5000$, $\phi_0 = 0.2$, $\delta = 0.05$, and $z = 7$. All results are obtained over 10^4 realizations.

become different. In this case, nodes are more stable to change state and the cascade size will be significantly suppressed. Nevertheless, if some of the nodes give positive feedbacks, the average threshold of their susceptible neighbors is lowered, meaning that more nodes would satisfy the threshold condition and change their state from 0 to 1^+ or 1^0. Hence, the parameter p has a significant influence on the spreading dynamics for larger z. As shown in Fig. 2 (b), we see that ρ_∞ grows from 0.2 to 0.8 as p increases from 0 to 1. The variation in ρ_∞^0 however is somehow intriguing: it first rises until a maximal value and then drops monotonously to 0 [see the orange curve in Fig. 2 (b)]. The reason is that ρ_∞^0 is determined by both p and ρ_∞: $\rho_\infty^0 \approx (1-p)\rho_\infty$. As p increases, ρ_∞ grows as well (for larger z), which contributes positively in ρ_∞^0; on the other hand, the factor $1 - p$ is a decreasing function of p. The competition between the two factors leads to the non-monotonous change in ρ_∞^0 as p increases. While for ρ_∞^+, both p and ρ_∞ contribute positively. As a consequence, ρ_∞^+ grows monotonously as p increases [see the blue curve in Fig. 2 (b)].

We then study how the parameter δ affects the cascading dynamics. Figure 3 shows ρ_∞ as a function of δ for different values of p. We find that ρ_∞ grows discontinuously as δ increases. The reason lies in the nature of the Watts model (or the threshold model), in which decreasing the average threshold of nodes could result in a step-like change in cascade size [15,28]. It is worth noticing that the effect of δ on the spreading dynamics is constrained to the parameter p. In particular, when p is small, only a small number of nodes reduce their threshold. Therefore, it is difficult for an innovation (or product) to spread out even if δ is large.

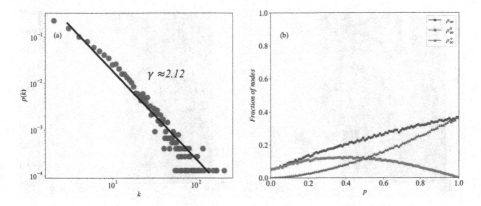

Fig. 4. (a) Degree distribution of the real social network. (b) ρ_∞, ρ_∞^+, and ρ_∞^0 as a function of p in the real social network. The simulation parameters are $\phi_0 = 0.2$, and $\delta = 0.05$. All results are obtained over 10^4 realizations.

Real networks are far different from ER random networks. Considering this, we finally employ a real social network to demonstrate the effect of the positive-feedback mechanism on the cascading process. In particular, we consider the LastFM Asia Social Network [29] collected from public APIs in March 2020. Nodes in the network represent LastFM users from Asian countries and links represent their mutual follower relationships. This social network includes 7624 nodes and 27806 links in total (hence the average degree is 7.29). The degree distribution of the real network is a power law [$p(k) \sim k^{-\gamma}$] with exponent $\gamma \approx 2.12$, as shown in Fig. 4 (a).

Figure 4 (b) shows how ρ_∞, ρ_∞^+ and ρ_∞^0 change with p for the real social network. We find that the phenomenon is similar to that of ER random networks, confirming that the positive-feedback mechanism can promote the spreading in heterogeneous networks. As a comparison, we consider ER random networks with the same number of nodes and links as the real network. Figure 5 (a) and (b) depict ρ_∞ as a function of ϕ_0 and p on ER random networks and the real social network, respectively. We see that, overall, the real social network is more difficult to propagate the initial perturbations due to the highly heterogeneous distribution in node degree. Specifically, in heterogeneous networks, the vulnerable nodes (those nodes that satisfy the condition $1/k \geq \phi$, i.e., one adopter neighbor is enough to make them change state) are poorly connected due to the block of high-degree nodes, which therefore hinders the contagion process. On the other hand, the number of vulnerable nodes (low-degree nodes) in the heterogeneous network is much greater than that in ER networks (with the same average degree), these nodes may form small clusters (though they are poorly connected overall), which can cause an additional effect: for relatively large ϕ_0 (especially $\phi_0 > 0.2$), there are more adopters eventually in the heterogeneous network.

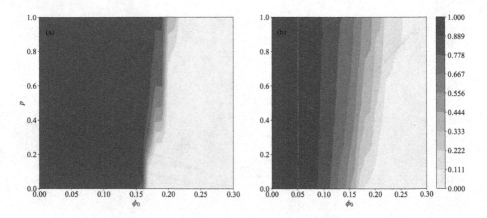

Fig. 5. ρ_∞ as a function of ϕ_0 and p on (a) ER random networks, and (b) the real social network. The simulation parameters are $N = 7624$, $z = 7.29$, $\phi_0 = 0.2$, $p = 0.6$, All results are obtained over 10^4 realizations.

4   Conclusion

In summary, we have modified the conventional Watts model by incorporating the positive-feedback mechanism, where each adopter may give positive feedbacks with a certain probability, and its neighbors would reduce their threshold values adaptively. On the basis of this model, we explored the effects of different model parameters on the final cascade size on both ER random networks and a real social network. The simulation results show that positive feedbacks could significantly facilitate the spreading process, making it easier for global cascades to occur. Furthermore, we find that network heterogeneity plays a complex role here.

Acknowledgements. This work was partially supported by the Zhejiang Provincial Natural Science Foundation of China under Grants No. LY21F030017.

References

1. Romero, D.M., Meeder, B., Kleinberg, J.: Differences in the mechanics of information diffusion across topics: idioms, political hashtags, and complex contagion on Twitter. In: Proceedings of the 20th International Conference on World Wide Web, pp. 695–704 (2011)
2. Törnberg, P.: Echo chambers and viral misinformation: modeling fake news as complex contagion. PLoS ONE **13**(9), e0203958 (2018)
3. Rogers, E.M.: Diffusion of Innovations. Simon and Schuster, New York (2010)
4. Jackson, M.O.: Social and Economic Networks. Princeton University Press, Princeton (2010)
5. Easley, D., Kleinberg, J.: Networks, Crowds, and Markets: Reasoning about a Highly Connected World. Cambridge University Press, Cambridge (2010)
6. Barrat, A., Barthelemy, M., Vespignani, A.: Dynamical Processes on Complex Networks. Cambridge University Press, Cambridge (2008)
7. Zhang, Z., Liu, C., Zhan, X., Lu, X., Zhang, C., Zhang, Y.: Dynamics of information diffusion and its applications on complex networks. Phys. Rep. **651**, 1–34 (2016)
8. Daley, D.J., Gani, J.: Epidemic Modelling: An Introduction. Cambridge University Press, Cambridge (2001)
9. Ruan, Z., Tang, M., Liu, Z.: Epidemic spreading with information-driven vaccination. Phys. Rev. E **86**(3), 036117 (2012)
10. Ruan, Z.: Epidemic spreading in complex networks. Sci. Sinica Phys. Mech. Astron. **50**(1), 010507 (2020)
11. Zhang, X., Ruan, Z., Zheng, M., Barzel, B., Boccaletti, S.: Epidemic spreading under infection-reduced-recovery. Chaos, Solitons Fractals **140**, 110130 (2020)
12. Centola, D., Macy, M.: Complex contagions and the weakness of long ties. Am. J. Sociol. **113**(3), 702–734 (2007)
13. Schelling, T.C.: Hockey helmets, concealed weapons, and daylight saving: a study of binary choices with externalities. J. Conflict Resolut. **17**(3), 381–428 (1973)
14. Granovetter, M.: Threshold models of collective behavior. Am. J. Sociol. **83**(6), 1420–1443 (1978)
15. Watts, D.J.: A simple model of global cascades on random networks. Proc. Natl. Acad. Sci. **99**(9), 5766–5771 (2002)
16. Galstyan, A., Cohen, P.: Cascading dynamics in modular networks. Phys. Rev. E **75**(3), 036109 (2007)
17. Dodds, P.S., Payne, J.L.: Analysis of a threshold model of social contagion on degree-correlated networks. Phys. Rev. E **79**(6), 066115 (2009)
18. Yağan, O., Gligor, V.: Analysis of complex contagions in random multiplex networks. Phys. Rev. E **86**(3), 036103 (2012)
19. Weng, L., Menczer, F., Ahn, Y.Y.: Virality prediction and community structure in social networks. Sci. Rep. **3**(1), 1–6 (2013)
20. Nematzadeh, A., Ferrara, E., Flammini, A., Ahn, Y.Y.: Optimal network modularity for information diffusion. Phys. Rev. Lett. **113**(8), 088701 (2014)
21. Dodds, P.S., Watts, D.J.: Universal behavior in a generalized model of contagion. Phys. Rev. Lett. **92**(21), 218701 (2004)
22. Gleeson, J.P., Cahalane, D.J.: Seed size strongly affects cascades on random networks. Phys. Rev. E **75**(5), 056103 (2007)
23. Singh, P., Sreenivasan, S., Szymanski, B.K., Korniss, G.: Threshold-limited spreading in social networks with multiple initiators. Sci. Rep. **3**(1), 1–7 (2013)

24. Ruan, Z., Wang, J., Xu, J., Zhang, M., Xuan, Q., Fu, C.: Effect of indirect social ties on cascading diffusion of information. In: 2017 International Workshop on Complex Systems and Networks (IWCSN), pp. 96–101. IEEE (2017)
25. Huang, W., Zhang, L., Xu, X., Fu, X.: Contagion on complex networks with persuasion. Sci. Rep. **6**(1), 1–8 (2016)
26. Ruan, Z., Yu, B., Zhang, X., Xuan, Q.: Role of lurkers in threshold-driven information spreading dynamics. Phys. Rev. E **104**(3), 034308 (2021)
27. Duan, W., Gu, B., Whinston, A.B.: The dynamics of online word-of-mouth and product sales-an empirical investigation of the movie industry. J. Retail. **84**(2), 233–242 (2008)
28. Ruan, Z., Iniguez, G., Karsai, M., Kertész, J.: Kinetics of social contagion. Phys. Rev. Lett. **115**(21), 218702 (2015)
29. Rozemberczki, B., Sarkar, R.: characteristic functions on graphs: birds of a feather, from statistical descriptors to parametric models. In: Proceedings of the 29th ACM International Conference on Information & Knowledge Management, pp. 1325–1334 (2020)

Discover Important Paths in the Knowledge Graph Based on Dynamic Relation Confidence

Shanqing Yu[1,2(✉)], Yijun Wu[1,2], Ran Gan[1,2], Jiajun Zhou[1,2], Ziwan Zheng[3], and Qi Xuan[1,2]

[1] Institute of Cyberspace Security, Zhejiang University of Technology, Hangzhou 310023, China
yushanqing@zjut.edu.cn
[2] College of Information Engineering, Zhejiang University of Technology, Hangzhou 310023, China
[3] Zhejiang Police College, Hangzhou 310053, China

Abstract. Most of the existing knowledge graphs are not usually complete and can be complemented by some reasoning algorithms. The reasoning method based on path features is widely used in the field of knowledge graph reasoning and completion on account of that its have strong interpretability. However, reasoning methods based on path features still have several problems in the following aspects: Path search is inefficient, insufficient paths for sparse tasks and some paths are not helpful for reasoning tasks. In order to solve the above problems, this paper proposes a method called DC-Path that combines dynamic relation confidence and other indicators to evaluate path features, and then guide path search, finally conduct relation reasoning. Experimental result show that compared with the existing relation reasoning algorithm, this method can select the most representative features in the current reasoning task from the knowledge graph and achieve better performance on the current relation reasoning task.

Keywords: Knowledge graph · Knowledge graph completion · Relation reasoning · Dynamic relation confidence · Path feature

1 Introduction

Knowledge graph (KG) can be considered as a variant of semantic network with added constraints, or a programmatic way to model a knowledge domain. Knowledge graph reasoning, which focuses on inferring new unknown knowledge from the existing KG, has been widely deployed in KG completion. For knowledge reasoning, commonly used methods concentrate on representation learning, rule, graph structure, and deep learning methods.

The KG reasoning method based on path features is an important part of the graph structure reasoning methods. This kind of method usually includes path search and reasoning. Since the path features is composed of the relation

X. Meng et al. (Eds.): BDSC 2022, CCIS 1640, pp. 341–358, 2022.
https://doi.org/10.1007/978-981-19-7532-5_22

sequences in the KG, it has strong interpretability. The KG reasoning method based on path features can be traced back to the path ranking algorithm (PRA) proposed by Lao et al. [1], which extracts the relation sequences between entities as features. Later, a series of improved algorithms for path search has emerged.

This paper observes and analyzes a series of typical path reasoning algorithms. In general, there are three problems that cannot be avoided in the path search and reasoning: 1. There are too many relations in a large KG, resulting in an inefficient path search. 2. Due to the sparsity of the KG, some reasoning tasks cannot find enough path features for reasoning. 3. Some path features are not relevant to the current reasoning task, so they are not helpful for reasoning.

Although some algorithms have noticed these problems and made effective improvements, there are still some shortcomings. Lao et al. [2] took data-based path walks to improve the efficiency of path search, but it only evaluates and filters the path features at the end of the path search. Gardner M et al. proposed the SFE algorithm [3] which divides the path search process into two subgraphs and searches for the intermediate entity at the same time, thereby improving the efficiency of path search. In addition, it binarizes the probability matrix to reduce the calculation. However, it still cannot choose the path related to the reasoning task and only improves efficiency. Xiong W et al. proposed the DeepPath algorithm [4], which applies reinforcement learning to search paths. Its disadvantage is that the method of reinforcement learning depends on the quality of the embedding method used. Meanwhile, the reinforcement learning network needs to be pre-trained which consumes more time.

Based on the above, this paper proposes a method that uses dynamic relation and path confidence to evaluate the path and guide the path search. Its characteristic lies in dynamically evaluating relations and paths during the path search. In the whole search process, with the search strategy is continuously optimized, the search space is continuously reduced to the area most relevant to the reasoning task. Finally, the path is selected according to the path confidence and other indicators to retain the most important path features for the reasoning task. The main contributions of this paper are as follows:

- We define the dynamic evaluation indicators to evaluate the quality of relation and path in KG. This method includes path search, path selection, and finally perform relation reasoning tasks based on dynamic confidence indicators is called Dynamic confidence path (DC-Path).
- We define dynamic relation confidence to guide the path search and narrow the path search space. Experiments show that path search through DC-Path can more effectively find the most important path for the current reasoning task.
- We use different strategies for path selection to observe its impact on the reasoning results and discover which paths play a decisive role in the reasoning task.

The rest of this paper is composed as follows: Sect. 2 briefly introduces related work about KG reasoning algorithms. Section 3 introduces our method, and Sect. 4 show our experiments and analysis. Section 5 summarizes the full text.

2   Related Work

2.1   Reasoning Method Based on Path Features

Path ranking algorithm (PRA) is the earliest and classic algorithm based on path features reasoning in KG. Lao et al. further improved the PRA algorithm in paper [5]. In this paper, a method of adding a reverse random walk is proposed to expand the original walking strategy, and a path containing constant is added to the path features. The DeepPath algorithm applies reinforcement learning to path search for the first time, and its core ideas are as follows: Get the current state according to the embedding of entities, and select which relation to search according to an action matrix. Set three types of rewards to continuously strengthen the strategy of walking, and finally extract the path features with the best performance. It improves the accuracy of relation reasoning tasks and uses fewer path features than PRA. After that, some new reinforcement learning methods for graph reasoning or path search were proposed [6–9].

2.2   The Reasoning Method Based on Representation Learning

The reasoning method based on representation learning maps the entities and relations in the KG to a low-dimensional space and set a score function to evaluate the correctness of a triple. Translation models are typical KG reasoning algorithms based on representation learning such as TransE [10] and its series of improved TransH [11], TransR [12], and TransD [13]. Another type of KG reasoning method that represents learning is the semantic matching model, and its typical algorithms include Analogy [14]. The advantage of this type of method is that after completing the embedding of entities and relations, reasoning can be performed efficiently through the scoring function. Compared with the reasoning method based on path features, the reasoning performance is better when facing sparse KG.In recent years, more KG reasoning methods based on representation learning have been proposed [15–19].

2.3   Reasoning Method Based on Association Rules

Association rule mining is another type of KG reasoning method. Association rules were first proposed for shopping analysis to indicate the shopping association in the market. There are also many association rules in KG. AMIE is a typical knowledge graph association rule mining system [20]. In the AMIE system, rule confidence based partial completeness assumption is proposed to replace the traditional indicators in the field of original rule mining. It does not assume any fact that does not appear in the KG but assumes that it is missing. This inspired us to make similar confidence definitions for the paths and relations in the KG. At the same time, AMIE+ [21] also proposed a prediction method based on the partial completeness assumption confidence of association rules, which has achieved a remarkable effect on the yago3 dataset. Many rule-based KG reasoning methods have been proposed in recent years [22, 23].

2.4   Reasoning Method Based on Neural Network

Recent studies have shown that the neural network coding model has a good effect on the completion of the KG [24]. Encoding models with linear/bilinear blocks can also be modeled by neural networks, such as NAM [25]. CNN are utilized for learning deep expressive features in recent years, its representative algorithms are ConvE [26], ConvKB [27] and HypER [28]. GNN encoder [29]is also used to reasoning.

3   Method

In this section, we propose a path search algorithm based on dynamic relation confidence, to search effective path features which are further used for relation reasoning. In general, the dynamic confidence of the relation will determine the search strategy.

For a specific reasoning task, if a relation appears frequently in high-quality path features, we will gradually increase the search probability of it and vice versa. In doing so, we can narrow the search space to be more relevant to the target task, and obtain the most representative path features. The framework of path search and reasoning is shown in Fig 1. Firstly, traverse the entity pairs in the training set for path search, during which both the path pool P_l and the relation matrix C are dynamically updated to adjust the search probability. The path pool saves all the currently searched path features and their dynamic path confidence and the relation matrix saves the path dynamic confidence that each relation has participated in. After obtaining all the path features via traverse, we conduct path selection based on dynamic confidence and pairs coverage. Finally, we train a simple linear regression model using the final path features to perform relation reasoning tasks.

3.1   KG Preprocessing

Considering the sparsity and incompleteness of the existing KG, we conduct preliminary processing via inverse relation generation which is commonly used to expand the KG. Specifically, we generate the inverse relation triples for the existing triples and add them to the KG, which can alleviate the problem that some reasoning tasks cannot find enough paths for reasoning due to the sparsity of KG.

For example, we will add an inverse relation triple $(t, hasspouse^{-1}, h)$ for the triple $(h, hasspouse, t)$. However, instead of adding an inverse relation triple for each triple directly, we first evaluate the relation in the KG. If a relation is frequently connected to the same tail entity through different head entities, we do not add an inverse relation triple for it. First of all, the triples composed of such a public entity usually represent common sense in the KG. In addition, adding such triples will generate an entity with a larger out-degree, which will affect the efficiency of path search. Meanwhile, we do not remove redundant relations from semantic information, the reason is that the relation in the KG is extremely incomplete.

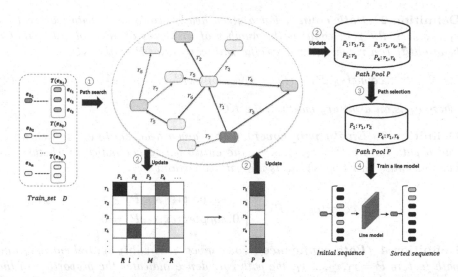

Fig. 1. The framework of path search and reasoning. The workflow proceeds as follows: 1) traverse the positive sample entity pairs in turn for path search; 2) update the path pool and the relation confidence matrix, and adjust the path search strategies; 3) make path selection based on dynamic confidence and pairs coverage; 4) train linear regression model using the final path features to perform relation reasoning tasks.

3.2 Path Evaluation

Although the addition of inverse relation triples helps us expand the path features, it makes the existing path features more miscellaneous. To evaluate the quality of various path features and select effective ones for relation reasoning, we define several evaluation measures as below: path-entity support, path count, path confidence, and entity pair coverage. Notably, different from association rules, we only focus on the path and use dynamic confidence for approximate representation.

Definition 1 (*Path-entity support*). *For a given head entity e_h, tail entity e_t and path feature $P = r_1, r_2, ..., r_l$, the path-entity support is the number of instances of target entity pairs (e_h, e_t) satisfying the path constraint P in the KG:*

$$support(e_h, e_t, P) = \text{ the number of } \{e_h \xrightarrow{r_1} e_i \xrightarrow{r_2} \cdots \xrightarrow{r_l} e_t\}, \quad (1)$$

where e_i is an arbitrary entity in the KG.

Under the constraint of a specific path feature, the head entity can reach the tail entity through different entity sequences, so this indicator is usually greater than one.

Definition 2 *(Path count).* *For a given head entity e_h and path feature $P = r_1, r_2, ..., r_l$, the path count is the number of instances of any tail entity that a head entity can reach under a specific path constraint P in the KG:*

$$count(e_h, P) = \text{ the number of} \{e_h \xrightarrow{r_1} e_i \xrightarrow{r_2} \cdots \xrightarrow{r_l} e_j\}, \tag{2}$$

where e_j is an arbitrary entity in the KG.

Definition 3 *(Entity pair cover).* *For a given head entity e_h, tail entity e_t and a path feature $P = r_1, r_2, ..., r_l$, the entity pair cover indicates whether the current entity pair (e_h, e_t) meets the path constraint P:*

$$cover(e_h, e_t, P) = \begin{cases} 1, support(e_h, e_t, P) \geq 1 \\ 0, support(e_h, e_t, P) = 0 \end{cases} \tag{3}$$

Definition 4 *(Path confidence).* *For a given head entity e_h, tail entity e_t and path feature $P = r_1, r_2, ..., r_l$, the path confidence indicates the proportion of the target entity pairs (e_h, e_t) to all entity pairs starting from the target head entity e_h under a specific path constraint P:*

$$confidence(P) = \frac{\sum_{i=1}^{|D|} support(e_{h_i}, e_{t_i}, P)}{\sum_{i=1}^{|D|} count(e_{h_i}, P)}, \tag{4}$$

where $|D|$ represents the total number of entity pairs in the training set.

The path confidence measures the overall reliability of a path in all entity pairs in the training set. When this value is 1, it means that the head entity of the positive sample can walk to the correct tail entity under the path constraint.

Definition 5 *(Entity pair coverage).* *For a given head entity e_h, tail entity e_t and path feature $P = r_1, r_2, ..., r_l$, entity pair coverage represents the proportion of all entity pairs (e_h, e_t) in the training set that satisfy the specific path constraint P:*

$$coverage(P) = \frac{\sum_{i=1}^{|D|} cover(e_{h_i}, e_{t_i}, P)}{|D|} \tag{5}$$

3.3 Path Search and Strategy Update

The indicators proposed in Sect. 3.2 can evaluate path feature well, but they cannot be calculated during path search, and only can be calculated after path search, which brings great computational consumption. Therefore, we use dynamic path and relation evaluation indicators, which can constantly update during the path search and ultimately guide our path search strategy. Specifically, we build a path pool P_l to save the searched path. When a path is discovered for the first time, we initialize its dynamic path indicators involving path support, path count, path confidence, and entity pair coverage based on the current head entity. When searching for an existing path feature, we dynamically update its indicators. In this way, the path pool is constantly updated during path search, in which new paths are constantly added, and existing paths are constantly updated with dynamic path indicators. The dynamic confidence and dynamic entity pair coverage are approximate as follows:

$$\text{D-confidence}\,(P) \approx \frac{\sum_{i=1}^{k} \text{support}\,(e_{h_i}, e_{t_i}, P)}{\sum_{i=1}^{k} \text{count}\,(e_{h_i}, P)}, \tag{6}$$

$$\text{D-coverage}\,(P) \approx \frac{\sum_{i=1}^{k} \text{cover}\,(e_{h_i}, e_{t_i}, P)}{k}, \tag{7}$$

where k represents the kth entity pair currently traversed. At the same time, we set a dynamically changing relation matrix $C = \{c_{ij}\}_{m \times n} \in \mathbb{R}^{m \times n}$, where m is the total number of relations in the KG, n is the number of paths in the current path pool, the entry c_{ij} represents whether the current relation r_i participates in the path P_j as follows:

$$c_{ij} = \begin{cases} \text{D-confidence}\,(P_j)\,, & r_i \text{ in } P_j \\ 0 & , r_i \text{ not in } P_j \end{cases} \tag{8}$$

The confidence vector of relation r_i is denoted as:

$$C_{r_i} = [c_{i1}, c_{i2}, \cdots, c_{in}]. \tag{9}$$

Such a relation matrix can reflect the current importance of different relations and guide path search. We use the following three strategies to narrow the path search space: 1) Probabilistic searching based on dynamic relation confidence, 2) Sampling the entities connected by the same relation. 3) Stopping immediately after finding any tail entity.

Figure 2 provides a simple example of path search in the KG, where the target task is to reason athlete's home stadium, the current head entity is the athlete: Kobe Bryant and the tail entity is the Staples stadium. The number marked below the relation in the figure is the probability of continuing the deep search for the relation, which will be introduced below. In general, we use such simple examples to illustrate our three path search strategies.

Probabilistic Search Based on Dynamic Relation Confidence. For each relation r_i that exists in the KG, the relation confidence is defined as:

$$A_{r_i} = (\text{Max}\,(C_{r_i}) + \text{Average}\,(C_{r_i}))\,/2 \tag{10}$$

This is the combination of the maximum confidence and the average confidence of the path that the current relation has participated in. If the relation confidence of a relation is close to 1, it means that the average confidence and maximum confidence of the path it has participated in are both high, and this relation will be given priority when searching for the path. Among them, we use a probability function $prob(r_i)$:

$$prob\,(r_i) = (\alpha A_{r_i} + \beta)^\gamma, \tag{11}$$

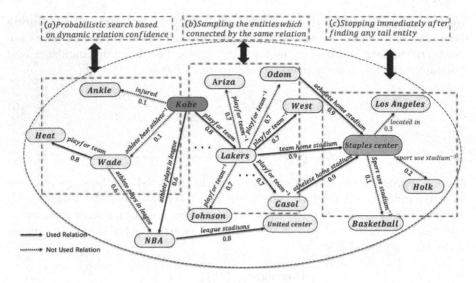

Fig. 2. A simple example of a path search. Reasoning task: the player's home stadium, the starting head entity e_h is Kobe Bryant, and the correct tail entity e_t is Staples stadium. Three strategies are shown in the three red dotted boxes. (Color figure online)

which represents the probability of continuing the deep search along with the relation r_i. α, β, γ are used to control the degree of change in probability with the relation of confidence. During the search process, such a probability function generates the probability between 0 to 1 according to the relation confidence of the current relation. Such a probability function will ensure that we can continuously search for those important relations and terminate the search for irrelevant ones in times. As shown in part (a) of Fig. 2, for the reasoning task of the stadium, the relation between the athlete's injury and the athlete's opponent hardly participates in any path feature, so they have a low search probability. In the process of traversing entity pairs and updating the path pool, the search target gradually focus on those important relations with a high search probability, to narrow the search space and change the path feature evaluation. Particularly, if a path contains only one relation, the search will not continue. Because such a relation may be a synonym of the target relation. We will start the probabilistic search based on relation confidence after a certain number of entity pairs are traversed.

Sampling the Same Relation of Entities. In order to further narrow the search space, when an entity is connected to multiple entities through the same relation, we only search for some of them by sampling. Through such sampling, the efficiency of path search can be improved without losing too much information. As shown in Fig. 2, Lakers have a large number of players. Therefore, we can only sample and search some of its players to approximate the overall effect. This ability strategy allows us to efficiently perform path search in the KG space with a large entity out-degree value and will not completely discard the information of these height out-degree entities.

Stopping Immediately After Finding Any Tail Entity. Once we find any target entity, we will stop the path search. Although it is possible to find another target tail entity from the target entity, such a strategy can simplify the path to a certain extent. As shown in Fig. 2(c), we will not continue to search after searching Staples stadium to avoid redundant path features.

The probabilistic depth search algorithms we called DFS-conf are shown in Algorithm 1.

Algorithm 1: DFS-conf

Input: Head entity e_h, tail entity set $T(e_h)$, max path length l, out-degree threshold θ_o

Output: Path pool $\mathbf{P}_l$

1   Initialization $step$=0;
2   **for** relation in e_h's conjunction **do**
3   generate a random number a in $[0,1]$;
4   calculate search probability of relation by formula 11
5   **if** $prob(relation) < a$ **then**
6   contine;
7   **end**
8   **else**
9   entity set $\leftarrow$ entities connect with head entity by relation;
10   **if** $|$entity set$| > \theta_o$ **then**
11   entity set $\leftarrow$ random sample k entities from entity set;
12   **end**
13   **if** find path **then**
14   Update $\mathbf{P}_l$,C;
15   contine;
16   **end**
17   **if** $step >= l$ **then**
18   **return**
19   **end**
20   **for** entity in entity set **do**
21   step += 1;
22   DFS-conf(entity,$T(e_t)$);
23   **end**
24   **end**
25 **end**
26 **return**

3.4 Path Selection

After path search, we select the path features in the path pool and set the entity pair coverage threshold θ_p to delete those path features with high confidence but extremely low coverage. Although the confidence of these path features is high, the scope of application in the knowledge is narrow. And we use segmentation thresholds θ_c to filter paths based on the confidence of the path. Therefore, we usually set different thresholds for paths with a length of 1 and greater than 1.

3.5 Train Linear Regression Models for Relation Reasoning Tasks

Similar to algorithms such as PRA and DeepPath, we perform path search and get the filtered path, and finally, train a simple linear regression to perform the relation reasoning task. The input feature is a probability matrix representing the probability of the current head entity being able to walk to the correct tail entity through the current path. The higher the final output score, the more likely the entity pair has the relation.

4 Experiments

4.1 Dataset

We evaluate the proposed method on two datasets: NELL-995 [4] and FB15K-237 [30]. The NELL-995 dataset is a subset of the 995th iteration of the NELL system, and the frequent but meaningless relations are deleted. The FB15K-237 dataset is a subset sampled from FB15K [10]. During path search, we only delete the corresponding triples and inverse triples from the KG for the currently searched head entity and tail entity set. The specific information of the datasets is shown in Table 1.

Table 1. The basic statistics of the two knowledge graph datasets.

Dataset	Entity num	Relation num	Triple num	Task num
NELL-995	75492	200	154213	12
FB15K-237	14505	237	310116	20

4.2 Baseline and Details

We compare our method with the following methods: translation models, Analogy, Rescal, and DeepPath.

- Translation models. We use the following translation method as the baseline:
  TransE [10]. It regards the relation as the translation of the head entity to
  the target entity and map entities and relations to the same vector space by
  constraining the difference between vectors.
  TransR [12]. It improves on TransE [10] and embeds entities and relations
  into different spaces. For the relation, an additional matrix M_r is added to
  describe the space where the relation is located.
  TransH [11]. It embeds entities and relations into the same vector space, but
  the representation of entities in different relations is different.
  TransD [13]. It simplifies the TransR [12] model, uses two vectors to represent
  entities or relations. One of the vectors represents the entity and relation, and
  the other is used to construct the dynamic mapping matrix.

- Rescal [31]. It is a semantic matching model that performs reasoning by
  matching the underlying semantics of entities and the relations in the vector
  space. Its scoring function is bilinear and uses a matrix to represent relations.
- Analogy [14]. It further models the analogy properties of entities and relations.
  At the same time, Analogy proved that DistMult [32], HolE [17], ComplEx
  [33] and other models can be regarded as its special cases.
- DeepPath [4]. It use reinforcement learning to search for paths and set up
  three different rewards functions: global accuracy rewards, path efficiency
  rewards, and path diversity rewards to find paths. Its reasoning performance
  has been proved to be better than the path ranking algorithm.

4.3 Experimental Setting

Reasoning Task. For a head entity and target relation, we try to find the tail
entity that is most likely to form a triple from the candidate tail entity. For the
relation r_t to be reasoned, the set of positive samples is denoted as D, which is
further split into training and testing sets.

We use the training set for path search and linear model training and the
reasoning performance is evaluated based on the testing set. A positive sample
and its corresponding negative samples together form a sequence. The trained
linear model can calculate the score of each candidate triple in the sequence and
sort the sequence in descending order. We evaluate the performance of relation
reasoning according to the ranking of positive samples in the sequence using
mean average precision (MAP) index: If there are k pairs of correct triples in
sequence, the MAP could be calculated as follows:

$$MAP = \frac{\sum_{i=1}^{k} rank\left(e_h, e_{t_i}\right)}{k} \tag{12}$$

Finally, we get the average MAP of all entity pairs in the testing set.

Details and Parameter Settings. The code of translation models comes from *Fast-TransX*[1]. For each reasoning task, we delete the positive sample entity pairs in the testing set from the KG to perform the embedding task. The learning rate is set to 0.01 and the margin is 1, the relation and entity embedding dimensions are both 100, and the training is performed 1000 times. For Analogy and Rescal, we get the result based on the provided code in *OpenKE*[2] and use the default parameters. The DeepPath algorithm is based on Xiong's code at *DeepPath*[3]. For our method DC-Path, the maximum path length is set to 3. In the probability function, α, β, γ are set to 0.99, 0.01, 0.5 respectively. Four threshold parameters are set for path selection: θ_{c_1} and θ_{c_2} represent the confidence threshold with path length equal to 1 and greater than 1 respectively. θ_{p_1} and θ_{p_2} represent the entity pairs coverage threshold with path length equal to 1 and greater than 1 respectively. In the NELL-995 data set, we set the above four thresholds as {0.3, 0.5, 0.01, 0.1} and {0.2, 0.3, 0.02, 0.2} for FB15k-237. In FB15k-237, we are lowering the threshold to {0.2, 0.2, 0.02, 0.02}.

4.4 Results and Analysis

Relation Reasoning Accuracy and Paths Used. In this part, we report the reasoning results of each method and the analysis of the used path number. Table 2 reports the results of performance comparison between our method and baselines, from which we can see that DC-Path significantly outperforms most baselines in most cases. The reasoning results in the NELL-995 data set show that in most tasks, DC-Path can get higher reasoning accuracy than these baselines. Although the reasoning results on FB15k-237 show that not every task performs better than these baselines, the average accuracy of the method is still leading. Therefore, we can conclude that DC-Path can get better reasoning accuracy than these mainstream reasoning methods. Table 3 shows the number of paths used in the final reasoning of DeepPath and DC-Path. DC-Path greatly reduces the number of path features used and achieve better performance. Meanwhile, we also found that there are more path features in FB15k-237. On average, there are nearly 33 path features for each task. And the number of path features of different reasoning tasks is very unbalanced. There are nearly a hundred paths for task: *personNational* but only 1 path for task: *orgFounded*. This is why in sparse reasoning tasks, path-based reasoning methods are usually inferior to representation learning methods.

Time Consumption of Path Search. We ran our code on a computer with 16 GB of RAM and an i7 8th generation processor. For the NELL-995 dataset, the average time consumption on path search for each target relation is about 21 s, while for FB15k-237, the average time is about 1100 s. We also discover that DeepPath usually spends more search time. Since the reinforcement learning

---

[1] https://github.com/thunlp/Fast-TransX/.

[2] https://github.com/thunlp/OpenKE/.

[3] https://github.com/xwhan/DeepPath/.

strategy of the DeepPath algorithm can discover longer path features, its path search cost is also greater, usually more than 10000 s. The reason may be that it needs to train the neural network many times. Therefore, our method can greatly reduce the time consumption in path search and use path features with a limited length to achieve good reasoning results.

Table 2. Results of relation reasoning. The best results are marked in bold.

DateSet	Task	Method							
		TransE	TransR	TransD	TransH	Analogy	Rescal	DeepPath	DC-Path
NELL-995	agentBelongsToOrg	0.746	0.747	0.723	**0.759**	0.708	0.669	0.576	0.650
	athleteHomeStadium	0.711	0.757	0.656	0.680	0.751	0.662	0.848	**0.904**
	athletePlaysForTeam	0.685	0.739	0.618	0.641	0.714	0.602	0.712	**0.818**
	athletePlaysInLeague	0.921	0.814	0.941	0.919	0.848	0.911	0.955	**0.975**
	athletePlaysSport	0.982	0.943	0.981	0.950	0.909	0.952	0.896	**0.984**
	orgHeadquaterCity	0.652	0.711	0.623	0.616	0.784	0.566	0.790	**0.803**
	orgHiredPerson	0.707	0.724	0.710	0.707	0.726	0.696	0.745	**0.780**
	bornLocation	0.795	0.711	0.802	**0.819**	0.807	0.812	0.742	0.727
	personLeadsOrg	0.766	0.771	0.765	0.735	0.796	0.746	0.780	**0.811**
	teamPlaysInLeague	0.907	**0.933**	0.913	0.918	0.873	0.895	0.857	0.910
	teamPlaySports	0.818	0.881	0.734	0.799	0.705	0.733	0.708	**0.886**
	worksFor	0.702	0.695	0.696	0.684	0.722	0.692	0.700	**0.743**
	Average	0.783	0.785	0.764	0.769	0.779	0.745	0.776	**0.833**
FB15k-237	teamSport	**0.968**	0.967	0.939	0.931	0.891	0.972	0.868	0.963
	birthPlace	0.411	0.390	0.383	0.386	0.398	0.310	**0.510**	0.441
	personNationality	0.662	0.719	0.493	0.664	0.681	0.773	0.840	**0.842**
	fimDirector	0.458	0.470	0.448	0.439	0.452	0.393	0.358	**0.490**
	filmWriteenBy	0.623	0.625	**0.642**	0.628	0.571	0.570	0.558	0.493
	filmLanguage	0.546	0.553	0.424	0.523	0.494	0.642	0.691	**0.705**
	tvLanguage	0.955	0.960	0.956	0.942	0.918	0.954	0.964	**0.967**
	capitalOf	0.520	0.539	0.541	0.556	0.527	0.501	0.743	**0.837**
	orgFounded	0.383	0.388	0.383	**0.451**	0.444	0.375	0.302	0.279
	musicianOrigin	0.426	0.434	0.423	0.416	0.484	0.385	**0.506**	0.446
	serviceLocation	0.483	0.514	0.530	0.541	0.523	0.470	**0.556**	0.492
	filmCountry	0.610	0.565	0.450	0.584	0.630	0.644	0.693	**0.708**
	filmMusic	0.507	0.500	0.526	0.499	0.384	**0.538**	0.251	0.465
	orgHeadquarters	0.580	0.584	0.606	0.591	0.422	0.503	**0.616**	0.415
	orgMember	0.437	0.437	0.443	0.441	0.444	0.389	0.261	**0.457**
	professionSpecializationOf	0.484	0.478	0.448	0.464	0.466	**0.607**	0.485	0.425
	languagesSpoken	0.404	0.415	0.461	0.461	0.417	0.405	0.327	0.402	**0.421**
	timeEventLocations	0.355	0.386	**0.395**	0.329	0.307	0.370	0.431	0.350
	tvProgramGenre	0.401	0.369	0.386	0.395	0.412	0.340	**0.511**	0.438
	tvProgramCountryOfOrigin	0.886	0.837	0.913	0.859	0.904	0.853	0.878	**0.915**
	Average	0.555	0.556	0.539	0.553	0.538	0.546	0.571	**0.576**

Table 3. Comparison of the number of paths

Dataset	Task	Method		Dataset	Task	Method	
		DeepPath	DC-Path			DeepPath	DC-Path
FB15k-237	teamSport	17	11	NELL-995	agentBelongstoorg	15	19
	birthPlace	4	8		athleteHomeStadium	9	3
	personNationality	86	52		athletePlaysForTeam	23	2
	filmDirector	2	2		athletePlaysInLeague	31	34
	filmWriteenBy	6	2		athletePlaysSport	15	21
	filmLanguage	53	94		orgHeadquaterCity	5	19
	tvLanguage	44	101		orgHiredPerson	9	12
	capitalOf	3	6		bornLocation	5	1
	orgnFounded	2	1		personLeadsOrg	15	9
	musicianOrigin	17	2		teamPlaysInLeague	8	27
	serviceLocation	52	16		teamPlaySports	10	17
	filmCountry	54	113		worksFor	15	11
	filmMusic	2	35		/		
	orgHeadquarters	8	2		/		
	orgMember	8	60		/		
	professionSpecializationOf	5	1		/		
	languagesSpoken	9	1		/		
	timeEventLocations	10	4		/		
	tvProgramGenre	51	3		/		
	tvProgramCountryOfOrigin	45	137		/		
	Average	13.3	14.5		Average	23.9	32.6

The Impact of Different Confidence Thresholds on the Results. In this part, we explore the influence of different path confidence thresholds on the reasoning results. We keep the paths whose path length is one and the path confidence is greater than 0.3, and the entity pair coverage is greater than 0.01.

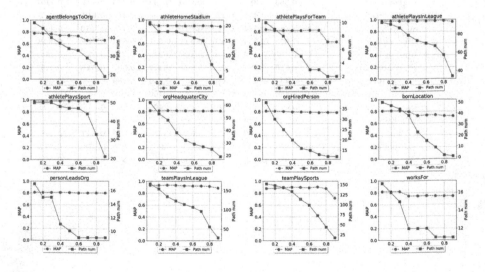

Fig. 3. MAP and path number in different path confidence threshold in NELL-995.

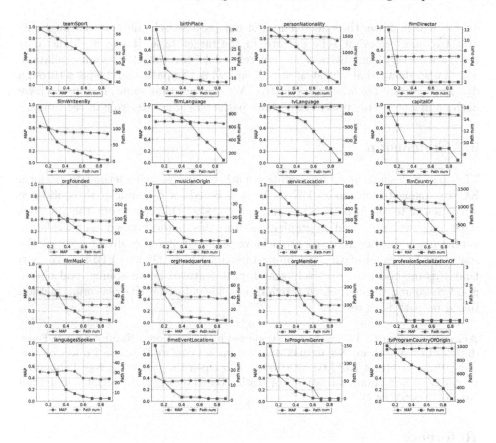

Fig. 4. MAP and path number in different path confidence threshold in FB15k-237.

On this basis, we fix the entity pair coverage threshold to 0.01 and test the accuracy of relation reasoning with different confidence thresholds. Figure 3 and Fig. 4 shows the number of path features retained by different path confidence thresholds and the reasoning accuracy (MAP) when using these path features for relation reasoning. We can find that the MAP of many target relations does not decrease significantly as the threshold increases, which means that those paths whose path confidence is greater than 0.5 or even higher play a key role in relation reasoning.The performance of some reasoning tasks is poor because of that there are too few effective reasoning paths that meet the confidence threshold.

Display Some Paths and Relations. In this part, we show some high confidence paths in several tasks and the most relevant top-2 relations among them. Table 3 shows the important paths and their confidence in some tasks. These paths are of high quality in terms of semantic logic analysis and path confidence, which shows the effectiveness of our path search method. Through the first two most relevant relationships in the target task. It can be found that they are usually semantically closely related to the target reasoning relation, which also shows that our strategy of narrowing the path search space through dynamic relation confidence is effective. We can find that some short paths have high confidence. This proves that short paths play a greater role in reasoning.

5   Conclusion

This paper designs and implements a path feature search method to perform KG reasoning tasks named DC-Path. It is based on dynamic path confidence and uses it to perform relation reasoning tasks. Different from the previous reasoning methods based on graph structure , this method uses dynamic relation confidence and other indicators to achieve path search and evaluation during the searching process. Relation reasoning tasks on NELL-995 and FB15K-237 show that this method can effectively search path features for reasoning, and obtain good reasoning results, which provides new ideas for the KG reasoning method based on path features.

Acknowledgment. This work was supported by the National Natural Science Foundation of China (Grant No. 62103374),Basic Public Welfare Research Project of Zhejiang Province(Grant No. LGF20F020016) and Open Project of the Key Laboratory of Public Security Informatization Application Based on Big Data Architecture(Grant No. 2020DSJSYS003).

References

1. Lao, N., Cohen, W.W.: Fast query execution for retrieval models based on path-constrained random walks. In: Proceedings of the 16th ACM SIGKDD International Conference on Knowledge Discovery and Data Mining, pp. 881–888 (2010)
2. Lao, N., Mitchell, T., Cohen, W.: Random walk inference and learning in a large scale knowledge base. In: Proceedings of the 2011 Conference on Empirical Methods in Natural Language Processing, pp. 529–539 (2011)
3. Gardner, M., Mitchell, T.: Efficient and expressive knowledge base completion using subgraph feature extraction. In: Proceedings of the 2015 Conference on Empirical Methods in Natural Language Processing, pp. 1488–1498 (2015)
4. Xiong, W., Hoang, T., Wang, W.Y.: DeepPath: a reinforcement learning method for knowledge graph reasoning. arXiv preprint arXiv:1707.06690 (2017)
5. Lao, N., Minkov, E., Cohen, W.: Learning relational features with backward random walks. In: Proceedings of the 53rd Annual Meeting of the Association for Computational Linguistics and the 7th International Joint Conference on Natural Language Processing (Volume 1: Long Papers), pp. 666–675 (2015)
6. Das, R., et al.: Go for a walk and arrive at the answer: reasoning over paths in knowledge bases using reinforcement learning. arXiv preprint arXiv:1711.05851 (2017)
7. Fu, C., Chen, T., Qu, M., Jin, W., Ren, X.: Collaborative policy learning for open knowledge graph reasoning. arXiv preprint arXiv:1909.00230 (2019)

8. Lin, X.V., Socher, R., Xiong, C.: Multi-hop knowledge graph reasoning with reward shaping. arXiv preprint arXiv:1808.10568 (2018)
9. Shen, Y., Chen, J., Huang, P.S., Guo, Y., Gao, J.: M-walk: learning to walk over graphs using monte carlo tree search. In: Advances in Neural Information Processing Systems, pp. 6786–6797 (2018)
10. Bordes, A., Usunier, N., Garcia-Duran, A., Weston, J., Yakhnenko, O.: Translating embeddings for modeling multi-relational data. In: Advances in Neural Information Processing Systems, pp. 2787–2795 (2013)
11. Wang, Z., Zhang, J., Feng, J., Chen, Z.: Knowledge graph embedding by translating on hyperplanes. In: AAAI, vol. 14, pp. 1112–1119. Citeseer (2014)
12. Lin, Y., Liu, Z., Sun, M., Liu, Y., Zhu, X.: Learning entity and relation embeddings for knowledge graph completion. In: Twenty-Ninth AAAI Conference on Artificial Intelligence (2015)
13. Ji, G., He, S., Xu, L., Liu, K., Zhao, J.: Knowledge graph embedding via dynamic mapping matrix. In: Proceedings of the 53rd Annual Meeting of the Association for Computational Linguistics and the 7th International Joint Conference on Natural Language Processing (Volume 1: Long Papers), pp. 687–696 (2015)
14. Liu, H., Wu, Y., Yang, Y.: Analogical inference for multi-relational embeddings. arXiv preprint arXiv:1705.02426 (2017)
15. Balažević, I., Allen, C., Hospedales, T.M.: Tucker: tensor factorization for knowledge graph completion. arXiv preprint arXiv:1901.09590 (2019)
16. Sun, Z., Deng, Z.H., Nie, J.Y., Tang, J.: Rotate: knowledge graph embedding by relational rotation in complex space. arXiv preprint arXiv:1902.10197 (2019)
17. Xue, Y., Yuan, Y., Xu, Z., Sabharwal, A.: Expanding holographic embeddings for knowledge completion. In: Advances in Neural Information Processing Systems, pp. 4491–4501 (2018)
18. Zhang, S., Tay, Y., Yao, L., Liu, Q.: Quaternion knowledge graph embeddings. In: Advances in Neural Information Processing Systems, pp. 2735–2745 (2019)
19. Zhang, W., Paudel, B., Zhang, W., Bernstein, A., Chen, H.: Interaction embeddings for prediction and explanation in knowledge graphs. In: Proceedings of the Twelfth ACM International Conference on Web Search and Data Mining, pp. 96–104 (2019)
20. Galárraga, L.A., Teflioudi, C., Hose, K., Suchanek, F.: Amie: association rule mining under incomplete evidence in ontological knowledge bases. In: Proceedings of the 22nd International Conference on World Wide Web, pp. 413–422 (2013)
21. Galárraga, L., Teflioudi, C., Hose, K., Suchanek, F.M.: Rule mining with amie+ fouille de règles avec amie (2015)
22. Guo, S., Wang, Q., Wang, L., Wang, B., Guo, L.: Knowledge graph embedding with iterative guidance from soft rules. arXiv preprint arXiv:1711.11231 (2017)
23. Yang, F., Yang, Z., Cohen, W.W.: Differentiable learning of logical rules for knowledge base reasoning. In: Advances in Neural Information Processing Systems, pp. 2319–2328 (2017)
24. Ji, S., Pan, S., Cambria, E., Marttinen, P., Yu, P.S.: A survey on knowledge graphs: representation, acquisition and applications. arXiv preprint arXiv:2002.00388 (2020)
25. Liu, Q., et al.: Probabilistic reasoning via deep learning: neural association models. arXiv preprint arXiv:1603.07704 (2016)
26. Dettmers, T., Minervini, P., Stenetorp, P., Riedel, S.: Convolutional 2D knowledge graph embeddings. arXiv preprint arXiv:1707.01476 (2017)
27. Nguyen, D.Q., Nguyen, T.D., Nguyen, D.Q., Phung, D.: A novel embedding model for knowledge base completion based on convolutional neural network. arXiv preprint arXiv:1712.02121 (2017)

28. Balažević, I., Allen, C., Hospedales, T.M.: Hypernetwork knowledge graph embeddings. In: Tetko, I.V., Kůrková, V., Karpov, P., Theis, F. (eds.) ICANN 2019. LNCS, vol. 11731, pp. 553–565. Springer, Cham (2019). https://doi.org/10.1007/978-3-030-30493-5_52
29. Jung, J., Jung, J., Kang, U.: Learning to walk across time for interpretable temporal knowledge graph completion. In: Proceedings of the 27th ACM SIGKDD Conference on Knowledge Discovery & Data Mining, pp. 786–795 (2021)
30. Toutanova, K., Chen, D., Pantel, P., Poon, H., Choudhury, P., Gamon, M.: Representing text for joint embedding of text and knowledge bases. In: Proceedings of the 2015 Conference on Empirical Methods in Natural Language Processing, pp. 1499–1509 (2015)
31. Nickel, M., Tresp, V., Kriegel, H.P.: A three-way model for collective learning on multi-relational data. In: Icml, vol. 11, pp. 809–816 (2011)
32. Yang, B., Yih, W.T., He, X., Gao, J., Deng, L.: Embedding entities and relations for learning and inference in knowledge bases. arXiv preprint arXiv:1412.6575 (2014)
33. Trouillon, T., Welbl, J., Riedel, S., Gaussier, É., Bouchard, G.: Complex embeddings for simple link prediction. In: International Conference on Machine Learning (ICML) (2016)

The Comparative Landscape of Chinese and Foreign Applications on Blockchain in E-government

Rongxuan Shang[1](✉) ⓘ, Bin Zhang[2] ⓘ, and Jianing Mi[1] ⓘ

[1] Harbin Institute of Technology, Harbin 150001, China
564047413@qq.com
[2] Hunan Agricultural University, Changsha 410000, China

Abstract. This research assessed the use of blockchain in e-government, to provide a useful overview for future research. To compare the research landscapes in China and abroad, We select a few publications from the CNKI and Web of Science Core Collections and choose to manually audit these publications by reading the abstracts to ensure the data's reliability. To examine the information in the title catalog that fits the requirements, as well as to study the research hotspots and research trends eligible, visual analysis tools such as Citespace are utilized. The following are the major findings: Firstly, foreign research on e-government involving blockchain focuses more on technical and practical analysis, while Chinese research focuses more on theoretical analysis, with specific technical practice yet to be implemented. Secondly, a foreign study in this subject was undertaken earlier than Chinese research. Finally, the Chinese should strengthen exchanges with international counterparts and institutions, and aim to synthesize experience that can be coupled with China's distinctive reality to better promote the deployment and application of blockchain in China's e-government.

Keywords: Blockchain · E-government · Bibliometrics · Comparative analysis

1 Introduction

From the late 20th century to the early 21st century, information technology has been closely integrated with public administration [1]. E-government development is considered an important component of the national informatization strategy. From information government to electronic government to e-government, information technology not only enriches the governance means of government but also plays a unique role in the digital reform of government [2], the change of government management and governance concept. In 2016, the government work report proposed "Internet + Government Services" [3], indicating that China gradually began to apply digital technology to all stages of government public services; in the same year, the Ministry of Industry and Information Technology and Application Development White Paper (2016) as the first official guidance document; in 2019 [4], the fourth Plenary session of the 19th CPC Central

Committee proposed "promote the construction of e-government, strengthen data sharing", indicating that China has raised e-government construction to the level of national governance [5]. The innovation and popularization of digital technology are closely related to the construction and development of e-government. Especially in the past two years [6].

Blockchain technology, has been the subject of much attention in many countries and different fields in recent years. The government sees blockchain as a potential solution to these challenges, because blockchain itself is secure against online attacks, can be verified by anyone. The use of blockchain technology in e-government systems is part of this development; it is necessary to discuss the relevant key issues. Meanwhile, the applications and research of blockchain have shown a blowout trend [7], and the technological change is the key factor and important driving force to promote the transformation of the government in the digital form [8]. Therefore, it is particularly important to analyze and understand the research status and situation of blockchain in the field of e-government at home and abroad and to summarize it in time [9]. Therefore, Citespace was selected to perform a visual and comparative analysis of the literature on landscape of Chinese and foreign.

2 Description of Literature

Although blockchain was first proposed in 2009 and is only more than ten decades now, the development of blockchain has gone through three stages from programmable currency to programmable finance to programmable society. In the past ten years, the Chinese research on blockchain in the application of e-government has achieved preliminary results. To be specific: Zhan Guobin [10] analyzed its values, technical tools, and related technical support in the process of e-government transformation, and summed up the aspects from which China can get enlightenment and experience; Yang [11] analyzed the transformation process of e-government in Japan from the technical level, believed that China can form the broad thinking from a strategic platform, strategic concept, strategic unit, and strategic node; Hu [12] clarified the definition of e-government, summarized the experience of developed countries, and China should pay attention to the use of modern information technology to improve e-government and technology to guarantee digital security and privacy; Yao [13] Shuiqiong summarized the experience. Zhou Jason [14] and Ding Huang [15] took the e-government construction in Guizhou Province, and analyzed the current situation, difficulties, and countermeasures; Wang Weiling [16] pointed out the path to solving the dilemma of e-government construction in China; Liu Shuchun [17] discussed the strategic implication and technical architecture of e-government construction and verified the accuracy of Zhejiang Province, studied the governance logic of Shanghai experience as an example [18]; and Chen Tao [19] and Song Kai [20] discussed the internal path of government data assets in Dongguan and Weifang.

The application of blockchain in the field of e-government mainly focuses on the three dimensions of strategic planning, technical system, and digital governance. Sotoudehnia, M [21] analyzed the Canadian government's plan for blockchain in the transformation process of e-government, and believes that digital leadership, digital management, and technology authorization are the three main factors affecting strategic planning; Oliveira, TA [22] and other scholars believe that the rational use of digital technology can promote the innovative development of cities and society. From the perspective of technology application, Lykidis I [23] believes that blockchain promotes the non-denial and transparency of transactions in the construction and transformation process of e-government, And there is a great potential to continue to play; Truby, J [24] analyzed the application of blockchain in the field of climate control and low-carbon emission reduction, It is pointed out that the development of blockchain promotes the social and economic benefits, And believes that it should be improved in the policy field, Greater areas that will ensure that blockchain works; Hassija, V [25] points out that the blockchain means to provide a secure and effective technical framework, Help governments improve technical traceability and reduce technology costs, It guarantees the cost performance of government digital construction investment and income.

Based on the above literature content, it can be seen that scholars at home and abroad have conducted considerable in-depth research on the role of blockchain in the construction of e-government to ensure that the construction of e-government is more efficient, fast, and convenient. However, the research of social science has always attached great importance to reflection and summary, to better find and solve problems, and ensure that there is no deviation in the direction of relevant research. Therefore, this study adopts the bibliometric method to analyze the title information of articles in the field of e-government, understand the status of relevant research at home and abroad, and provide reference and references for subsequent research.

3 Research Methods and Data

3.1 Research Methods

To complete the research purpose of this paper, combined with the actual situation, we decided to use the bibliometric method combined with the visual analysis software for the research.

The bibliometric method refers to the cross-science of quantitatively analyzing all carriers of knowledge by using mathematical and statistical methods [26]. It is a comprehensive knowledge system that integrates mathematics, statistics, and philology and pays attention to quantification. The measurement objects are mainly: the number of documents (various publications, especially journal papers and citations), the number of authors (individual collective or group), and the number of words (various literature labels, among which the majority are narrative words).

We choose Citespace [27] as the visual analysis software which can be used for massive literature including Web of Science, Scopus, Pubmed, CNKI, and other databases for topics, keywords, author units, cooperative networks, and journals, publication time, literature citation, and so on. The software was developed by Dr. Chaomei Chen, then a tenured professor at Drexel University, and requires a Java environment. Therefore, the Java virtual machine is downloaded to ensure the smooth operation of Citespace-related software before formal data analysis.

3.2 Data Acquisition

According to the research purpose of this paper and the proposed research method, to more comprehensively and accurately obtain the research content and research trend of the blockchain articles involved in the e-government fields at home and abroad. Decided to obtain Chinese and foreign literature from the CNKI (CNKI) and Web Of Science (WOS) databases as the analyzed data sets.

Acquisition of Chinese Literature. The acquisition and processing process of Chinese literature is as follows: advanced search in CNKI, search conditions are condition 1: full text = blockchain and theme = e-government, database: core journal and CSSCI journals, time limit, 134 papers; condition 2: theme = blockchain and full text = e-government, database: core journal and CSSCI journals, time limit, 55 papers. The retrieved information of the articles was manually screened twice, and after removing the articles with poor academic notice, meeting notices, meeting minutes, news reports, and the research purpose of condition 2 and condition 1, a total of 184 articles met the requirements. The title information of these 184 articles was exported as a database for the analysis of Chinese articles.

Acquisition of Foreign Literature. The foreign article chose WOS as a data source, because of the foreign words and Chinese subtle differences, and combined with the meaning of different words, so the foreign literature search conditions as shown in Table 1, related search results are according to the same standards with the Chinese literature after secondary manual confirmation, a total of 724 meet the requirements of the literature.

Table 1. Conditions for foreign literature.

Search condition	Conditions constitute	Results
#5	#4 AND #3 AND #2 AND #1	38
#4	TS = (blockchain) and TS = (e govern*)	346
#3	TS = (blockchain) and TS = (digit* govern*)	339
#2	TS = (blockchain) and TS = (smart govern*)	346
#1	TS = (blockchain) and TS = (digital govern*)	300

4 Data Analysis and Results

4.1 Descriptive Statistical Analysis

Title information of 784 articles obtained from CNKI and 724 articles obtained from the WOS database was processed and counted by annual and source journals. The results are shown below (see Fig. 1 Table 2 and Table 3).

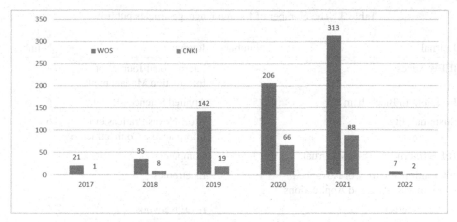

Fig. 1. Statistical chart of the number of published articles.

Table 2. The number of articles published in Chinese by sub-journal.

Journal	Number	Journal	Number
E-government	**21**	Theory and Reform	3
Chinese Public Administration	**12**	Theory Monthly Magazine	3
Administration Reform	**9**	Taxation Research	3
Leadership Science	**8**	The World of Survey and Research	2
Administrative Tribune	**8**	Comparative Economic & Social Systems	2
Governance Studies	6	Theoretical Investigation	2
Probe	5	Renmin Luntan · Xueshu Qianyan	2
People's Tribune	4	The Journal of Shanghai Administration Institute	2
Reform	3	The Journal of Tianjin Administration Institute	2
Guizhou Social Science	3	Journal of Information Resources Management	2
International Taxation	3	Study and Practice	2
Hubei Social Science	3	Journal of the Party School of Tianjin Committee of the CPC	2

The application research of blockchain in the field of e-government shows an increasing trend year by year, and the number of foreign research is more than that of Chinese research, but the growth rate of Chinese research is faster than that of foreign research (see Fig. 1). From 2017 to 2022,120 articles were published in the foreign sector and about 30 articles in the Chinese field. By average value, foreign countries grew in 2017

Table 3. The Number of foreign language articles published.

Journal	Number	Journal	Number
IEEE Access	66	International Journal of Information Management	7
Frontiers in Blockchain	25	Applied Sciences-Basel	6
Sustainability	22	AtoZ-Novas Praticas em Informacao e Conhecimento	6
IEEE Internet of Things Journal	13	Computers	6
International Journal of Advanced Computer Science and Applications	10	Electronics	6
Future Internet	9	IEEE Network	6
Technological Forecasting and Social Change	8	Information Technology for Development	6
Computer Law & Security Review	7	International Journal of Production Research	6
Information Polity	7	Journal of Cleaner Production	6
Information Processing & Management	7	Journal of Medical Internet Research	5

and 2018, laying the technical foundation for subsequent research, and the literature volume has increased rapidly since 2019; from 2017 to 2019, and since 2020, the growth trend is lower than that in foreign countries. On the one hand, is the closer and closer related scholars at home and abroad, draw lessons from foreign-related disciplines or technical methods to solve the problem of the Chinese situation, on the other hand, is the country of the government itself digital transformation and construction needs also prompted Chinese relevant scholars to increase research size of Chinese problem, produced a lot of high-level results.

The journals mentioned in Table 2 only involve journals with several publications more than 2. Among the 95 journals, 24 journals had more than 2, and the remaining 71 journals published one related literature. The sources of journals in Table 2 are ranked in descending order of the number of publications. The largest number of posts is *E-government*, with a total of 21 articles published, and the top five are *E-government*, *Chinese Public Administration*, *Administration Reform*, *Leadership Science,* and *Administrative Tribune*. In addition to the *Guizhou Social Science* (3) and, *Hubei Social Science* (3) for comprehensive social science journals, most of the remaining journals are management journals, management, especially public management for e-government application block chain more attention, also shows that public management discipline for new information technology application in traditional fields also maintained high attention.

The number of foreign journals involved in Table 3 ranks the top 20 journals in descending order of the number of articles, accounting for about 10% of all 366 journals, but the number of published articles accounts for about one-third of the total number of articles. Among the foreign journals, *IEEE ACCESS* has the largest number of published articles, with a total of 66 related articles published, significantly more than the number of articles published in the *Administrative Tribune*. At the same time, the style of the journal is also inclined to the technical field, and most of the journals in Table 3 are inclined to data, big data, computer analysis, and related technologies, and there are fewer journals in the management field. It fully shows that foreign articles on blockchain technology in the field of e-government are more inclined to conduct research from the related technical fields, which presents different characteristics from the Chinese related research.

4.2 Research Hotspot Analysis

Using Citespace5.8R3 software, the obtained journal-title information was analyzed, the node type was selected as "keyword", and the research hotspots of Chinese and foreign journals are shown in Fig. 2 and Fig. 3 respectively.

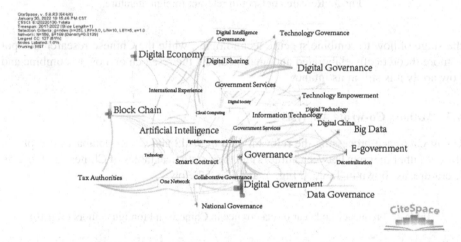

Fig. 2. Research hotspot of the Chinese-related literature.

Each node in the figure above represents a keyword, the closer the connection between the nodes, the closer the connection between the two keywords; the node size represents the frequency of the keyword in the whole research field; the darker the color in the node, the earlier the keyword of the node appears. Comparing Fig. 2 and Fig. 3, it can be seen that in terms of density, the density of keywords in Fig. 3 is significantly higher than that of keywords in Fig. 2, which shows that foreign research on applying blockchain and other technologies in the field of e-government has become a system than that in China. Moreover, the size of the nodes in Fig. 2 is larger than that in Fig. 2, which shows that in the relevant research hotspots, foreign research should be deeper than in China. Moreover, a considerable part of the hot spots in the relevant foreign literature involves the specific technologies of blockchain, such as smart contracts; blockchain application; ledger technology; communication technology and blockchain platforms, etc. It shows that the foreign research on blockchain in e-government has gone deep into

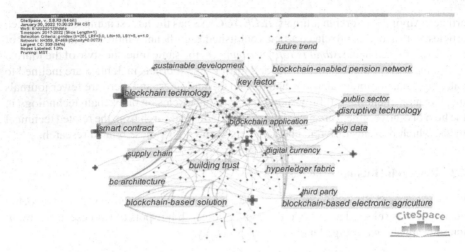

Fig. 3. Research hotspot in relevant foreign literature.

the stage of how to combine specific technologies, while the Chinese research hotspot is more theoretically elaborated and analyzed, and the research on how to combine and how apply it is still in its infancy.

4.3   Authors Co-wrote Analysis

Using Citespace processing the relevant data in WOS and CNKI databases can obtain the co-author diagram between authors and their statistical tables of Chinese and foreign literature, as shown in Table 4, Fig. 4, and Fig. 5 below.

Table 4. Frequency and year of occurrence in Chinese and foreign authors (Top 10)

Foreign author	Frequency	First year	Chinese author	Frequency	First year
Khaled Salah	14	2018	Huang Huang	4	2020
Raja Jayaraman	9	2019	Tian Tian Hou	3	2020
Junaid Arshad	6	2018	Qi Liu	3	2020
Samer Hassan	5	2021	Tianguang Meng	3	2020
Neeraj Kumar	5	2020	Wei-ling Wang	3	2019
Ibrar Yaqoob	4	2020	Wen-zhao Li	2	2020
Mazin Debe	4	2020	Xuexiang Qi	2	2018
Sudeep Tanwar	3	2021	Haijun Cao	2	2021
Dharmender Singh Kushwaha	3	2021	Yalin Kuang	2	2021
Amrendra Singh Yadav	3	2021	Minjuan Jiang	2	2021

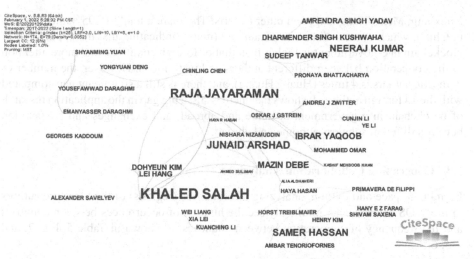

Fig. 4. Foreign co-wrote authors' relationship diagram.

In Fig. 4, each node represents an author, the size of the node represents the size that the author can play in the field, and the thickness of the connection between the nodes represents the closeness between the two authors. As can be seen from the figure above, Khaled Salah appeared 14 times, as the most frequent author; the least occurrence was 1 and 130 authors, accounting for 74.7% of all authors. However, the connection between the authors is relatively sparse, indicating that there has not been a system and network for the application of blockchain technology in the field of e-government, and there is a deep research potential to be explored.

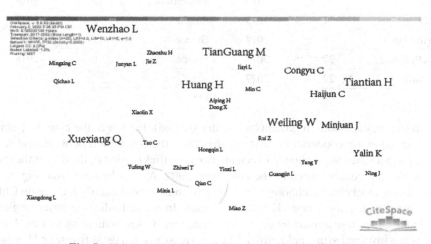

Fig. 5. Chinese co-wrote the authors' relationship diagram.

As can be seen from Fig. 5, the co-wrote authors' relationship with domestic authors is relatively scattered, with the main authors including Huang Huang, Xu Xiaolin, Qi

Xuexiang, Meng Tianguang, and other experts. There are a total of 105 authors (units) in China, which is more than foreign authors (units), indicating that the application of blockchain in e-government is higher than that of foreign countries, and more attention to the cooperation between different authors and institutions. However, the number of domestic authors is 4 times (Huang Huang), and there is still a significant gap compared with the 14 foreign authors. It shows that there is still a big gap in the application research of blockchain in e-government at home and abroad, and exchanges and cooperation between different scholars at home and abroad.

4.4 Geographic Collaboration Analysis

Using Citespace and Python, analyzing the countries (regions) of the literature authors in the WOS database can intuitively see the number of occurrences between countries and the frequency of cooperation between countries, as shown in Table 5, Fig. 7, and Fig. 6 below.

Table 5. Statistics table of occurrence frequency of countries (regions)

National (regional)	Frequency	First year	National (regional)	Frequency	First year
USA	92	2017	Germany	26	2017
Peoples R China	66	2017	Saudi Arabia	23	2020
England	48	2017	Taiwan	21	2019
India	45	2018	U Arab Emirates	21	2018
Australia	37	2017	Pakistan	20	2018
Spain	31	2019	Switzerland	13	2018
Italy	31	2018	Russia	13	2017
Netherlands	28	2017	Greece	12	2019
South Korea	27	2019	France	10	2018
Canada	27	2017			

In Fig. 6, each node represents a country (region), the larger the country (region) plays in the entire cooperation network; the closer the connection between nodes, the more frequent the cooperation between the two countries (regions); the darker the color, the earlier the country (region) the node represents. As can be seen from Fig. 6, the research on blockchain technology in the e-government field mainly focuses on China, the United States, the United Kingdom, Canada, India, and other countries (regions), while the nodes represented by the United States are darker, indicating that the United States was involved in this field earlier. The main reason is that the software and hardware construction and ideas involved in e-government all started in the United States, and a considerable number of enterprises such as Internet facilities and digital facilities are in the United States, objectively leading to the stronger strength in the field of e-government construction compared with other countries. Although China started late, it represents

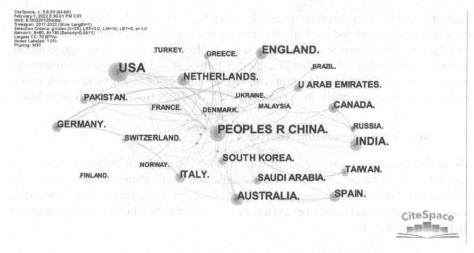

Fig. 6. National (regional) cooperation diagram.

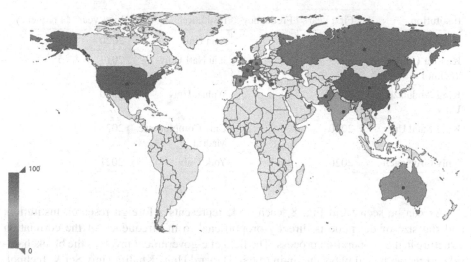

Fig. 7. Country (region) occurrence frequency diagram (greater than or equal to 10). (Color figure online)

large nodes, which shows that China is developing blockchain in e-government; while the nodes represented by China and other countries are closely connected, which shows that China pays more attention to cooperation with researchers from different countries and regions, strengthening international exchanges and promoting common development between different countries and regions.

In the map of Fig. 7, the values increase from blue to red (red dots are only used for national and regional markers and do not represent the capital city). Listed in Fig. 7 are countries and regions arranged in descending order of countries (regions) with more than or equal to 10 occurrence times. As it can be seen from the figure, the areas of the Chinese mainland and the United States are marked red, indicating that the Chinese mainland and the United States have a position in blockchain research in e-government; second, countries in the UK, Russia and other European regions are more concentrated on blockchain research in e-government, but the number of scientific research results produced is relatively small, so the color of these countries (regions) tends to be blue.

4.5 Institutional Cooperation Analysis

Using Citespace5.8R3 software, analyzed the author institutions in the literature description information obtained in the WOS database and CNKI database, and counted the number of related structures and their first occurrence year, the cooperative relationship diagram and statistical results between the institutions can be obtained below, as shown in Table 6 and Fig. 8.

Table 6. Institution appearance frequency statistics (Top 10 digits)

Institution	First year	Frequency	Institution	First year	Frequency
Harvard Univ	2018	10	Asia Univ	2020	5
Khalifa Univ Sci & Technol	2019	7	Jeju Natl Univ	2019	5
King Abdulaziz Univ	2020	7	Wuhan Univ	2020	5
King Saud Univ	2020	6	Univ Complutense Madrid	2021	4
Univ Groningen	2020	5	York Univ	2021	4

As can be seen from Fig. 8, each node represents a foreign research institution, and the size of the node is directly proportional to the frequency of the correlation structure in the cooperation process. The field of e-government involves the blockchain-related research, and plays the main role in Harvard Univ, Khalifa Univ Sci & Technol, King Abdulaziz Univ, and other foreign well-known foreign universities, for how e-government construction, development, and transformation of blockchain technology, foreign has begun to explore, and the related research presents the tendency of hot spots. And domestic and foreign cooperation only more colleges and universities are Wuhan Univ (Wuhan University), in the field of e-government involving the blockchain research in the first cooperation in 2020, after a total of five articles, although began cooperation time is short, but still located in the top 10, related universities and research institutes in China has great scientific research potential in this category.

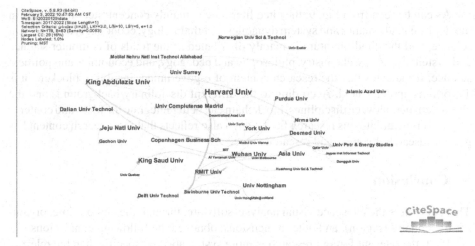

Fig. 8. Cooperative relationship diagram of relevant foreign institutions.

4.6 Journal Overlay Analysis

In cite space 5.7, the overlay analysis of journals is performed using the "JCR Journal Map" (Fig. 9). The left part represents the cited journals and the right part represents the cited journals, which are categorized according to the categories provided by cite space 5.7, respectively, and are represented by different colors. The number of lines between them indicates the strength of the cross-citation relationship between the journals of that type, while the vertical axis of the ellipse in the figure represents the number of papers in the journal and the horizontal axis represents the number of authors of the journal papers.

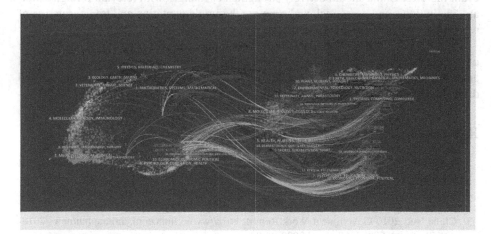

Fig. 9. Journal overlay analysis.

As can be seen from Fig. 9, the cited literature is mainly concentrated in journals in the fields of mathematics and system dynamics, ophthalmology, economics, and political science, and the cited literature is mainly distributed in the fields of computer science and system dynamics, chemistry, philosophy and pedagogy, and economics and political science. It indicates that the research content of e-government involving blockchain is a cross-disciplinary field. According to the different disciplinary backgrounds and the characteristics between disciplines, blockchain can better integrate the ideas and contents of e-government into this research field, which also reflects that the research content has greater research potential and research value.

5 Conclusion

This study uses the citespace visual analysis software, through the author, time, organization, country (region), and other dimensions, obtained the following conclusions:

First, the relevant foreign research is more systematic and specific than the relevant domestic research. The research of relevant foreign scholars and institutions is more focused on how to apply specific technologies in the construction of e-government, and how to better combine related technologies with the concept of e-government construction. There is less related research on e-government theory and more attention to the related research on e-government theory.

Second, although the domestic relevant research started late, it makes rapid progress, which can better learn from the relevant foreign technologies and combine the specific practice situation of China to understand how to better combine it with the domestic situation. While summarizing the foreign advanced experience, it can promote the domestic relevant research to avoid detours.

Third, the application research of blockchain in the construction of e-government requires both the exploration of relevant technologies and the innovative research of relevant theories. China should actively strengthen exchanges with relevant foreign scholars, institutions, and personnel, and promote the implementation and transformation of relevant domestic experience and theories.

The main deficiency of this paper is that the short occurrence time of relevant research objects and the research data is not very rich. A more comprehensive research and analysis will be conducted by combining the content of other relevant databases and data visualization and analysis tools.

References

1. Yutao, H.: Local government data collaborative governance from the perspective of digital transformation. Learn. Pract. **6**, 69–77 (2021)
2. Shuijin, L., Xinfeng, Z.: The evolution logic and future trend of the reform of "delegating power, delegating power and serving." China Admin. **4**, 15–17 (2019)
3. China Net: 2016 Government Work Report. http://www.china.com.cn/lianghui/news/2018-02/27/content_50484682.shtml.2022/02/02
4. Sohu.com: https://www.sohu.com/a/224324631_711789.2022/02/02
5. Xinhuanet clien: http://www.xinhuanet.com/video/sjxw/2019-10/31/c_1210335880.htm. 2022/02/02

6. Yinxi, L., Miao, Z.: Public value creation: a new perspective of e-government governance research: theoretical framework and path selection. E-Government **2**, 65–74 (2022)
7. Yun, Z., Minjuan, J., Weiling, W.: Theoretical explanation and operational mechanism of China's digital transformation. E-Government **6**, 67–84 (2021)
8. Ying, Z.: The practice and thinking of the social participation of the elderly under the blockchain technology. Chongqing Soc. Sci. **12**, 120–131 (2021)
9. Chuangchuang, D., Haijing, L., Xueying, Y., Xiaobing, G., Zhonghua, L., Beibei, N.: A review of blockchain technology research. Comput. Sci. **48**, 500–508 (2021)
10. Guobin, Z.: Transformation of British e-government: value concept, technical tools and institutional guarantee. Admin. Forum **28**, 136–143 (2021)
11. Da, Y., Li, L.: "Green Linkage": a strategic perspective of Japan's e-government transformation. China Admin. **11**, 138–144 (2021)
12. Shuigen, H., Jingnan, Y.: Exploration and experience reference of e-government construction in developed countries. Exploration **1**, 77–86 (2021)
13. Shuiqiong, Y., Yinzhi, Q.: Practical research and experience reference of e-government construction in the United States. Gov. Res. **35**, 60–65 (2019)
14. Yasong, Z.: Construction of e-government: current situation, dilemma and countermeasures——taking "Guizhou on the Cloud" government affairs data platform as an example. J. Yunnan Univ. Admin. **21**, 120–126 (2019)
15. Huang, D., Xiaocheng, M.: The governance logic and innovative approach of data elements driving the development of the digital economy: taking the construction of a comprehensive pilot area for big data in Guizhou Province as an example. Theory Reform **6**, 128–139 (2021)
16. Weiling, W.: Dilemma of e-government and cracking path. Informatization Constr. **1**, 57–60 (2021)
17. Shuchun, L.: Promoting the modernization of government governance with e-government construction. Audit Obs. **12**, 62–66 (2020)
18. Yongsheng, C., Muhui, W., Huanning, S., Qianqian, Y.: Document filing and management based on internet government service platform: governance view. Arch. Res. **6**, 4–11 (2019)
19. Tao, C., Ahlong, G.: Research on optimizing the business environment driven by the digital transformation of the government—taking Dongguan as an example. E-Government **3**, 83–93 (2021)
20. Kaiye, S., Yaqian, X., Tianxiang, C.: Innovative development, internal mechanism and path optimization of governmental data assets: taking the Weifang model of governmental data asset management as an example. E-Government **1**, 14–26 (2022)
21. Sotoudehnia, M.: 'Making blockchain real': regulatory discourses of blockchains as a smart, civic service. Reg. Stud. **2**, 1–11 (2021)
22. Oliveira, T.A., Oliver, M., Ramalhinho, H.: Challenges for connecting citizens and smart cities: ICT, e-governance and blockchain. Sustainability **12**, 1–21 (2020)
23. Geneiatakis, D., Soupionis, Y., Steri, G.: Blockchain performance analysis for supporting cross-border e-government services. IEEE Trans. Eng. Manage. **99**, 1–13 (2020)
24. Jon, T.: Decarbonizing Bitcoin: law and policy choices for reducing the energy consumption of blockchain technologies and digital currencies. Energy Res. Soc. **44**, 399–410 (2021)
25. Hassija, V., Chamola, V., Krishna, D.N.G., Kumar, N., Guizani, M.: A blockchain and edge computing-based secure framework for government tender allocation. IEEE Internet Things J. **10**, 1–10 (2020)
26. Junping, Q., Fangfang, W.: Visual analysis of the hot spots and frontiers of library and information science research in the past five years: a quantitative study based on 13 high-influence foreign language source periodicals. Chin. Libr. J. **37**, 51–60 (2011)
27. Yue, C., Chaomei, C., Zeyuan, L., Zhigang, H., Xianwen, W.: The methodological function of CiteSpace knowledge graph. Sci. Res. **33**, 242–253 (2015)

Research on Medical Question Answering System Based on Joint Model

Yong Li[1]($\boxtimes$), Yunyu Bai[1], and Hai Jia[2]

[1] College of Computer Science and Engineering, Northwest Normal University,
Lanzhou 730070, China
15735659344@163.com

[2] Department of Pharmacy, Gansu Provincial Hospital, Lanzhou 730000, China

Abstract. With the global outbreak of virulent infectious diseases such as COVID-19, the lack of medical resources has become a serious social problem. More and more online users who encounter physical discomfort will first choose to look up the relevant symptoms on the Internet. Some online platforms have been able to understand the symptoms entered by users and provide auxiliary diagnosis suggestions. However, the professionalism and accuracy of online health and medical Question Answering (QA) systems are very insufficient. How to obtain and utilize massive medical symptom data from multiple data sources such as the Internet, medical symptom libraries and medical professional electronic books has become a difficult problem. The development of big data, artificial intelligence, and especially knowledge graph technology has provided ideas and methods to solve this problem. In this paper, a medical knowledge graph NWNU-KG is constructed on the basis of multi-source data, and the BiLSTM-CRF-CNN-Dict (BCCD) joint model is used for entity recognition and relationship extraction of user-asked questions to implement a healthcare knowledge QA system. Numerous experiments have found that the joint model BCCD proposed in this paper has a higher accuracy rate compared with the best available models, and can filter the answers to questions and return them to users in multi-source, heterogeneous and massive healthcare data, which has some practical value.

Keywords: Knowledge graph · Question answer system · Natural language processing · Entity recognition · Entity relationship extraction

1 Introduction

In recent years, with the outbreak of global infectious diseases such as Ebola, Middle East Respiratory Syndrome (MERS), and COVID-19, insufficient medical resources have become a serious social problem. The willingness to search for information online is more urgent than ever, and search engines and intelligent question answering have become the two main ways for people to obtain medical information. Most existing search engines are based on character matching technology and lack the ability to mine knowledge from a semantic perspective,

X. Meng et al. (Eds.): BDSC 2022, CCIS 1640, pp. 374–388, 2022.
https://doi.org/10.1007/978-981-19-7532-5_24

resulting in high redundancy and poor accuracy of search results, requiring users to filter out the desired results from a massive list of search results. Compared with search engines, intelligent question answering is closer to the actual needs of users. It can analyze the questions raised by users from the semantic level, accurately locate the user's intention, and directly return the desired answer to the user. Although fruitful research findings have been achieved in the field of intelligent question answering, Chinese healthcare automatic QA technology is still under investigation. Most of the existing mature online QA systems are built based on rules, and most of them are for English and open fields, which cannot be applied to the Chinese healthcare field.

Due to the rapid advancement of knowledge graph technology, humans have entered the "Web 3.0" era of knowledge interconnection [1]. Knowledge graph-based healthcare QA systems can quickly respond to questions asked by patients and give accurate and effective answers [2], which is expected to solve the shortcomings of intelligent QA in the Chinese healthcare field. In recent years, several Chinese medical knowledge graphs have been built in academia and industry, such as Ali Health's "Medical Knowledge Deer", Sogou's medical knowledge graph APGC. However, the application of the existing Chinese healthcare knowledge graph in the field of intelligent QA is still under investigation, and there are several problems such as low data volume, low efficiency, and poor scalability.

To address these problems, this paper extracts data from multiple data sources such as the Internet, medical symptom libraries, and medical professional electronic books to construct a more comprehensive healthcare knowledge graph; combines deep learning and lexical methods to improve the effectiveness of medical named entity recognition; and combines deep learning and template-based methods to improve the accuracy of entity and relationship extraction. Based on the constructed health and medical knowledge graph, a more accurate healthcare intelligent QA system is constructed by using the BILSTM-CRF-CNN-Dict joint model for entity recognition and relationship extraction of the questions asked by users.

The main contributions of this paper are summarized as follows.

(1) We have constructed a more comprehensive health and medical knowledge graph NWNU-KG. Data are extracted from multiple data sources such as vertical medical sites, medical symptom libraries, and medical professional e-books to construct a knowledge graph supporting the QA system, which contains 7 types totaling 44,000 entities and 10 types totaling 300,000 relations.

(2) We propose the intelligent medical question answering joint model BCCD (BILSTM-CRF-CNN-Dict). The model consists of an embedding layer, a bidirectional LSTM layer, and a CRF layer. If the BILSTM-CRF model fails to recognize, the dictionary is used for secondary entity recognition.

(3) We propose a questioning intent recognition method that combines textCNN and rules. For user input questions, first, use the textCNN model to classify the question. If successful recognition, the answer is matched into the knowledge graph database; if unsuccessful recognition, the user intention is

matched by invoking the rule set to obtain the user intention for secondary intention resolution.

(4) Experiments show that the proposed model is better than the known optimal benchmark model in terms of accuracy, recall and F1 value, and optimizes the user intention recognition model, which can effectively improve the accuracy of the medical question answering system.

2   Related Work

2.1   Progress in Medical Knowledge Graph Research

Generally, knowledge graph is a powerful tool for knowledge representation and management. The general knowledge graph is focused on a broad field and includes a substantial body of practical common sense knowledge. A knowledge base that is focused on a particular field and made up of expert data in that field is referred to as a domain knowledge graph, also known as an industry knowledge graph or vertical knowledge grap.

Currently, most knowledge graphs are constructed using the bottom-up approach [2]. Reference [3] proposed a primary liver cancer knowledge question answering system based on a knowledge graph and selected the Neo4j database as the storage system of the knowledge graph. Reference [4] creates a medical graph using the Neo4j graph database that takes into account the connections between hospital departments, illnesses, and symptoms and offers medical advice based on the graph of knowledge. In this paper, we combine the existing research work and consider the problem of retrieval efficiency of the knowledge graph-based healthcare question and answer system, and use a graph database (Neo4j) with a triadic representation to store entities and relationships.

2.2   Question Answering System Based on Knowledge Graph

The main implementation methods of knowledge graph-based QA systems can be divided into three categories. The first category is based on semantic parsing, which mainly parses the semantics of natural language interrogative sentences so as to transform the question asked into a logical expression that can be understood by the knowledge base, and then infer the answer from it. Although some common semantic parsing models are more effective in the application of QA systems, they also have disadvantages, such as the large labor cost required for tagging data and poor generalization ability [5].

The second category is based on information extraction [6], which is similar to the process of humans answering a question by first detecting the main entities in the question, then querying the candidate paths connecting these main entities from the knowledge base, calculating the semantic similarity between all candidate paths and the question sentence, and finally returning the path with the highest similarity to generate the answer [5]. However, as compared to the conventional NLP method, this method's accuracy is somewhat subpar.

The third category consists of vector-based modeling techniques, which map natural language problems and entities from the knowledge base to the same vector space and compare the similarities of the vectors to arrive at solutions. This method is a straightforward data-driven modeling approach that doesn't require much pre-processing of the data [7]. However, this method ignores the impact of context, which can influence the accuracy of retrieval results, and instead uses keywords to represent knowledge in isolation.

2.3 Medical Named Entity Identification

The main purpose of biomedical named entity recognition (BioNER) [8] is to identify entities with specific meanings in medical texts and to annotate these entities. At present, there are three methods for named entity recognition in medical texts.

Reference [9] used two medical dictionaries, CHV and SNOMED-CT, to identify medical information in electronic medical records, and obtained good experimental results. However, due to the limited size of the dictionary and the need to update it in time, only using the dictionary often cannot achieve better results. Luo [10] et al. applied both CNNs and RNNs to the i2b2-VA challenge dataset for entity recognition and showed that CNNs and RNNs with word embedding features can achieve better performance. However, CNN in the NLP tasks pooling layer will discard the relative position relationship retained by the convolutional layer to a certain extent, which leads to a certain degree of information loss; RNN, on the other hand, with the continuous accumulation of time series, the gradient will show exponential decay, making it difficult to record historical information at longer distances, so the performance is constrained.

Currently, BiLSTM-CRF is the most dominant deep learning model for entity extraction in the medical domain [1]. Referenc [11] experimentally compared the entity extraction performance of the BiLSTM-CRF model and other machine learning models in the medical domain, and the results showed that BiLSTM-CRF is more effective in improving the entity recognition accuracy. Combined with existing research work, this paper uses a combination of dictionary and deep learning approaches for entity recognition of user interrogative sentences.

2.4 Medical Relationship Extraction

After identifying the entities in the user's online question statements, the extracted entity relationships and attributes must be mapped into the knowledge graph. At present, the main methods of relation extraction include rule-based, traditional machine learning, and deep learning-based methods [12].

Chun Wen et al. [13] proposed an extended association rule approach for extracting Chinese noncategorical relations, using ordinary association rules to extract noncategorical relation concept pairs, and then extracting the corresponding noncategorical relation names by linguistic rules. However, the rule-based relation extraction method has disadvantages such as poor portability, high cost of manual annotation, and low recall rate. Ning Shangming et al. [14]

computed attention weights for each channel of text features and achieved good results in the extraction of relationships of electronic medical record entities. However, the method of deep learning is less scalable and portable, and the model performance still needs to be improved.

Convolutional neural network textCNN is a commonly used model in text relationship extraction to obtain key information in sentences and enable better access to local relevance [15]. Previous studies have shown that textCNN has better performance in the task of medical entity relation extraction [16]. In this paper, we focus on entity-relationship extraction of natural interrogative sentences of users' short texts. This paper combines textCNN model and rule-based approach for entity relationship extraction and achieves better results.

3   Construction of Medical Knowledge Graph NWNU-KG

3.1   Medical Data Acquisition

The Chinese medical knowledge graph data constructed in this paper comes from multiple data sources, mainly including structured data from medical symptom libraries, semi-structured data from medical websites (such as seeking medical advice), and unstructured data from medical professional literature. The specific data acquisition process is shown in Fig. 1.

3.2   Classification and Storage of Medical Knowledge

In this paper, a more comprehensive healthcare knowledge graph NWNU-KG is constructed, which contains 7 types of consultation items, departments, diseases, drugs, food, symptoms, and drugs on sale, with a total of 44,000 entities, as shown in Table 1; and 10 relationship types, with a total of over 300,000, as shown in Table 2.

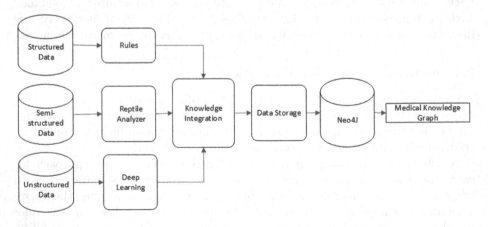

Fig. 1. Flowchart for building medical knowledge graph.

Table 1. Entity type and quantity.

Entity type	Number of entities	Example
Disease	8785	Gastric asthma
Check	3350	Electronic dermatoscope
Department	53	Gynecology
Symptom	5988	Fever
Drug	3727	Liuwei Zhuanggu granules
Producer	16998	Tai Chi Sheng Li Xiong Wan
Food	4863	Ginkgo chicken soup

Table 2. Entity relationship types and examples.

Relationship type	Quantity	Example
Common-drug	14599	Influenza, commonly used, ibuprofen
Do-eat	22240	Strong spondylitis, suitable for eating, chicken liver
Not-eat	22251	Pneumonia in children, avoid eating, greasy food
Belong-to	8842	Stomatology, belonging to, ENT department
Drugs-of	17323	Ibuprofen, on sale, ibuprofen tablets
Disease-check	39452	Cerebral infarction, required tests, fibrinogen
Drug-recommand	59477	Cough, recommended medication, Nakachos
Eat-recommand	40235	Mentally retarded, suitable to eat, peanut kernels
Has-symptom	5898	Foot crumples, symptoms, foot dampness
Accomptom-with	12033	Children's cough, complications, whooping cough

The visualization of local entities and relationships in the constructed healthcare knowledge graph NWNU-KG is shown in Fig. 2. Taking cerebrovascular disease as an example, there are 6 entities directly related to cerebrovascular disease, in which green are foods to be eaten and avoided for cerebrovascular disease, blue are corresponding drugs, brown are items to be examined, purple are corresponding symptoms, orange is complications, and red are corresponding departments.

4 Construction of Question Answering System Based on BCCD Model

This paper proposes an online question-answering system based on the BCCD model of the medical knowledge graph using the constructed Chinese medical knowledge graph. The main framework is shown in Fig. 3.

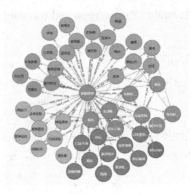

Fig. 2. Example of knowledge graph. (Color figure online)

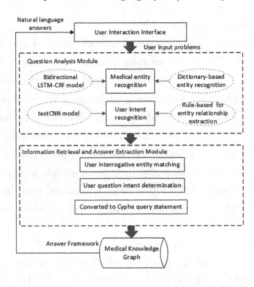

Fig. 3. Question answering system framework based on the medical knowledge graph.

4.1   Question Analysis Module

In this paper, the user's short text natural language questions are first identified based on the deep learning model. If there is unrecognized text, the AC multi-pattern matching algorithm [17] is immediately invoked to extract entities such as disease symptoms in the dictionary.

User Question Preprocessing. Since the research data in this paper involves the medical field and there are more medical proper nouns, the main tool used for word separation in this paper is pkuseg's word separation toolkit on the medical field [18], and the "stop words list of Harbin Institute of Technology" [19] is used as the basis for deactivating words.

BiLSTM-CRF Model. The BiLSTM-CRF model mainly consists of an Embedding layer, a bi-directional LSTM layer, and a CRF layer. The key technologies of the model include the CBOW word vector training model, BiLSTM model, and BiLSTM joint learning model.

CBOW Word Vector Training Model. Among all vectorization tools, One-Hot encoding is the simplest word vector representation, but the word list is too large leading to too large vector dimension, and the individual words are isolated from each other, which cannot represent the semantic information among words. Usually, the CBOW model is chosen for word embedding when the training sample data is small, so this paper chooses the CBOW word vector model for vectorizing medical text.

BiLSTM-CRF Medical Entity Recognition Model. LSTM can solve the problem of gradient disappearance in traditional RNN, and BiLSTM is an improvement of LSTM, which can use both forward sequence information and reverse sequence information in named entity recognition tasks. In this paper, a CRF layer is added after BiLSTM, and the features obtained by BiLSTM using word information and position information are input to the CRF layer for label prediction. The frame structure of the BiLSTM-CRF model is shown in Fig. 4.

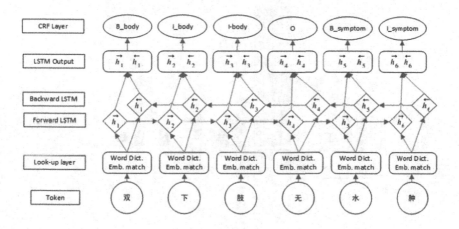

Fig. 4. Schematic diagram of the framework structure of the BiLSTM-CRF model.

Dictionary-Based Medical Entity Recognition. Most domain-limited automated QA systems retrieve only from the domain knowledge base, and cannot answer the questions asked once no candidate question is retrieved or no predefined pattern is matched [20]. In this paper, the deep learning method and the dictionary-based medical entity recognition method are integrated, and when the deep learning method cannot recognize an entity, then the system automatically enters the dictionary for matching and returns the correctly recognized entity if the matching is successful, and prompts the user to change a term to re-recognize it if it cannot be recognized.

Dictionary-based medical entity recognition usually relies on a terminology dictionary and uses a matching algorithm for medical entity recognition. The size and quality of the dictionary play a key role in the task of dictionary-based medical entity recognition. Therefore, in this paper, we use the DomainWords-Dict [21] dictionary in the field of Chinese medicine and medical science, which contains 549008 medical-related words.

User Intent Recognition Model

textCNN Short Textual Relationship Extraction Model. The textCNN model uses the convolutional neural network to extract the relationship of the text, uses the textCNN network to perform semantic analysis on the questions asked by the user, and uses the medical entities and semantic relations to achieve relationship extraction. The network structure of the textCNN model is shown in Fig. 5.

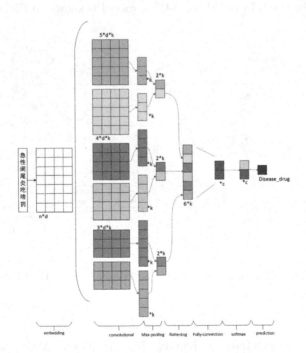

Fig. 5. textCNN intent recognition model.

Rule-Based Entity Relationship Extraction. Since the questions asked by users for personal diseases are relatively small in the field of medical expertise, when the textCNN model cannot recognize the user's intention, this paper designs a rule-based matching method for secondary intention recognition. Specifically, the user's query is first classified and the corresponding template is constructed, and then the AC algorithm is used for multi-pattern string matching.

4.2   Information Retrieval and Answer Extraction Module

User Question Entity Matching. Through entity recognition and question intent recognition, entities can be obtained from the user's question statements and the user's question type can be identified. If the matching fails, the Jaccard similarity algorithm [22] is used to find similar words. Jaccard's calculation formula is as follows:

$$Jaccard(X,Y) = \frac{|X \cap Y|}{|X \cup Y|} = \frac{|X \cap Y|}{|X| + |Y| - |X \cap Y|} \tag{1}$$

Cosine similarity [23] measures how different two angles are from one another by taking the cosine of the angle that separates their two vectors in a vector space. The following is the cosine similarity formula:

$$Similarity = \cos(\theta) = \frac{\sum_{i=1}^{n} A_i B_i}{\sqrt{\sum_{i=1}^{n} A_i^2} \sqrt{\sum_{i=1}^{n} B_i^2}} \tag{2}$$

TF-IDF (term frequency-inverse document frequency) [24] method is a statistical method for determining the significance of a word for a document set or one of the documents in a corpus. The word frequency (TF) indicates how often a word appears in the text and is given by the following formula.

$$TF_{i,j} = \frac{n_{i,j}}{\sum_k n_{k,j}} \tag{3}$$

The Inverse Document Frequency (IDF) measures the prevalence of a keyword. The greater the IDF and the fewer documents containing the term, the better the term's ability to distinguish between categories. The IDF for a particular term is calculated as:

$$IDF_i = \log(\frac{|D|}{1 + |j : t_i \in d_j|}) \tag{4}$$

After calculating the TF and IDF values separately, multiply them together to get the TF-IDF values. The formula is as follows:

$$TF - IDF = TF \cdot IDF \tag{5}$$

User Question Answer Extraction. Converts the extracted entity categories and the specific entities involved into 'entity type': [entity], ... into a dictionary format. Finally, it is translated into the Cypher query language in neo4j to perform the query and send the results back to the user.

5   Experiment

5.1   Experiment Environment

The experimental environment of this paper is shown in Table 3. dummy

Table 3. The experimental environment of medical QA system.

	Parameter	Configure
Hardware environment	CPU	AMD Ryzen 5 5600H
	Total physical memory	16 GB
	Hard disk	512 GB
Software environment	Operating system	Windows 10
	Python	3.8.11

5.2   Experimental Results and Analysis

BILSTM-CRF-Dict Medical Entity Recognition Model. To verify the effectiveness of the proposed model in thin paper for medical entity recognition, a private dataset cEMR and the ChineseBLUE dataset [25] published by Alibaba Cognitive Intelligence and NLP team were used for validation experiments. The private data set cEMR comes from 15,000 electronic medical records provided by a tertiary hospital, 500 of which are randomly selected, and 70%of them are used as training data and 30% as test data. The model proposed in this paper is compared with three baseline algorithmic models for experiments, including the current common approaches in machine learning as well as deep learning.

Named entity recognition task is evaluated by using recall, precision, and F1 metrics. Each evaluation metric is calculated as follows:

$$precision = \frac{e}{k} \times 100\% \tag{6}$$

$$recall = \frac{e}{n} \times 100\% \tag{7}$$

$$F1 = \frac{2 \times precision \times recall}{precision + recall} \times 100\% \tag{8}$$

In formulas (7) and (8), e is the number of correctly identified entities, n is the total number of entities, and k is the number of identified entities. The experimental results are shown in Table 4.

The BILSTM-CRF-Dict model proposed in this paper has the best performance in terms of accuracy, recall, and F1 value, and has a better performance compared with the previous baseline model, and the model proposed in this paper has been improved in all three metrics.

Table 4. Experimental results of each model on public and private datasets.

Model	ChineseBLUE			cEMR		
	Precision	Recall	F1	Precision	Recall	F1
HMM	84.44%	70.45%	76.38%	82.43%	71.23%	76.42%
BILSTM	88.88%	70.48%	77.87%	87.65%	71.54%	78.78%
BILSTM-CRF	89.21%	74.77%	80.70%	88.19%	75.58%	81.40%
BILSTM-CRF-Dict	**90.29%**	**83.29%**	**86.42%**	**89.99%**	**84.67%**	**87.25%**

Relation Extraction Joint Model. 150 natural interrogatives were designed manually, corresponding to five types of questions in QA. The three basic evaluation metrics commonly used in the field of relationship extraction are: accuracy, recall, and F-value [26]. The experimental results are shown in Table 5.

Table 5. Results of ablation experiments for different problem classes.

Question	Rule-based			textCNN			Rule-based+textCNN		
	Precision	Recall	F1	Precision	Recall	F1	Precision	Recall	F1
Symptom	89.65%	78.35%	83.62%	82.55%	72.33%	77.10%	91.22%	80.12%	85.31%
Reason	85.13%	75.68%	80.13%	81.35%	74.35%	77.69%	89.35%	79.65%	84.22%
Diet	86.74%	77.58%	81.91%	75.69%	73.65%	74.65%	88.95%	78.99%	83.68%
Prevention	81.58%	77.46%	79.47%	74.33%	74.68%	74.51%	86.74%	80.15%	83.32%
Check	84.79%	76.35%	80.35%	77.64%	72.68%	75.08%	90.12%	79.68%	84.58%

The results show that the rule-based entity relationship extraction effect is better than the textCNN model, which is because the questions asked by users for the medical QA system are generally in a smaller range of medical domains, and the textCNN model cannot cover all the questions asked due to the insufficient training corpus. It is found that the relationship extraction effect is greatly improved by combining the rule-based approach with the textCNN model.

QA System Performance Evaluation. Based on the question and answer statements designed in the literature [27], this paper designs five types of questions to evaluate the system performance according to the question framework of "disease + category question words", and the accuracy rate is calculated as shown in formula (9).

$$A = \frac{t}{T} \tag{9}$$

A denotes the accuracy of the results returned in the test; t denotes the number of correct answers returned in each type of test; T denotes the total number of tests in each type of test (the value of T in this paper is 30).

The evaluation results in Table 6 show that among the five categories of questions designed in this paper, the symptom category has the best test results and the preventive category has the lowest test accuracy. The average response accuracy of the system is 88.0%. The accuracy of the automatic responses to the examination-type questions and the preventive questions was lower than the average accuracy of the system because there were more missing values in the data set for these two types of questions.

Table 6. Evaluation results on the private dataset NWNU-KG.

Question	Number of test questions	Number of correct answers	Accuracy rate
Symptom	30	29	96.7%
Reason	30	28	93.3%
Diet	30	26	86.7%
Prevention	30	24	80.0%
Check	30	25	83.0%
Total	150	132	88.0%

6   Conclusion

In this paper, based on multi-source medical data, a relatively complete medical knowledge graph NWNU-KG is constructed. Combining the deep learning and the dictionary entity recognition method, a medical entity recognition model - BILSTM-CRF-Dict is proposed. The accuracy, recall and the F1 metrics and other aspects have achieved the best known performance; the textCNN model and the rule-based method are combined to optimize the user intent recognition module in the question answering system and build a medical question answering system with high accuracy.

In the future, end-to-end learning methods will be applied to entity recognition and relation extraction to learn different contextual representations of entities and relations to improve the performance of medical question answering systems. In addition, the model proposed in this paper fails to fully exploit the advantages of intelligent reasoning with knowledge graphs, and conversation management, as well as vectorized analysis models, will be added in the future to improve the reasoning capability of the medical question answering system and its accuracy in multi-round conversations.

Acknowledgments. This research was partially supported by the grants from the Natural Science Foundation of China (No. 72161034, 61863032); Major scientific research projects of Northwest Normal University(NWNU-LKZD2021-06).

References

1. Hou, M., Wei, R., Lu, L.: A review of knowledge graph research and its application in medical field. Comput. Res. Dev. **55**(12), 2587–2599 (2018)
2. Tan, L., Haihong, E., Kuang, Z.: Key technologies and research progress of medical knowledge graph construction. Big Data **7**(4), 80–104 (2021)
3. Cao, M., Li, Q., Yang, Z.: Knowledge graph-based knowledge quiz system for primary liver cancer. Chin. J. Inf. **33**(06), 88–93 (2019)
4. Deng, W., Guo, P., Yang, J.: Medical entity extraction and knowledge graph construction. In: 2019 16th International Computer Conference on Wavelet Active Media Technology and Information Processing, pp. 41–44. IEEE (2019)
5. Xue, X., Jiang, J., Zhang, W., Huang, Y., Wu, X.: A Chinese knowledge base question answering system. In: Proceedings of the 30th ACM International Conference on Information & Knowledge Management, pp. 4813–4816. Association for Computing Machinery (2021)
6. Bao, J., Duan, N., Zhou, M., Zhao, T.: An information retrieval-based approach to table-based question answering. In: Huang, X., Jiang, J., Zhao, D., Feng, Y., Hong, Yu. (eds.) NLPCC 2017. LNCS (LNAI), vol. 10619, pp. 601–611. Springer, Cham (2018). https://doi.org/10.1007/978-3-319-73618-1_50
7. Wang, Q., Liu, J., Luo, Y., Wang, B., Lin, C.Y.: Knowledge base completion via coupled path ranking. In: Proceedings of the 54th Annual Meeting of the Association for Computational Linguistics, vol. 1, pp. 1308–1318. Association for Computational Linguistics (2016)
8. Wu, Z., Bai, K., Yang, L.: A review of electronic medical record text mining research. Comput. Res. Dev. **58**(03), 513–527 (2021)
9. Wu, S.T., et al.: Unified medical language system term occurrences in clinical notes: a large-scale corpus analysis. J. Am. Med. Inform. Assoc. **19**(e1), e149–e156 (2012)
10. Luo, L., Li, N., Li, S., Yang, Z., Lin, H.: DUTIR at the CCKS-2018 Task1: a neural network ensemble approach for Chinese clinical named entity recognition. In: Proceedings of the Evaluation Tasks at the China Conference on Knowledge Graph and Semantic Computing (CCKS-Tasks 2018), pp. 7–12. Springer (2018)
11. Jagannatha, A.N., Yu, H.: Structured prediction models for RNN based sequence labeling in clinical text. In: Proceedings of the 2016 Conference on Empirical Methods in Natural Language Processing, vol. 2016, p. 856. Association for Computational Linguistics (2016)
12. Li, D., Zhang, Y., Li, D.: A review of research on entity relationship extraction methods. Comput. Res. Dev. **57**(07), 1424–1448 (2020)
13. Wen, C., Shi, Z., Xin, Y.: Chinese nonclassified relation extraction based on extended association rules. Comput. Eng. **35**(24), 63–65 (2009)
14. Ning, S., Teng, F., Li, T.: Multi-channel self-attentive mechanism-based entity relationship extraction for electronic medical records. J. Comput. Sci. **43**(05), 916–929 (2020)
15. Zhu, X., Wang, J., Zhang, X.: YNU-HPCC at SemEval-2021 Task 6: combining ALBERT and Text-CNN for Persuasion detection in texts and images. In: Proceedings of the 15th International Workshop on Semantic Evaluation (SemEval-2021), pp. 1045–1050. Association for Computational Linguistics (2021)
16. De Angeli, K., et al.: Class imbalance in out-of-distribution datasets: improving the robustness of the TextCNN for the classification of rare cancer types. J. Biomed. Inform. **125**, 103957 (2022)

17. Wang, X., Pao, D.: Memory-based architecture for multicharacter Aho–Corasick string matching. IEEE Trans. Very Large Scale Integr. (VLSI) Syst. **26**(1), 143–154 (2018)
18. Luo, R., Xu, J., Zhang, Y., Ren, X., Sun, X.: PKUSEG: a toolkit for multi-domain Chinese word segmentation. arXiv preprint arXiv:1906.11455 (2019)
19. Stopwords Homepage: https://github.com/goto456/stopwords
20. Zhao, Y., Liu, D., Wan, C.: A review of retrieval-based automatic question and answer research. J. Comput. Sci. **44**(06), 1214–1232 (2021)
21. DomainWordsDict Homepage: https://github.com/liuhuanyong/DomainWords Dict
22. Li, X., Li, P.: Rejection sampling for weighted Jaccard similarity revisited. In: Proceedings of the AAAI Conference on Artificial Intelligence, vol. 35, No. 5, pp. 4197–4205 (2021)
23. Thongtan, T., Phienthrakul, T.: Sentiment classification using document embeddings trained with cosine similarity. In: Proceedings of the 57th Annual Meeting of the Association for Computational Linguistics: Student Research Workshop, pp. 407–414. Association for Computational Linguistics, Florence, Italy (2019)
24. Yahav, I., Shehory, O., Schwartz, D.: Comments mining with TF-IDF: the inherent bias and its removal. IEEE Trans. Knowl. Data Eng. **31**(3), 437–450 (2019)
25. Zhang, N., Jia, Q., Yin, K., Dong, L., Gao, F., Hua, N.: Conceptualized representation learning for Chinese biomedical text mining. arXiv preprint arXiv:2008.10813 (2020)
26. Zhang, H.E.W., Xiao, S., Cheng, R., Hu, Y., Zhou, X., Niu, P.: A review of deep learning entity relationship extraction research. J. Softw. **30**(6), 1793–1818 (2019)
27. He, L., Jiayu, L., Shiyu, L., Di, W., Shuaiqi, J.: Optimization of automatic question and answer system based on disease knowledge graph. Data Min. Knowl. Discov. **5**(5), 115–126 (2021)

Author Index

Printed in the United States
by Baker & Taylor Publisher Services